national service

BY THE SAME AUTHOR

UTOPIA AND OTHER PLACES

CHANGING STAGES (with Nicholas Wright)

national service

diary of a decade

RICHARD EYRE

BLOOMSBURY

First published 2003

Copyright © 2003 by Richard Eyre

The moral right of the author has been asserted

Bloomsbury Publishing Plc, 38 Soho Square, London WID 3HB

A CIP catalogue record for this book
is available from the British Library

ISBN 0 7475 6589 9

10 9 8 7 6 5 4 3 2 1

Typeset by Hewer Text Ltd, Edinburgh
Printed by Clays Ltd, St Ives plc

ACKNOWLEDGEMENTS

Many thanks to Helen Osborne for allowing me to quote letters from John Osborne.

Extract from *The Complete Poems* by C. Day Lewis, published by Sinclair-Stevenson (1992), copyright © 1992 in this edition, and the Estate of C. Day Lewis.

Lines from 'The Mistake' by James Fenton from *Out of Danger* (Penguin) reprinted by permission of PFD on behalf of James Fenton.

Lines from 'I Think I Am in Love with A. E. Housman' by Wendy Cope reprinted by permission of PFD on behalf of Wendy Cope.

Lines from 'I Think Continually of Those Who Were Truly Great' by Stephen Spender from *Collected Poems* by Stephen Spender; and lines from 'Another Unfortunate Choice' by Wendy Cope from *Serious Concerns* reprinted by permission of Faber and Faber Ltd.

Lines by Louis MacNeice from *Collected Poems* reprinted by permission of Faber and Faber Ltd.

CONTENTS

INTRODUCTION

My grandfather – an Antarctic explorer – wrote diaries in meticulously clear writing even when on a ship rolling in a gale or in a hut battered by a blizzard. There was never any doubt of his intended audience: he wanted to leave a testament for his family in the event that he failed to return from his journey. I had no such exalted motives. I wrote my diaries in a barely legible blue biro in large black notebooks late at night or early in the morning in the comfort of my house, partly for fun, partly for practice, and partly for solace – to remind myself that what is unbearable today will be bearable tomorrow.

Writing is not my profession but I'm enough of a professional to recognise that I'm the author of a text which, from a literary point of view, has a number of shortcomings: the narrative is exasperatingly intermittent and incomplete, the judgement is uncertain, the style is inconsistent, and the tone is the essentially Pooterish one that afflicts any conversation with oneself.

'A journal exists only if you put into it, without reservation, everything that occurs to you,' said Cocteau. Even if I have always tried to follow Cocteau's dictum, I have found it as hard to write unreservedly of my feelings as it is to suck my own toe. I have always felt guarded – even with myself – about objectifying some of my more disturbing, louche, disloyal, violent, and ungenerous thoughts. So, like most diaries, the problem with mine is that, if true, it is never quite true enough.

I can't understand why I've frequently not recorded events that I know were important at the time and even more so now, but I take solace from the fact that in Kafka's diaries, written from 1914 to 1918, there is not a single line that refers to the First World War. In my case there is little enough about the things that devoured most of

my days – meetings and rehearsals – and there are conspicuously few entries which refer to my immediate family – my sister Georgina (Gorg) and the people who shared most of my life and much of the burden, my wife Sue and daughter Lucy.

In editing my diaries I have been given help by some of the friends who feature in these pages, not always to their credit. I'm very grateful to them for their friendship and for their disinterested generosity. I'm also grateful to Liz Calder, friend and publisher, who encouraged me to think that the decision to publish these diaries was something more than vanity and less than folly. For better or worse, this is a prejudiced and wholly unobjective account of my life at the National Theatre over a decade.

I was first courted by Peter Hall, then Director of the National Theatre, to become one of his associates in 1978 when I left Nottingham Playhouse to join BBC TV as producer of *Play for Today*. I was content for a while with television and for two years didn't work in the theatre at all. In 1980 I was asked by Max Stafford-Clark, the Director of the Royal Court Theatre, to direct a play there. I think he hoped that I might suggest a new play or a timely revival, a 'play for today', but he accepted my suggestion of *Hamlet* with Jonathan Pryce with no visible ideological struggle.

After that I started to feel drawn to the theatre and when Peter Hall asked me again in 1981 to join him at the National Theatre I accepted. I directed three productions there in 1982 – *Guys and Dolls, The Beggar's Opera* and *Schweyck in the Second World War* and then I left to direct a film for the newly created Channel 4: *The Ploughman's Lunch*. I remained an associate at the National Theatre and returned in 1985 to form a company with the playwright David Hare. He directed his (and Howard Brenton's) prescient satire on the rise and rise of Rupert Murdoch, and I directed a production of *The Government Inspector* with Jim Broadbent and Rik Mayall.

One day while we were preparing that season, after a lengthy, frustrating and inconclusive meeting with Peter Hall and fellow associate directors, I walked with David Hare into the office I shared with him. The office was then occupied by Howard Brenton, who was still writing, or rewriting, *Pravda* with David. Howard paused for a moment in his two-fisted assaults on the typewriter. 'How was your meeting?' said Howard. 'Mmmm,' I grunted, for once rather

sympathetic to Peter Hall's problems. 'I wonder if I could ever run the National Theatre?' 'But you must,' said Howard. 'It's your destiny.' And so it became.

Peter was restless after twelve years as Director, and he sounded me out. 'Would you,' he murmured, 'ever think of yourself as my successor?' 'Only,' I said, 'if I could find someone to run the theatre with me, someone who would share the job with me of being both impresario and administrator.' I suggested the Director of the Haymarket Theatre in Leicester, David Aukin, and Peter, who had had some bruising experiences with administrators at the National Theatre, warmed to the idea. So much so that he approached David to take the job. David accepted, and I assumed that there was a tacit strategy, which Peter had yet to sell to the Board, for me to succeed Peter with David in place.

By the autumn of 1985 press speculation seemed to confirm my supposition. So did Terry Hands, then running the Royal Shakespeare Company, who invited me to a meeting in November 1985 in order, as it turned out, to deter me from the National and hitch my wagon to the Royal Shakespeare Company.

We met in an empty restaurant looking out over the tundra of the Barbican courtyard. He looked, as usual, like a worker priest: black polo-neck and black jeans. He was nervous with me, and I with him, but he made a spirited attempt at geniality. After ten minutes the entire directorate of the Royal Shakespeare Company walked in and peered suspiciously at us; I waved ambiguously at Howard Davies, who looked both bemused and amused. Possibly Terry had arranged for me to be seen with him *pour encourager les autres*. He described the glories of the Royal Shakespeare Company with an evangelical fervour: 'There is literally nothing that the company can't achieve; we've even started marketing a programme for box office and theatre accounts. Our work can extend infinitely – a New York offshoot, a film studio.' He talked of the National Theatre as a cottage industry, marginal, somehow pointless, a building not a company. But the more he talked of the Augean stables of the National Theatre, the more I felt attracted to the ordure. I realised that I was hooked: I really did want to run the National Theatre.

Why? Even at this distance, I'm not sure I can improve on the mountaineer's laconic defence: 'Because it was there.' Is there any answer less adequate than this, but is there any more sufficient? Was

it vanity? Hubris? Devouring ambition? Certainly, but they don't
quite offer a full explanation of why I should have wanted, as my
father put it, to 'nail my balls to the wall'. Theatre directors don't
embark on their professional lives with the aim of running the
National Theatre in the sense that cardinals aspire to be Pope, or
politicians Prime Minister. They don't plan their working lives
strategically. They don't have 'careers'. They drift from one piece
of work to another like itinerant carpenters. Occasionally though,
wearying of the life lived out of the suitcase, they become aware that
their work (and their lives) can improve if they are attached to the
same group of actors, writers and designers over a prolonged period;
in short, if they are guaranteed continuity of employment. The best
way of ensuring that is by becoming one's own employer: running a
theatre. But running a theatre – at least one the size of the National,
which has three auditoriums and employs over 800 people – obliges
you to add the bureaucrat, the diplomat, the politician, the manager
and the impresario to the role of artist.

Shortly after my meeting with Terry Hands I received a letter from
the cartoonist Raymond Briggs, dominated by a large skull and
crossbones. Above it Raymond had written these words:

Dear Richard,
Rumour has it that you are to take
over from someone called Peter Hill [sic]
at the National Theatre.
DO NOT DO IT!
You are a ĉréativè ârtişte and
must not become a boring civil servant.
All artistes who get anywhere are
in danger of getting SUCKED OFF
into Administration.
IT IS DEATH.
Yours 'Very concerned'
Tunbridge Wells.

I didn't take Raymond's warning lightly but I became convinced,
rather through wilful determination than innate self-confidence, that
I could do the job without sacrificing my soul or my sanity.

*   *   *

For all Peter Hall's advocacy I was far from being the inevitable candidate, and my appointment was not straightforward. Although I had run theatres in Nottingham and Edinburgh, I hadn't worked extensively in London and only once, unhappily (my fault not theirs), at the Royal Shakespeare Company. Added to that, the Chairman and the Board of the National Theatre, uniquely among British arts organisations, were then appointed by the government of the day and my politics were not to the taste of the Thatcher government. But the National Theatre Board followed one of the laws of the British Establishment as immutable as gravity: loyalty to the organisation will always transcend political, religious, or personal bias. Or in other words, governing bodies will always go native and assert their independence from the ministers who have appointed them. In this respect Max Rayne and his Board were true to form when they appointed me in 1986.

Apart (with David Aukin) from supervising the welfare of the building and balancing the books, my job, as the Board construed it, was to decide artistic policy and execute it. In doing that I relied on George Devine's adage, when he started the English Stage Company at the Royal Court in the 1950s, that 'policy is the people you work with'. This wasn't the dizzy optimism of the child who believes that if you see a pile of horse manure and it's your birthday then there must be a pony. It was more wilful: a belief that if you choose the right people to work with and if you encourage them to do their best, they will succeed more often than you might have a right to expect.

If I had an initial, instinctive plan of action it was this: to encourage a sense of community, a sense of 'family', a desire to share a common purpose; in short, to make the National Theatre into something that was more than the sum of its parts. That's the point of institutions: you do together what you can't do alone. I had some specific aims – touring more widely, doing more co-productions with regional theatres (replacing the upper-case 'National' with the lower-case 'national'), recruiting a new generation of writers, directors, actors and designers, enfranchising a generation of small independent companies – but I was diffident about trumpeting an artistic manifesto. I wanted my principles and my sensibility to be inferred from what appeared on stage and how good it was.

I have often heard theatres described as 'autocracies', benign or otherwise. While they are invariably led by one person, a theatre as

large and diverse as the National, staffed by intelligent and talented people, is an organism that cannot be despotically controlled by one person. It's ignorance – or wishful thinking – to believe otherwise. But it is true that the Director, in having the power to choose the play and the manner of its production, exercises an autocracy of taste, whatever the influence of associates, script committees and advisory groups. And to a rejected playwright or director, this power can seem an offence against natural justice. One playwright whose play I turned down wrote to the Prime Minister and the European Court of Human Rights.

The Board expected to be told what plays we were going to do and why I had chosen to do them but, while they discussed the merits of my choices, they never acted, as do some other theatre and opera boards, as surrogate artistic directors. They gave me autonomy, whose price was that if I failed – if the public and the critics rejected my policy – they had a perfect right to fire me. I was never uncomfortable with this even if I was often anxious about the outcome of my decisions, and although I sometimes made righteous protestations about the right to fail (and the Board supported me) I never believed there was virtue in empty houses and large deficits.

I can see now that with an unsympathetic government and wide-spread public scepticism about the arts, the '90s weren't the best time to run a subsidised theatre, but I think it was part of my luck to have had to work hard to make a case for the theatre as an art form and the National Theatre as an institution. If I had been told when I started that I would do it successfully and moreover that I would eventually enjoy it, it might have seemed to me more miracle than luck. I found out that to work at something that you feel is worth doing, in the company of people for whom you feel admiration and affection, for the benefit of people who endorse what you do, is just about as good as life gets. It's true that some of the time it was awful but, as Ingmar Bergman wrote of running the National Theatre of Sweden, it was also 'fun in an insane way, both awful and fun'. For all my complaints, my doubts and my occasional despair, I had the time of my life.

February 2003

1987

17th January   Yesterday I became Director Designate of the NT. A bizarre sensation. I don't know whether I expect people to commiserate or congratulate. It's like being in *Metamorphosis*, waking up as Director of the National Theatre instead of as a cockroach. I felt very sick after the press conference, where I'd felt as if I was performing a character called Richard Eyre about whom I didn't have enough information to give a credible performance. At first I put sickness down to nerves, but I got home and was violently, painfully sick. Photos in most of the papers of this elusive Richard Eyre character. I hardly recognised him. I feel no stirrings of epic purpose, no sense of destiny, and my ribs still ache from being sick. I talked in a TV interview about why I liked theatre and why I am daunted but unbowed (ha ha) by the prospect of running the NT. I like danger. I like the feeling of having a gun pointed at my head: dance, perform, live a bit.

18th January   Feeling surprisingly optimistic in spite of hearing David Steel saying on the radio that we now live in a Third World country. In which case is there less reason for having a National Theatre or more? I talked to Howard [*Davies*]. He's very contained, reined in, self-aware and watchful. Welsh, slightly Nordic-looking, and very fit. Slightly self-regarding and self-conscious about his politics – as if they were a badge of credibility. Rather naive about money. He's very good director and very much my constituency. He wants to do Wederkind's *Lulu* and Goethe's *Faust*, both practically unperformable. Also *Cat on a Hot Tin Roof*, performable if we could cast it. He's a veteran of the RSC and describes Trevor Nunn [*ex-Director RSC*] as the perpetual sixth-former, but surely the RSC has

always had more of the Cambridge college than the sixth-form. The two strongest intellectual influences have been two Cambridge dons: Dadie Rylands, Shakespeare scholar and aesthete, and Leavis, ideologue and scourge of dilettantism – two men united by mutual detestation.

19th January   Dinner with Tony Harrison. Tony's a baker's son from Leeds but he's probably the most cosmopolitan man I know. He looks like Holbein's drawing of Erasmus – pale, chiselled, ascetic. He speaks Greek, ancient and modern, Latin, Italian, French, Czech and Hausa, and is much travelled. He lives precariously between London, Florida, New York and Newcastle. He's fastidiously knowledgeable about food, wine, music and the theatre. He's witty, wry, volatile and tender. He lives up (or down) to the Yorkshire stereotype only in his rare but formidable stubbornness and intransigence. Says all translation is 'carrying across' – it has to be remade in a new language, given new life. 'There is no method except to be very intelligent,' said T.S. Eliot, who Tony despises as a poet and man.

25th January   Go to *Evening Standard* Film Awards. An unexpectedly genial evening. Greeted by many people who congratulate (or is it commiserate?) with me on running the NT. The last awards ceremony I went to was at the Sorrento Film Festival, which was held in the Naples Opera House. I got kissed on the stage by Gina Lollobrigida, who must be well over sixty but still very sexy. She was wearing a red sequinned sheath dress; I was only aware of the prickliness of the sequins and the acres of magnificent peach skin of her breasts which spilled over her dress like fresh dough.

26th January   Had a long meeting with David Aukin at my house. We played table tennis for a while, until it became obvious that David would always win. Then we discussed a number of writers, actors and directors, agreed that we should commission a play from Mike Leigh, talked about how to run the different auditoria, the desirability of seasons – closing the theatre in the summer rather than keeping it open fifty-two weeks a year – our timetable for action, the need to make the auditoria more attractive to the audience and some ideas for productions. And the company system. Does it work? It's attractive: a 'company' provides an aesthetic (or appears to) and it

gives a coherent identity to a body of work. It has to be one of the core justifications for the NT or RSC. But – and it's a big but – more often than not it's for administrative convenience, institutional homogeneity. No writer wants their new plays performed by a company: they want the best possible actors for each part. We have to find a way between the two: continuity without dogmatism. What are our criteria for doing plays? What do we do with our successes (if we have any)? How can we avoid being a creature of the brochure? How do we use each of the three auditoria?

Then we gossiped and told jokes. I told him Al Clark's [*film producer*] latest: three dogs and their owners boasting in a park. They see a pile of bricks. Look what my dog can do, says the mathematician. And his dog arranges the bricks into the formula $e = mc^2$. Look what my dog can do, says the architect. And the dog arranges the bricks into a geodesic dome. Look what my dog can do, says the film producer. The dog grinds up the bricks, snorts them up his nose, fucks the other two dogs and goes off without saying thank you.

27th January Can't sleep. Read and listen to Berwald's First Symphony which Richard Armitage gave me just before he died. I'd never heard of Berwald, never imagined there was a Norwegian composer, let alone a sort of a bland Mozart. And I'm reading now about Charles Fourier who I'd never heard of either. He was an eighteenth-century social reformer who imagined a Utopia in which the sea would lose its salt and taste like lemonade, or that the world would blossom with thirty-seven million playwrights all as good as Molière.

30th January Dinner with Jamie Muir [*BBC arts producer*]. Pete Townshend was there. Very droll and rather serious. He reminded me of Spike Milligan. Told story about Roger Daltry. Said to him: 'Roger, you're so mean you've probably got a bundle of money hidden under the bath.' Enter Roger's wife (American). 'Roger, why did you tell Pete about the money?'

31st January Last night of *High Society* [*my musical adaptation from the films* Philadelphia Story *and* High Society] in Leicester. Relief that it's ended, and dread about London. I'm told that London

audiences will respond differently to it, i.e. be more responsive because they're more sophisticated. This is a consoling fiction. I don't have the appetite for it. I'm creeping forward, dragging a disappointed and depressed cast behind me. The heart went out of me when Richard Armitage [*producer*] died on the first day of our technical. He'd been so touchingly enthusiastic about the show during rehearsals and – as is often the case – it was at its best then. His was the driving passion. It was a back-breaking technical week, followed by hideously unsettling problems. Hope on the first night followed by a certainty of failure and of overwhelming quantities of work to be done. Robert Fox [*producer*] came up to see the show on the first night and thought it was so bad he could only laugh. But at least he made me laugh, as he does invariably. He told me that after his brother James became a Christian he was driving up the motorway with him and Robert was reading *Oz* magazine. James stopped the car on the hard shoulder and threw it out of the window. 'Jesus wouldn't approve.'

1st February Talk to Bill Bryden [*director and NT associate*] about the NT. He confirms my sense that it needs to be more about theatre, less about the organisation. It's not an institution, it's not a kind of cultural cathedral, a Vatican where aesthetic edicts are dictated, it's not a politburo, it's not a parliament for cultural politics. It exists to put plays on, and it's defined by the taste and talent of its directors, actors, designers and writers. Its aims should be coherence and continuity. A theatre is a theatre is a theatre. People who work in the theatre do it for sentimental reasons: they want a sense of community, of 'family'. They want to share the excitements, to respond to the tensions and rhythms of putting on plays. The architecture and geography of the NT militate against this. The building doesn't revolve around its stages. They should be the epicentre of the building. That puts an even greater onus on the people running the place to ensure that not only are as many people as is practical included in decision-making, but also that when decisions are made people are informed of them.

3rd February I've been re-reading Peter Hall's Diaries. Suddenly they start to make sense. They're a catalogue of misery: Peter's tied to a rack of anxiety about his imagination. He says at one point: 'I often

sat in a theatre and prayed that the building would be burnt down that night.' I've thought that recently during *High Society*. A year ago Peter decided he was going to stay on for another three years; he said at an associates' meeting that he'd 'resolved his great dilemma'. Like Lear, he couldn't bear to lose his power. He thanked us for supporting him through the 'difficult times' and I felt a bit like Goneril or Regan: a terrible sense of defeat because he'd encouraged me to think that he was leaving and that I'd be his successor. I felt angry, but also found myself admiring his dogged persistence.

6th February   Olga Knipper asked Chekhov: 'What is the meaning of life?' He replied: 'It's like asking what a carrot is. A carrot is a carrot and nothing more is known.' I feel everything's slipping out of our fingers beyond our control. It has something to do with this being the first atheistic age in history. We're supposed to be capable of knowing and doing anything, so we no longer respect the mysterious, the absolute, any power beyond our knowledge. Of course the more that we want to control, the more despairing we feel when we're unable to control anything in the world outside our homes – let alone within them. When I say 'we' I suppose I mean 'I', like most people I live in a Ptolemaic universe: the planets revolve around me.

10th February   *High Society* sounded unbearably thin and austere tonight. Natasha [*Richardson*] has been astonishingly brave and stoical, with the occasional lapse of stoicism because I haven't been able to help her enough by making the show better. She's very gifted, quite obsessive, and altogether heroic: her father's said she's miscast, her sister's discouraged her, her boyfriend thinks the show's a dog, and she feels responsible for her mother.

I go home to watch a debate on TV about subsidy. Peter Hall was vivid and convincing, with a politician's assurance in spite of his transparent rawness. His attackers seemed Neanderthal. 'Tell me what's special about art,' they cried. Various defences offered: it's special (bit lame), highest aspiration of human spirit, pursuit of excellence and meaning, making sense of world, God speaking through man, etc. Peregrine Worsthorne, seeing the way the debate was going, tried to subvert it by claiming that art was too special to be 'controlled' by the state. I have to work out all the arguments for

subsidy: it's always a mistake to argue on the basis of it being a good investment.

28th February *High Society* has opened. The reviews range from the ecstatic (well, one) to the vitriolic (most), but all good (deservedly) for Natasha. Success and failure is always more exaggerated in one's own head than in others'. It's possible to feel that you have become an irredeemably disgraced figure when you aren't acclaimed, but usually only a few people have read more than one review and most don't care anyway.

9th March Filming *v.* [*Tony Harrison poem for the* South Bank Show] in Leeds has cleared my head. I try to console myself by believing that my over-exposure and hubris acted as a poultice for critical bile, but actually there was no shortage of goodwill: the show just wasn't good enough. We're filming in Leeds in the churchyard where Tony's mother is buried, high above the city. When he wrote the poem her tombstone had been defaced by graffiti. It's been cleaned and we have to do our own graffiti with washable spray-paint, but it's impossible to fake the real thing. It looks slightly art-school. Weather perfect: as if by magic or command it starts to snow just as we start filming. On Friday afternoon Tony got a lift with the crew, and they got stuck in a traffic jam. 'It's poets' day,' said one of the crew. 'Poets' day?' said Tony incredulously. 'In Leeds?!?' 'Yes, POETS – Piss Off Early Tomorrow's Saturday.'

13th March Dinner with Peter Hall. He was warm and voluble. Amazing appetite and energy: after a day's hard and vexed rehearsal, then a bitter union meeting, he shrugged it off and surfaced full of joy and anticipation. He talked a lot about sex – in metaphor and in gossip – and a lot of the death of culture, his alienation from today's pop culture, about Jenny [*daughter*] becoming a pop singer, about Maria's [*opera singer and wife*] genius and eccentricity, and about his other children. I remember John Gunter [*designer*] watching Peter and Maria's daughter drawing a picture during rehearsals. What was the picture of? I asked John. A man walking through an open door with two suitcases, said John. We strolled for a taxi. Peter feels liberated from the NT, I feel oppressed by it.

16th March Woke at 3.45 a.m. Sat listening to Schubert Quintet, then the dawn chorus. I'm still worried about *High Society*. It's work still undone and although it's doing well at the b.o. I can't collect the money without guilt. And the NT – so much to do and I can't feel where to start. With the plays, of course. What classics? Goethe: 'I call classic what is healthy and romantic what is sick.' Degas: 'A classicist is a romantic who has arrived.'

26th March Went to Caryl Churchill's *Serious Money* about the commodities and futures market, the City boys. It was like a wall newspaper: very funny, roughly (and rightly) acted and directed (by Max [*Stafford-Clark*]) with a wild, crude energy, perfectly matched by Ian Dury's songs. On the way back a car ran into the back of mine: a pissed young b(w)anker in a Merc with no proper insurance.

2nd April Drive to Fishguard, then a night on the ferry to Cork. The last time on this ferry was when Lu was two; a priest blessed her and she was sick over his shoes. My neck is agony; it must be whiplash.

8th April Trip to Mallow cottage hospital for X-ray. I've got a trapped nerve apparently. 'You'll not be dancing tonight,' said the nurse as she gave me a neck support. If I had a frock coat and a jabot I'd look like a Regency buck.

10th April Flew back from Ireland wearing a neck brace. It's a certain guarantee of an upgrade, even if it hardly compensates for the chronic pain. Ice pack and neck support don't alleviate the agony. And Sue's dad is very ill. He's the cornerstone of her life: constancy, dependability. When I told him I wanted to marry Sue he said: 'Look after her.' And now when I should be, she's looking after me. She raced round London trying to get chemists to issue pethidine which I've been prescribed as a painkiller and then her car got clamped.

14th April Frank's died. He was a very good, very nice and very gentle man. When I told Lu she looked blank, then her face broke and she ran into my arms knocking the breath out of me.

16th April Lunch with Nick Hytner [*director*]. He has a face like a mime – Barrault from *Les Enfants du Paradis* – oval face, arching

eyebrows, animated, almost *over*-animated. Flights of ideas and gossip, riffs of enthusiasm, indignation, then repose; latent violence, subverted by a childlike smile. He's prodigiously talented, has a great facility for staging and a great appetite for work. He's from a completely different constituency from me and thinks I should work with new people.

20th April   Frank's funeral. Family blasted by grief. A big turnout at the church: family, friends from the railway, from the tennis club, from the dancing club. Loyalty and undemonstrative affection. The crematorium was bleak, unbearably impersonal, muzak, the next shift queuing as we came out. At the wake I saw Sue's Uncle Bob throw a sandwich on a flowerbed, as if he was making an offering. Like throwing earth on a coffin lid. I envy their sense of family.

5th May   I've been flat on my back in hospital having traction, stretching my spine. It's the rack – a sling under my chin and a Heath Robinson pulley system with weights attached, increased day by day. I get released once an hour for five minutes. Alan Bennett came to see me. He's the perfect hospital visitor, did most of the talking, was funny, didn't offer excessive sympathy, and didn't stay too long. He said the worst possible taste would be a T-shirt saying: I HATE JUDI DENCH. We saw one in Liverpool when we were filming *The Insurance Man* [*BBC TV film by Alan Bennett*] soon after the Italian football fans were killed in Turin: LIVERPOOL 39 TURIN 0. Alan's writing about Judas. He says Judas betrayed Christ because he believed him infinitely. He couldn't wait for the ascension for him to display his divine power: he betrayed him in order to hasten his victory. Alan says there's a new disease that attacks the immune system called Screenwriter's Disease – caught from dialogue rather than intercourse.

Charles Wood and Richard Broke came to talk about me directing Charles's Falklands War screenplay, *Tumbledown*, which I've agreed to do for the BBC. Charles was like a large heron in the small room. With him, Richard's wheelchair and the hospital bed and its pulley system I feel trapped in a *New Yorker* cartoon. Satisfying irony having a meeting in a hospital room, which is where much of the film is set.

12th May   Saw Peter Stein's production of *The Hairy Ape* at the NT. Incomparably well performed and well choreographed. Stein has taken O'Neill's stage directions, word for word, and realised them brilliantly. But it's over-emphatic, portentous and monomaniacal; a remorseless allegory of mechanisation of man and yet caught up in its own deadening process of alienation. It's very decadent, like the Radio City Rockettes. Much of the action is played near the top of the proscenium. I still have my neck brace so it's sheer agony to watch.

13th May   Dinner with David Hare. It's odd that people think of David as a hard-edged, pure intellectual, when his romanticism is his most conspicuous characteristic: he believes that people have the capacity to change society and each other – that love is a force of redemption. People often mistake belief in the redeeming power of love for sentimentality, much as they think that David's admiration for women is insincere – the 'men in drag' argument. But his writing is always in good faith. My politics are less defined than his: like most people who work in the theatre, I'm drawn to *any* vision of unity and social justice. I envy – but am wary of – the certainty of his opinions, which gives him the confidence to be a moralist, although a moralist, at least in private, unwilling to judge. He has a necessary self-belief, an absolute conviction of his own singularity, but if a writer doesn't have that, how *can* he write? It's clear that he doesn't want to direct any more because he can only hear one voice (his) in his head, and can't bear the endless banter and negotiation and patience required to work with the actors. He admires (and so do I) the writers who year after year stick at their craft. And he certainly does that. Many playwrights surprisingly aren't concerned with technique; David's almost too concerned. He tells me a story of Ivan Boesky, recently convicted of massive insider trading. He went to Joe Papp [*Producer New York Public Theater*] with the offer to finance the Public Theater for life. His condition: that he be allowed to play Stanley Kowalski [*in* Streetcar Named Desire].

14th May   Visit from Christopher Morahan [*theatre and TV director, associate of Peter Hall*]. Christopher always has gravitas, like a bishop or general. He's always seemed to me rather genial and very generous, like a large pink bear, but actors call him 'the

Brigadier' because of his severity and love of discipline. He made a handsome offer: to put to the associates the proposition of resigning en masse so that I don't have to face the dilemma of who to keep and who not to. 'It's going to be an exciting time for all of us,' he says as he offers himself up for sacrifice.

15th May   I met Robert Lawrence for the first time. He's the subject of *Tumbledown*, shot in the head at the end of the battle to retake Port Stanley, victim partly of his courage and partly of his vanity: he was on a ridge overlooking the town when he was shot, celebrating impending victory by holding two rifles above his head as if he was in a movie. He became paralysed down one side of his body but he conceals it brilliantly. He's dapper, slight, a rugby fly-half. He has blond hair, possibly streaked, and looks more like an actor than an actor. His accent is new City, a patina of upper class put on over a classless one. He's very worried about the possibility of losing his name in the film. Charles says it's his last act of heroism, to stand up in public and be identified with the character. He's having a hard time from the Army. He talks coherently about the Army as an institution and the friend that his senior officers wanted to dump on Ascension Island: Robert was asked to go on deck and beat him up for being insubordinate. He talks about fitness, about being trained to kill, and about how no one understood what to expect when battle came. They watched war movies on the way down in the *QEII*; the favourite was *Apocalypse Now*. When they were going into battle they saw themselves as the stars of the movies in their heads. The Guards no longer hold on to the old regimental ways, but still closed ranks to exclude Robert when he came back to the Regiment. He was asked to leave the barracks quickly when he went to say goodbye to his men.

16th May   A thought for David Aukin. When asked why she and Sidney had always appeared to agree, Beatrice Webb said: 'Sidney was to decide the way we voted, and I was to decide which were the great issues.' But who's Beatrice and who's Sidney? Three jokes from George Fenton [*composer*] who harvests jokes from musicians: A man goes into a restaurant, orders a drink. He waits for a long time, then sees a waiter: 'How long have you been here?' Waiter: 'About six months.' 'Then you couldn't be the man I ordered my drink

from.' Woman coming out of variety show in Leeds. 'How was the show?' 'All right if you like laughing.' What's the difference between James Last [*bandleader*] and a cow? In a cow the horns are at the front and the arsehole's at the back.

17th May At a party, feeling unconfident, I meet the novelist Paul Bailey. He asks: 'Were you surprised when they offered you the job at the National?' I should have said: 'Were you surprised to find out that Patrick White calls you Pearl Barley?'

20th May Dad came to see *High Society* and had a good time. I must have directed well over a hundred shows; he's seen two.

22nd May I sat on the Baylis Terrace for two hours until the sun went down with Peter Radmore [*head NT lighting department*], and he spoke with the unelected but unmistakably authentic voice of the theatre's staff. He told me that if I gave them my support I need never doubt that it would be repaid.

30th May Gala for Olivier's eightieth birthday. Peter [*Hall*] and I wait by the stage door for Olivier, pretending diffidence but both as anxious as Billy Bunter waiting for his postal order. Peter is leaning against the side wall. Nikki Frei, who's the press officer for the occasion, is standing next to him. He strokes her bum with a casual, haphazard air, like patting the flanks of a horse. There's an enormous crowd and hordes of paparazzi in the street. The car pulls up and there's a wail from the crowd as Olivier steps out. He looks almost unrecognisable: smaller, a very, very frail man supported by Joan [*Plowright*]. There's an eruption of flash bulbs and hoots and screams and for a moment he's completely dazed. He steps towards the crowd, then hesitates between terror and intense joy. Peter moves to welcome him, his arms outstretched in greeting. There's a moment when Larry looks at Peter as if he's unsure why he's being approached by a large genial man with a beard and benign smile. Then they shake hands. Larry's now certain who he's meeting. Then Max Rayne shakes his hand, and Peter pushes me forward. Larry turns, looks politely bemused, stares at me as if I was the wrong suspect in a police identity parade and for a few seconds my hand lies in mid-air as if in rigor mortis. The three of us are then prodded into a line for

the 'photo opportunity'. We all feel uncomfortable and stare mirth-
lessly at the cameras in almost total embarrassment.

At the end of the show, the audience stood to applaud Olivier. He
smiled an enchanting, childlike smile of pure pleasure and acknowledged the applause in a beautiful gesture, raising his right hand and
turning it as if he were cupping butterflies. Joan made several
attempts to lead him out but he wouldn't be led. The applause went
on and on. And on. He was asked once what his policy was for the
National Theatre. 'To make the audience applaud,' he said.

2nd June   Talk to Peter who says. 'I've gone from the NT,' and
wants to formalise it. I'm not supposed to start officially until
September of next year, but I suggest that I start in January. Saw
View from the Bridge with Michael Gambon, an immense Balzacian
welter of humanity, violence and love. He's a genius, more capable of
giving and receiving love on stage than any other actor. Seeing him I
feel that a number of unperformable plays become possible. Not that
he'd ever want to be in them.

8th June   Just seen Peter [*Hall*]'s production of *Antony and Cleopatra* and really admired it. A very finely tuned and well-thought-out
production, and Judi [*Dench*] was really remarkable, even by her
standards. It has complete authority and most of the actors – particularly Judi and Michael Bryant – have an innate sense of how to treat
the language. There's a temptation with Shakespeare to provide a
visual conceit that tidies up the landscape, or to impose unity through a
rigorously enforced discipline of verse-speaking, as Peter does. For me
verse-speaking should be like jazz: never on the beat, but before, after,
or across it. All the same I'd rather have Peter's emphasis on the life of
the play being in the language, than an arhythmic, naturalistic shuffle.
My neck is still painful; I was sitting on the centre aisle and flinched
every time a soldier dashed down to the stage with a spear in hand.

9th June   Saw *Yerma* [*Lorca*] in the Cottesloe. It made me think of
well-meaning Westerners wearing saris, or of tourists doing Zorba's
dance.

10th June   Meeting with Robert Lawrence. He talks of the similarities between the 1914–18 War and the Falklands: the wet, the

wrong equipment, the jingoism, the lack of readiness for the conflict, the incompetence of the senior officers, the fear, the bitterness of the aftermath, the gap between reality and propaganda. The men in his platoon burned copies of the *Sun* because of its lies. 'Training doesn't produce soldiers,' Robert says. 'Character does.'

11th June Went with Dan [*Day Lewis*] to see the Bergman *Hamlet*. It's very clear and distilled, and Peter Stromare an excellent Hamlet. We went to the Swedish Embassy afterwards. Ingmar didn't turn up. 'He's very depressed,' we were told, which is like being told that the Pope is a Catholic.

12th June Thatcher's back. On *News at One* she was speaking not as if she thought she was in absolute control for ever but as if she knew she was. Day One of the Fourth Reich. I remember hearing a story in Munich about Hitler from a location manager. He was filming in Braunau, Hitler's birthplace, where the local beer was dark brown and powerfully strong. Over a few weeks it had a disastrous effect on everyone in the crew who drank it. They became irascible, megalomaniac and paranoid – in short, Hitlerian. What's Thatcher drinking? I had a dream that I'd written to ask for a meeting and I met her for five minutes. I talked very quickly without stopping, trying to justify subsidy to the arts. Then the dream faded.

16th June Dinner with the caucus of the NT Board at the Savoy, a necessary flamboyance of Max Rayne's to demonstrate where the real power lies. He's a very engaging (and generous) man who seems, in the presence of Victor Mishcon [*Deputy Chairman, NT Board*], to be vulnerable and almost childlike. Engaging because of his charm and his unwillingness to be pragmatic. Mishcon is a Jonsonian figure, serpentine and portentous. Each sentence of his begins with a prefix: 'In my humble opinion . . .' 'Maybe it's just my stupidity . . .' 'Maybe it's just my old head . . .' He arrives, takes up what he regards as his natural place in the centre of the room and ostentatiously drops a rumour ('in deepest confidence') that the next Minister for the Arts is to be Peter Palumbo who is about to be elevated to the Lords. 'Of course one of the recent candidates is shortly to face imprisonment . . .' It's Ernest Saunders, of Guinness scandal fame. Victor implores me to put on plays that have no

violence or explicit sexuality or four-letter words. This is the same as
the Board at Nottingham except they have more power in the world
– if not in the theatre.

But Max is no Cyril Forsyth [*Chairman Nottingham Playhouse
Board*], who used to bang the table and pull my hair at the Board
meetings. 'Get your hair cut, lad.' Max has the air of a charming and
dapper bounder: suede shoes, silver hair and silver cigarette lighter,
blue pinstripe, silk socks, perfectly polished shoes. He told me he had
difficulty controlling Peter. 'He ran rings around us,' he says. And he
talks of his own background: Jewish, radical, philanthropic. He can't
understand how anyone can pursue money and power for their own
sake. When he tells me his grandmother used to say: 'If he says he's a
communist and he has holes in his shoes, he's a communist,' I hide
my feet under the chair. He said Peter wants to be one of the boys but
can't wear the blue jeans.

23rd June   To *Lady Macbeth of Mtensk* at ENO. Inspiring piece of
theatre. Makes me aware of how in the theatre expressiveness is
usually sacrificed to utility. But opera productions so frequently
decline into a form of camp: high seriousness dressed up in im-
plausible costume – like postmodern architecture, pop videos, and
High Church liturgy.

24th June   Saw Al Clark, who's getting married to an Australian.
Two New Zealander jokes, which are the Aussie equivalent of Polish
jokes. 'How does a New Zealander get to run a small business?'
'Give him a big business and wait.' 'What do you call a New
Zealander in a suit?' 'The defendant.' He told me about a visit to
LA Film Festival. He met a distributor who said: 'I don't want to sell
you coleslaw when I can sell you Cole Porter. I've got this picture, it's
called *Puccini*. It's got loads of girls and fast cars and music by
Maurice Jarre.'

26th June   Mum's birthday. She's sixty-six. She's old before her
time, actually about a hundred years old. It's a terrible illness,
Alzheimer's disease. If there's a physical disease it resembles it's
leprosy, which eats away the body as Alzheimer's does the brain.
We've watched her personality disappear for years and with it her
humanity, leaving only her body to breathe and be fed. She's been

losing her mind for years, slipping away little by little. I wonder if we'd still get on, and if she and Dad might have separated. I really miss her.

8th July   Long letter from Tony Harrison, who is teeming with new ideas. Must attempt the Greeks and Molière, particularly *Le Bourgeois Gentilhomme* as a contemporary satire. Tony says this is probably the least propitious time *ever* to run a subsidised theatre with an adventurous policy. Richard Luce, Minister for Arts and Libraries, has just made a speech about the arts having to escape their 'welfare-state mentality' and having to 'give the public what they want'. Hard to do better than full houses. What does he mean? That they should be self-supporting? That 'business' should be a partner? The trouble with business sponsorship is that it forces the artist into the position of begging to the plutocracy. It's supposedly a way of testing the market – of seeing if there is a real demand for the 'product' – but of course the product will be determined by the sponsor in the sense that they will only subsidise what is anodyne and unexceptional. Shaw said: 'The State should endow all forms of art to the extent necessary to place its highest forms above the need for competition.' Yes, but who decides what are its 'highest forms'? Apropos sponsors, who said: 'When I hear artists making fun of businessmen I think of a regiment in which the band makes fun of its cooks'? Auden?

9th July   To *Small Family Business* [*Alan Ayckbourn*] which is about a world situated at the epicentre of the heartland of Thatcherism. It's not a 'state of the nation' play – it's more anthropological than political – but it gives an acerbic view of the social corrosion of the very people who Thatcher is alleged to be enriching.

11th July   Party at Max Rayne's house. Wonderful paintings (Monet, Pissarro), Giacomettis on the terrace, Degas maquette on the piano. 1960s Bauhaus-style house and furniture. The cast list included Richard Luce. He's not a great reader: he said he was going on holiday and wanted to take a book. Could I recommend one? He's amiable, confused about subsidy, but rather pro the arts, which is just as well considering he's Minister for them, but by no means inevitable. Woodrow Wyatt told me we should abolish arts sub-

sidies. 'I saw your *Guys and Dolls* three times. But last time you had a black man in the cast. Quite unacceptable.' At dinner the widow of Charles Douglas Home [*Editor* The Times], attacks me without restraint at the news that I'm doing a film about the Falklands. She's a Spartan, instantly ready to damn 'softness', liberalism, woolly thinking.

8th August　　Starting to get nervous about *Tumbledown*. There are strenuous attempts to prevent it being made by the Ministry of Defence, the Home Office and the Scots Guards. We'd arranged to have some full-dress uniforms made by military tailors who have been making uniforms for the Guards for 200 years. They were told that if they worked for us their contract would be terminated. Also we're having problems with the lawyers over fact/fiction and libel. Alan [*Bennett*] says BBC lawyers are like ships' doctors. Says when he was doing *An Englishman Abroad* he had advice from the lawyers that the line 'Laertes looks as though he's got a couple of King Edwards down his tights' could be defamatory. Can it be defamatory to accuse a man of having big balls?

25th September　　Lu's thirteenth birthday. We were talking about getting a cat. I said we'd need to get a cat flap in the basement door. 'Oh dear,' she said, 'he'll keep getting sent letters asking him to join the Labour Party.' She says that she dislikes people who are violent and people who think they're great.

7th November　　I've emerged from filming *Tumbledown*. Drive back from Wales with Colin Firth. We both feel like battle victims, insensible with tiredness and resentful of anyone who hasn't shared our experience. I was never able to imagine myself emerging from filming having completed the film that Charles had written. Like a soldier I could prepare, I could train, but the only experience that would equip me to deal with the battle was the thing itself. Like all good work I've been connected with, the film was a series of happy accidents – the right decisions made at the right time. We made our luck and our luck was good. But I still can't be clear that we've made a good film, even if during filming I was convinced that it would be remarkable. One gets consumed by *folie de grandeur*, an inevitable consequence of feeling that what you're doing is at the centre of the

universe (and it is, of your own universe), and if it's good it must be the summit of everyone else's. My fear is that it's something less than the sum of its parts. Now back to the NT. I love the protective womb, the privacy and camaraderie of film-making. To run the NT seems in comparison to be going into fire naked, caught on the barbed wire.

21st November Beginning to make headway at the NT and at the same time confronting the fear that it will consume me. And my family. Elizabeth Hardwick in *Seduction and Betrayal: Women and Literature*: 'In the long run wives are to be paid in a peculiar coin – consideration of their feelings. And it usually turns out that this is an enormous, unthinkable inflation few men will remit, or if they will, only with a sense of being overcharged.' This thought is a companion for something Shaw said (quoted by Louise Brooks): 'No man who is preoccupied in doing a very difficult thing and doing it very well, ever loses his self-respect . . . An actor, a painter, a composer, an author may be as selfish as he likes without reproach from the public if only his art is superb; and he cannot fulfil this condition without sufficient effort and sacrifice to make him feel noble and martyred in spite of his selfishness.' Mmmm . . .

23rd November Board meeting. Max finds it hard to delegate to the others. I feel quite relaxed, not least because Max goes on and on, tetchy with Douglas Gosling [*head of finance*], who stays mute as he's criticised for being opaque about the financial position. Ian Brown, the Arts Council Drama Officer, stumbles over an answer as to why the Arts Council is eroding the grant to the NT: 'I'd need notice to think that through,' he says with preposterous gravity.

3rd December I saw Deborah Warner's production of *Titus Andronicus*. It has a wonderful unselfconscious enthusiasm and bravura about it, and is quite without any of the mannerisms and affectations that decorate most RSC productions. Brian Cox is straight from the heart, and there are several actors whom I could have sworn couldn't act at all but in this production are convincing. Deborah has a real gift for animating the company: she's the real thing. There's a lot of sentimental and specious nonsense talked about 'companies' as if in themselves they were any guarantee of good work. This is a 'company' – the Royal Shakespeare Company –

but in other shows these actors are listless and mutually apart; under Deborah's baton they meld together.

18th December   Lunch with Peggy Ramsay [*literary agent*], who was in fine form. Apart from a mild amnesia, particularly over names – 'Who is that downtrodden nice fat man who runs the RSC?' Me (baffled): 'Trevor? Terry?' 'No, dear,' 'David Brierly?' 'Yes, dear, I think he's the house manager . . . And who is that man who does all Caryl's plays at the Royal Court? Very ambitious man.' 'Les Waters?' 'No, dear, no.' 'Max?' 'Yes, dear. Father was a famous psychiatrist.' Peggy has a stream of gossip and observations which shock me by their complete unsentimentality: 'Will Hare ever write a *really* good play, dear?' 'I wish I'd never given Christopher that book [*Les Liaisons Dangereuses*], it's distracted him.' She talks about Michael Meyer and Graham Greene going off as a pair to pursue women around the world, and Peter Hall: 'A nice boy. Can he still do it, dear?' I had food poisoning in the evening and was sick in the interval at the Barbican: a perfect response to a dismally poor production of *The Wizard of Oz*.

23rd December   Visit to Dorset. Dad's girlfriend [*Margaret*] asks me several times if I'm ill. A week ago, I say. Dirt, chaos, cat hair, smell of decay. She and Dad seem to be unaware of it. Dad tells her to shut up frequently and she smiles as if she's used to this form of affectionate banter. In the morning she asks if I'd like China or Indian tea. Indian, I say. 'Well, you would be difficult,' she says. 'Your son has no taste,' she cries out to Dad. I clear a small corner of the table to put a teacup down, brushing aside the accumulated glacial deposit of letters, old food, newspapers, magazines, photographs, a sewing machine, clothes and crockery, while the dogs snuffle around my feet. She asks me if I'm going to visit Mum. She says fools *will* ask how she is and one has to have an answer. 'If there's a case for euthanasia,' she says, 'Mrs Eyre is it.'

   Go to see Mum in the new hospital, which is all red-and-blue ironwork, like a giant Meccano set. She lies on the floor on a beanbag. No sight, no hearing, no sense at all. She breathes and eats and week by week wastes away, but remains incredibly resilient. What do I feel? Guilt. Grief. Regret. When people are ill, they say, 'I'm not feeling myself.' It's been years since she's been herself, or had

a 'self' to feel. Occasionally I can see in her mouth the hard shape it became in the later years when she became settled in her bitterness with Dad. And I recoiled from her then, although she was right to feel bitter. If only she'd left him. Perhaps he was right that she wouldn't have been able to survive on her own. But I doubt it.

28th December   Been reading Kathleen Tynan's book on Ken. It's very well written, and in spite of some obvious cosmetic work on her character and motives, is very honest and very sad. Ken was crippled by the scourge of early celebrity. What he most craved became a mercilessly recurring burden. He wrote, he said, to be sexually desirable, a plea for identity. When he'd found his identity, what was left? He was self-advertising, vain, and frustrated; a vicarious performer, who was condemned to write about an ephemeral medium. It all combined to drive him into a cul-de-sac with nowhere to develop. He always longed to be above his class but to criticise the class to which he longed to belong. And in the end his self-mockery, if a man who wore mauve suits could ever have any, deserted him. The role of the *enfant terrible* is wearing for everyone – the *enfant* and the audience.

He was a brilliant critic: what he wrote was always alive, opinionated, provocative and intelligent. He really made theatre seem as if it mattered. He responded to the right sort of life in it. Harold Hobson said the other day: 'The trouble with our successors is that nothing seems at stake for them.' But Ken's attempts to break out of the critic's prison were feeble – those ghastly sex shows – and his advice at the NT when he was literary manager was often wildly off target. I don't think the story of the first night of *The Architect and the Emperor of Assyria* is apocryphal: Olivier and Ken were standing in the foyer during the interval as a mutinous audience defected to the street. 'Such a good idea of yours to put this play on, Ken,' said Olivier, with the crisply projected diction that could be heard well down the Cut. When I went to Nottingham I asked Ken if there were any plays that he'd wanted to do but hadn't. 'Yes, if you want a hit do Molnar's *The Play's The Thing*. You can't go wrong.' He must have told Tom Stoppard the same thing because Tom adapted the play for the NT and I think it's the only disaster he's ever had.

31st December   New Year's Eve. I can't make predictions. All I know is that the NT will be more difficult than I can anticipate. And

I'll start to make enemies. I must try to act in good faith, and I mustn't give up. Last year on New Year's Eve I was on a rattling train from Leicester, pissed and maudlin, looking at a wonderful sunset – deep azure sky, sea-green grass, peach-red sun and low flat clouds, canal bridges, church spires, trees in silhouette – thinking you go on to see what the hell is next. When Oscar Wilde was at school he was translating a few verses of the Bible from Greek aloud – Judas selling Jesus for thirty pieces of silver.

TEACHER: That will do, Mr Wilde.
WILDE: Hushh . . . let us proceed and find out what happened to the unfortunate man.

1988

3rd January Tomorrow is my first day at the NT with my own office. 'Beware of any enterprise that requires new clothes,' said Thoreau. I haven't worn suits for years, except on special occasions. Nowadays I have 'suit' days – Board meetings, funding meetings, lunches, dinners, and more often than not feel the suit wears me. I sometimes step outside myself and marvel that it's me doing this job. I'm not steeped in theatre lore and I'm not sure I like theatre enough to act as its propagandist and evangelist. I don't *love* it. It can be inert and dispiriting, and clubby, self-regarding, tacky and embarrassing. You can sometimes be ashamed of being in the audience on those occasions, let alone in the same profession as the people on the stage, let alone part of the human race. But when it's good? Oh well, then it makes its own argument.

6th January Peter has told David Aukin that he no longer wants to be bothered with the details of running the NT, he's too involved in his productions. David is anxious about his role. It's hard for him to accept second fiddle. I think that he's already spent too long waiting, and his natural instinct is to be at the front, not behind my shoulder: he's a producer. Max had warned me not to let David become my boss, but I wouldn't have wanted to work with David if he *wasn't* ambitious. We went to see a Pinero play at the Royal Exchange, which seemed anti-Semitic to David and badly done to both of us. I felt churlish not liking it. I love going to the theatre and enjoying myself, but more often than not I travel in hope and arrive in gloom.

8th January I met Declan Donnellan. I'd seen a few of his productions: elegant, light-footed, iconoclastic, some fine performances,

and sometimes some perverse choices. I'd imagined a svelte, self-contained, mournful Celtic boy. But he's round, tubby, bucolic and jolly. Occasionally he becomes serious, grave, almost solemn, and then breaks into a charming and infectious laugh. We talk about Catholicism, being Irish, his father, and his partner (also his designer). I like his transparent honesty and his emotionalism. We talk about *Fuente Ovejuna* [*Lope de Vega*], which he wants to do with his company [*Cheek by Jowl*], but I want to do it at the NT and have a very good translation, which I commissioned from Adrian Mitchell. The play was robust enough to be performed during the Russian Civil War on the streets of St Petersburg.

11th January   The spectre of the *Royal* National Theatre walks abroad. Max clearly wants it desperately – 'an accolade' for the theatre. Bit like Judith Hart accepting a Damehood on behalf of the Third World. Max thinks that the NT's image would be enhanced. I disagree and say so. It's a useful distinction from the Royal Shakespeare Company, and the demotic 'National Theatre' is attractive. To allow it to be assimilated within the orbit of the monarchy is to bang another rivet into our theocracy: monarchy's our religion. Victor Mishcon supports Max. 'We walk in troublous seas,' he says. Blimey. Most of the Board seem to support me, but in a public vote Max would win.

17th January   Last night of *High Society*, thank God. Jean-Louis Barrault: 'Whenever I did anything mainly because I thought it was going to be commercial, it was a failure, and whenever I did something only because I thought it was good, it turned out to be commercial.'

18th January   I see the possibility of making administrative sense of the NT building but not artistic sense. How to make meaning of the work? That's why it's so hard to decide which plays to do. And how to do them. I'm reading *Candide* (Voltaire not Bernstein):

> Candide turned to the Abbé: 'How many plays have been written in French?'
> 'About five or six thousand,' replied the Abbé.
> 'That's a lot,' he remarked, 'How many are good?'

'Fifteen or sixteen,' replied the other.

'That's a lot,' said Martin.

Talk to David [*Hare*] about the programme. We agreed that the problem was to define what the approach was to the classics – i.e. what is our voice? Peter's approach was to have a clear text, and be morally neutral and visually uninflected. Ours must be more inclined to spectacle and interpretation, but maintain a responsibility to the text. We need to introduce a note of anarchy to the theatre; but it's hard to make an anarchistic gesture now that isn't immediately assimilated. The climate is dark and savage, and we should respond to that, not engage in the chummy humour of the times: them grinning at us grinning at them.

19th January A bitter attack in the *Independent* on Adrian Mitchell, who's just done a reading in the Cottesloe. It showed a real animus against what it saw as the privileged protectionism of the NT and the hegemony of 'official' culture.

20th January Max has written to me that he hopes the issue of the 'Royal Appellation' won't become 'emotional'. But his side of the argument is nothing but emotion. He's obsessed with obtaining the 'accolade' for the theatre, the blessing on his chairmanship. Only understandable in the light of the incredible difficulty of getting it open and the unbelievable hostility to it then.

21st January I met Deborah Warner, who is very confident and very likable, and quite certain of her destiny. She's a handsome woman, slightly haughty, with a nineteenth-century patrician bearing, which would have served her well with the Bedouin in the Empty Quarter or with Florence Nightingale in the Crimea. A woman of action. She has an endearing self-confidence allied to a sort of youthful bashfulness. We talked about Shakespeare and Brecht.

25th January Appeared at a demonstration against Clause 28 in the Local Government Bill – to stop the 'promotion' of homosexuality. How can anyone believe you can promote any kind of sexuality? If you could the world would be full of raging heterosexuals, given the oceanic mass of propaganda for straight sex in

EVERY advertisement. I said that the legislation is the forerunner of censorship – it's about what we think and feel and do in private.

26th January Preview of *Cat on a Hot Tin Roof*. Howard [*Davies*] has staged it well, but the play seems creaky and melodramatic and needs to be more florid and stylised. The older actors understand this, the younger ones have seen too many Hollywood movies, so play it in quotes. But it's an occupational hazard with Williams' plays – to misread 'intense' and 'Southern' for camp.

31st January Directors' meeting. Bill Bryden was in provocatively belligerent mode, or tone. He's an inspired impresario and sometimes – as in *The Mysteries* and *Lark Rise* – a marvellous director. He can be simultaneously very rash and very pedantic.

7th February In Sheffield to do an assessment on the Crucible Theatre for the Arts Council. It reminded me of how hard it was holding it all together at Nottingham, and how it can so easily crumble. To keep the work consistently good seems more difficult than ever. Resources to the regions have diminished and a whole generation of directors has stuck at the RSC and NT without ever running regional theatres. And we've lost that haphazard apprenticeship for actors: those that might have done a year or two in a regional theatre now look for parts on TV, in films, or the national companies, while they're still at drama school, helped by the massive proliferation of casting directors. And this country is so oppressively London orientated; we've lost the sense of shared experience between theatres in Newcastle, Nottingham, Exeter, etc and London. We watched a very self-consciously postmodern production of *Winter's Tale*, admirably ambitious but almost wholly unachieved, even if redeemed by Jim Broadbent.

8th February *Cat on a Hot Tin Roof* first night. The actors rose to the occasion, so did the audience, but in spite of its visceral energy, the construction still seemed creaky, even though there's something really attractive about the waywardness and the raggedness of the play. It's a cruel play but it's not a neurotic one: 'Life has got to be allowed to continue even after the *dream* of life is – all – over . . .' says Maggie. Williams never judges his characters or evangelises for

a life less ordinary. I'm sure Howard will have (and deserves) a success with it, and will I be generous enough to enjoy his success? This is the nub: if I can't, then I shouldn't be running the NT. The most important attribute for *anyone* who runs a theatre is generosity: you've got to be prepared to enfranchise people who are more talented, more successful, and just *different* from yourself.

9th February   Flurry about the Arts Council grant and their assessment. Standstill instead of the expected 2 per cent rise. I feel resigned. Everyone outside the NT feels that it's been comparatively over-funded, so I'm not surprised we've been penalised, even if it doesn't make my life any easier. Peter's in a fury; he says the Arts Council assessment is disgraceful and mean-spirited. I had a visit from a Telecom fitter at home. He talked about his son, how he couldn't get a grant for college. 'And he's six foot two, you know.' He went out of the room, then popped back in. 'Have you ever met that Peter Ustinov?'

16th February   I went to Maria St Just's house in Pimlico (next to Noel Coward's) to be auditioned, to see if I'm fit to direct one of Tennessee Williams' plays. Maria's like a rather ferocious bird, angular, small-boned, brightly coloured; she pecks about, fluttering her wings, preening her feathers, crowing and, just occasionally, purring like a pigeon. Deeply opinionated on every subject, and unforgiving to those who defy her, whose number includes Howard Davies who finds her a pain. She told me her life story: born in Russia into a family that she called 'ordinary nobility', she came to this country when she was nine. She trained as a ballet dancer and then decided to become an actress. She was understudying in a West End play when she was invited to a party given by John Gielgud. She claims to have been standing silently in a corner, which seems improbable, and was drawn to the red-and-blue socks of a small man who sat by himself on a sofa. The stranger turned out to be Tennessee Williams and she became a friend for life – and beyond it: he appointed Maria his literary executor. She gave me a rigorous cross-examination. I ended up liking her, partly because she made me laugh, partly because I thought she liked me.

17th February   Lunch with Jerome Savary [*French theatre and opera director*] and Tony Harrison. Jerome says it's unnecessary to go to the theatre if you're running one: 'Don't go and see the plays,

get someone to do it for you who you trust. And make sure you have a good restaurant: people care more about eating than theatre.' Actually I'd like to do both: good theatre and good restaurant, and will resist all pressure from the Board to contract out the catering. First the cleaning, then the security, then the catering, then the office services, then the art . . .

18th February   Peter Stein on his production of *Torquato Tasso*: 'I feel we never escaped from the ghetto of language.' That's what I'm facing: directing three seventeenth-century plays – *The Changeling*, *Bartholomew Fair*, and *Hamlet*. Why am I doing them? Because I'm obsessed with that period and I've done them before successfully and so feel indemnified, but of course that's the worst reason: you should never go back.

20th February   Long meeting with script committee followed by dinner at Rules with the associates. This is ancien régime stuff – we can't afford this in the future. There's a picture of Marvell on the wall of the restaurant. Tony recites 'To His Coy Mistress'. 'You should be able to taste the language,' says Tony, 'the whole body as well as the mind, and the mouth should savour it.' And with his work you do. When we were doing *v.* the film editor was a man who'd been turned off poetry at an early age. I watched him become drawn into the poem so that he felt each nuance, rhyme, rhythm, shift of thought. 'Fucking amazing,' he said.

28th February   Meeting with Jonathan Powell [*Controller BBC1*] about transmitting *Tumbledown* on BBC1. He keeps talking of getting it on the air 'cleanly'. Not sure what he means and fearful that the swearing and the legal problems are never mentioned.

2nd March   Lunch with John Mortimer. He talks about the Moral Tutor of New College, who is alleged to have written a venomous preface to *Crockford's*, the Church's *Wisden*. John said that A.N. Wilson went to see him for a talk about God. 'Oh no,' said the churchman, 'I don't like your looks.' John says that Lord Chandos [*ex Chairman NT Board*] would complain about Victor Mishcon saying at NT Board meetings 'through the Chair . . .' 'I thought he was going to penetrate me,' said Chandos.

12th March   Meet with Richard Pulford who runs the South Bank Centre. He says: 'Don't let the National be *worthy*.' I've lost the battle of the 'Royal Appellation'. How do we avoid being tainted by it?

16th March   Meeting with Bill Gaskill [*director*]. It's probably hard for Bill to come to me to ask for a job. He doesn't show it, but then it's always hard to know Bill's feelings. I've known him nearly twenty years, and been in admiration, or awe, or fear, or exasperation of him ever since. He was generous to me at Nottingham and he doesn't patronise me, for which I'm immensely grateful. It's hard to know Bill: he's removed, you always feel it's your turn, that he's waiting to see you fall into a trap. He wants to do something that isn't 'like' him. He suggests a play by Pirandello, which I don't know: *Man, Beast and Virtue*. I've been reading his autobiography. He's a great teacher and his productions of *Saved* and *The Sea* are among the best productions I've ever seen. There's a slightly miserable sense in his book of deliberately setting himself on the *edge*, a self-justifyingly arid aesthetic. There's much in common, though I don't think Bill would concede it, with this from Peter Brook: 'I became increasingly interested in whatever is a direct element in performance. When you set off on that path everything else falls away . . . I want everything to be seen, everything to stand out clearly . . . I have not come to this conclusion through puritanism, nor do I want to condemn elaborate costumes or ban coloured lights. Only I have found that the true interest lies elsewhere, in the event itself as it happens at each moment, inseparable from the public's response.'

17th March   Max Rayne asks me to go to a function to celebrate the sponsorship of Foyer Music by Robert Maxwell. One of his sons is deputising for the great man. Max tells me of being in a taxi with Maxwell coming from a do at Burlington House with another Jewish potentate. Maxwell spoke Yiddish during the journey, and the next day Max saw him on TV talking about reading the lesson on Sundays at his local church. Max talks about the desire of the immigrant to belong, and how he'd said to his father in 1947: 'We've got £50,000, we're secure.' But the horizon keeps moving.

23rd March Last Supper with Peter and his associates. Rich in irony, macabre humour, absurdity and pleasure, and real affection for Peter. There's gratitude from him for the fact that we've turned up, Harold [*Pinter*] in particular. And that we've gone along with him – some, like John Goodwin [*head of press*], for most of a lifetime. Michael Kustow initiates speeches, provokes Peter to his feet. Peter makes an elegant speech and ends: 'There is no chance that what is great in the theatre today will also be great tomorrow. Tomorrow it will become something different.' Then he sits down insisting that there are no speeches in reply. Kustow prods me and I reply: 'None of us would be here . . . etc.' Then speeches round the table, but by this time we're all very pissed. So Harold is confused and incoherent, Peter Gill [*director and writer*] tearful but focused and fastidious: 'Peter *was* a fine director,' Christopher [*Morahan*] is careful, dignified and hopeful, Michael Rudman [*director*] droll, Michael Bogdanov [*director*] bullish, Bill Bryden elegiac. All were self-mocking except for Kustow. I take Bill home and I'm more drunk than he is.

12th April Mary Soames [*writer, Churchill's youngest daughter*] has been appointed Chairman to succeed Max. Derek Mitchell [*NT Board member*] said she would more appropriately have been appointed Governor General of Bermuda.

13th April Lunch with David Hart, adviser to Thatcher, who says he'll get me a meeting with her to talk arts policy. He's a dilettante playwright; a curious figure – louche, heavy-jawed, balding, faintly dangerous. He says the theatre's job is to be the Court Jester, to raise two fingers to society. He's a combination of Tory anarchist, ideologue and rake. Very vulnerable: he considers himself a writer, a thinker, who is obliged to deal in property in order to live as a man of letters. Says the coming struggle will be between the libertarian and the authoritarian right. Thatcher is in politics, according to him, because she is interested in the difference between good and evil. She has no irony, hates class, stops her ministers doing the occasional outlandish thing because 'it's immoral', and she's a snob. His evidence? 'She calls the Duke of Grosvenor "Gerry Grosvenor". No one calls him Gerry.' He says that there's a rational explanation to the Peter Wright affair: Wright is the Fifth Man. His book was ghosted by the KGB.

14th April Meeting with Mary Soames at the Minister's office. Huge nineteenth-century rooms decorated with contemporary paintings. She reminds me slightly of my mother in her looks and her nervousness and her slight sense of being out of her depth. And thinking of her as my mother, I warm to her immediately. She appears pleasant, conscientious, tenacious, with a 'manner' that can deal with any occasion and raise it to her reference points. She never used to go to the theatre – 'Christopher didn't like it' – but says she's going to have to take a crash course and asks me to help her.

15th April Grisly row with the finance department. There don't seem to be any detailed budgets for individual shows, or at least the budgets all seem to be post hoc. Money is allocated to departments, who then distribute it as they think fit. To me it looks like all money and all control is spread horizontally. Each department is a barony, there is no systematic control of production expenditure from the centre – unless of course it's the finance department, but how would we know? They guard the figures like masonic secrets. The subtext of our row is: Who's in charge? Who trusts whom? They are incredibly obstinate and patronising. The message is: 'We do it THIS way, don't interfere.' I need to know the figures: I want to be able to control them.

24th April I'm directing *The Changeling*, which I did for the Edinburgh Festival in 1971, when the notion of madness as a social phenomenon was current. Now, in spite of its wildness, the play – written in 1622 – feels oddly unfashionable. Nevertheless, this week has been a joy in the rehearsal room and misery outside it. The Late Shakespeares are moving into the Cottesloe like an aircraft carrier into a small pond. I chaired a meeting at the ICA on Writing in the Theatre with three playwrights: Christopher Hampton, Ann Devlin and Timberlake Wertenbaker. OK until Hanif [*Kureishi*] piped up from the back: 'Can I ask R.E. how many black plays he'll be putting on at the NT and how many black actors and directors he'll be employing?' I should have commissioned him on the spot. He said afterwards that he was only trying to irritate me. The most interesting thing to emerge was Christopher's two questions:

1. Why is there no opposition to the status quo when in the '70s there was so much with less provocation?
2. Does subsidy, or at least excessive subsidy, breed indulgence in the artist and indifference in the audience?

11th May   First night of *The Shaughraun* [*Boucicault*]. Howard's done it beautifully, and Bill [*Dudley*]'s designed it magnificently – making sense of the Olivier revolve for the first time – and Stephen Rea's wonderful, and I think it'll be successful enough to run it (*force majeure*) as our Christmas show, which will vindicate the money we've spent on it. So what was born out of chaos will look like policy.

23rd May   *Tumbledown* showing at the NFT. After the film Charles [*Wood*] and I answer questions from the audience. Someone asks if the film is political. Of *course* it is, I say. How can you make a film about war without being political? But is it biased? they ask. Of *course* it is, I say. Afterwards, I'm collared by two men with a tape recorder. Did I mean what I said? Is it proper for the BBC to be biased? They reveal themselves as representatives of the Aims for Freedom movement – right-wing activists.

30th May   The *Sunday Telegraph* has a headline: 'DIRECTOR SAYS FILM IS BIASED'. I curse myself for my big mouth. ITN ring for an interview. I tell them I'm not in London. No problem, we'll send a crew. So on a gloriously hot day a crew comes down from London, through narrow country lanes, and I'm interviewed in front of a cascade of clematis in bloom about the politics of *Tumbledown*. I attempt to try and present it as fair and balanced, so that people see it without prejudice, but feel as if I'm pissing in the wind.

5th June   Directed the Clause 28 show, a Sunday 'gala'. Alan Bennett said that he'd been asked if he'd contribute to the show and what, if he didn't mind them asking, was his sexual orientation? 'I'm like a man dying of thirst in the Sahara being asked if he'd prefer Perrier to Malvern water.' I spent the day getting the names of the Pet Shop Boys the wrong way round and trying (and failing) to keep every act short.

6th June   *The Mahabharata* in Glasgow. Beautiful *mise en scène* and costume and lighting. Peter [*Brook*] is a brilliant showman as well as director: it's a coup to 'consecrate' the building as a theatre with this show. Fantastic images – a snake of flame twisted out of the dark, pulling a dancer in its wake, a torch-lit battle ended with a nuclear flare; arrows appeared to fly across the stage, horses to gallop; the elements of the production were the elements of life – earth, fire, air and water. The staging had the flair, brilliance and bravura that could have been attention-seeking were it not so obviously the consequence of trying to find the most expressive way of telling the story. The length of it, the shared experience, the daylight vanishing, the dawn rising, made it very moving. The meanings of the play were opaque, and the actual *text* of the play was quite bland. What did it mean to us? Were we tourists? Of course the play spoke to the audience as a cultural *event*; beyond that, what? A sense of spiritual redemption?

8th June   Sponsors' lunch at the NT. Mary Soames pushes a note across the table to me. It reads: 'Who is Ian McKellen?'

9th June   *Tumbledown* has provoked extraordinary ferocity: front page of the *Mail* and questions in Parliament. It was salutary to be reminded just how seriously and how dirty the Right are prepared to fight. It's tainted my view of the film. I now regard it as something of a poisoned chalice because I'm not sure, when it comes down to it, if I have the appetite or the courage to be in the front line of controversy. It isn't as easy as it looks. I've been outed as a socialist and a pacifist but I'm not truly either. I'm forced to see the film as a weapon which has gone out of control. It's impossible now to separate the film from Robert's life, so it's viewed as a biography of Robert rather than a film about soldiering – which is how Charles and I see it. I didn't help with my indiscreet remarks at the NFT – but I wasn't to know that Aims for Freedom had tape recorders running. And of course the film *is* political: war always has an inevitable political context – it's the apotheosis of politics – and the response from the Army, the papers, and MPs to the film is a political one. It'll make my life harder at the NT, and harder to raise funds from the government and the business world, and harder to live up to the expectations of the Left.

Lunch with Mary Soames reminds me of this. She's clearly nervous

of the mockery from her friends. We have lunch, and she spills her handbag on the floor. She picks up a tape measure and puts it around her neck where it remains for the rest of the meal. She becomes garrulous, but she's nobody's fool and I remind myself not to patronise her.

10th June   Depressing meeting with Denys Lasdun [*architect of NT*] after a meeting with Nuria Espert [*Spanish actress and director*] and Joan Plowright about *Celestina* [*Fernando de Rojas*]. Joan would make a fearsome opponent. She's very tough but Lasdun could outdo both of them. I tell him I admire the building (as I do) – its nobility, its classicism, its beauty, in fact. I get a thrill out of all its public spaces. But I also say that the Olivier is a difficult theatre to present plays in, which I suppose is a bit like saying that you have a watering can that doesn't hold water, but he doesn't want to discuss it. We work in his building, we know its problems, and so do the audiences. The acoustics are bad because the volume of space is so huge in proportion to the number of people in the audience, and it's enormously difficult to design for. It's an unfocused space: you either leave it bare or create a form of false proscenium, and whatever you do the concrete jaws either side of the stage intrude ostentatiously on the actors' space. I don't of course say all this to Lasdun but nevertheless he refers to me as a 'barbarian'. In spite of his abuse I can't help liking him and his building. He's still defending himself against the gross and gratuitous abuse he received when the building opened.

11th June   *Tumbledown* shown on TV. And for once, with a piece of my own work, I'm inordinately proud of it: I think it's a really good film – a better film than *Platoon*, which I watched time after time to study the battle scenes, and it seemed more callow each time – all that 'first casualty of war is innocence' crap and breast-beating about finding meaning in their lives (at the expense of the Vietnamese). Reviews very good, except of course from the *Telegraph*, which I suppose is a kind of battle honour. Their military correspondent, John Keegan, wrote a patronising and wilfully misleading review. Alan [*Bennett*] wrote a letter to the *Telegraph* asking if they were setting a precedent: would the crime correspondent be sent to review *Macbeth*? I had a letter from Neal Ascherson [*journalist*] saying he'd had a letter from John Keegan about the film. Keegan

talked about my failure to understand the 'military caste', but he revealed his real objection: 'I'm all for knocking the Establishment, but I'm choosy about who does it.'

Two weeks ago Jan Younghusband [*NT head of planning*] was asked to Chelsea Barracks for lunch by an officer of the Scots Guards. She was standing with a glass of sherry talking to her friend when the Colonel joined them. He asked what she did; she owned up to working for me. A frosty silence. Then he turned his back on her and said to her friend: 'Your guest won't be staying for lunch.'

12th June   Went to the Free Mandela concert at Wembley. Huge turnout. Crowds are thrilling and fickle and terrifying. Very few black faces and a frightening capacity of the crowd to display all the characteristics of, well, a crowd. They give the impression that they could be persuaded to chant 'Kill the black bastard' as easily as 'Free Mandela'. Salman Rushdie is very excited at sitting next to Daryl Hannah. The crowd below the front row start pointing at the front row of the VIP section and applauding. Trevor Huddleston stands up, thinking, reasonably enough, that the applause is for him. Actually it's for Annie Lennox, who's sitting next to him.

14th June   The 'Royal National' nonsense has burst like a fat blister. I haven't yet had to publicly defend it, and am not looking forward to having to lie in public. Sean French in the *New Statesman* compares the 'Royal National Theatre' to 'The Ploughman's Lunch', a completely synthetic piece of memorialising, another page in the 'Britain as theme park' catalogue. Neal Ascherson writes to me that 'everyone is looking to you to stop this royal nonsense'.

19th June   *The Changeling* has started previewing. I'm moderately enthusiastic, but it feels not really alive. It looks beautiful, it all makes sense, the staging is striking, but I fear it doesn't quite add up.

26th June   *The Changeling* has opened. Bill [*Dudley*]'s done a wonderful set and the theatre looks and feels very different. It seemed to me that the play was clear. Howard says he's seen the play five times and this is the first time he's understood it, but I think he's just offering me comfort. Derek Mitchell said he was proud to be on the board of a theatre that did such work. Anthony Everitt [*Secretary-*

General Arts Council] said it was among the best work he'd ever seen at the NT. Valerie Profumo said it was 'my calling card – magnificent and uncurled at the edges'. But I don't think I've pulled it off.

6th July   Deluge of reviews, some very good, but I'm coming to the conclusion that *The Changeling* isn't really achieved, and once again I marvel at my capacity for self-deception. The theory of the production is fine, it's the execution. I haven't cast it right, and I've let Miranda [*Richardson*] down. David [*Hare*] sends me a letter – 'nothing less welcome than the advice of an honest friend' – castigating me for failing to get a company, to get actors who can live up to the demands of the text, etc. I feel wildly hurt and rail in fury. But we must work out a policy for actors. It's all too ad hoc.

Met Maggie Smith and Albert Finney last week. They were both enthusiastic, though neither has much fondness for the building. They both want to work outside the West End and yet not get institutionalised. I tell Albert that Peter Brook says that a theatre should be like a violin: its tone comes from its period and age, and tone is its most important quality. 'Yes,' says Albert, 'and who'd build a violin out of fucking concrete?'

14th July   I had a meeting with Professor Bain who's been the Arbitrator for ACAS in the negotiations between the NT and the union in the light of the Rayner Report [*on NT over-manning*]. Bain's a Canadian, an expert in Industrial Relations, who lectures at the LSE. He says that the labour relations at the NT are the worst he has ever seen, worse even than between the National Coal Board and the National Union of Mineworkers.

19th July   Meeting with Harold P. about *Mountain Language*. We go for a drink at the Lyttelton bar.

HAROLD: This wine's disgusting.
ME: It is, isn't it? Who do we blame?
HAROLD: You.

25th July   David rings to apologise. He says he's giving me the criticism because he feels I can take it, and because I'm the only director he respects enough to do it. Of course I can't take it, who

can? We talk about self-doubt. He says that artists with a working-class background have no self-doubt, or at least don't show it. If they fuck up they blame other people; the middle class, like us, blame ourselves.

30th July To New York to see David Mamet's *Speed-the-Plow*. New York, or at least the theatre and publishing circles and of course 'society', is an extraordinary hermetic world, circled by myths of 'style', 'class', 'old and new money', parochial and unforgiving to outsiders. Its literary indicator is *The New Yorker* – locked in a seamless '40s, arch, obscure, austere. But much of the US seems stuck in the '40s – their clothes, their cars, their foreign policy, their theatre, their graphic design. The good thing in the States is the much greater social confidence at all levels. People feel they have a right to be wherever they are; no cringing deference as in England, just open envy. It's hard to understand the determined efforts to maintain social standards when they're being constantly invented, or re-invented. A man in the lobby on the way in to the show was reading his ticket as if he was just discovering what he'd come to see. The play was very enjoyable. Mamet's not a satirist, even if it is a lethally accurate comment on Hollywood – two scam merchants running a film studio trading a commodity that happens to be a 'buddy film'. The play really asks the question: are we capable of change? Madonna plays the girl, adequately, her lack of charisma on stage a definite plus in the part. Her knees (knobbly and school-girlish) seem the most affecting thing about her.

5th August First preview of Nick Wright's play, *Mrs Klein*. The play is like Nick: it's careful, touching, intellectually ambitious, elegant, droll, and a bit diffident. Peter [*Gill*] has done a faithful production, but he could have raised the temperature, rather than endorsing the play's caution by making the character of Melanie Klein more of a monster.

20th August Back in the theatre this week after two weeks' holiday. Felt totally dislocated. I could as well have been on Mars or in Mexico City. Overwhelming feeling of the oddness of my doing this job. I told David [*Aukin*], which was unfair: he looked terrified. I've been reading Peter's Diaries again. So much fear and corrosion

and self-doubt. At least he has a prodigious energy, a kind of devouring greed and an edge of madness.

1st September   Today I am officially The Director. It seems ironical, having been doing the job for at least nine months. I was interviewed by a lively, uncomfortably intelligent young woman from Breakfast TV. She asks: 'Aren't you daunted by following two very BIG men?' Then I started rehearsing *Bartholomew Fair* [*Ben Jonson*], and I knew that I shouldn't be doing it. 'It's a big play for a big theatre,' I tell myself. But I'm doing this play just because the giant mouth of the Olivier Theatre wants to close its jaws on it, and because I can't find a large-scale comedy and none of the directors I've approached wants the Olivier. I'm doing a re-tread without the daring and excitement of the production I did at Nottingham. I'm doing the things I swore I wouldn't do. It's a terrible note to start on.

5th September   Weekend in Dorset, beautiful weather, ruined for me by problems at the theatre: rehearsals of *Bartholomew Fair*, a production that's going off the rails – *The Father* [*Strindberg, adapted by John Osborne*], what to do about the future repertoire, what to do about failing box-office. And when I open the sunroof in the car I notice that my hair has started to go grey. But I haven't changed quite enough though to justify the photograph of me in a magazine captioned: 'HAROLD PINTER'.

7th September   Peter's affair with Nikki Frei has surfaced in the press. Why should I be surprised by the press? They look through keyholes because there's enough of the voyeur in all of us. Recently in Peter's office my eye was caught by a black dress hanging on the back of his door. Peter caught me looking at it. 'Who on earth has left a dress in here?' he said. The *Express* has a feature ('THE EYES HAVE IT') about the demonic force of his attraction which ends up: 'Or is it merely that there is nothing quite like being wrapped up in those huge arms and being able to whisper in his ear – "Where to now, Sir Peter?"'

10th September   If you run a theatre, there are only four decisions worth making:

1. What play?
2. Who will direct it?
3. Who should be in it?
4. Who should design it?

In that order. And then the question: will anyone come and see it? To ignore that is to court disaster. As Craig Raine says: 'The task of the artist at any time is uncompromisingly simple: to discover what has not yet been done and to do it.'

17th September There was a mean-spirited piece about me in the *Sunday Telegraph*, arguing that Peter's committee style (?) of running the theatre would be replaced by an autocracy: 'ENTER THE NATIONAL DICTATOR' was the headline. I had to go with Peter to have my photo taken with him in front of a blow-up of Olivier. Peter was like a student, without money, or a home, or a wife. He was dressed almost identically to me – black shirt, grey-and-white-flecked jacket. We look like a Country and Western duo. Peter's boyish and undentable. He giggles at the newspaper articles about him and his love life. 'Nikki's been offered more money than you can dream of,' he says. I think Peter's got a real horror of silence and a fear of loneliness. He's not gregarious; he obliges himself to paper his life with activity.

18th September Long associates' meeting. I despair about:

(a) ad hocery
(b) being too eclectic
(c) my own abilities

The conclusion of the meeting is that we should do what we said we'd do – have a company in the Olivier and Cottesloe, develop new work, pursue a policy of children's theatre, have a clear response to classical work, and tour. If we do this we'll justify ourselves. If not we'll be a supermarket trolley that from time to time carries products of great quality.

19th September I saw Max, who talked interminably about the Royal Gala. On the way to the lift he said that he'd heard that

Winston Churchill [*Mary Soames' nephew*] had said that Mary had been put into the NT to clear out the pinkos.

20th September   Gathering of the June 20th Group – named, I think, after the date of its inception rather than the Haiti military coup which happened on the same day. Harold and Antonia risk mockery and provide hospitality to a group of people all concerned with loss of freedom, which tonight includes amongst others Melvyn and Cate Bragg, Ian [*McEwan*], Salman, Germaine, Margaret Drabble and me. Why should it be mockable to try to find an alternative to our present government? Very good speech from Geoff Robertson [*barrister*] and one from Denis Foreman [éminence grise *Granada TV*]. It was an intelligent, gentle and constructive discussion. Slightly sixth-formish as most of us were rather self-conscious and ill at ease with the formula. Could easily be hijacked by the politicos – rules, agendas, motions, etc. Antonia was a very good chair. She brought Harold to order: 'Harold, or darling, as I sometimes call you . . .' Geoff talked about how the rhetoric of free speech was always invoked but the reality of free speech was more elusive. I said I might need practical support in the area of free speech: Max is starting to be obsessed with the issue of *lèse-majesté* and Alan [*Bennett*]'s play because the Queen is a character in it.

21st September   It's all more difficult than I imagined. It's the sheer size of the NT – three plays in repertoire in each of the three auditoriums and maybe another nine productions being planned, plus touring, transfers, education, not to mention platform performances, FOH music, catering and the bookshop. I seem to have an infinity of meetings – management, planning, finance, scripts, directors, associates, heads of department, plus production, casting, press, poster and programme meetings. I remember a review of a show called *Do It* at the Traverse by Cordelia Oliver. It was about the American revolutionary (now turned banker) Jerry Rubin. Eight men took off their clothes and pranced about the small stage waving their cocks at the audience. This, remarked Cordelia, was seven too many for her. With me it's auditoriums – two too many for me.

25th September   Lu's birthday. She's fourteen and I wish I could have spent the day with her instead of at the NT where there seems to

be nothing but bad news. Poor houses (and massive over-expenditure) for the Late Shakespeares in the Olivier, poor advance for *The Secret Rapture [David Hare]*, Jenny Hall [*actress*] hasn't turned up (now my problem), Ken Stott [*actor*] is ill (also my problem), production managers are up in arms over late designs, and the production we're doing with Field Day is a disaster.

1st October The week started with an F and GP [*finance and general purposes committee*] where it looked as though we were heading for a £750,000 deficit. Then on Tues a meeting with Max and Victor Mishcon about the appearance of the Queen in *A Question of Attribution*. 'A matter of protocol,' said Max. 'And precedent,' said Victor. Both Labour peers, both in an agony of shame about embarrassing the monarchy. Threats were discreetly made, indelible matters of principle stated. I remained obdurate if terrified, but for all the pain of it, I wouldn't have missed the opportunity of hearing Victor read the part of the Queen (and of Blunt) in his finest courtroom baritone. Derek Mitchell was immensely clear-headed and clearly loathed by Victor, who was inflamed by Derek's defence of my position. David Aukin was marvellously forthright – he's a good lawyer – and appeared unruffled. I started to see the real possibility of resignation (only hinted at by Derek). My resignation was intended to be pre-empted by the hint that 'Larry didn't resign over *Soldiers*'. By conviction rather than gamesmanship, I refused to budge. Suddenly I realised that they were playing poker, trying to force my hand, expecting me to do the decent thing and concede. When they realised I wouldn't, they were keen to knit together a compromise: don't tell the Board, face the consequences when the play's on, put a note in the programme. And then the meeting was closed, cordiality resumed and Victor was off to the opera.

6th October Been reading Melvyn Bragg's biography of Richard Burton. He was a melancholy phenomenon. He always promised more than he delivered, always gave the impression of being capable of greatness had he not been inhibited by inferior material, or drink, or bad directors, or any other specious cause. He had presence, ambition, a wonderful voice, no reflectiveness and a great flair for being Richard Burton. He seemed like an actor embarrassed by his

trade because (a) it felt unmanly, and (b) because it felt childish. In his Notebooks he says that Olivier wanted him to be his successor at the NT. I've never heard that from anywhere else. When he died, on the pad were lines from *Macbeth, The Tempest*, and, last, an unfinished fragment of Marcellus' description of the Ghost of Hamlet's father: 'Cap a pi . . .'

8th October *The Secret Rapture* has opened and is a success. David's become admired, established, respected by the critics who have cavilled for years. I wanted to direct it but was already committed, but Howard's done it with great flair and one beautiful and haunting image (not in the play) – the oak tree and the ghost. David has a capacity to put his finger on the pulse of the time; previously he's been resented for this by the critics. Now he's being treated like Shaw and they'll expect an annual dose of moral castigation like Spanish penitents.

9th October Rehearsals for *Bartholomew Fair* have been fun this week and my spirits soar. John Wells is marvellous company: he loves Ben Jonson and we agree he's the complete writer. John says Denis Thatcher calls the TV channels M1, M2, M3, M4 – Marxist 1, 2, 3, 4.

10th October *Tumbledown* is being repeated this week. It had an audience of 14 million first time. There's barely an atom in the press of the violent controversy over its first showing. There's always a sense of disappointment about anything one's done being shown on TV: even if millions have watched it you still feel as if you are putting a message in a bottle and throwing it in the Atlantic Ocean.

12th October Card from John Osborne asking if he can have ten minutes to talk soon. 'It's to do with *Look Back* and my new play. It's rather important that I speak to *you* about it.' I feel excited, but also a wave of anxiety – if I don't like the play I'll be faced with his legendary scorn. John's generous about *Tumbledown*, which he's now seen three times. I offered him the part of The Writer but he couldn't or wouldn't do it.

14th October   A party to say goodbye to Peter, rather oddly timed given that Peter officially left weeks ago and unofficially months ago. He's very statesmanlike about the magnificence of the NT building and very generous to me. We present him with a Hasselblad camera – 'Something small, and no fuss' – which we've all contributed to. 'Typical Peter,' says Tony Snowdon, who was charged with buying it (and getting a discount). 'Top of the range.'

17th October   Meeting with John O. I've never talked much to him before and had, I suppose, expected an acrid, snarling, misanthrope. But I find myself with a lanky, dapper Edwardian gentleman, wry and immensely courteous, like a soldier whose wars were a long time ago. Which in a sense they were. John was vastly successful in his late twenties for about fifteen years – *Look Back in Anger, Luther, The Entertainer, Hotel in Amsterdam, Inadmissible Evidence* (his best), and of course the screenplay of *Tom Jones*. To keep on writing is the hardest thing and perhaps even harder if you're successful. On the other hand writers are probably corrupted as much by failure as success.

20th October   Opening of *Bartholomew Fair*. I retreated to my office where I listened on the tannoy, drank champagne and took Valium. I wandered to the loo where I met Yolande Bird [*secretary to the NT Board*] and Peter Gill in the corridor. We all went down to the VIP room where Yolande gave small and enticing gobbets of her memoirs of the NT Board. At the end of the show David [*Aukin*] told me it had gone really well, but I think he was being generous. I fear the worst from the press.

22nd October   My fears were amply justified. What felt as though it might have been a true popular success – I mean large numbers of people laughing and applauding in a very big theatre – shows itself to be dismal and unachieved. Peter always said I took the press too seriously; I do.

24th October   Spirits improved after the weekend. Booking is good and reviews are half terrible and half glowing. But I'm not convinced. Comedy is more risky than anything, and classic comedy the riskiest of all, and this production doesn't deliver. My fault: wrong play, wrong

time. Half the critics describe the show as vibrantly alive and the other half as flat and dead – i.e. it's neither a hit nor a disaster but in the Olivier we need hits. Which we have in the Cottesloe with *The Father*. It was nothing but trouble but has had wonderful reviews, which, as John Osborne says, proves that the critics know nothing. I can't take comfort from it. I still feel raw about my mishandling of it.

27th October   The Royal Gala performance of *The Tempest* to mark the twenty-fifth anniversary of the NT. It proved to be the wrong play (but what would have been the right one?) and the evening provided a few laughs, Bubbles Rothermere being one of them; she'd come as the Christmas Fairy, with a huge flounce skirt, and her hair done as a sort of Ugly Sister wig. 'Just look at that Rothermere woman,' said Prince Philip to Prince Edward as I walked behind them. Peter [*Hall*] next to the Queen during the performance, which unsurprisingly failed to soar, to Peter's visible agony. During the interval she and Prince Edward did 'funny' Cockney voices when they met up. I had to introduce Edward to a group of people, one of whom was Denys Lasdun who had no idea at all whom I was introducing him to. I was astonished at the eagerness of everyone else to meet the Prince. The limits to which people will go to touch the hem of royalty is just astonishing. Mary Soames was amazed by the fact that I was surprised by this.

In the second half I set next to Prince Philip. We had an excellent view of Tony Haygarth as Caliban, or at least of his large bum. His costume consisted of a giant nappy, stained with blood, mud and shit. Prince Philip chuckled gamely at any vaguely funny line. I gave him high marks for concentration. He repeated every line that took his fancy. Trinculo: 'They say there's but five upon this isle: we are three of them; if th' other two be brained like us, the state totters.' Prince P. hooting with laughter, 'the state totters . . .' No doubt this technique has served him well over the years. Repeat the line, chuckle, nod.

8th November   Meeting with Denys Lasdun. Slight cause for optimism. 'God preserve Prince Charles and God preserve us from his views on architecture,' he says. After Prince Charles's criticisms of the National Gallery extension the architect became a pariah – he was unemployed, gave up his architectural practice, became a

teacher. Denys was upset about a bad review of *Bartholomew Fair* because it said the Olivier Theatre was the culprit as much as the production. Quite unconcerned about whether the review would have hurt me, he wanted me to write and complain about the insult to the architect. Bill [*Dudley*] and John [*Gunter*] and I have been talking about how to improve the Olivier and the Lyttelton – or as Bill says, 'how to turn it into a theatre'. John's made a model of the Olivier which shows how the acoustics could be improved by cutting down the volume and making it one tier of seating (thereby, of course, making it *more* like Epidaurus), but we don't show it to Lasdun. He tells us we are 'custodians of the building': we can change the 'fittings' but not the 'room'.

14th November   To Dublin to see Brian Friel's *Making History* which I'm co-producing, and spent a day with the actors trying to sort the wood from the trees, which is always easier to do when someone's cleared the ground. I spent two evenings with Brian Friel and Stephen Rea. We seem determined to fulfil the 'when in Rome' adage, and get wildly drunk, singing the entire Rodgers and Hammerstein canon in the lounge of Buswell's Hotel until at least four in the morning. Stephen gleefully tells me a (possibly) apocryphal story of 7:84 [*independent theatre company*]: John McGrath [*writer and director*] in his Volvo Estate pulls up at a garage. Attendant asks him what the 7:84 sticker is for. John: '7 per cent of the country own 84 per cent of the wealth.' Attendant: 'Aye, but there's no need to flaunt it.'

18th November   Saw Ibsen's *Enemy of the People* at the Young Vic. Tom Wilkinson very good as Stockman, but the play promises much less than it delivers. I'd wanted to do it at the NT but David Thacker got in first. He's used Arthur Miller's version, which irons out many of Ibsen's ironies and turns Stockman into a Milleresque hero. Talked to David Thacker about running the Young Vic. He said if he totted up the days that he'd been happy running the Young Vic and weighed them against the unhappy, misery would win out.

1st December   Lunch with Trevor Nunn, amiable and voluble as ever. He said Peter's view of Shakespeare had been transformed by

meeting John Russell Brown, who was afflicted with the notion of 'free Shakespeare', which sounded as if it should have been administered with orange juice and cod-liver oil. He wished me well with the NT, and I wanted to ask him about the letter he'd written me a few years ago when I made *Country*. He congratulated me on turning to film-making, and I wondered whether he thought I should have stuck at it rather than turned back to the theatre.

2nd December   Meeting with Lindsay Anderson [*theatre and film director*], who, as always, manages to make me feel as if I have a contagious skin disease. He breathes misanthropy. But his best work – on David Storey's plays – has been anything but: generous and humane.

4th December   *A Question of Attribution* and *An Englishman Abroad* have opened in triumph. It was painful to see Alan [*Bennett*] so nervous. I'd somehow always counted on him to be beyond nerves, but hardly surprising given that he'd written the plays, was directing one of them and playing the lead in the other. Beautiful acting from him and Pru Scales. The Queen ought to be deeply flattered by Alan's characterisation of her – very canny and knowledgeable about art and history – and by Pru's brilliant performance. She's utterly convincing, and no one was anything but delighted with the show. Even Victor came near to apologising for having mistrusted my judgement and good faith: 'One was worried about the precedent.' A friend of Lu's saw the plays and said of Alan: 'I didn't realise he had to put on an accent to be English,' meaning, I suppose, talking posh.

6th December   Dinner for Max Rayne, a farewell. I had to act as MC, which I think I did fairly ineptly. And Max thought so too. I failed by Swift's standards: 'A public speaker should aim at that simplicity without which no human performance can arrive at any great perfection.' Peter had flu and found it hard to rise to the occasion. Not least, I suppose, because he had rather ambivalent thoughts about Max. I said that having Max as Chairman after Cyril Forsyth was like having died and gone to heaven, which at least had the virtue of being true.

7th December   Party at Kathleen Tynan's. David introduced me to Charlotte Rampling. We were talking about Denis Foreman. I said what a nice man he was, how he invested everything in the person he was talking to, and in the middle of that sentence she was distracted by someone and turned away without apology. The true privilege of the beautiful.

8th December   Another meeting of the June 20th Group at Harold and Antonia's to discuss Charter 88. At the moment a Bill of Rights, proportional representation, etc are all said to be constitutional impossibilities. Talk about the possibility of a popular front. Much discussion about the calling it a popular front. Was it historically correct? Was it invoking the French or the Spanish one? To me it seems vainglorious for Charter 88 to invoke the Czech movement, Charter 77. People actually suffered, went to prison for years, to defend constitutional rights. Penny McEwan made a plea for the underprivileged: children, animals, the countryside, and the sea . . . There was a long, long, silence.

14th December   It's very difficult to run the theatre and to concentrate on *Hamlet*, but that's the job. I describe what I'm thinking about the play to Dan [*Day Lewis*], all in terms of Eastern Europe, of the Romania of Ceauşescu. But why aren't I doing it like that? Out of a perverse sense of 'classicism'. It isn't my voice. Casting goes well: Judi Dench will play Gertrude, and I've cast John Castle as Claudius. He's dark and unpredictable.

15th December   I'm living the life of a politician, meeting after meeting: lunch at the Savoy with Peter Palumbo [*Chairman Arts Council*], who is a charming but opinionated amateur, and Victor Mishcon, who is not. Victor is still auditioning me. Meeting with Adrian Noble [*associate director RSC*], who is commendably unwilling to be disloyal to the RSC, although the more he talks about the RSC's problems the more I feel sorry for Terry Hands. Meeting with Ian Brown, Arts Council Drama Officer, who is more than usually cagey. And lunch with Richard Luce at the Admiralty. Michael Billington is there. I tax him with the effect of critics. 'Surely no one could be hurt by a critic for more than five or six days,' he says. I tell him that Patrice Chereau [*French theatre and film*

director], who doesn't speak fluent English, can apparently still quote word for word a dismissive review of Billington's from 1974. And lunch with Michael Blakemore, who still can't forgive Peter [*Hall*]; he says for the dullness of the work but that somehow seems like less than the whole story. Michael's generous to me but must feel that he hasn't had his just deserts: a very good director who seemed a natural successor to Olivier.

16th December Harold gave a dinner for the cast of *Mountain Language*. I sat at the end of the table with Michael Gambon. I told him a joke and as he laughed he slipped off his small chair on to the floor; with his belly, his legs stretched out and his seismic laughter, he looked like Falstaff. 'Will you play Falstaff?' I said. 'Of course,' said Mike. Of course he won't.

1989

7th January   About to start *Hamlet*. Nervous, well, afraid. I must stop worrying. David [*Hare*] tells me about going to see Lord Goodman at the Arts Council when the grant to Portable Theatre was being withdrawn. David started: 'Aren't you worried –' 'Let me stop you,' said Goodman. 'I'm never worried. When I leave this room I stop worrying.' George Kaufman [*American playwright and director*] used to time his rehearsals so that he would start a scene a few minutes before rehearsals were due to end. He'd work his way to the back of the auditorium during the scene, wait till it was finished, say: 'Thank you, everybody,' and dart through the foyer into the street before any actor could catch him to share their problems with him. It's not a tactic that would work if you run a theatre.

I spend a lot of time talking to Declan, who's in rehearsal for *Fuente Ovejuna*. He demands – and gets – absolute commitment from his actors. He's fond of a form of vernacular Freudianism, which he tries out on me. I suppose Freud (and maybe Declan) would say that I'm his father-figure. Whatever, it's a pleasure to share his anxieties. We talk about how to start rehearsals. There's always the problem of how to get a disparate set of individuals to work together within a few days; British actors are good at this, but you still have to find means of mutual familiarisation, ways in which they can legitimately sniff each other out. Declan does a lot of exercises, games and improvisations. I change my approach for each production. It never works to give the actors – who are always numbed to deafness by nerves – a lengthy lecture about the background to the play and its meaning. It never encourages actors to be made to feel that the director holds all the cards and they hold none.

8th January Card from Dan [*Day Lewis*]: 'Each time it's an adventure working with you; each time the gradients gain severity. Each time we've worked with new plays and this seems like the newest, richest, most wonderful, most intriguing, most irresistible of them all. I wouldn't have ever considered doing this, had you not suggested it. It goes beyond thanks.' And on the other side: 'three o'clock Father's Funeral/five o'clock Mother's Wedding.'

10th January Opening of *Fuente Ovejuna*. Declan's done a beautiful production: utterly true to the play, with a sinuous energy and freshness that defines what every production of every classic should aim for. It's the best production of a classic I've seen for years. Well, about twenty years.

14th January The first week on *Hamlet*. I was very nervous and got ill – first stomach, then a cold. The cast are strong and enthusiastic. I'm wary of John Castle; he's quite prickly although I think his heart is in it. He wears a suit to rehearsals and clearly despises anything that smacks of 'modernism'. Judi is utterly game and loyal; I still feel slightly in awe of her even though I've known her for over twenty years. She's given me a beautiful present: Stanley Wells' edition of the Complete Works. And written in it: 'What larks, Pip!' I hope there are. Dan is determined and immensely committed. He bikes to rehearsal, looking like a Basque dancer – breeches, knee socks, ribboned garters.

15th January Al Clark tells me the difference between commitment and involvement: in a ham omelette the pig is committed but the chicken is involved.

20th January *Speed-the-Plow* has started to preview. It's very funny, well acted, but with rather leaden sets. It'll have a mixed press and will be popular with what Americans call 'savvy' audiences. I hate that word even more than I hate the word 'feisty'. The box office is quite healthy with *Secret Rapture*, *The Shaughraun*, *Single Spies*, *The Father*, *Mrs Klein* and even *Bartholomew Fair*. It's possible we'll make up the deficit by the end of the financial year. The Late (unlamented) Shakespeares cost us dear. There is much talk at meetings about 'marketing', 'knowing our audience'. This is a

prelude to 'give them what they want'. They don't *know* what they want until we give it to them. We should never try to second guess our audience. When we were doing *Kafka's Dick* at the Royal Court they decided to 'market' the play and tested the potential audience by having a girl walk round Sloane Square with a clipboard showing a photo of Alan Bennett to passers-by. Most people identified him as Jonathan Miller.

22nd January   Another week of *Hamlet*. More confidence and some excitement. I'm trying to give the feeling of a court strapped by convention and hierarchy, so we've been doing work with movement – the body language of courtly behaviour: bows, 'reverences', deportment, etc. Never forget Hamlet's a prince; Denmark's a prison for him – of class, of status, of manners, of duty. Michael Bryant is unconvinced of the usefulness of these exercises. For him all the work has to be directly related to the scene; that's the only hard evidence. Dan is showing flashes of great intelligence and daring.

Hamlet has to learn how to die; he has to learn how to live with death – with killing and being killed. Is he 'mad'? Well, he's at least extraordinarily highly strung, what we'd call 'neurotic' now – his extreme grief, his reaction to the Ghost, his behaviour (on and offstage) to Ophelia, his self-laceration: 'Oh what a rogue and peasant slave', his manic exhilaration after the play, his hysteria with Gertrude, his wild fury at Ophelia's funeral . . . And he says he was punished with a 'sore distraction'. He's labouring under an overwhelming fault: incipient insanity. He's mad because politics is mad when it destroys all feeling and affection. His madness is a protective carapace. Why did all seem so much simpler to me when I did the play at the Royal Court? When I was preparing that production I used to look at Dürer's portrait of Melancholia – a drooping, long-haired, androgynous figure slumped amidst the scientific artefacts of Renaissance science: compasses, a sextant, a globe, a telescope; a figure encircled by technology, immobile in the face of progress. I read an interview by Günter Grass. 'What will the '80s be like?' he was asked. 'If you want to know what the '80s will be like,' he said, 'look at Dürer's picture of Melancholy.'

28th January   *Speed-the-Plow* has opened, moderately well received by the press, although Michael Coveney castigates me for

casting 'another woefully inexperienced recruit' in Rebecca Pidgeon. But she's better than Madonna, who was a perfect example of how, unless a stage performance is animated by the breath of real talent, beauty, intelligence or sexual charisma, it can seem gauche and leaden. David Mamet has a confident, slightly over-awing manner – diffident, but hard, charming and slightly clubby. He's very ordered; gives the appearance of total contentment but writes about the aching limbo of desire and frustrated ambition. His play seemed colder with the first-night audience than when it started previewing: at its heart a hole.

Greg Mosher [*director*] told me about a writer who was recently phoned by a producer about his script: 'It's not going to be read by the third assistant, or the second, or even the first. Dan himself is going to read it. It's here in his diary: Thursday afternoon, read K.'s script.'

29th January   This week I had a sense of how good *Hamlet* could be, even though I've got severe doubts about my choice of setting it within its period – I think it's caution, not classicism. I convinced myself that to make absolute sense the play had to be set in a world where the court, the religion, the hierarchy, the politics had an exact meaning. But I feel inhibited by it, and by the company, although they seem to have settled. John Castle is still a conundrum; Dan says he's a natural iconoclast, instinctively contradictory. Oliver Ford-Davies [*Player King*] unerring in his loyalty and his willingness to try anything. The Players have to be so distinct from the Court. For better or worse, it was right to have Christopher Logue as the Player King when I did the play before – he palpably came from another world.

4th February   Howard [*Davies*]'s production of *Hedda Gabler* has opened in the Olivier. It raises the old questions of how to use that theatre and how to do the classics. The auditorium forces Howard into an expressionistic design and the actors are pulling in the other direction. The NT seems as intractable as ever. I've started to take on critics when they talk about my policy. Fruitless endeavour, why don't I keep quiet.

Robert Graves on Wilfred Owen: 'All that stuff about "the poetry is in the pity" – really it's as if you and I were looking at a battlefield covered with the bodies of beautiful girls.'

5th February   This week I've felt great optimism about *Hamlet*. I had the feeling on Friday, a quite overwhelming and moving one, that for the first time I was rehearsing a Shakespeare play with a company who could actually do it. Shaw on acting Shakespeare: 'Shakespeare should be played on the line and to the line with the utterance and acting simultaneous, inseparable, and in fact identical.' But so few can do it. It was like finding myself conducting a professional orchestra for the first time. I told the cast, and afterwards regretted it. I was probably overreacting, but Oliver Ford-Davies, characteristically, thanked me for what I'd said: 'It gives us confidence,' he said. With Michael Bryant he's the moral compass of the company. There always has to be one.

14th February   Salman has been threatened with death by the Ayatollah Khomeini, who has ordered Muslims to kill him on sight. It's an appalling testimony to the power of words, and an even more appalling testimony to the endemic meanness of spirit, hardness of heart, and foulness of soul of competing religions. A sentence of death is a living hell, it's a daily inferno. Salman's sentence brings the world of *Hamlet* nearer to us. Hamlet wants people to tell the truth, to stop people lying. Lying entails the loss of natural feelings. He tries to waken Gertrude's feelings. On his return from England he becomes obsessed with death; he goes to a cemetery. He welcomes death – why should he go on living? His father is dead; Ophelia is dead; he is estranged from his mother. And he can't overthrow the tyranny.

15th February   More than usually fictitious piece in the *Standard* ('EYRE GOES FROM RED TO PINK') about how I wanted to 'ascend into the squirearchy' by starting to hunt in Gloucestershire and that I'm a friend of Prince Edward.

16th February   Talk to Mark Henderson [*lighting designer*] after the run-through of *Hamlet*. 'It's there,' he says. 'What are you going to do now?' Two weeks to go and I feel that it's a good piece of work – if I can translate it from the rehearsal room to the stage. It's like carrying water in your hands. Dan is a thrilling and self-effacing actor: wise, with great beauty of speech and movement. I went with him to have his photo taken by Snowdon, whose technique of

relaxing the subject is to feign anxiety about whether he's doing the right thing. It's obvious that he does know: he played with some skulls and then he shot Dan looking every inch a Renaissance prince haunted by death. Dan and I were too tired, and a poor audience for Snowdon's repartee – jokes about girls' names: Salmonella, Listeria, etc.

18th February Peter Gill's production of *Juno and the Paycock* has started previewing. It's very spare, minimalist, anti-naturalistic. Peter's trying to find a way of doing O'Casey that doesn't require everything including the kitchen sink. It should give breath to the play, but at the moment the Lyttelton is sinking it. Peter and I talk about writing diaries. He says we should record the minutiae – conversations in the bar and phone calls – but by the end of the day I'm usually too tired and have forgotten the details. But the 'Today war broke out . . .' stuff is never interesting.

20th February The *Standard* have offered a sort of 'apology' for their story by quoting my father. 'Someone's been pulling your whizzer,' he was quoted as saying. 'My son is grown up and I don't dictate to him whether he should go hunting, or drink a bottle a day, or have three women a week.' That certainly sounds like him.

25th February *Hamlet* still on course but I still can't seem to make the whole greater than the sum of the parts. Every time we do the closet scene, we end in a sort of stalemate. Judi and Dan give it all the energy and attack that one could hope for, but it never quite adds up. The scene should be like a wild vertiginous argument in a car going downhill, crashing – the killing of Polonius – and the two survivors finding themselves intact and mutually terrified, fired by adrenalin, ascending into an emotional territory that they've never explored before. I fear that the problem is that Judi never quite convinces herself that she's Gertrude. In fact she says so.

26th February *Juno* has opened to universally damning reviews, a catastrophe. On the first night I thought the reviews would be dismissive but not abusive. But now everyone's an Irishman and it's a play, like *Hamlet*, that everyone has stored in their inner eye. And the Lyttelton is a *big* theatre; it needs very strong, clear, large

acting that resonates, but at the moment it's imploding. Peter Gill is very down and I'm not being supportive enough. I'm afraid of falling out with Peter. He'll always walk alone. I've always loved his productions – and his writing always surprises me, though I don't know why it should; it's like his productions, detailed, tender and unsentimental.

27th February   Salman rang to ask if he could use the cottage that we rent. He sounded desperately low, and why would he not? He's looking for somewhere safe to spend the rest of his life. He's accompanied by four Special Branch men, two of them armed. Their department will check out the cottage. It'll probably be too conspicuous. A few authors – including John Le Carré – have condemned *The Satanic Verses* and appear to be implying that death is a just punishment for what they think is bad art.

5th March   I have a feeling of near certainty about what *Hamlet* meant to Shakespeare. He was writing about rejecting your parents, about taking on responsibility, about growing up. He charts one of the great human rites of passage – from immaturity to accommodation with death. Hamlet grows up, Barbara Everitt says, in effect to grow dead. He is bound to 'grow dead' in the alien world of court politics and inherited duty – to make accommodation with that world is to be obliged to accept its 'adult' values: male and militaristic. Idealism gives way to expediency.

7th March   Mary Soames rings me at 7.45 a.m. in a state of undisguised panic. She asked me why the NT is putting on a show for Nicaragua – a late-night show organised by the actors in *Fuente*. She's very disturbed. What will happen when we have a real crisis? At least we've made up our deficit so we won't end the financial year in the red.

15th March   Technical and preview week for *Hamlet*. At times I'm certain it's good but then I think this is the usual *folie de grandeur* that precedes opening night, only to dissolve into recrimination, depression and despair when the critics and the public pass their judgement. In the Green Room someone from the education department who has just been to see the show asks me if I'm happy with it.

'Well, yes,' I reply, wrong-footed. 'Mmmm,' she says, implying, 'Well, if I were you I wouldn't be . . .' What does the production lack? The audience can't identify with Dan. They admire him, they are awed by him, but they don't yet love him. He must break their hearts. Dan tells me that a friend of his, young Spanish woman, came to see it and felt she couldn't reach him.

16th March *Hamlet* opens tonight. I'm sitting looking at a postcard of a statue of Hamlet in Elsinore that Sue gave to me last time I did the play, nine years ago, almost to the day. I sent Dan a book for the first night with a quote from a poem of his father's, 'A Time to Dance'.

> For all that have won us wings to clear the tops of grief,
> My friend who within me laughs bids me to laugh and sing.

17th March Sleepless, early morning. Haunted by *Hamlet*. Michael Bryant told me before the show that he thought it was wonderful, and I thought: if Michael thinks that, it can't go wrong. And David Aukin sent me a hugely encouraging card: 'For the second time you have directed the *Hamlet* for our generation.' But the show was only OK, it never soared. The audience was peopled with the sponsor's guests – Ladbroke's the bookies, now hoteliers, bemused at why they'd been dragged to this of all plays. Reluctant to get in for the start, practically mutinous at being pushed back after the interval. And patronising at the end. 'What did you think?' asked one woman. I opened my mouth to reply, but she did it for me. 'Interminable,' she said.

Mary Soames rang me again at 7.45 a.m. to tell me there was a dreadful review in *The Times* (actually it turned out to be the *Telegraph*), and then I found out the *Mail* was bad. And then there was the *Standard*. I feel numb at the moment, too stunned to despair. David Aukin and David Hare are very supportive, and are as bemused as I am. David H. thinks the other reviews will be brilliant. I just don't know what to think. Dan is being very stoical.

22nd March Card from Dan's mother. She says: 'After a lifetime of *Hamlet* productions yours is THE one . . . it's wonderful having

D. here to spoil a little and his attitude to his reviews is wholly admirable . . .'

24th March I'm trying to understand my feelings after *Hamlet*, reeling from the critical drubbing. It's all the more painful for having been unanticipated. I find that my production is 'old-fashioned', 'mainstream', 'has failed to find a visual syntax', etc, etc. Exactly the opposite of what was said the last time I did the play. Have I been neutered by the NT?

1st April Feeling stronger now, even combative. The reviews are actually (just) more good than bad and word of mouth is much more favourable than the reviews. I should shrug it off; Howard [*Davies*] says he knows of no director who is more self-critical and more self-doubting.

2nd April Calmer now, more philosophical. I was much too cautious; everything in the production should have been much more explicit: the court formality, the militarism, the spying, the politics, the sex. I've been reading Peter's Diaries on *Hamlet*. He said, before his NT production opened, that it was as close as he'd ever got to realising his intentions in a production. Then it started to preview and he began to be alarmed. 'I confronted for the first time the possibility of failure. And I mean it – for the very first time. Up to now I have always been supremely confident about this work . . . I thought it was going to be a breakthrough . . . What happened? . . . Some of the critics are wonderful, some are dreadful. Why are they so angry?' I still have bursts of rancid and bitter feelings about the *Hamlet* reviews. Like Saul Bellow's Herzog, I want to write to everyone who criticises it. I'm angry and hurt. It'll wear off. I've had a letter from Will Boyd, very detailed and generous account of *Hamlet*. He ends up: 'I sometimes think that the perfect fate for these types [the critics] is what they did to the dead pharaohs before embalming them – having their brains drawn out through their noses with a long hook.'

7th April David Storey's *The March on Russia* has opened. It doesn't have the force of *In Celebration*, its prequel, but I love David's writing: it's not nostalgic, but it's all about loss – of youth, of

way of life, of community, of hope. Lindsay [*Anderson*] and Jocelyn [*Herbert, designer*] have done it in what is now a wildly unfashionable style: old Royal Court – unmannered acting, devotion to the text, unostentatious direction, simple and expressive design.

9th April   Gloucestershire. I rode along the side of the airfield, soaked in wartime echoes – old hangars, weed-infested tarmac and the ghosts of planes limping in and young men going to die. Idyllic countryside, down a glacial valley, then a river valley, rushes and willow, past a lake, through a wood. As David [*Hare*] says, a day when you could see the point of England.

10th April   I was confronted by all the reviews of *Hamlet*. They were less violent than I had imagined. In most of them the strongest emotion was disappointment, which is a compliment of a sort. The production was variously interpreted as 'bland', 'over-dressed', 'economically staged', 'lavishly over-extravagant', 'well-spoken', 'badly spoken', 'adventurous', 'mainstream', 'highly intelligent', 'devoid of any ideas', 'utterly lucid', 'confused', 'thrilling' and 'dull'. The reviews weren't sufficiently discouraging to warrant jumping out of the window but not sufficiently effusive to guarantee lifting the depression that follows opening a play as sure as tonic follows gin. So, *en avant*.

11th April   Denys Lasdun did a platform lecture in the Olivier. He announced he had no intention of changing an atom of 'the room' (i.e. the Olivier), a space that embraced audience and actors in a unifying hug. He was mandarin, combative, vague, lyrical and occasionally incomprehensible. But right about fashion and to say about the building: 'It is what it is.' He quoted Arthur Clough:

Pure form nakedly displayed
And all things absolutely made.

Someone asked him: if concrete is the medium of our century and its pure form is nakedly displayed, why was the concrete shuttered and is therefore impregnated with the pattern of a million pine planks?

15th April   Ninety-three people have been killed in an accident in a football stadium. Once again it's Liverpool involved, but it could

have happened any time, anywhere, in the last few years and astonishingly hasn't. Bad facilities, thoughtless treatment of fans, lax safety conditions. If such things happened in a theatre things would be changed soon enough. It's class, of course, as always.

16th April The RSC is in turmoil. Terry Hands has resigned; he's leaving in 1991. There's a frantic scrabble for power. My money would be on Ian McKellen. I don't know if Adrian [*Noble*] will want it. Good director, but I don't know if he'd have the appetite for taming the colossus. The RSC suffers from what historian Paul Kennedy describes as 'imperial overreach'. Now there'll be a power struggle, which will seem inexplicable to the outsider. 'The politics of the art world are only a diminutive parody of the real power,' said Tristan Tzara.

17th April Variety Club Lunch for Lulu's twenty-five years in showbiz. A room full of showbiz folk tanned like handbags. I got introduced in a roll call as a 'celebrity'. I felt (and was) an utter sham.

18th April I went to the House of Commons with Mary for a Back Bench Members Arts Committee. Toby Jessel [*Tory MP*] told a joke about a Scots Guards officer seeing a down-and-out in Waterloo with a sign reading 'FALKLANDS VICTIM'. He gave him a ten-pound note. '*Muchas gracias*,' said the down-and-out.

19th April We had a reading of *Racing Demon* at the Studio [*NT research and development facility*. David [*Hare*] visited the Church of England Synod in York in 1987, with a vague idea that the spectacle of vicars playing politics might make good theatre, and he was right. I had no higher expectations than a satirical look at a largely irrelevant expiring British institution, but this is something really exceptional and wildly original, about love really, sexual and spiritual. And faith of both sorts. The play's still missing what David describes as a *scène à faire*. Oliver Ford-Davies and Stella Gonet read beautifully.

20th April John O. has given me his play; it's called *Déjà Vu*. He's haunted by the spectre of mediocrity and loss (or lack) of talent, and consumed by fury and despair. I think he expects the best of people – perhaps including himself – and is always disappointed by them. He

sees himself as an aristocrat, dragged down by the middle class, the commonplace, the mundane, the unambitious, the unassertive, the mediocre. This from Jimmy Porter in the new play: 'I should settle down if I was you. Pretend it isn't happening. You're a lucky fellow. Mediocrity is a great comforter, my little funny ursine friend. And very democratic. It's all yours.' Charles Wood, who loves him, says you can only understand him if you think of him as a rep actor – meaning formed by that experience. He's sufficiently self-aware to know that his prejudices and his passions are incurable: he's a sort of demonic Peter Pan.

21st April Max Rayne took me to lunch with Lord Goodman. He's a mountainous creature like a prehistoric animal – mammoth or coelacanth – with hair sprouting from every extremity. He said Harold Wilson never went to the theatre and had only read one novel: 'The Spreading of – something or other. A Yorkshire tale.' Goodman stopped Wilson from appointing John Betjeman as Poet Laureate. He appointed Cecil Day Lewis instead. I told Goodman that I'd once asked Mary Wilson if she was still writing poetry. 'Alas, no,' she said, 'the muse has flown.' Much talk between the Lords Rayne and Goodman of other lords, and much talk of putting people in the way of jobs, chairmanships of boards, etc. This is the world of realpolitik. It feels like a casting session.

22nd April Meeting with Deborah Warner. She's deeply concerned with doing things for the *right* reasons. It's almost a religious thing with her, it can't be casual or opportunistic or haphazard. She thinks – and she's right – that there's too much of theatre, too much of everything. The audiences are spoilt for choice and the directors are corrupted by quantity. She tells me that after making *Tumbledown* I could have retired. 'It's so achieved,' she says. She'll definitely do *The Good Woman of Sezchuan*. Much discussion of whether the title should be 'Good Woman' or 'Good Person'. I asked Maggie Smith when I last had lunch with her if there was any difference between women and men directors. 'Well, I've only worked with one. But she's the only director who's ever asked me if my corset is pinching.'

23rd April I wrote to John O. about his play. I said I couldn't remember looking forward to receiving any play more than his, and

my disappointment was perhaps due to my exaggeratedly high expectations. The play is really Jimmy Porter's speeches, essentially monologues, which are depressing, heroic cries from another world. I suggested to John that he should perform the play, or Jimmy Porter's speeches, as a monologue prior to a performance of *Look Back*. Old and new Jimmy Porters could speak for their respective generations. But I know this suggestion will add insult to injury.

1st May   I ended the week in exhaustion and thought seriously of cancelling my production of *The Voysey Inheritance* which I start rehearsing in two weeks' time. My heart isn't in it.

2nd May   Talk to Peter Palumbo about changing the face of the Arts Council. He says it's desperately difficult to do anything: they want to close down Northern Ballet on the grounds that in the AC's view they're terrible. They've had about 10,000 letters and been castigated by MPs. Saw Caryl Churchill's new play, *Icecream*, at the Royal Court. She can't write uninterestingly even if it doesn't feel like she's convinced by it. There's an argument that women artists are unlike male in that they're essentially conservationist, not concerned with overturning the past. Caryl defies this, but she's not competitive like male writers.

3rd May   I'm beginning to feel like a courtier. Went to *Aspects of Love* with Princess Margaret and Max and Jane, with Norman St John-Stevas in attendance. The show is clunky and humourless, with pitifully bad lyrics ('I dined with Garbo/Translated La Bo/Heme'). But it does have a well-meaning heart and its premise isn't a contrived one: that love changes everything. It's operetta – cursory characterisation and storyline, driven forward by the music rather than character, and by a generalised demand to FEEL and LOVE. Lloyd Webber's forte is myth or fairy-tale: *Phantom of the Opera* is 'Beauty and the Beast', *Joseph and His Amazing Technicolor Dreamcoat, Evita* and *Jesus Christ Superstar* are Cinderella stories. In the interval Princess Di appears with her friends and, one gathers, her lover, giving us the opportunity to compare and contrast two princesses at close quarters. Princess Margaret gestures emphatically and rather self-consciously, keen to establish the persona of a 'jolly' girl, but if it weren't for the sharp English upper-class voice, you'd

say she looks like a Maltese landlady: small, frowning, drawn and unhealthy. Diana is pretty but not beautiful, tall, slightly awkward and faintly pitiable. Margaret talks to me about opera: 'Can't stand it. A lot of frightfully boring people standing still on stage and yelling.' I ask her if she'd seen *A Question of Attribution* and she's quite tart about it. She didn't approve of putting the Head of State on stage, but would like to watch it from the wings. She's wary of 'Bennett', she says.

4th May   Opening of *Ghetto*. A triumphant evening even if the play *is* occasionally thin and sometimes teeters on the edge of bathos. It's a triumph for Nick [*Hytner*] and Bob [*Crowley*], and deservedly so. They've staged it brilliantly and it's musically superb, but the writing often lacks substance and is only given ballast by its subject. The material acts like a trampoline: the actors with weight rebound significantly, the lightweights just bounce off, so that there's an occasional sniff of Nazi kitsch. Peter Gill tells me he thought of resigning when I decided to do it, which dismays me because he was unwilling or unable to express his reservations at meetings when the play was discussed. Or at least nothing more than a discreet sneer. I'm sure he would say that it wouldn't have made the slightest difference. It doesn't make the slightest difference what I say to him about the Studio, but it doesn't stop me speaking about it. It raises the question of whether Peter wants to be part of a theatre that he disapproves of.

5th May   David Aukin wants me to take a week off rehearsals for *Voysey*. I want to cancel the show.

7th May   Dan's exhausted, stretched on the rack. If it weren't for his pride and his loyalty he'd be off tomorrow. He's completely lost heart. I couldn't tell him that I felt just the same. For him it's partly the subject matter – his father and suicide, but it's much more that he's determined to investigate the truth of the part and he has to do it in a great barn with hopeless acoustics to 1,200 people who are craving spectacle. How *can* he reconcile this? Every day, *every* day, even when he's not playing, he's confronted with these feelings, and they aren't purged by playing the part. Just aroused and toyed with. And it's not even continuous. Now the pain in my neck has started to

come back. The body's way of making metaphor. From *The Mistake* by James Fenton:

> With the mistake your life goes in reverse
> Now you can see exactly what you did
> Wrong yesterday and wrong the day before
> And such mistake leads back to something worse.

9th May   I haven't cancelled *Voysey*. David [*Aukin*]'s been very stalwart in the face of my chronic cowardice. I went to see *Hamlet* again. It had energy, passion and detail, but I'd failed to create a world that was expressively realised. It was too static, too realistic, too solid, and for the first time I could clearly see that the audience didn't take Dan to their hearts because although he does let the audience in, they're intimidated by what they find. I felt depressed and dissatisfied by the production: so nearly good, but so nearly dull.

13th May   Mary rang me this morning about her meeting with Peter Palumbo at the Arts Council. Just as it was about to start Luke Rittner [*Secretary-General*] came in, a smile just visible above a pile of papers. He put the papers down, and then demonstrated the number of documents that the AC had sent to the NT and the NT's responses. Palumbo was baffled by this intervention. 'I get the message,' said Mary to Luke. But she didn't, and I didn't. He might have been signalling to Palumbo, For God's sake rid us of this bureaucratic baggage.

We've advertised for a new literary manager. From an application: 'At present I'm applying the theories of Julia Kristeva to the work of Edward Bond, in an effort to see what avant-gardism can offer in an examination of Bond's political work.'

14th May   I went to the ruins of the Rose Theatre, a stone's throw from the Thames, uncovered in excavations for a new office block: mud, a few stone foundations, a hint of wooden columns that look as if they've been chewed by a giant dog, but in spite of it all a feeling of being there in the sixteenth century. You could feel the theatre: a rough platform, a raked auditorium, a gallery, all smaller than the Cottesloe. Peter Hall was on hand to say that it proves that Shake-

speare was written for chamber theatres. True, but why have we got these aircraft hangars to do the plays in? It's just economics. They're about to fill in the site: a sign of the times, concreting over our history.

17th May   I feel like I'm in a Balzac novel – I seem to do nothing these days but dinners. A few days ago I sat next to the Japanese Ambassador's wife. When she went back to Japan people asked her why she talked so strangely. She was so habituated to years of diplomatic talk – feigning pleasure, surprise, interest, retaining a diplomatic smile – that she seemed to them to talk like a foreigner. And a dinner in the city in Mercer's Hall – grand and Jacobean, full of self-regard and self-indulgence. I sat next to one of the Tate family who was well pleased with himself, and Charles Moore of the *Spectator*, once described by Willie Donaldson as looking like the juvenile in a '30s musical. He was slightly fogeyish, slightly school-boyish, but very pleasant. We both felt equally out of place. He said he'd introduce me to James Goldsmith, who he was sure would endow the NT. On the way out I bent down to do up my shoelace and stumbled on the stair. I got a very left-handed look from two women who were certain I was drunk.

18th May   I saw Joe Papp who's just been in Poland. He's indefatigably enthusiastic and energetic, running an organisation at least as large as the NT – or at least doing as many productions – with no subsidy. But with no building. 'Let me tell you a secret,' he said. He's planning a production of *Kiss Me Kate* with Kevin Kline and Meryl Streep, and Mike Nichols directing, and Neil Simon doing the rewrites. But will it happen? 'Oh sure,' said Joe. Joe asked me a few years ago to direct *Lear* with Lee J. Cobb in the Park. 'Are you ready for *Lear*?' he said. 'No,' I answered. He asked me again, and my answer was the same.

I went late (10.30 p.m.) to the House of Commons for an Adjournment Debate. It's apparently a way of putting a point on record and forcing a minister to answer it. Alastair Goodlad [*Tory MP*] made a good (well-briefed) speech about the NT to an audience of two Tory back-benchers, the Minister Richard Luce, and his PPS, David Aukin, Stephen Wood [*head of press*] and myself. He gave us a very good review and argued for increased funding from the Arts

Council and for the AC's allocation from the Treasury. Luce was wholly non-committal but wholly respectful.

21st May   I talk to Bill Dudley [*designer*] about the rise of the new orthodoxy, the opera ethos – camp and self-referential. There really is a reluctance to engage with any feeling or humane detail or ambivalence. Expressionism is a fascist aesthetic.

23rd May   Read an interview with Jean Mohr where he said that we should look at a photograph of ourselves once a month to assess one's mental and physical health. I'm looking at a photograph of myself taken by Snowdon about six months ago. At first glance I see someone I don't like very much. At second glance I see fear (is this hindsight?). And an attempt to assert confidence. The subject is trying to detach himself from the occasion, trying to second-guess the photographer.

28th May   Rehearsals for *Voysey* chug along – a good run-through. The play is satisfying and I revere (well, worship) Granville-Barker, and with a perfect cast it would be transcendent. But at the moment it's patchy and although it will be an honourable, detailed piece of work I fear it will be reverently endured by the audience and damned with faint praise by the critics.

30th May   I had to talk to the cast of *Hamlet* to tell them Dan was withdrawing from the show. It was painful and embarrassing. Then I went to *Hamlet* with Lu, who'd touchingly brought me a sandwich and an apple. She knew I was in agony and she broke my heart with her generosity. At the age of fourteen. I didn't like my production: I thought Dan seemed obviously uncomfortable in it and that really crushed me. My injury was compounded by seeing Chris Morahan who was sympathetic, but clearly hated the show. I saw Denys Lasdun in the interval. He castigated me for not understanding taste, or not having it. He's immensely dogged but right about one thing – you can't just add on to the building: it is what it is.

3rd June   I'm rung by a friend of Dad's to say that he's had a serious stroke and is in Yeovil Hospital. I ring the hospital and am put on to a 'relative', actually Margaret. She tells me it's not worth

coming down at the moment because he won't recognise me. Then she tells me he has been pinching her bottom, so he must be all right. He went up for a sleep in the afternoon, and when she went up at seven to see why he hadn't come down, he was lying on the floor. 'I didn't know whether he was drunk or something more serious.' He was paralysed down the left side and could barely talk. I went down to see him after rehearsals, drove like a madman, utterly unaware of the road. Dad could barely speak. Nor could I. However confused one's feelings about one's parents, when you're confronted with them – weak, vulnerable, mortal – it's terribly hard not to feel very shaken. He barely knew I was there. But then that was nothing new.

6th June   Went to see Dad again after rehearsals. Down on the train, in the hospital for an hour, train straight back to London. He didn't say much, seemed in terrible pain and depression. He seems hugely diminished.

11th June   Sunday. Went down to Yeovil Hospital. Left London early – about seven-forty-five. Clear roads. I drove in a dream and I was stopped for speeding. Dad was sitting up in a chair, slumped over, sleeping, his glasses about to fall from his hand. He woke up; we talked a bit. He told me his mother had died of a stroke at the age of forty-three. And his father had died of a stroke. He seemed a very sad, defeated figure, and I felt desperately sorry for him.

12th June   Drove back late last night, rehearsed this morning and in the evening we did the first preview of *Voysey* to an audience who loved the play and the company.

19th June   Saw Dad again yesterday. He talked more coherently. I don't think he'll recover the use of his limbs, although he talked confidently, or defiantly, of doing a lot of exercise. I told him I was going to take a play to Dubrovnik. He said he'd been there in a battleship.

20th June   In Dubrovnik for a recce. It's an enchanting city. Like Siena and Venice, it's free of traffic inside the walls and it gives the impression of having been designed as a whole. It's small but perfectly formed, like an Oxbridge college, slightly claustrophobic

and infested with tourists, very well preserved, with no trace of the brain-numbing hand of the State that you see in Czechoslovakia and Romania. Misha, who runs the Festival, is like an amiable and intelligent gigolo. He says that things haven't been the same since the old king died.

21st June   *Voysey* still goes well, and I marvel at the fragility of my judgement and my confidence that a few weeks ago I was pleading to be released from the obligation of doing this play. The cast have pulled together and are doing very good work. I love the way that a production can turn around in rehearsals in a few days. I so much prefer Granville-Barker to Shaw, who was a brilliant polemicist who dealt with certainties and assertions. Sometimes – but not often enough – Shaw breathed life into his sermons, whereas G.-Barker was a committed sceptic who started from the premise that the only thing certain about human behaviour is that nothing is certain. *Voysey* is a virtuoso display of stagecraft (his best play): the writer showing that as director he can handle twelve speaking characters on stage at one time, and that as actor he can deal with the most ambitious and unexpected modulations of thought and feeling. I think he's the English Chekhov. He never got the credit he was due, and must have been galled by the way that Shaw's insatiable ego sucked up attention. No wonder he retired into exile with his millionairess.

22nd June   *The Grapes of Wrath* in a production by Steppenwolf at the Lyttelton Theatre. This is thrilling work and a triumph for Thelma [*Holt, producer*] who's got them here. It's the best of American theatre acting in an elegant production that mercifully doesn't try to mimic the film. It's naturalistic – real water, etc – but makes beauty out of the thingness of things. Wilde: 'This unfortunate aphorism about art holding up the mirror to nature is deliberately said by Hamlet in order to convince the onlookers of his absolute insanity in all art-matters.' Well, he was wrong. No theatrical naturalism – if taken seriously, as opposed to being a half-hearted convention – is without poetry.

25th June   Peter Brook asked me to a seminar that he was giving for the Directors' Guild. He spoke of the importance of the

audience, of previews, of small spaces, of privacy in rehearsals, of
the need of the designer always to be present. 'What does a director
do?' he was asked. 'Get the actors on and off stage,' he said. I
remember what he told me he'd learnt when he did *The Mahabharata* for the first time. He said: 'Never have a press night.'
Afterwards he talked about a project that he said we could work
on together, about Meyerhold.

29th June Lunch at the *Spectator*. The cast included Norman
Tebbit and James Goldsmith. Tebbit talked of God as a WASP and of
'our Froggie friends'. He's imperialist, sexist, but not fascist. He
discriminates between freedom and democracy – the one not ensuring the other. He speaks of common sense – 'the sense of the ruling
class' – and admires the way that Labour conducted the last election.
His three M's are: Muddle, Mortgages and Mandelson. Says Tory
European policy is a mess, no clear objectives, and the European
Parliament is an irrelevance. Goldsmith is tall, very striking, with a
strong sense of subdued violence. He's anti-nuclear and anti-colo-
nialist. Talks of '*civisme*' lacking in England, but strong in France.
Says Mitterrand is a crook and France has an elected monarchy.
Tebbit looks envious at that. Goldsmith senses that I'm going to ask
him for money for the theatre. 'Don't ask me about theatre,' he says,
'I never go. My legs are too long.' Nigel Lawson's children – Dominic
and Nigella – are confident and articulate and charming. She wanted
to be a pop singer or a ballet dancer, but became a journalist,
propositioned early in her career by the editor of a Sunday newspaper who gave her a stone as a present. Frank Johnson talks of his
love of opera and his nostalgia for the great days of the *Daily
Telegraph*. Do they go together?

7th July I went to Berlin to see Peter Stein's production of *The
Cherry Orchard*. Much of it was wonderful, alluring and illuminating, but much was massively self-indulgent. Brilliantly lit by Wolf-
gang Goebbel, but in a style that we'd never tolerate: real dark, real
shadow, real silhouette. The first act was lit only through the shutters
at the back of the room without any front light and there were some
characters whose faces we never saw at all, and most of them only a
third of the time. It was played at a pace that doubled the length of
the performance; the last act, which Chekhov specifically wanted to

be played urgently – they have a train to catch – was played at funereal tempo. A lot of the detail was wonderfully observed, and often there were wholly unexpected and spontaneous moments. What the production did was to take everything in the play and push it to its logical conclusion – the farce, the polemic, the naturalism, the expressionism, the poetry, the symphonic orchestration.

9th July *Voysey* has had a very good press. The work was so painfully difficult to do – not because of what it was, but because of my lack of will. Day after day crawling into rehearsal and showing a good face to the world while inside I was screaming. I dreamt last night that Peter Hall was looking after Mum.

11th July Went to Lu's prize-giving to see her collect her form prize. I was daydreaming when somebody pushed a card under my nose: 'PHONE CALL FOR RICHARD EYRE'. I went out to the secretary's office and spoke to David Aukin. He told me that Olivier had died and could I come to the theatre straight away. I knew this was a significant historical moment, but didn't at the time feel anything except mild exasperation and sadness. Only after I had spoken to half a dozen journalists about his legacy and how I didn't really know him, did I start to feel that it was truly the end of an era, the last great buccaneering actor-manager. Brecht said: 'Happy the land that needs no heroes.' Maybe happier perhaps, but duller. Olivier was mercurial, had energy, a remarkable presence, was funny, charming, devious, vain, and occasionally laughably hammy. He willed himself to greatness, but I'm not sure that a 'great' actor is always a good one. He satisfied a desire that audiences have for actors to be larger than life and to be able to be seen acting at the same time as they move you to tears or laughter – the desire to be knowingly seduced.

17th July Meeting with Peter Nichols, who is like a cardinal inquisitor, short grey hair, flinty eyes, an unforgiving stare. I feel that I have been judged guilty before I have been charged. He is jumpy and so am I. I feel that he regards my emollience as evasion and my admiration of his previous work as mere flattery. There's only one compliment from a director that can mean anything to a playwright: 'I like your play and I'm going to put it on.' It must be

exasperating for Peter after years of success and demand to find that now he's a supplicant.

19th July   Joan Plowright has pulled out of *Celestina*. I can't blame her for that, but what will we do instead?

20th July   Talked to Gorg about Dad today after she'd been to see the Consultant. I wrote this on a notepad:

> can't read
> can't walk
> won't try
> incontinent
> despairing

We talk about Mum. She says that Mum once said to her that she couldn't recognise the planet we'd descended from.

22nd July   I'm strolling around Gatwick with Lu (who's travelling with me) looking for actors. The clothes ('leisure wear') of the Brits have changed so much in the last few years that suddenly everyone looks like an actor. C & A and Benetton and Next have stopped Brits abroad looking like refugees from a McGill postcard. John Castle is still wearing his suit. The exchange rate is plummeting as we're in flight, so much talk about being dinar millionaires by the time we reach Dubrovnik. At the castle nothing is as we asked for: the seating, the entrances, the dressing rooms. The winch that we were going to use to lift the statue into the courtyard has been dismantled since our recce. A helicopter is being sought. In the evening Dan, Lu and I go to see a local show which is a parody of a parody of a memory of a Lloyd Webber-style musical. Lu adores Dan and he's very good with her.

23rd July   Dubrovnik. An endless sequence of threats, cajolery, ultimata and fevered conferences. Finally we had what we asked for with the seating: an army helicopter appeared from out of nowhere and lifted the statue, like a flying Christ (or Lenin) into the courtyard. On Monday night we lit the show, working until 4 a.m, anxiously chasing the dawn. Then went back to the hotel for an hour or two of

sleep. When I came down to breakfast I saw Roger Chapman [*head of touring*]. 'We've had our first incident,' he said. One of our actors had got drunk, provoked some local psychopath to violence and had his eye almost gouged out by a broken bottle. I went to see him in hospital. It was like a First World War dressing station in Gallipoli, blood-soaked bandages, beds in the nicotine-stained corridors, dust, dirt, and the smell of poverty, pus and despair. He apologised, acknowledged his drink problem and wants me to put him in touch with Tony Hopkins, so at least something positive has emerged from this diplomatic debacle.

I watched the dress rehearsal of *Hamlet* with something approaching despair. It seemed a lifeless, unconnected costume parade. But the next day, the first night, it was coherent and animated and Dan was incandescent. In the last scene when Claudius sent him off to England, he banged his head against the castle wall. In the interval a frightened interpreter came to find me and took me to the dressing room. 'There is trouble,' she said, 'between the King and Hamlet.' And trouble there was. They were shouting at each other surrounded by the rest of the cast in the vaulted cloisters that we were using for dressing rooms.

The second half of the show was charged with static. Afterwards, when I asked how Dan's head was, Roger Chapman said: 'Someone should have told Dan that the stonework has been around a lot longer than he has.' The whole incident further convinces me that there's something profoundly wrong with the show – a cast that has never cohered. I feel defeated. I told Judi this, and she nodded: Yes, you're right to be. But the party after the performance was cheerful, and in spite of a scar and a bruise on Dan's forehead he was buoyant. Lu got drunk. I thought she'd had one glass of champagne, but apparently she'd had five more when I wasn't looking. She had sat next to me during the performance and whispered to me just before it started that she was very proud of me, and I turned away from her in tears.

24th July   Dubrovnik. Dan and I had a long lunch with Misha at a restaurant about an hour away. Lovely meal, swimming in clear water, we felt a galaxy away from an East European communist country. There's an island off the coast that belonged to the Hapsburgs. A gypsy put a spell on it – whoever owned the island would

die an unnatural death: Rudolph, Maximilian of Mexico, and the Socialist Republic of Yugoslavia. Misha says the country will explode – there's a psychotic Serbian leader and there'll be violence between Serbs and Croats.

28th July   Went to see Dad who's been moved to the geriatric ward of Dorchester Hospital. When I first saw him he was being helped into a chair in exactly the same place in exactly the same room as Mum had been seven years ago. He's suffering more from despair than paralysis. He says: 'These things are meant to change people.' The man in the next bed keeps him awake shouting. 'I want a fuck.'

2nd August   Scarborough to see Alan Ayckbourn's new plays: *Revenger's Comedies*. The taxi driver who collects me from York tells me that a few months ago he'd picked up Peter Hall at the station when he was being chased by the press over his love life. 'How will I recognise him?' the taxi driver asked Alan. 'Oh he'll be travelling incognito,' said Alan. 'He'll be the only person stepping off the train wearing dark glasses.' Alan's plays are mathematically intricate; the plot logic is unimpeachable but the emotional logic is unclear. The characters, who are in extreme positions, don't seem to suffer pain. Like all Alan's plays the technique is dazzling, but in this one the bloodstream seems to have been thinned out. These plays would be brilliant if Alan would compress the two plays into one. Alan's very hospitable: the Duke in his domain, utterly confident and secure.

8th August   Meet with Ian Charleson at my house; in theory he'll replace Dan in *Hamlet*. I haven't seen Ian for a while, but I know he's been ill and I've heard rumours about him being HIV-positive. I'm shocked when he appears: he's had pneumonia and he's still got a chronic sinus complaint which gives him large, swollen bags under his eyes. It's barely possible to glimpse the face beneath the swelling, a malicious parody of his beauty. But he seems to be without vanity. We don't talk about him being HIV-positive, but it's there as an unspoken subtext. He says he's sure that his eyes will respond to treatment. We talk about the parts that he desperately wants to play – Richard II, Angelo, Benedick – and Hamlet. I offer him the part, more with my heart than my head.

10th August   Lunch with Cameron [*Mackintosh*], Prospero and Pied Piper of the British musical theatre in the guise of an enthusiastic schoolboy. He's played a long game, investing big, marketing widely, creating a brand image – the 'Cameron Mackintosh musical' – which is perpetuated with successive casts and productions cloned throughout the world. Cameron's like Ziegfeld: with his shows there are only two stars – the show and the producer. We talk about the possibility of his trust endowing the NT, enabling us to put on a series of classic musicals with full orchestra and chorus. By 'classic' I mean that blend of drama, song and dance infused with optimism and wit which reached a perfect equilibrium for a few years (*Oklahoma!* to *Cabaret*) and then failed to re-invent itself. We agree on six classics: *Guys and Dolls*, *West Side Story*, *My Fair Lady*, *Oklahoma!*, *South Pacific*, *Carousel* and *Gypsy*. We argue over *Pal Joey* – great score, rotten book in the second half, decide that *Sweeney Todd* is in a class of its own, and totally disagree over *Oliver* which Cameron loves and I don't. I find it matey – fake Cockney – and dated.

3rd September   Back from holiday. An unexamined life is a life not worth living (the unlived life isn't worth examining), so I'm taking account. Even at the age of eight this prayer would mortify me: 'We have left undone those things which we ought to have done, And we have done those things which we ought not to have done, And there is no health in us.' I wish I'd studied harder at Cambridge (or at all), I wish I hadn't been satisfied with early success, that I'd travelled more, that I'd learned to speak French and Italian properly and remembered more Latin, that I'd learnt music, been more generous, given more of myself, listened more, spoken less, not been so callous and casual with relationships. In short, I suppose, not been myself. Auden: 'Between the ages of twenty and forty we're engaged in the process of discussing who we are, which involves learning the difference between accidental limitations which it is our duty to outgrow and the necessary limitations of our nature beyond which we cannot trespass with impunity.'

5th September   Coventry with Roger Chapman and David Aukin to see Peter Wood's production of *Beaux' Stratagem* [*George Farquhar*], which we're touring. On the journey we talk about *Richard III* which Ian McK. is keen for me to direct, and I tell David and

Roger that I'll do it. Peter's production is very enjoyable: he really understands these plays in a way that I don't and his temperament and talent is terribly well matched to the wit – of the language and structure. In the interval I'm told there's a phone call for me: Dan has walked offstage in the middle of the Ghost scene. He couldn't/ wouldn't go back on, so the show stopped. An announcement. Half an hour pause. Then Jeremy Northam went on, and finished the performance. Poor Dan. At least I've had the solace, or the distraction, of the work of running the theatre, but Dan has had to battle on night after night. When he left the stage I suppose it was because, with his remorselessly punishing honesty, there was nothing else he could do.

12th September Confirmation that Dan can't play *Hamlet* again, so Jeremy Northam will play in the interim, until Ian takes over. Dan's problem wasn't, as the papers say, his relationship with the Ghost of his father but his relationship with the play and that auditorium: it sucks you dry. He wrestled night after night in that vast space with the play's subjects – fathers, mothers, sons, grief, suicide, sex, love, revenge, intellect, violence, pacifism, discipline and death, and if they floored him he was guilty not of neurosis or incompetence, but of an excess of ambition to do justice to it.

14th September Occasional flashes of enjoyment in rehearsal working with Ian. *Beaux' Stratagem* and *Man, Beast and Virtue* have opened successfully. Elsewhere turmoil among the staff, and paranoia and fear of mutiny on my part. And I've heard today that the *Sunday Mirror* is asking if Ian is going to be able to open in *Hamlet* because he's got AIDS.

15th September Went to *Miss Saigon*, which makes me feel that we're a small American colony – Airstrip One. It's not my taste, but Nick [*Hytner*]'s staging is dazzling and Jonathan [*Pryce*]'s performance is excellent. It has a filmed sequence where Vietnam victims of bombing – children – are shown in an orphanage and their suffering is conscripted to make us feel that the show is authentic. The show is straining to be *Madame Butterfly* but the music is kitsch, orchestrated within an inch of its life. 'Just a wee bit manipulative,' said Billy Paterson in Jon's dressing room. 'People were sobbing in the

front row,' said Jon. 'Probably the backers,' said Billy. Actually the
show is one of those that theatre people will always complain about.
As Michael Codron [*producer*] said of a play: 'No one likes it. Only
the public and the critics.'

16th September Just talked to Dad, who was very tearful. I told
him I loved him. I've never said anything like that to him before, and
he never has to me.

17th September Dan is more philosophical about his collapse but
hardly less disturbed by it. Macready had to act after hearing of the
death of one of his children. He said in his diaries that 'an actor must
affect an immoderate buoyancy of spirits while perhaps his heart is
breaking'. For the first few days Dan was almost calm, and almost
indifferent to what he'd done. Numb with shock. It's the thawing
that's so painful.

18th September Early meeting with Anthony Blackstock [*head of
finance*]. We face a big deficit this year, and an apocalyptic model for
next year – redundancies, massive change of policy, turmoil, con-
vulsions and fear. Meeting with Richard Bullimore [*production
manager*] who tells me that the staff are disappointed that I couldn't
wave a magic wand and change their lives. Then meeting with Mary
Soames about the sponsorship we've been offered by Rothman's, the
South African tobacco company: £170,000. What is the price of our
moral purity? Mary agrees that we shouldn't accept it. *Hamlet*
rehearsals are sticky and very wearing. Ian's heard that Phil Sayer
[*actor*] has just died of AIDS, but he works on resolutely. Then to
Our Country's Good [*Timberlake Wertenbaker*], which is really
enjoyable, typically fastidiously directed by Max [*Stafford-Clark*], a
very good cast, inc. Jim Broadbent. The play and production make a
powerful argument for the resilience and necessity of theatre.

20th September Saw Trevor Nunn's production of *Othello*. With
his *Macbeth* he invented small-scale Shakespeare, which was reve-
latory and the only production of the play that I've ever seen that's
worked. At the moment – it was the first preview – this production is
extremely slow because each scene is staged with fastidious naturalistic detail and a profusion of props. The flow of the play is broken

by long shuffling in the dark as chairs, tables, beds, books, papers, etc are set up for the next scene. It's all clear from line to line – and no one more so than Ian [*McKellen*] – but there's no fluency. The urgent pulse and the terrifying helter-skelter into chaos become a studied and sedate progress. Willard White as Othello suffers from the inescapable equation of this play – the better your Iago, the more difficult it is for your Othello.

22nd September Meeting with Tony Harrison during which I floundered because I couldn't concentrate. We talk about doing *Le Bourgeois Gentilhomme* [*Molière*] together: a great social satire. Tony will update it. Gloom in *Hamlet* rehearsals looking at Ian's face. I talked to his doctor, who was far from optimistic: the swelling is AIDS-related, he said, it won't go away. I also talked to Tamasin [*his sister*] about Dan. She says she's very anxious about him; he seems to be making little progress and is suffocating from guilt at having let me down.

26th September Dinner with Natasha [*Richardson*] and Robert [*Fox*], who was churning with bile about *Miss Saigon* and gave an inspired precis of the show culminating with a demonstration of Jonathan ravishing a Cadillac. Robert is hugely entertaining, even when you're fearing that in other company it might be you that is the cause of his wit. Like most of us Robert wants to be an outsider but at the same time succeed on the inside.

28th September Party for the last night of the old *Hamlet* cast. I couldn't watch any of the performance. I'm sick of the production, embarrassed and angry and ashamed of it, but it's *there* and I have to support the actors who are going on and continue feeling guilty whenever people talk of it. I'm appalled by my current treachery.

4th October I've asked Ian [*McKellen*] to lead a company; Deborah [*Warner*] will direct *Lear* and I'll do *Richard III*. And Bob [*Crowley*]'s agreed to design it. I know what I want out of *Richard III* – or at least I know what I don't want: faux medieval posturing. Every line of the play must be explored in a rehearsal process that is open and exploratory. The process is as important as the result.

9th October *Hamlet* opened with Ian Charleson. He looks strange but acts beautifully – he's warm, accessible, and vulnerable, but a bit under-powered. Since he's become HIV-positive he's acquired real moral authority: courage, sangfroid, maturity. I admire him very much and feel that he's going to need every ounce of his courage, and a ferocious determination to survive. I've been painfully unsure about whether to let him go onstage or replace him. I hope I've taken the right decision for the right reasons.

10th October I saw the Ninagawa production of a Chikamatsu play, *Suicide for Love*, which we've got visiting in the Lyttelton. Hugely acclaimed but I found it entirely meretricious, very badly performed and glutinously kitschy – mountains of snow and wall-to-wall muzak.

11th October Board meeting. We discuss the purpose of the NT and its future. I describe the aim of the NT to provide continuity of 'investment', employment and theatrical tradition, at ticket prices which aren't punitively expensive, and to present what couldn't or wouldn't be done in the commercial theatre both in content and style. Tom [*Stoppard*] says it's for the best of everything: our greatest asset is our integrity. We mustn't be seen to concede to pressure of any kind. Sarah Hogg points out that my definition of doing anything that couldn't or wouldn't be done in the West End is implicitly Thatcherite. Well, it's a response to Thatcherism certainly, and perhaps I'm guilty of conspiring with the opposition by being defensive. I think we're going to have a huge deficit at the end of the financial year, but I feel oddly optimistic.

12th October I saw Tom Clarke [*TV writer*] in hospital. 'These fucking doctors, they don't know *anything*. But I'm going to write *the* play about them – that'll fix em.' He told me about David Mercer visiting Cuba: he was taken to the sugar-cane fields to see workers, the intelligentsia sent by Castro to mingle with the peasants. A foreman came up to him. 'Do you know Fidel?' 'Yes,' said Mercer. 'Well, please ask him if he would take the intellectuals off the fields, then we can get on with our work.'

13th October Working with Bob [*Crowley*] on *Racing Demon*. We're trying to stage it in as simple a way as possible – bravura

minimalism, we call it. We went to Whippel's, the ecclesiastical costumiers, and wandered round looking admiringly at copes, surplices, rochets and chimeres. 'Are you professionals? We get all sorts here,' said the shop assistant, as if we might have been looking for frocks for private use. We discovered that there's a detailed iconography involved in the size of the dog collar and the colour of the shirt – shades of grey, black, green and purple denote degree of high and low church, conservative or evangelical.

20th October   I had three sessions of meeting separate departments, trying to explain what was happening and why. It's all very well talking about shortage of resources, but in the end the problem is shortage of income from the box office. And I fear our plans for the next few months won't be our salvation. Woody Allen: 'What do you do to make God laugh? Tell him your plans.' We'll be short of about £1m. I had a long, disturbing row with Richard Bullimore, who accused me of profligacy, of going behind his back, or perpetuating the habits of the ancien régime. He said we could be faced with bankruptcy. He also said that doing *Sunday in the Park* was a mistake. He may well be right. All of this was set against our Student Day which was wonderful – the whole building teemed with activity and energy and young people.

21st October   Olivier's Memorial Service in Westminster Abbey. A lot of Walton, but a synthetic concoction of ritual: actors inc. Albert Finney and Peter O'Toole carrying Olivier's memorabilia like holy relics to the altar – a sword that had belonged to Kean, a prompt-script of *Hamlet*, a crown from *Richard III*. Alec Guinness gave an address: very skilful tightrope act balanced between obsequiousness and acerbic wit. He said rather pointedly that it was unkind to compare young actors to Olivier, there was no second Olivier. Peggy Ashcroft read *Lycidas* beautifully, and John Gielgud stumbled over 'Death be not proud'. Albert read Ecclesiastes with actorish vigour, and John Mills read Corinthians without meaning. At the end of the service we filed out down the aisle. I saw Brian Ridley (who started as an electrician at the Old Vic when he was sixteen) sitting with a few colleagues from the early days, looking thoughtful and mournful. I caught his eye and he smiled wryly. For me Olivier was a symbolic loss: the death of a heroic actor of the kind never to be seen again. For Brian it was the loss of part of his youth.

There was a party afterwards at the NT, which was like a celestial casting session. I saw Joan [*Plowright*] who said the service was nice but there could have been a few more jokes. I talked to Frank Dunlop [*director*] who was waspish about everyone, Ronnie Corbett who was genial, Melvyn Bragg who was distracted, Jill Bennett who was droll, Shirley Ann Field who said she was a fan of mine, Judi who said she missed the NT, and Eileen Atkins who said she'd come and work at the NT any time. She said she was in the ghastly Jeffrey Archer play; the great mystery was that Paul Scofield seemed to be enjoying himself in it.

23rd October   We're facing an £850,000 deficit. I have two reactions – the first is to want to run, the second is to want to succeed in our own terms, beat the deficit and achieve a surplus. I'm most scared of shame: being the man who closed the National Theatre.

24th October   David [*Hare*]'s father has died. He'd been expecting it for some time. Says it was a good death: he died holding his wife's hand. David says the funeral can't be for a while. 'You can't get buried quickly in Bexhill-on-Sea,' he says, 'it's like getting a table at the Caprice.'

25th October   First night of *Ma Rainey's Black Bottom* [*August Wilson*]: Howard [*Davies*] has done an exemplary production, Bob's used the Cottesloe in a really striking way, and the actors are outstanding, particularly Clarke Peters. It's a wonderful play – an oral history of blacks set to music. The music is appropriated, marketed as entertainment for whites, but it's as much about the differences between black and black and white and white as between black and white.

26th October   A Mexican anthropologist found that in small villages the witches who were accused always lived in the end of the village furthest from the accuser. I saw the arch witch Thatcher on the TV. She's gratingly intrusive, and makes me feel like a cat with an arched back. She's constantly defensive and constantly aggressive.

28th October   Saw *The Plantagenets* at the RSC. Adrian [*Noble*]'s production and Bob [*Crowley*]'s designs had a bravura energy, but

they've not found a way of presenting the histories in a way that transcends *The Wars of the Roses*. Too many choric advances to the front of the stage with banners waving, too much smoke, too much tankard-clashing. But the most worrying thing about them was the acting, which was often unspecific and treated the verse as an alien and unapproachable obstacle.

30th October Breakfast meeting for the heads of the national companies – RSC, ROH, ENO, etc – at the Savoy. Somebody must have a sense of irony: we're meeting to discuss our shortage of money. Party in the evening at Sonia Sinclair's [*NT Board member*]. Max Hastings [*Editor* Daily Telegraph] says he can't understand why the government don't see that they can buy the silence of the arts lobby for a very small price.

5th November Saw Dad. His memory is going. He says he lies in bed trying to remember the names of destroyers in 1938 in all different classes. And the names of all the members of the Hawke Term at Dartmouth in 1929. He's afraid: rage and despair alternate. Margaret is being very patient with him. He behaves like a child and she treats him as one. As we talk in the kitchen she heats her hair rollers in a saucepan and picks them out with cooking tongs.

6th November Ian [*Charleson*] is on the brink. He's had flu and is very frightened, but he hasn't got pneumonia. He said to me: 'I lie awake thinking what a terrible lot of trouble I've given Richard.' I spoke to his doctor, who wasn't encouraging. What can it be like to live through day after day wondering where the next mark or lump will develop?

7th November Opening of Steven Berkoff's *Salome*, which has replaced *Celestina* in the Lyttelton. Wilde's purple (well, puce) prose is handled like fragile jewellery being passed ritualistically from hand to hand. It's slow and relentless but mesmerising and unquestionably its own thing – admirable for that, but I wish (a) it were shorter and (b) it were better in its *own* terms. But it's successful and I'm grateful at least for that at the moment, even if it's at the expense of my conscience. Steven's a curious mixture of the courteous and companionable, with the defensive aggressiveness of the pit bull terrier.

He's taken a stand early against his critics and carved out his work from a rock of rejection – the last of the Victorian actor-managers. I feel shifty about Berkoff on Alan [*Bennett*]'s account. I hate Berkoff's take on Kafka: manic and melodramatic. Alan's Kafka was a realist, a poet of common sense, a visionary of the detail of daily life. He chipped away at the Kafka seam and extracted mountains of material, which he melted down into *Kafka's Dick* and *The Insurance Man*. Joan Washington [*dialect coach*] told me that John Huston had seen *The Insurance Man* on TV when he was casting in London. He said it had an actor who's going to be a star and it ought to win an Oscar. Well, he was right about Dan Day-Lewis.

10th November   I went to the Synod debate on the ordination of women. A vivid concentration of purple in the centre of the round hall – the bishops, many of them reading the papers for the reviews of yesterday's debate. The purple silk of their shirts is an absurdly anomalous flash of Carnaby Street colour. The bishops are mostly bald, mostly wear glasses with perspex rims and are mostly fifty-fiveish. Grey suits, grey woollen socks with thin pale calves exposed when they cross their legs. They all stand for prayers at the beginning of the debate: the Lord's Prayer in the New English Prayer Book version, bland and clinical. A boomingly male gathering. The Bishop of Durham looks like an old character actor, Miles Malleson perhaps; the Archbishop looks like a melancholy golden retriever. It's a surprisingly good-natured debate until a high-powered evangelical speaks against the ordination of women: he says there'll be trouble 'when the rubber hits the road'. Then a radical woman says: 'When I look round here I don't see much of this Jesus but I do see a lot of bleeding Pharisees.' People are not pleased by this. When they're not pleased they're 'anguished'; when they're pleased they 'rejoice'.

Then I had lunch with Dan and Tamasin. Dan is pink, healthy, wry and coming to terms with himself. I feel at times overwhelmingly sad at what has happened and had to avoid crying when we said goodbye.

13th November   Watched *Hamlet*. Ian hadn't played the Saturday shows. I saw him before the show, and he looked very weak and pale, his face now deformed by swelling. He apologised for his lack of

professionalism. 'If they pay you, Richard, you should turn up,' he said. His performance was possessed. He wasn't playing the part, he became it. By the end of the performance he was exhausted, each line of the last scene wrung out of him. He stood at the curtain call like a bruised boxer after sixteen rounds, battered by applause.

14th November   At the *Evening Standard* Awards Ian McK. got the Best Actor Award. He said he'd been to very few plays this year but had been to the theatre last night and seen the most brilliant performance of Hamlet and for him the Actor of the Year was Ian Charleson. There were a lot of people in the room who knew what Ian was saying, who loved him for saying it, and grieved for Ian Charleson. I went back to the theatre for a run of the *Good Person*, which was promising, full of good performances but a tendency to make it a star vehicle for Fiona Shaw – who is certainly a *tour de force*. Then Patsy Pollock [*casting director*] rang to say that Ian wouldn't be able to do the tour to Hong Kong in ten days. I rang Ian and he said he couldn't, he was sorry, he knew he'd let me down. I knew what I was doing when I cast him and I don't regret it. I love and admire Ian and giving him a chance to play Hamlet was the least, and also the most, that I could do for him. He's starting to get carcinomas on his face; in a week, he says, they'll go purple. It's all beginning to close in, this disease raging at his body. Ian McK. said that it seemed as if Ian had been preparing all his life for Hamlet.

24th November   Hong Kong. *Hamlet* went surprisingly well. A huge relief and a triumph for Jeremy [*Northam*]. I've got bad jet-lag. I feel as if I've got a lizard in my head, thrashing its tail. HK has changed beyond recognition since I was here nearly twenty years ago. Not a single building remains. This is a monument, a temple, to free enterprise: Thatcher's Utopia. An oligarchy, no unions, hardly any tax, no elected government, and a servile, hard-working under-class with enough emergent and successful Chinese to allow it to look as though it's not a colony. Most of the ex-pats are an underclass, middle-class émigrés from a world which never existed except in their imaginations. Shopping is what makes HK the developed world's Utopia. Its heart is like most towns in the US or Britain – a shopping arcade. They're the contemporary cathedrals and you can

worship here in the same way as you can in Leicester or in Tokyo or in any town in the US, and maybe now even in China.

Hear some Oz-speak: 'the verandah over the toyshop' = a beer belly. Also: 'Happy as a bastard on Father's Day'.

28th November   Tokyo confuses me. I can't get a purchase on it. It's not just the language and the alphabet, it's the city. It was razed to the ground in the war and rebuilt, so its features are almost wholly post-war, utterly bland and uniform. Extreme courtesy and generosity from the people. Also suppression, or repression, of violence or anger – the insane work ethic, the inferiority of women, the fascination with sado-masochism. The Tokyo Globe is an awkward space, a pointless exercise in historical re-creation, almost certainly wrong in every aspect – scale, proportions, sightlines, materials and roof. But it has got a remarkably faithful audience who show a passionate keenness for *Hamlet* and, freed from the physical production, the actors invent the space instead of being defined by it, leaving the audience able to concentrate on character and relationship, which was the idea in the first place.

30th November   Thurber was trying to improve one of his cartoons: 'Don't do that,' said a friend. 'If you ever got good you'd be mediocre.' Picasso to Gertrude Stein: 'You do something first, then someone comes along and makes it pretty.'

1st December   Ion [*Caramitru, Romanian actor*]'s in London. He says he's my spiritual brother. He's here to give a poetry reading at the Barbican to celebrate the centenary of the poet, Eminescu. Ion was once summoned to read a poem in front of Ceauşescu. He refused, but the Bulandra Company persuaded him to do it, otherwise their theatre would be closed down. Ion went along to read the piece of official doggerel and at the rehearsal he read it like a child. Everyone laughed and he wasn't allowed to perform in the evening. He wants me to make an official offer to invite the Bulandra Company to the NT with their *Hamlet*, the production, as Ion says, that I should have directed. It's a diplomatic manoeuvre because they won't be allowed to bring it out of the country. But everything can change. It took ten years in Poland, ten weeks in East Germany, and ten days in Czechoslovakia. But Romania, says Ion, is different. 'The

Berlin Wall has moved to the Romanian border. There won't be any changes in Romania.' His friend, the poet, Mircea Dinescu, says: 'Who will intervene in Romania? God does not get involved in politics.'

We have dinner with Deborah and Declan and I get Ion to tell the story of being on tour in Moscow and sharing a room in a hotel with a friend, a middle-aged actor. When the concierge on their floor saw the actor she had a *coup de foudre*: she became obsessed, wouldn't leave him alone, stalked him, harassed him, haunted him. He reminded her of her boyfriend who had been killed in the war.

3rd December   Went to see Dad with Gorg. It's all on the edge. He's confused but sufficiently coherent to understand everything but himself. He rages with impotence and despair. He has a variable memory and is, mostly, resigned to his fate, longing, longing, for the deliverance of death. Margaret treats him with exaggerated patience and he becomes furious with her; she becomes maddened with him, he can't respond and she screams with frustration. Their relationship hasn't changed much, but instead of sustaining banter and mutual abuse, it's become unresolved torture for both of them. She tells me that she loves him, that he's given her a few happy years, that he wants to die, that she wants to help him die if she can and that he wants to resume their sex life. Then, sobbing, she collapses on my shoulder and, sobbing too, I hold this stranger in my arms and feel ashamed of my churlishness about her.

8th December   Went to a meeting at the Queen Elizabeth Hall in honour of National Arts Advocacy Day, organised by the National Campaign for the Arts. I sat next to Jenny McIntosh [*administrator RSC*] before I went up on stage, and wished she was working for us. I said that the arts should make their own argument – part of our life, language, way of seeing, etc. I exhorted the audience to complain loudly and quoted Napoleon (I bet he lived to regret he'd said it): 'When people cease to complain, they cease to think.'

10th December   I start *Racing Demon* tomorrow. I'm eager but cautious. I read this remark of Nureyev: 'A great dancer is not one who makes a difficult step look easy, but one who makes an easy step look interesting.'

14th December Staff party. I spent much of my time talking in a subdued shout to Mary Soames, who was having trouble hearing with the noise of the band, a lot of time having my ear bent by actors, an inordinate time doing the raffle draw, and then I was made to dance by a girl in wigs who kept saying you don't know who I am and I've been here for eighteen months. I wanted to say I've been here eighteen months and I don't know who I am.

16th December Ian has gone to hospital, near to death but still fighting. His father, who's had a struggle with AIDS and a Calvinist conscience, wrote to me today, thanking me for letting Ian do Hamlet, and he said: 'He is also a very remarkable young man, and he is doing his best to defy the doctors and hang on to life.'

17th December There have been riots in the north of Romania. I try to ring Ion to find out what's happening, but can't get through. Is it all starting to unravel?

18th December A week into *Racing Demon*. Extremely benign atmosphere at rehearsals. It's partly the actors, presided over by Oliver Ford-Davies – slightly donnish, ineffably goodwilled; he's like a really effective vicar. But the mood really comes from the play. What's so unusual to find in a play is that, with the exception of the journalist (natch), all the characters are trying to do good in the world – even if they're doing it in ways which we may not identify with. The play's addressing the question: How does a good person change people's lives for the better? We're working very slowly and very carefully.

22nd December Samuel Beckett's died. I walked through the Green Room when an Irish barman was watching the TV before the show. 'Ah well,' he said cheerily. 'That's another one gone' – stoicism that Beckett would have appreciated.

29th December Christmas came and went and I hardly felt as if I'd stopped to enjoy it. I drove to Nottingham from the theatre on Christmas Eve. Utterly deserted streets: it felt like the aftermath of a neutron bomb. An eerily empty M1 and I realised halfway I'd left the Christmas presents in London.

30th December   Romania is now a free country. I tried to ring Ion many times but haven't got through. I hope he's safe. I did talk to Ian, who's very near death. He'd rallied, and sounded weak but optimistic. I'd said I'd be seeing him soon. He sent me a Christmas card:

> One day when I'm better I'd love to attempt Hamlet again, and all the rest; and together we can revitalise Shakespeare. Anyway I hope this is not a dream and I can't tell you how much of a kick I got out of doing the part, if only for the short time I could . . .

I remember sitting in the canteen with him when he was talking wistfully of wanting to play Lear, saying, 'If, God willing, I live long enough . . .' Well, God hasn't willed it and when I rang to speak to Ian yesterday I talked to Richard Warwick 'He's very ill,' he said. It sounded near the end. No more of his grace, his mocking wit, his beauty and his talent.

31st December   The edge of a new decade, and the end of a grisly year, public and private. If this year has taught us anything (at least in politics) it's that things *can* change: nothing is immutable. And nothing can be predicted; no one saw the collapse coming in Eastern Europe. Now communism is dead; nothing in its life became it like the leaving of it. I was disturbed by the death of Ceauşescu. His wife's hand was on his knee during their trial, and they were holding hands before their execution.

I've been reading Chekhov's letters to Olga Knipper: 'Art, especially the stage, is an area where it is impossible to walk without stumbling. There are in store for you many unsuccessful days and whole unsuccessful seasons, there will be great misunderstandings and great disappointments . . . You must be prepared for all this, accept it, and nevertheless stubbornly, fanatically, follow your own way . . .'

1990

1st January The New Decade, or the old one shaking its tail, started with an ominous incident. After a party we came home and found we'd forgotten our keys and had to get a locksmith at 1.30 a.m. We waited in the freezing drizzle and were made painfully aware of the faint line between comfort and desolation. It's not exactly Lear in the storm but to be locked out of your home – even if it is your own fault – is to face the wilderness. 'Home is the place where, when you have to go, they have to take you in,' said Robert Frost. At the party I talked to some friends of friends whose daughter had tried to slash her wrists just before Christmas. She's just fourteen, adopted quite young from a very violent home. She's been thoroughly loved but still fights, still resists. She was there, pale, smiling optimistically, very sad and very sweet. I spoke to a girl who said that she'd been anxious about her boyfriend in Hong Kong after the Tiananmen Square massacre and had phoned him: 'How are you?' she'd said. 'Oh, I'm up on one ski now,' said her friend. Reading Mark Twain's Journals: 'When we remember that we are all mad, the mysteries disappear and life stands explained.'

2nd January I read an assessment of the decade in the *Observer*. It named ten highlights of fiction, film, theatre, etc. *Guys and Dolls* featured and – I'm sure to the fury of its many detractors – *The Ploughman's Lunch*. I remember Alan [*Bennett*] being asked by a journalist (as they do) if there was anything bad he could think of to say about me, and Alan saying ruefully: '*The Ploughman's Lunch*.'

6th January I saw Ion on the TV News, standing beside the poet Mircea Dinescu, who was addressing a crowd. He looked tired and rather frightened.

7th January   Went to Dorset for Dad's birthday. We did a dinner for him and invited a few friends, and it was cheerful. He dressed in his mauve velvet suit and looked dapper and frail, like a nineteenth-century man of letters. He barely noticed me, or if he did he barely showed that he did. After dinner he tried to make a speech, gasping, choking with feeling, like an over-charged light bulb – shining for a moment with great intensity, then breaking down in shuddering flickers. It was as if any feeling, happy or sad, overloaded his system. Perhaps because he's spent so much time concealing his feelings. When I saw him in the morning, he'd only just got up, tired from the night before. He looked very sad and confused, and when I left him I felt as if I was leaving him for ever. 'Parting is the younger sister of death': Mandelstam. I went to see Mum who looks more peaceful than ever. I can't allow the possibility that she can feel or think. She seems insensible, just ready for food, drink and sleep.

When we got back to London there was a message from Patsy Pollock on the answering machine that Ian had died. He died peacefully on Saturday night with his family and friends. Apparently everyone who dies in their bed dies peacefully. I hope so. Does it matter how you go? 'Death is no different whined at than withstood.' I wrote a tribute to Ian for the *Guardian*. It took ages, listening to the Mozart Requiem over and over, and spotting the paper with tears.

8th January   Somebody has scrawled a black cross over Ian's face on a photograph of him in the corridor near the Stage Door. Who could be so crude and so cruel? There's a tribute to Ian from Richard Attenborough in one of the papers. He said that if he had to cite the best British acting of the past fifty years he would say it was a scene in, yes, *Gandhi* with Ben Kingsley and Ian. Read an interview with Edmund White: he says of AIDS literature that it 'must begin in tact, avoid humour, and end in anger'. Under the shadow of Ian's death, rehearsals are a bit cowed but being in the company of half a dozen actors playing priests is comforting. The only uncomfortable note is struck by the appearance of the Theatre Chaplain, who comes in uninvited to offer advice. Since he's usually only seen on first nights popping into dressing rooms when the boys have their underpants off, he doesn't offer the most uplifting example of pastoral care. There's a long silence when he comes into the room. His visit reminds me of rehearsing *The Shawl* in a church hall in Pimlico. We were

sitting round a table in the large room, when a man opened the door and stared at us for an eternity. 'Is this Alcoholics Anonymous?' Very long pause from us. 'Downstairs,' said Mickey Feast. The man looked unconvinced.

11th January   Ion rang from Bucharest. A very bad line and I could hardly hear him, but I could hear that he's OK, his family are OK, and, 'Richard, this is so exciting. I have great news,' he said. 'Are you running the Bulandra Company?' I said. 'No, no, bigger than that.' 'Is it the Cultural Ministry?' 'No, no, bigger than that. I'm in the government, close to the centre.' He's become a member of the ruling Executive Committee of eleven, and one of five Vice-Presidents, Head of the Commission for Culture, which includes Education, Art and Leisure. He wants me to go over soon.

12th January   Ian's funeral in Edinburgh. A cold, clear, sunlit day. We arrived early at the house, inadvertently taking the family by surprise, his mum in her dressing gown. They're remarkable people, and in spite of Ian's frequent antagonism to his father, and his father's horror at Ian's 'perversions', Ian had spoken to them every day of his life. They were desperately sad that they only reached London just in time to see him die. His father said that, when he took his hand, Ian's eyes opened slightly and he seemed to smile. There was a small service in the living room. The Minister made conventional noises and gradually hardened our hearts as he spoke of Ian returning to Edinburgh to 'his ain folk'. After the service we went to the graveyard, tilted on the side of a hill by a railway line, butter-yellow sun and iridescent green grass. It's a terrible thing to see a parent bury a child. I'll never forget the sight of Ian's father teetering on the side of the grave, sobbing helplessly, as the Minister intoned: 'God so loved the world that he gave his only begotten son.' There were reporters at the cemetery gates and on the plane back to London, sitting behind Ian McKellen, scavenging for gossip. Back at the theatre in the evening for a meeting with Stephen Sondheim. We talked about writing for musicals. The songs, he said, always have to move the show forward. I told him about the debacle of *High Society*. 'Oh sure,' he said, 'that would never have worked.'

14th January There are two difficult scenes in *Racing Demon* with Stella and Oliver – the first because there's so much story, the second because there's so much mood. Both scenes show the classic dilemma of the director, suspended between the writer's need to push the play forward, and the actor's desire to stand still and create a character. We rehearse the second scene – a sort of love scene – in candlelight with the lights off and the problems fall away; it seems real, unforced and very touching. Is it possible to love God and love Man, the scene asks?

15th January Lu has just asked me if I write nice things about her in here, and she wants me to remember to buy her a car when she grows up.

17th January Meeting with Terry Farrell, putative architect for the restoration, renovation, and improvement of the NT building. I say that's it's unfortunate that it's practically impossible to see St Paul's Cathedral from my office without sitting on the window ledge and craning my neck. He explains that it's because the building is aligned at a right angle to Waterloo Bridge rather than parallel to the line of the river.

20th January Maggie Smith, Joan Plowright and Jill Bennett together at the first night of *Bent*. They looked like the Supremes. Maggie said that I seemed so much better than when she'd last seen me; she said I seemed to have grown into my skin. I picked up David Aukin's copy of *Variety* today and reminded myself how remote I am from the land of showbiz. Varietyese: 'outfronters' = the audience, 'hand to hand music' or 'mitting' = applause, an '88er' = a pianist, 'nsg' = not so good, 'wk' = well known, HIP NIP IN HUB = a Japanese pianist in Boston, a 'helmer' = a director. Actually, nobody uses this slang except *Variety*, which is what makes it an enjoyable read – like Flann O'Brien.

22nd January Dad has had several fits and it probably means another stroke. He's not conscious at the moment and I hope for his sake he doesn't come round. Half there or less would be an unbearable agony for him. I drove down after rehearsals to the small cottage hospital in Bridport. He was lying on his right side, on

his paralysed arm. The left side of his face was puffed, red, the skin stretched parchment tight. His eye flickered open and he seemed to see me but I can't be sure. He nodded occasionally at things I said and even, at one moment, squeezed my hand, but I don't know if he knew it was me and if he's knows he's dying.

24th January   David Aukin's frustrated by the job, so he's in a state of restlessness and irritability. I know he feels his hands are tied, and of course I understand that, but it's unsettling. I told Mary Soames that we're being threatened by a visit from the National Audit Office who will examine our affairs and decide whether we're worth keeping. She's been to see *Bent* which she found unconvincing: 'But there were masses of gaggles of nancy boys in the audience,' she says entirely genially.

27th January   Dad has improved a little. Margaret is in agony but says: 'It would be much nicer if he'd died.' Nicer? 'Of course he's not ill enough to kill,' she adds.

When I'm not rehearsing *Racing Demon*, I'm working with Bob [*Crowley*] and Ian [*McKellen*] on *Richard III*. We've tried to avoid rushing to conclusions or 'solutions'. We work simply, day by day, reading the play aloud to each other. Otto Dix: 'One slogan has been vital for artists in the last few years – "Create new forms of expression!" . . . What I see as the new element in painting lies in the expansion of subject matter, in the intensification of those expressive forms which, after all, were already present in the works of the old masters.'

29th January   It's the middle of the night; I'm having a panic attack about *Racing Demon*. I'm afraid I've misjudged the play and the production, provoked largely by David Aukin's response: loved the second half, but bored by the first. Maybe the first is too laid back and staging it in the round doesn't help it. Terrible anxiety that it's irrevocable. When I last opened a play – in June last year – Dad had just had his first stroke. When I opened *Beggar's Opera* in '82 Mum was in her first serious phase of Alzheimer's.

2nd February   First preview of *Racing Demon*. The show was extraordinarily exciting; the audience leapt on it. They went on

applauding after the house lights went up, which Michael Bryant said he'd never seen before. The cast is immaculate and the staging works. It's David's best play. We wait now for the inevitable disappointment that will come next week, when the press fail to match our aspirations. But I've loved doing it, the public love seeing it, and it's made me feel confident about the NT.

4th February   Dad is fading. He seemed pleased to see me but was often uncertain who I was. At one moment he said: 'My memory's going, I can't remember a thing.' I tried to get him to talk about the past. He seemed very lucid and occasionally very sharp and then drifted away again. I asked him if he'd rather be at home or at the hospital. 'I've got to be somewhere,' he said.

6th February   I talked to a friend of Ion today who said that he was now very depressed. There are demos against him and then counter-demos, and he wants to go back to acting.

8th February   Letter from Christopher Hampton: '*Voysey* made me think a good deal about the necessity of energy in the matter of writing plays, not to mention brooding on the fact that Granville-Barker gave out at forty-three.'

9th February   The first night of *Racing Demon* was a good performance, which I managed to watch throughout, wholly sober. It's a really original play and has been a joy to work on. Meanwhile frantic activity casting for *Richard III:* meetings, rows, placation, plans, crises and weariness.

10th February   Lunch with Peter Brook. He was amiable, impish and practical. He wants to do a project with me – a history of modern theatre: Stanislavsky, Meyerhold, Craig, Artaud, Brecht. I don't know how it would work. He talked of Olivier – 'less heart than Stanislavsky', of Peter Hall – 'he always used to be very jolly', and of *The Tempest* – 'I want to do something that is purely theatrical, and pure theatre.' I'm not sure I know what that means.

11th February   The RSC have announced a deficit of £4m., and are closing the Barbican for four months in the autumn. I don't see

how that saves them much money – they still have the staff but no box office. They've become prisoners of an expansionist philosophy that emerged through years of success. They've occupied more territory, because larger means more power and more status. A few years ago the RSC had a large display ad: '44 NEW PRODUC-TIONS THIS SEASON'. The opening of the new NT, with its three auditoriums, locked them into a pattern of emulating that model. The result is that they can't go back and they can't go forward.

12th February   The daily reviews for *Racing Demon* were good without really giving full credit to the play or the production, as if, being in the Cottesloe, it were somehow marginal, but the Sundays are really good, as in 'brilliant', 'funny', 'fascinating', 'uplifting', 'a classic', 'perfect'. *The Times* religious correspondent castigates the play, or at least its writer, for not having 'been there' – i.e. not being a Christian in the grip of theological despair, an odd criterion of judgement. The show's a success, the right play at the right time in the right theatre, but there's all the difference between a success and a 'hit' – which is what several reviews call it. Peter Hall told me on the first night of *Guys and Dolls* that its success would buy me five years' critical immunity. And he was about right. On his index, may be I've got a year or so with *Racing Demon*. Now we'll have to find a way of exploiting that success, and for now I don't feel any trepidation about the future. As Harry says in the play: 'We get by on so little.'

13th February   Terry Hands says in the *Independent* that the RSC is a company and at the NT no one knows who anybody else is. Deborah Warner tells me that Terry was asked if he'd be at the birth of his son. 'Only if it's a Caesarean,' he said.

14th February   Talk to Declan about rehearsals for *Peer Gynt*. He's having difficulty with a few of the cast. We talk about the familiar phenomenon of carrying two or three actors who just won't go with the whole. It always seems like such a personal rejection. Declan looks to me for calming advice. I don't know if I provide it.

22nd February   Went to the *Guardian* with Terry Hands (who apologised for his *Independent* gibe) to meet the staff. Q and A for about three-quarters of an hour. Melanie Phillips asked why I put on

plays which supported the IRA. I wasn't the only person in the room
to be baffled. Then we went to Bertorelli's with Peter Preston [*Editor
Guardian*], Michael Billington and Nick de Jongh. Terry complained
of everyone telling him what to do: critics, journalists, sponsors,
boards, the Arts Council, the government, even the audience. He
made a case for Trevor [*Nunn*]'s thesis – that there is a large
untapped audience to whom we don't speak and that we should
address them through the medium of the 'new' musical, i.e. *Carrie*
and *Les Misérables*. I asked him why the RSC did *Kiss Me Kate* and
Showboat. 'To make money,' he said.

23rd February Off to Bucharest. I ran into Ken Campbell at
Heathrow. We talked of the shows we did at Nottingham. He
reminded me of the woman who he'd heard in the interval of
Bendigo [*musical about a nineteenth-century Nottingham prize-
fighter*]: 'I can't imagine the sort of person who would enjoy this
sort of thing.' Ken also told me that he'd met a descendant of Bendigo
who told him that for training Bendigo used to go into pubs and spit
in blokes' beer to annoy them. That would provoke a fight and he'd
get a free sparring partner. He once did it to a ballet dancer who
pranced about so much that Bendigo couldn't get near him: that's
how he got his technique.

I got stuck in Frankfurt, delayed for a day by a strike at Bucharest
Airport. I booked into a hotel and wandered round the town, which
is featureless but not unpleasant. The taxi driver, a woman with
excellent English, gave me a run-down on the hotels: 'The Inter-
continental,' she said, 'the prices go up, the service goes down.' In the
cathedral there's a notice giving information about its history, which
said that its artefacts attempted to answer the questions: 'How can I
bear suffering and death?' and 'What is the source of hope?'

24th February The flight was five and a half hours late. I'm used
to the airport being half lit, wreathed in a grubby gloom and
populated by dour faces. Now lights, smiles, crowds, deafening
TV sets, and 'La Bamba' over the PA system. It feels like the children
have been allowed to take over the house and are marvelling at all the
fun that can be had with its machinery. I'm met by Victor, who I
knew from years ago, a pleasant old apparatchik from the Cultural
Ministry. He finds it difficult to break the habit of enthusing about

all Romanian theatre. I ask if the Ministry allocates money to theatres as they used to. 'The Ministry does not control, it is there to help,' he says with the same forthright certainty that he used to have when the policy was the opposite.

I managed to see the last half-hour of *Hamlet* at the Bulandra Theatre. It seemed quite slow and low in tension, and I felt wholly detached from it. But the theatre was full, the audience passionate. Ion, not surprisingly, seemed very tired. I'm astonished that he has time to play Hamlet. He said that he wished I had directed the production when he asked me in 1982. And so did I. After the performance we went to a painter's house – an artist who operated within the parameters imposed by the state. He actually didn't seem to be any more restricted artistically than the artist dependent on a commercial gallery. A beautiful flat, full of lovely objects and nineteenth-century paintings. Ion and I went into a small room (the daughter's?) to talk. This is what he told me or at least how I remembered it:

He had to go to Cluj, in the north, to give a talk and while he was there he heard rumours of a massacre in Timisoara, flew back to Bucharest and on the TV at the airport saw Ceauşescu speaking from a balcony to a huge crowd. Suddenly the TV broadcast stopped. Ion left the airport but could barely drive his car for the crush of coaches filled with riot police heading for the centre. He joined the crowd and the square was surrounded by soldiers and Securitate. He was recognised by students and teenagers who asked him to help them persuade people to join the opposition. 'It was the beginning of a new world.'

Next day students came to his house and they insisted he go with them to a demonstration. They put a guard on his house – three sixteen-year-old boys with sticks, stopping and searching people and cars in the street. He was surrounded by kids, who had chosen him as their leader, and clung to him like monkeys. He joined up with the poet Mircea Dinescu. By ten o'clock it was known that the Commander of the Army had either committed suicide or had been executed, and there were groups of people emerging all over the city. The soldiers embraced the people and the Securitate started to fight, killing hundreds. Helicopters hovered overhead, scattering leaflets: 'DON'T LISTEN TO FOREIGNERS'. Nobody knew what to do. Nobody knew where to go. There was no order, no plan.

A general said to Ion: 'My army is at your disposal, tell us where to go.' 'The TV station,' said Ion, thinking: Well, isn't that what people do in revolutions? And off they went. There was fierce fighting round the TV station but by the time Ion went in, the crowd parted for him and they found the TV studio guarded by only one Securitate man, who was trembling too much even to raise his hand in a salute. 'Then we opened a programme, but it was the same announcer who had been broadcasting all these lies for YEARS. So I said no. But the TV people said yes, let him speak. We are all guilty. I told him to apologise for his past. He did and then I went on and I said we're free, we've won. God was with us. Don't shoot anyone. Join us . . . I was too full of emotion to speak properly.'

25th February   I drove round Bucharest in the morning in beautiful soft sunlight. There are weeds in the concrete, iron bars bent and rusted, *fin de siècle* houses pitted by flaking plaster, grime and grey tiredness everywhere, but the streets are full of people who talk as if they'd just found their tongues. When I first came here, in 1970, the city could still pretend to the title of the Paris of the East but Ceauşescu plagued the city with hideous baroque apartment blocks and a monstrous boulevard which culminates in a preposterous palace of Oz, which makes Stalin's architectural taste look restrained. Workmen used to fall off the scaffolding in the cold and were brushed away, their bodies laid out in a room reserved solely for coffins.

Around the parliament building and burnt-out shells of official buildings, the dome of the library is resting on the street: of 500,000 books only 200 survived. An effigy of Ceauşescu hangs from a tree. I could see where people died: in the square outside the CP HQ, on pavements, on street corners, in shop doorways – small clusters of candles and bunches of flowers. Often they describe the outline of a body like the shadows of the vaporised bodies in Hiroshima. There used to be a giant statue of Lenin in front of the huge Stalinist wedding cake of the Ministry of Culture. It's been torn down. There's a small placard in its place which says: 'GOD HELP ROMANIA'.

28th February   *Peer Gynt* has been declared a success and Declan is very pleased – or relieved. The production is inventive but it has serious flaws, some weak performances and a poor translation. It's

not been easy and the Olivier gives little help – in the Cottesloe it wouldn't be so cruelly exposed.

4th March   Saw Dad. He was quite lively, witty for a while, and wary of me as always. I felt constantly that I was disappointing him by not being part of his constituency. After an hour he felt tired and bored and wanted to go to bed. Margaret told me he's been seeing the local vicar, in search of absolution, and he's been phoning the hospital to speak to Mum, who hasn't spoken for over ten years.

6th March   The first preview of *Sunday in the Park* was cancelled and it opened with a cold, cautious and clumsy performance. Next day I preside over a meeting with Stephen Sondheim, James Lapine and Stephen Pimlott; they indict with unanswerable charges. Stephen P. is torn between staying loyal to the conceit of the design for the show and the expediency of making it work. They've tried to change the idiom from American to European and it won't conform. It appears to be a long way from the conventional Broadway musical but it still makes many of the same demands on the audience. 'Would you allow a new play by David Hare or Tom Stoppard to be treated like this?' says Stephen S. When I first talked to him about the show I said that I thought the first act was wonderful but the second act seemed unfinished. Could he think of looking at it again? 'I have to tell you, Richard, that I'm entirely happy about the second act.'

7th March   Lunch with Dirk Bogarde. He's flirtatious, charming and amusing. Quite tart and quite self-analytical. Says several times that he knows he's good at his craft. He's very bitter about his rejection by the British movie establishment and compares his billing, his homages, his status here, to France where he is a 'real' star. He's very assiduous about demonstrating his familiarity with the Connaught staff, who he says (nostalgically?) never used to let black people stay here until Ella Fitzgerald. He said, apropos acting being visible: 'Larry was a terrible actor, I've always thought so. So did Vivien.'

8th March   I've had a letter from a vicar called Tim West who's been going to see Dad. He says he has made peace with his creator and has received Holy Communion. He invites me to help him 'put

his house in order' before he faces 'the evening light' by recognising that he has not been 'an ideal father'.

9th March   Lord Cottesloe came to see *Racing Demon* to celebrate his ninetienth birthday. He's on his third wife, who tells me that she is taking Catholic instruction and will send her priest to see the play. Lord C. says it's 'a rather curious play, very beautifully performed'.

10th March   Peter [*Hall*] wants a life for himself in the theatre: can I give him some sort of home in the NT? I dithered. I can't see how we could operate compatibly; his time here is much too fresh.

12th March   Went to see Dad, to make my peace with him. He was pleased to see me, coherent and shy of me. He knew, I think, what he wanted me to say and that I was probably going to say it. We circled around each other for a bit. He kept asking me about the Cheltenham Gold Cup. I asked him about seeing the Vicar. He was silent for a while before he said he'd got a great deal of comfort from him. 'One of the straightest men I've ever met. You'll find it a rich joke coming from me but I've been taking Holy Communion.' He struggled with the words, tears threatening. Until his stroke I'd never seen him cry. 'Was I as bad a father to you as my father was to me?' 'No, of course not. I wish we'd got on better, that's all.' 'He was a tyrant.' 'You weren't a tyrant, just a bit neglectful perhaps. But I don't feel any anger against you. I love you.' He gripped my hand, almost spasmodically. 'I don't know if I was neglectful, I just didn't appreciate you. I'm sorry if I made you unhappy. When is the Gold Cup on?' 'In two days' time, Dad. In two days' time.' Then he paused. A long time. Minutes perhaps, and when my tears dropped on his hand, he gripped me tighter and smiled gently. 'Is Lucy a happy person? I hope so.'

In the evening I went to see our NT education tour of *Tartuffe* performed at Sherborne, in the school theatre. The performance is less than half good but more than half popular. The show (and I) was welcomed with unaffected generosity. The last time I was here I was expelled, and however much I might try and glorify it now, it was humiliating. I can see the danger of falling into that familiar love/hate, it-didn't-do-me-any-harm mistiness about school, even if I did

hate it and do feel damaged by it. Auden: 'I hope there will be some kind of boarding schools after the war – or what will happen to English romanticism?'

13th March Dinner with Tom Clarke. He's shrunken, cruelly crippled with arthritis. He's still keeping up his remorseless banter, mercilessly exploiting his script editor, who murmurs pathetically: 'He doesn't always treat me like this.' I have to leave early to see *Sunday in the Park* again. Pimlott suggests some cuts, I talk to Sondheim who appears to approve them, then I discover they're more radical than we thought, and Sondheim doesn't approve, and now Pimlott is not speaking to him. Rows ensue, and I have to arbitrate.

14th March Princess Margaret comes to the show. I have to stand in the foyer waiting for her. As she comes in she announces to me quite loudly that she can't STAND Sondheim. She demonstrates this quite conspicuously throughout the evening. She raps me, quite painfully and only half jokingly, at the end of the National Anthem, which Jeremy Sams has rearranged in a slightly arch fashion. She shifts restlessly during the show. At the interval grim comedy getting her a drink. Ice! Whisky! Water! and more whisky. She wasn't hard work after the show. She talked to me about public speaking, which she hates. She said that Reagan enjoyed it; he knew he was a bad actor but was properly trained. Mary was very touched by Princess Mgt saying that she'd liked Christopher Soames. I didn't tell Mary that she'd also said that she hadn't liked Churchill, who had no time for her and her sister when they were children and she'd found him rude and self-interested.

16th March *Sunday in the Park* had the sort of first night that is the stuff of myth. For the first time everything came together and the show was much more than the sum of its parts. The audience was made for the show and willed it into success. The reviews, with the exception of the ones which point out the absence of the Emperor's clothes in the second act, are excellent. We have successes with *Ma Rainey's Black Bottom*, *Racing Demon*, *The Good Person*, and *Peer Gynt*, so we're due for a disaster. We've talked about the possibility of taking *Ma Rainey* to the Hackney Empire to find a new audience

(i.e. black/working class). How do we change our audience? We leaflet, we advertise, we have contacts, we evangelise in schools, but still our audience is overwhelmingly white and middle class. Do we have to wait for a revolution, in which apartheid in class and education are abolished? Clarke Peters says we should bus them in to the NT.

24th March   Bucharest again. It's spring here, hot and full of light and blossom. And hope. Everything is now described as 'free', and a standard joke is that there's a knock at the door at two in the morning. 'Who is it?' 'It's the Free Securitate.' I talk to Dan Jitianu, an old friend, about the locked-door theory: do they feel guilt for not having tried to push open the door and for finding it wasn't locked when they did? 'No,' he says. 'You have to understand the over-whelming influence of oppression – fear, mutual suspicion. Who stood up to Hitler?' Ion has a long-term view. 'Remember,' he says, 'that Romania has always been too rich to be free, and that our character is sad but also funny.' I ask about the future. He tells me an old joke: 'What is COMECOM policy? – the goodwill of Russia, the stability of Poland, the organisation of Romania.' Romania's great-est natural resource is irony.

25th March   Rupert Murdoch has been to Bucharest in his private plane. He wanted to buy Ceauşescu's palace. Why? No one knows. People say that a revolution is like being in love – exhilaration and intoxication, followed by habit, disappointment and broken pro-mises. Ion became one of the twelve-man Executive Committee (the only one who hadn't been a member of the Party) to administrate the country until elections could be held. On the night of victory, he tried to persuade Iliescu [*Prime Minister*] to go out on the balcony in front of the huge crowd, tear up his Party card and scatter the pieces in the wind; a simple theatrical gesture that could have changed the history of his government.

29th March   *Trackers* [*Tony Harrison*] has gone well, even if Tony was irritated by the amount of time and attention that was siphoned away by the musical. His show is exhilaratingly ambitious, and I can remember few sights as exciting in the theatre as the twelve priapic satyrs bursting out of their crates and clog-dancing. Tony's one of the

few playwrights who's prepared to write for the Olivier – it defies naturalistic presentation and demands that the actor acknowledge the audience's presence. It calls on huge resources of energy from the writer and the actor; the timid need not apply. Tony's nerve is like Victor Hugo's, who wanted to overturn the rigid conventions of French classical theatre and, like Berlioz, to emulate Shakespeare.

5th April   John Neville [*actor and director*] to dinner, and David [*Hare*]. John offered me my first real job as a director. He came to see my Sunday night production of *The Knack* [*Ann Jellicoe*] with Judi, and wrote to me within two days to offer me a job directing a schools' tour of *Mirandolina*. I saw him play Richard II at Nottingham Playhouse, and it's one of the best Shakespearean performances I've ever seen. John must have been fortyish then – tall, aquiline, a natural aristocrat with feline grace which disguised the roaring boy underneath. He'd matched Richard Burton part for part and drink for drink at the Old Vic. He's the only figure in recent British theatre history to defect to obscurity, from stardom at the Old Vic and running the new Nottingham Playhouse to the smallish town of Edmonton in Canada. He turned down Olivier's offer to join the NT. It wasn't for him, too Royal Courtish with Bill Gaskill and John Dexter and Ken Tynan. He regarded them as too smart, too modish, too avant-garde; I imagined they regarded him as part of the old actorish world.

7th April   There's a *Guardian* article about the links between stress and success. The theory is that ruthless men are mentally arrested in the adolescent stage of development, making them unstable, restless and in constant fear that someone will find them out and overtake them. Stress releases powerful chemicals in the brain which can become as addictive as heroin. You become hooked on excitement. Stress opiates create a perpetual state of emergency and fear. But all men are engaged in a desperate search to be somebody.

11th April   We've got eight awards out of eighteen in the Oliviers. Napoleon's mother was congratulated on the unique distinction of being mother to an emperor, three kings and a queen. '*Oui, pourvu que ça dure.*'

13th April   Good Friday and Friday the 13th. I've started rehearsing *Richard III* and had a good week. Deborah has been working with the company on *Lear*. I have first priority now for three weeks, then we alternate. A confident, pleasant, easy cast. So far. I'm slightly wary of Ian [*McKellen*]. He monitors his effects and orchestrates them very carefully. I'm proud of running the theatre at the moment. Two years ago I could never have imagined myself saying this.

21st April   Completed two weeks of rehearsals – one week of real exploration of the text. I'm finding it very tiring, partly because the play is so difficult, partly because the cast is so demanding. Ian is particularly exhausting. It's difficult to divine his true feelings and he fusses around and over-decorates. It's his way of sketching; then, I hope, he'll start to cut away. At the moment it feels like the text and the production are wide apart and I've got to yank them together.

23rd April   Sue gives me a newspaper clipping: 'Karoshi is death from overwork. The syndrome was identified in Japan in 1978 to describe sudden death from heart attacks or strokes associated with overwork or stress. But the main cause is very long working days.' My days start at 7.45 a.m. when (often) I have a phone call from Mary; I arrive at the office at 8.30, make phone calls until 9.30, have meetings – management, heads of department, budget, a director or writer, rehearse at 10.30, meetings at lunchtime, rehearse until 5 p.m.; then do letters, followed by script meetings or whatever, a show in the evening – NT or elsewhere – then (sometimes) a sponsor's dinner, home by 12.30 a.m.

25th April   Talk to the *Racing Demon* company about wanting to hold the company together, and how David [*Hare*] had a plan to write a trilogy. In the short term the company could stay together: David Edgar is going to write a play with them in mind about the Czech Revolution.

28th April   I drove to Dorset today to see Dad, who is slipping away little by little. I felt terribly upset afterwards. The weather was perfect, as perfect a day as I can remember, and it reminded me of my childhood. I can see what Saint-Exupéry meant about seeing through the heart. I looked, as if for the first time, at wild flowers:

celandine, dandelions and staggering rich bluey-purple bluebells. And little churches, sandstone villages, valleys, hills, downland, barrows, lynchets, burial mounds, earthworks, ditches and standing stones. I've never really valued it before; now I feel everything slipping away from me. When you're young there's always time for everything.

1st May   We've just opened *School for Scandal*, which is unexceptional, true to itself but just a well-mounted revival. (Samuel Butler: 'The history of art is the history of revivals.') But a revival shouldn't just *be* there; it should make the play come alive *in the present tense*. I should be grateful for it – and I *am*, it's got a number of excellent performances and Peter Wood's done us proud – but it moves nothing forward. But it gives pleasure to many thousands, and why should they be despised? And it fills the Olivier.

7th May   Get back from a weekend at a hotel in Hampshire to a phone call from Stephen Wood to tell me that Michael Attenborough [*RSC associate director*] has described the NT as a 'cultural whorehouse'. I splutter like Bertie Wooster. Within minutes Adrian Noble rings to apologise on Michael's behalf.

10th May   *Bérénice* has opened to justifiably bad reviews. It's intellectual tourism, sustained by a noble performance from Lindsay [*Duncan*]. Thoroughly bogus and thoroughly depressing, but John Peter in the *Sunday Times* says it's the most Racinean Racine he's ever seen. The only time I've ever seen a Racine work in English was in Tony [*Harrison*]'s translation/adaptation of *Phèdre*.

11th May   Dinner with Adrian Noble. He looked like an enthusiastic schoolboy when I arrived. We ate in the Caprice, and I was distracted throughout the meal by the presence of Joan Collins busy projecting her Joan Collinsness over his shoulder. I told Adrian about how difficult I found it all at the NT. He told me he was undaunted by the RSC and wanted to create the best acting company in the world. He said he was going to do the two *Henry IVs* in Stratford next year. I said I couldn't stand in his way but had been hoping to do them with Gambon. He played with the sugar in the bowl but didn't put it into his coffee and I wondered

whether I should tell the waiter that the sugar had been well fingered.

13th May Went to see Dad. He was pleased to see me when he knew who I was, but kept thinking I was someone else. I sat holding his hand for a long time. 'I'd like to be an oar,' he said. '?' 'Yes, an oar.' 'What, like in a brothel?' 'No, idiot, oar.' 'Why?' 'It would be a nice thing to be.' Then he said he'd seen a viper. Maybe this was inspired by his Bible readings. He talked about the Fall of France; said it was June 18th, the day he got married. 'Send Granny some flowers,' he said. He meant Mum. He said she was happy with lots of her friends. And that she was in debt. 'I'm bleeding in my brain,' he said.

14th May *Richard III* is exciting. A run-through of Part I was illuminating and, in parts, thrilling. Ian is a formidable actor at the height of his powers. I wish he would be more settled: when he does something really good and utterly truthful in rehearsals, he mistrusts himself and if we run the scene again he over-decorates. But it's because he always want to mine *more*; it's an exasperating virtue.

15th May Dinner at Lord McAlpine's house in Westminster, with Richard Luce and Geoffrey Howe – 'ministers friendly to the arts'. Beautifully furnished, narrow, panelled eighteenth-century house. The cast list – Jeremy Isaacs [*Director Royal Opera House*], David Puttnam, Richard Attenborough, Simon Hornby [*businessman*], Vivien Duffield [*philanthropist*], Christopher Gable [*ballet director*]. The idea was to put the case for the arts to the ministers. I probably talked too much, and Jeremy certainly did. It was perfectly obvious that there was going to be no more money for the arts forthcoming. Geoffrey Howe is a bit of a Bermuda triangle. He speaks very quietly and slowly, and by doing so compels attention. He thought that the main problem for the arts was convincing those within his own party that the arts were worth supporting. Do you mean convincing the Treasury? said Jeremy. No, said Geoffrey, convincing the Cabinet. He cited Norman Tebbit as the principal enemy of subsidy.

17th May   David Aukin's just told me that he's been offered a job at Channel 4 as Head of Drama. It's an irresistible offer. I know David's found it very frustrating being an enabler rather than the *abl*er, the impresario. So I'm partly relieved and I'm partly really depressed: I've depended on him probably more than he knows – for his friendship as well as the work. I'm very anxious about how I can find someone to replace him, without disturbing the eco system. It's a measure of my increasing confidence that I'm not panicking. Elizabeth Bishop: 'The crises of our lives do not come, I think, accurately dated; they crop up unexpected and out of turn, and somehow or other arrange themselves according to a calendar we cannot control.' *Richard III* continues to grow although I'm still not 100 per cent sure that Ian trusts me.

27th May   David's resignation is now public. Mary put a notice on the board about it. It ended: 'We shall miss him.' Somebody wrote 'Speak for yourself' underneath. Oh the meanness of spirit: it shocks me like the graffiti on Ian's photograph.

29th May   Dorset. We had a picnic on Eggardon Hill. Any day of the year in any weather this hill seems to me vast and mysterious and awesome but at the same time familiar, domestic and English. Sunlight hung over it like a benediction. Skylarks floated on thermals. Buzzards hovered above dozy cows. The smell of fresh cowpats mingled with the musk of cow parsley. I saw Dad later. He said he'd been dancing all night, but had hurt his ankles and had to take to his bed. He woke up with three large women beside him. Said it was like naval dances.

4th June   Lunch in the canteen with Arthur Miller. He talked about being in London with Marilyn in 1956, mobbed, escorted everywhere by police. They went shopping at Harrods and closed the shop down. 'She was as big as the Beatles before the Beatles,' said Arthur. After lunch we both watched a run of *After the Fall*. Michael Blakemore has directed it very well and Josette Simon was electric. I sat next to Arthur trying to avoid a feeling of prurient fascination. It's a very intimate and revealing play, very accurately observed, about the hateful vicious circle of love, disaffection, deceit and painful disentanglement. 'It's just like real life,' I said to Arthur

jokingly. 'It sure is,' he said solemnly, 'it sure is.' He says the play was destroyed when it first opened – partly by the misfortune of Marilyn's death and the opportunism of Kazan in making the play seem as much like unadulterated autobiography as possible.

7th June   *Richard III* still goes forward. Ian trusts me now and I trust him. The work is good.

8th June   Been reading Ian McEwan's new book, *The Innocent.* Ian's preoccupied with innocence as a state of 'not knowing', lack of knowledge, knowledge withheld, childhood: 'the imagination was even more brutal than in life'. He rang me when he was writing the book and had reached the part where the body has to be cut up. 'Do you think I should visit a morgue to research this?' he asked. I told him to do it from his imagination, and I'm sure I was right. He's got an admirable facility for doing what novelists should do – i.e. making it up, getting in the minds of other people. He writes very well of men's inability to come to terms with their emotions and the consequent implications of violence.

14th June   Ferociously hard work on *Richard III.* I've had a final run-through and stopped rehearsing for a week and a half to let *Lear* rehearse. It felt like a first night without the agony and the punishment. I'm proud of the work, and now am loving working with Ian, who's become a real collaborator and friend. Everything that I was interested in has matured in the production.

15th June   Meeting of associates. Started genial but later became slightly acrid. Ian [*McKellen*] argued for continuity and national responsibility. Howard [*Davies*] supported him but has yet to guarantee his own continuity. David [*Hare*] said we needed to find our new audience, speak with our own voice. David Aukin suggested asking Nick Wright to become an associate. Deborah [*Warner*] talked about wanting better conditions and got up Howard's nose. Howard said why don't we spend more money on new writing, rather than fourteen-week rehearsals. Peter Gill talked obscurely about Michel St Denis at the Old Vic. He's clearly unhappy with things, sadder and sadder and visibly on the periphery. I don't know how to draw him in. He wants me to leave him alone, but how can I

not do something about the Studio? I dread it because of the human cost and the consequences. I don't like conflict, but I feel more capable of dealing with it.

18th June   Run-through of *Lear*. The play in the rehearsal room is overpowering, huge and inchoate, like the weather. Brian [*Cox*] is very affecting; he just goes for it with unqualified gusto. A charging bull with occasionally shocking moments of extreme gentleness. The production is shapeless and large areas of it are entirely generalised. Somehow Deborah's ethos seems to preclude intervention: all is intended to grow like mushrooms in the dark, but the actors need help and the play needs shaping – particularly in the fourth act after the blinding of Gloucester.

23rd June   I might persuade Jenny McIntosh to take David's job. She's fairly newly appointed as Adrian's executive director – or similar title. I met her at the Savoy in an atmosphere heavily laden with corporate treachery. It felt dangerous and improper to meet her, but she's obviously very fed up with the RSC and can only contemplate making a change now because of the deep confusion and bewilderment (and despair) of the RSC management.

24th June   I had to pick my six favourite films for a magazine last week. I chose these and then regretted every one of them. They were: *La Grande Illusion, His Girl Friday, Andrei Rublev, On the Waterfront, Closely Observed Trains* and *Melvin and Howard* – the last because I'd only recently seen it and I thought it was a quintessentially American film – the little man and the American Dream. Brits just can't do that. Why didn't I pick *L'Atalante* and *La Regle du Jeu?* Or *A Bout de Souffle?* Or *M?* Or *Tokyo Story?* Or *The Tree of Wooden Clogs?* Or *The Godfather?* Or *The Hustler?* Or *Singing in the Rain?* Or any Bergman? Everyone always seems to pick *Citizen Kane* in their lists, but Welles is so insistently lapel-tugging. Look at ME! Brilliant but so self-consciously theatrical. Of the six films I chose, five are black-and-white. When we were filming *Past Caring* Denholm [*Elliot*] asked me why I thought black-and-white films were so alluring. I said I didn't know; he said it was because we dream in black-and-white.

25th June Dad died today at about 3 a.m., the day before Mum's birthday. Gorg rang me at about 7.30 a.m. 'He's gone,' she said. A lifetime's habit of deflecting feeling made it impossible for her or for me to express ourselves without putting our feelings in inverted commas. We learned it from him. He couldn't say anything without irony or self-reflexive punning, evolving a code that was elusive to strangers, and defensive with us. I went into the theatre and met Ian. I told him I was going down to Dorset and I wanted to talk to him about what I felt, I couldn't concentrate on anything else. He wanted to talk about the battle scenes, which I still haven't got right. I went to Dorset and I sat in the room with Dad's body for a while. I kissed his forehead. How I'd longed for him to embrace me when he was alive. He looked at peace. He'd shrugged off the tense, childlike, febrile look that he'd had in the past year, when he was tormented by physical pain and his inadequacy and his enforced reflection: guilt and suffering. When he first met the Vicar Dad asked him why we suffer. The Vicar, according to Dad, said that Christ bore our sins for us and we suffered for Christ. It didn't sound too convincing. I don't think he bought the Christian line but he did recognise one of the great moral truths, perhaps the only one, that all our actions have their consequences. Or the Buddhist teaching: 'No one's deed is lost, it comes back to him.'

He lay naked beneath a blanket, his arms crossed over his chest. He looked very dignified and for once he seemed to me utterly authoritative. He'd grown a beard, his last twitch of mild self-display. Perhaps it was the beard or perhaps it's the dead body I'm most familiar with from photographs, but he reminded me of Lenin. That would have amused him. The undertaker and his assistant arrived in a white van: a large, grave, portly man and a young apprentice with a cleft palate. They were bemused by Margaret who was explaining that she was his common-law wife, not his real one. I gave them his details. The undertaker tried his best to give the impression that this wasn't all in a day's work; it wasn't for us but was for him. They unpacked their fold-up bier and lifted his naked body off the bed. He looked very misshapen, mottled, white and unreal as they lifted him on to the stretcher. Margaret leapt forward to pick the catheter tube from between his legs. By sleight of hand she managed to transfer this to the bunch of roses which she'd picked earlier for me. Then she took a peach rose and sweetly laid it on his

chest. They closed up the body bag and carried him out and I held the gate for them. I watched as they pushed him into the carpeted back of the van. I closed the gate and Margaret and I went back towards the front door, where we collapsed on to each other like spent swimmers, sobbing for breath.

30th June   I told Mary about Dad's death, and my feelings of things undone and unsaid. Mary told me that she was sitting with her father in his old age late one evening. Long silence followed long silence. Then she asked him if there was anything in his life that he had wanted to do but hadn't, any honour that he'd wanted but hadn't received, anything that he regretted. And he said: 'I'd like my father to have lived long enough to have seen me do something good.'

1st July   It was a hard week, doing the tech, fielding expressions of sympathy, feeling ludicrously thin-skinned. A technically ragged first preview of *Richard III* but a powerful visceral response from the audience. There's a huge amount of work to do: the return from the '30s to the medieval isn't yet achieved, the coronation isn't an inventive enough solution to match the first half, the battle doesn't work, and there's too much woolly and unspecific acting. Ian loved the audience and they rose to him; even if it gets no better it's a remarkable performance.

2nd July   Dad's funeral. It was a beautiful day and I was as moved as ever seeing Portland Bay beyond Weymouth as we passed over Ridgeway. It had always been a treat to make that journey – visiting the beach, the cinema, Chesil Beach or the dockyard at Portland. At the crematorium we all seemed surprised at how strongly we felt. The service was very simple. We played the slow movement from the Mozart Clarinet Concerto, sang 'Eternal Father Strong to Save', 'The Day Thou Gavest Lord Is Ended', and 'Dear Lord and Father of Mankind'. Or at least we tried to sing them, small bursts of hymn, then spasms of grief. I read his favourite Masefield poem: 'Captain Stratton's Fancy' ('So I'm for drinking honestly and dying in my boots') and 'Fear no more the heat o' the sun'. I managed to do it by taking Ian's advice: just breathe. And by not looking at anyone. And at the end of the service Gorg and I held each other. Oh, the confusion of our feelings.

Back for the performance in the evening. The second preview of *Richard III*. It was chaos. Everything that could have gone wrong went wrong: flying cues and lighting cues seemed to happen randomly. The actors became unnerved and lost conviction. So did I. Bob left the auditorium, unable to watch as the silk tent got caught up and looked like a large burst red balloon. I felt immune to the disaster on stage, protected by the carapace of grief.

10th July   Dad's Memorial Service. A lovely day, once again the heart-tugging beauty of the landscape. A big turnout at Cattistock Church. They all arrived early to get a good seat. It was definitely an occasion to be judged by the highest criteria of social events, and was said by everyone to be a good 'do'. A lot of people told me how much they'd loved and admired Dad. He would have given the world to have been there.

12th July   Melanie Klein, or at least Angela Carter echoing Melanie Klein: 'Our lives are all about our childhoods.'

30th July   *Richard III* and *Lear* have opened. The whole venture has been well received – better than I could have hoped for, approval for the company, the two designers, Deborah and me, Ian and Brian. Some reviews love *Richard*, hate *Lear* and vice versa. *Richard III* is a 'controversial' production, which is to say that the reviews are enjoyably diverse ranging from 'definitive' to 'total disaster'.

2nd August   We've appointed Jenny McIntosh. *Piano [adapted by Trevor Griffiths]* is about to open in the Cottesloe, *Racing Demon* is about to transfer to the Olivier and I feel almost at peace. Many letters of sympathy for Dad. One from Gladys Mold who used to work in Grandpa's house in Devon: 'My brains don't catch things now very quickly owing to Advancing Years. My memory gets so bad but I never go out far from my chair as I have acute Rheumatism and I shall soon be 89. 'Tis a big age to be alone in the world.'

1st September   Back from holiday. I feel occasional shocking tremors of grief for Dad. Why? Unresolved guilt and sorrow that I never knew him better and didn't try harder. I really do miss him now. I've effectively lost both of my parents and ought to be mature. It's the most significant rite of passage.

10th September Tokyo with *Richard III*. The show has been devised to work in proscenium theatres of varying sizes throughout Europe, but the Globe proves to be unmanageable and there's really no way that I can unpick the production to make it work properly here. It's hell getting it on. Brian is less and less enthusiastic about appearing in it and wants only to play Lear. Understandable, but not what he signed up for. His diffidence is corrosive. Ian and I go to a reception for Japan/UK week. We meet Douglas Hurd, who's just come from Moscow, is jet-lagged, and *really* doesn't know what city he's in. Ian asks him if there'll be a war in the Middle East. 'No, it'll all be over by Christmas' – as Sir John French said of the First World War. To Kyoto and the Zen Garden which was spellbindingly peaceful, when you could ignore the shuffling and muttering of the tourists.

16th September Ion's in London and we asked Neil and Glenys [*Kinnock*] to dinner. Neil told him that he *mustn't* abandon politics, it's his duty, the acting will wait. This is not what Ion wanted to hear.

20th September Lunch with Andrez Pleszu, a friend of Ion. A philosopher and writer, he's now Foreign Secretary. He's been to see Douglas Hurd who told him they have to sort themselves out before they get aid. Hurd told him that he had to demonstrate – or his government did – that they were free of the taint of communism, to which Andrei replied: 'You have to play God with your two fists: with one fist you can chastise us, but with the other' – and he uncurled his fist – 'you must treat us with the hand of gentleness.' He said Hurd looked bemused.

1st October I finally bit the bullet and fired Peter Gill today. It was extraordinarily painful for both of us. He behaved with perfect dignity: angry, shocked, hurt but not yet bitter. 'I've been sacked before and I expect I'll be sacked again.' He said it was the logical consequence of my 'reforming zeal'. Reforming zeal? I'm just trying to make the fucking place *work*, let alone *reform* it. I said I thought the Studio had to have a wider remit, to have a much more eclectic spectrum of interests. We agreed to disagree. Peter's aesthetic is precise, fastidious, exclusive, which is his virtue as a director, but the Studio has to embrace talents that he disapproves of. I felt strongly

how much I'd miss him, his drollery, his waspishness, his scorn, his occasional generosity, and his perceptive intelligence, often wrapped in almost impenetrable obliquities. And his apparently psychic ability to know about shows in detail (and criticise them) without having seen them.

9th October   Cardiff for *Richard III*. Huge appetite and enthusiasm for the show. Ian is flourishing in his role of actor-manager, and loves the embrace he gets from the audiences who are genuinely pleased that he's shown up. I love the company of Ian on tour, the side of him that's the 'Stan McKellen' – Burnley's own. The stage management have a photo of him in their office, which makes him look like a '40s Northern comic: Frank Randle or Al Read.

10th October   First preview of *Dancing at Lughnasa* by Brian Friel. It's a charming, really affecting but faintly frustrating play. The high point of the play – the dancing at Lughnasa of the four aunts – is halfway through the first act, and after that it's an elegiac, heartbreaking descent into loss and rural bleakness, about the hair-cracks that appear in lives apparently in good shape. It's full of sensory detail – dancing, cheap cigarettes, cold floors, gloves being knitted – and it's beautifully played, and once again I thought that without the Irish the British theatre would be half dead. Small audience, and will the critics take to it? If not we're in trouble.

11th October   Brighton for the educational tour: Dario Fo's *Accidental Death of an Anarchist*. It's surprisingly effective, largely because of young Scottish virtuoso Alan Cumming, who reminds me a bit of a more innocent and less dangerous Jonathan Pryce.

12th October   A bomb scare in the theatre. Several hundred people piled out on the pavement for several hours. It seemed a daunting number of people to be responsible for. There was a search of the building, then the police gave me the choice of allowing people back in the building or staying out another hour to be absolutely sure. My nerve went and I took the extra hour, making all the shows go up late. During all this I had a meeting with Saeed Jaffrey. We sat on a bench by the river in the growing dusk and he read the part of Ibrahim in *White Chameleon* [*Christopher Hampton*] for me.

14th October   Peter Gill's assistant came to see me, trying to steer a line between betraying Peter by asking for a job and staying loyal to him. Rather more of former than latter. I've had a lot of aggro over sacking Peter, inevitable, I suppose. Someone has written to the Board comparing me with Saddam Hussein. 'Perhaps just a bit excessive?' said Mary Soames.

15th October   Jill Bennett has committed suicide. Lindsay Anderson wrote: 'Who do we know with such gaiety?' Or such pain. Or such loneliness. She was wayward, wise, perverse, painfully shy, arrogant, not big-hearted but she respected those who were. Feline, private, sad. Tim Spall was making a film with her in Morocco. They drove over mountains every day to the location. After three days of jolting and three days of silence, Jill said: 'This can't be good for the womb.' She told me once that she and John Osborne exhausted themselves; they told each other everything. By the end of twelve years there was nothing left. John was very hurt by their split. Jill also, but I think what really hurt him was her patrician contempt.

16th October   The row over Peter gets no calmer. Feel as if I'm swimming in hysteria and hyperbole. I just have to stick it out and keep my head above the waves. 'The lightest way of life is in the arts,' said Brecht. It doesn't feel like that.

17th October   We've made a breakthrough with the design of *White Chameleon*. Bob [*Crowley*] and I had got bogged down in trying to solve the technical problems of staging it. Jean Kalman [*lighting designer*] acted as a catalyst and started asking simple, Brookian questions. A work of art isn't *about* something; it *is* something. We have to find its meaning without reducing or diminishing it. Think of what Gauguin said to Vuillard: 'How do you see that tree? Very green? Then use the richest green on your palette.'

18th October   Went to Dublin for the day to do a press conference held in the Guinness Brewery for the tour of *RIII* and *Lear* to Cork, which at least gave me the opportunity of saying how pleased I was to be to have been able to organise a piss-up in a brewery. I was phoned by Roger Chapman in Dublin: 'We've got problems with the tour going to the Hamburg Schauspielhaus.' The Schauspielhaus is

run by Michael Bogdanov and he's having a hard time of it. He's had to cancel the opening of his show and move it to the night before our opening.

23rd October　Belfast for *Richard III*. I haven't been here since 1965, when I loved it. Don't recognise it now: soldiers on the street, men pushed up against the wall, but pedestrians passing by don't even turn their heads. Poverty, bleakness. It seems more foreign than anywhere in Europe and more inaccessible. But it's not Beirut: it's bearable for most of the people most of the time.

25th October　I went to the neurologist at the National Hospital to be tested for the cause of the tremor in my left arm, related to the whiplash. The insurance company wants to confirm that I don't have Parkinson's disease before they pay up. The doctor put electrodes all over me, and tested my response to objects and words. Apropos the difficulty of saying the word even when your brain recognised the object he said that when he was a student he'd thought Wittgenstein's 'Whereof one cannot speak, thereof one must remain silent' was a great truth. Now he thinks it's nonsense.

28th October　Piece in the *Observer* by Michael Coveney. He says he 'tried to rile me and failed'. I can't remember the incident. He does say that this year the NT has been an unbroken success. That's a relief, but I don't feel a wild sense of exhilaration. I'm used to a regular pattern of crises now, down and up, up and down, and I have the illusion of being able to cope.

29th October　Went to a meeting at the Young Vic to discuss 'Crisis in the Theatre'. There are severe problems with regional theatre (and with the big companies). There's been no strategic thinking on the part of the Arts Council: they've starved the regions at the expense of the big national companies but talked about 'equal misery for all', as if there were a virtue in a policy that's an absence of policy. The regions quite rightly complain but their most effective weapon – their work – hasn't been good enough often enough (to a large extent because of decline of funds) and they're caught in a vicious spiral.

　There's a litany of honest, well-meant, good-hearted, sanctimonious and sententious speeches about 'the crisis' to which I con-

tribute and I feel a slight sense of shame – I'm alienated from it, not because I don't feel that the government and the Arts Council have been feeble and philistine but because I think *we've* all been too supine and too pragmatic. We've brought trouble on our own heads by our complacency: we've blurred the distinction between subsidised and commerical theatre. We've got to be seen to exist to do the kind of work that, in content and execution, can't be done in the commercial sector: it should be an *aesthetic* choice to work in the subsidised theatre. There should be a positive desire from actors, writers, directors, designers to work there because it provides a unique framework in which to work, not for reasons of expediency or opportunism. The real issue is not about money, it's about art.

Peter [*Hall*] says: 'The Tories are trying to dismantle the whole of British theatre.' Actually, the Tories – or the Labour Party – don't care enough to want to dismantle anything in the arts, or mantle anything for that matter. 'I think art is a basic metaphor for all social freedoms,' said Joseph Beuys, 'but it shouldn't only be a metaphor, it should be a real means, in daily life, to go in and transform the fields of power in society.' But it isn't; or we can't make it so or we haven't. In my speech I said that 'the body of British theatre' is indivisible and being bled to death by amputations, and talked about 'shared experience', and about trying to put the small 'n' into the large 'N' at the NT, but what did this achieve? Mine is the fate of the politician. My sense of impotence drives me into self-important proclamations, boy-scout earnestness and hyperbole, while inside it all there's a mean little (Thatcherite?) voice saying to me: why not just get on with it and stop whingeing. You can *only* make your case on the stage BUT, as politicians say, the fact of the matter is that I've got the resources at the NT and others haven't. Politicians always say 'the fact of the matter is', whereas artists always know that the fact of the matter is that there is no fact to the matter.

31st October   Hamburg with *Richard III*. The Schauspielhaus is in a state of mutiny, and Michael [*Bogdanov*] is being threatened with the sack by the actors' collective who run the company. He's locked in meetings. Meanwhile we struggle with a recalcitrant, truculent and incompetent crew dressed uniformly in blue coats like lowly lab technicians. However did the Germans get the reputation for efficiency? But Hamburg is a wonderful city, the audience embraces the

show, and I get a lift to the airport from the Director's driver – a perk unaccountably unavailable to the Director of the NT.

2nd November   *Shape of the Table* has opened. David [*Edgar*]'s written a play in which all the ideas are fine, the arguments are clear, the subject is resonant, but its only flaw is that it doesn't quite generate the heat that the subject deserves. It feels slightly willed. And the audience seems to regard the Czech revolution as entirely some-one else's concern – 'a faraway country about which we know nothing'. It was hugely disappointing that my attempt to found a permanent company fell at the first fence with the refusal of the *Racing Demon* company to be in *Shape of the Table*. Actors talk a lot – and so do critics – about permanent companies, but how few are actually prepared to sign up for it. Big parts in big plays is what they mostly want and why shouldn't they?

3rd November   Review in German paper of *Richard III* says it is a ground-breaking production because it puts its actors at the centre of the performance. Where are they usually in Hamburg? Jean [*Kalman*] puts the blame on directors having too much power in Germany, being too concerned with the 'image' at the expense of the performance of the actor. This is connected to the relationship between the theatres and their public and the level of subsidy.

4th November   In urban architecture isn't there a latent totalitar-ianism, the desire to rob individuals of their identity? I heard on the radio today that when people buy council houses the first thing they do is change their front doors. Why is that less 'art' (apart from the lack of craft etc) than, for instance, Carl André's bricks in the Tate, which depend entirely on the gallery to identify it as 'art': an inert pile of bricks is transformed into a minimalist 'statement'. I worry about the growth of museum art: museums become so eager to propagate the new that they become the artist's accomplice, an almost equal partner, legitimising it as 'art'. Earlier art, without the aid of galleries and museums, never received such legitimacy.

8th November   To Milan via Paris. In Paris I met up with Glenn Close, who David Puttnam has arranged for me to meet because she wants to work at the NT. We met at twelve in Montmartre outside a

restaurant that turns out to be closed – it's Monday. We wandered up the hill and found another restaurant, which didn't open until twelve-thirty. I suggest that we knock at the door and that she says: '*Je suis Glenn Close.*' We knocked and she doesn't need to speak because the manager is thrilled to open his doors to a star. I tell her that if I employed her at the NT I'd be castrated publicly by at least five prominent English actresses.

Richard III goes well in Milan. Giorgio Strehler comes to the last twenty minutes of the show and tells me it is 'quite interesting'. After the show he holds court with his students and ignores our company, who giggle at his preposterously blue-dyed hair. No one suggests that he is not a great director – in my view the best in Europe – but why does he need to behave in such a childish way: we're no threat to him. The next day *La Stampa* says its a 'stupendous production' but fails to mention the name of the director.

16th November   *Evening Standard* Awards. Met David Mellor, who's the new Arts Minister. He made excessive protestations about his enthusiasm for the theatre and said we'd be rewarded for good housekeeping. 'I've been accused of dirigisme, but I think you'll approve of it.' He says we'll receive something from the Enhancement Fund. The RSC is to receive £8.7m. and they'll still complain. Joan Collins presented the Award for Best Comedy. She said she was appearing in *Private Lives* and 'As Edmund Kean said on his deathbed, "Dying is hard, comedy is easy."' The audience's jaw dropped but she seemed blithely unaware that she'd got it the wrong way round.

17th November   I was supposed to have gone to Madrid but the shows were cancelled due to a strike of the stage crew of the Teatro Nacional. They've been waiting for our visit to make the maximum impact. The company are in a bad state of depression: they're unmotivated and not led. Deborah is preoccupied and Ian can't rally them. There were a number of company meetings where there was extensive breast-beating and self-flagellation. Ian and Deborah were shocked to find that there were actors with vastly different impulses and priorities to their own. I'm relieved but guilty that I wasn't there. I was faxed the programme of *Lear* for a joyously inappropriate misprint: 'Brain Cox.'

18th November Dinner with the Kinnocks in Ealing. Politics thrives on gossip even more than theatre. Neil and I share the same birthday and to some extent the same character – well, we're both dogged, accessible and ambitious. And Neil wears his heart on his sleeve, which is probably not an advantage in a politician. We talk about how our generation has missed the defining experience of a war. Neil would have flourished in a war; he'd have made a good commander. He worries about his generation who he says are 'willing, almost eager, to use military force almost anywhere in the world. I wish they wouldn't be so keen to get into wars, because one day it will come back on your territory and God help you.' Of course they do it because they don't want to be seen as unmanly. Glenys is a model politician's wife – undeviatingly supportive, intelligently loyal but subversive. She kicked Neil firmly on the shin to get him to help clearing the table, when he was taken with his own anecdotage.

20th November Run-through of *Wind in the Willows*. It's been a very untroubled journey. Nick [*Hytner*] rang me from his rehearsal room in Stratford last year. 'I know what I want to do for you,' he said, '*Wind in the Willows*.' So I put him and Alan [*Bennett*] together, and Nick arrived for the meeting with his copy of the book, in which he'd written as a child: 'IF THIS BOOK SHOULD CHANCE TO ROAM, BOX ITS EARS AND SEND IT HOME.' Alan has adapted it beautifully, making something that is recognisably his without being a commentary on Grahame's book. He'd mentioned to me that he wanted to write a play about Kenneth Grahame when we were doing *The Insurance Man*, a play set in the Bank of England (where Grahame worked) with the Bank's staff mutating into animals. Nick has encouraged the actors to research their toad, rat, weasel, ferret, rabbit and badger personae. Only Michael Bryant has resisted. He has as much interest in 'research' as a cow has in veterinary science. But he took a video of a badger-watch away with him and returned a day or two later with this revelation: 'I have made a discovery about the habits of badgers: their movement and their posture have an extraordinary resemblance to Michael Bryant.' I think the show's going to be very successful. It's really well staged and it's funny and touching and is – well, it's the perfect Christmas show, thank

God, because we've spent a lot of money and I've told the Board that we plan to run it for several years.

22nd November   To Paris for *Richard III*. In the taxi from the airport to the Odéon we heard that Thatcher had resigned. We cheered, and the taxi driver did too. He wanted to know who would take over, and none of us knew. 'Michel Heselteene?? Jean Majeur??' When we reached the Odéon there was a message for me, asking me to appear on the French TV News to comment on the fall of the Tyrant Thatcher, but I didn't think my French would be up to it so I declined. The whole company are in a state of high jubilation. I feel a slight sense of the 'locked door syndrome': if she went so easily why wasn't the door pushed before. She *has* been an autocrat, inhibited thought, crushed imagination, encouraged greed, but haven't we been supine? After all it wasn't a real tyranny, even of the imagination. Playing *Richard III* in the Odéon was the realisation of an adolescent dream – to have a successful production playing in a great theatre in a great city. And it's my favourite auditorium in the world, where I saw Jean-Louis Barrault in 1966.

23rd November   Phone call from Ian early in the morning. 'Can you come to my room?' I did; Ian lay on his bed, looking anxious but elated. 'I've been offered a knighthood,' he said. 'Do you think I should take it?' I told him he should and he was relieved, but being Ian wouldn't show his elation. Later I walked with Peter Brook across Les Invalides. A beautiful soft light, a warm day, the city, the river, matchlessly beautiful. 'Is there anything you miss about England?' I asked Peter. 'The language,' he said. We talk about Deborah's production of *Lear*. 'Why doesn't she direct the parts of the play that need directing?' says Peter. The language is what I missed in Peter's production of *The Tempest* although it's eloquent and expressive – particularly an exceptional Prospero from a Sudanese actor and a Caliban from a Swiss one – the boy in the film of *The Tin Drum*.

24th November   Meeting with company about visiting Broadmoor with *Lear*. Brian Cox responds tetchily: 'I haven't decided yet.' 'But you agreed.' 'I don't want to go to Broadway!' 'Broadmoor, Brian, not Broadway,' sighs a weary chorus.

2nd December   I went to New York to try to sort out a transfer of *Racing Demon*. It's curious wanting to swim in the Broadway pool, which always seems to me archaic compared with London: it makes *All About Eve* seem like social realism – antique stage design, intense villagey gossip, critics afforded vastly too great an importance (they even name theatres after them). I went with Liz McCann [*producer*] to Jimmy Nederlander's [*Broadway theatre owner*] office. He called in his staff. 'It's a deal,' he said and we agreed on the theatre, shaking hands across his desk. I went for a drink in the Marriott Hotel. In the lobby, signs to various reception rooms: the Wilder Room, the Williams Room, the Inge Room, the Miller Room, the Albee Room, and the Brecht Room. The *Brecht* Room?

5th December   Back in London I had lunch with Noel Pearson [*Irish producer*] and learned that he'd had an identical meeting two days later with Jimmy Nederlander and been promised the same theatre for *Dancing at Lughnasa*, so *Racing Demon* has fallen through. Perhaps I should have pushed harder; perhaps I didn't want it enough. The trouble with the US and showbiz is that they make you want what you don't want and then make sure you can't have it.

6th December   *Tectonic Plates* [*Robert Lepage*] has opened. Robert's work has such grace and wit and invention. I'm still haunted by the face of George Sand coming out of the water: the sheet, the projection, the water tank, all so simple and so expressive. Robert has the ability to render the theatre poetic: images, verbal and visual, succeed one another, and accumulate resonance; they grow and harmonise, threads become themes, themes become narrative.

10th December   It's over thirty years since the Suez invasion, and we seem to be moving to another major intervention in the Middle East, another monument to bad faith. We started to rehearse *White Chameleon* – Christopher Hampton's autobiography – which is as much about history as himself. We look at videos and photographs of the Suez crisis, and Christopher talks about growing up in Alexandria during it. It seems a marvel that we're doing the play; only three months ago I sat in his room reading the first half, handwritten in ink in a black notebook, hoping that the second

half would materialise. There's no sign in the writing of anxiety; in fact there's a calm about it which seems to be reflected in the rehearsal room. And a sense of 'play' provided by the five boys in the cast, all about twelve, led by David Birkin, stick-like, like a tall and beautiful elf. Actually David seems older than I am. 'Do you think late Mozart is more interesting than early Mozart?' he asks me. The play is hard to get hold of, it's so delicate – mood and nuance like natural colours. Rehearsing it is like catching rare butterflies, or dusting off shards of pottery.

12th December   Outside rehearsals nothing but meetings about the budget and how we can balance it, and then meetings about how we can save and how we must cut, and then meetings about how it can be explained to the staff. Our problem at the moment: we can't run a deficit budget and our grant isn't increasing, our sponsorship income isn't increasing, and our box office is on the edge. We budget at 75 per cent capacity audiences, which translate – with concessions – to 67 per cent cash. So we need to have at very least one very successful show in each auditorium. If we don't we're faced, like Mr Micawber, with the result: misery. And if we do happen to do really well, with the result: happiness, we'll be penalised for our success. It's obvious, the Arts Council will say, you don't need so much grant. But our grant is our guarantee of continuity.

31st December   I'm worried about my fear of becoming bored, of my questionable commitment to theatre, and of my doubtful endurance. Some days I long to sit at home and read. I still feel as if I'm just getting ready for something, but life, as they say, isn't a rehearsal.

1991

8th January   I went to the Hammersmith Hospital for a brain scan. When I arrived at the hospital I sat nervously in the reception area talking to the receptionist about theatre, which she loved. She traced her fingers over her desk before she made phone calls and never looked at me as she spoke: she was blind. And the theatre? 'Oh, I don't miss the sets, my friend tells me what they're like. I just love the sound of the voices.' They made a mould for my head, a bag with a sort of polystyrene mixed with a chemical which fizzed for a while, got pleasantly hot and then set. I lay on the bed in front of the CAT machine – a long silver doughnut, like an iron lung – with my head held fast in the fitted headrest. They warned me to have a pee. I'm fine, I said, and then they slid me inside the machine, where I lay for three hours longing to pee and trying to imagine the inside of my brain.

12th January   We're on the brink of war in the Gulf. How? Why? If we go to war in six months' time we'll be facing the mutilated, the disabled, the grieving, and they'll ask: 'Was it worth it?' and we'll have to answer no. Again.

13th January   I went with Gorg to Dorset today to put Dad's ashes in the ground and plant an oak tree in his memory on the farm. He sold the farm a few years before he died; it's a nature conservancy zone now – home of rare orchids and butterflies. A quite perfectly beautiful day – clear azure sky, primrose sun.

14th January   Ian McKellen told me about the company's visit to Broadmoor with *King Lear*. The patients sat close to the action, which was played on the floor in a large room in daylight. They

concentrated with a rapt intensity. Silence. Until Lear's line: 'Is there any cause in nature that makes these hard hearts?' And a young woman slowly shook her head.

15th January   I saw Al Clark. We talked about the neologism 'toney', meaning a quality product. The NT, Al says, is 'toney'. A friend of his was in a supermarket in Australia. A woman was buying a large box of Tampax. 'Reg,' she called out, 'what's the price of these Tampax?' 'The ones you push in by hand or the ones you bang in with a hammer?' 'I said Tampax, not tintacks.'

18th January   I can't believe that we're going to war in the Gulf. The generation now in charge – i.e. my generation – have been shaped by a world war but not taken part in it. In some ways this new war is a rite of passage, a way of demonstrating that we can do it as well as they can, that we've grown up. Endless commentary on TV and radio about boys' toys: i.e. 'smart weapons' (there's an oxymoron) and 'strategy'. Deluges of experts and an infinity of talk to legitimise the whole exercise. It's all a massive hypocrisy. There have been so many times when the US and the UK have chosen to turn a blind eye to International Law – Panama, Grenada, Cyprus, Chile, Vietnam (where they used chemical weapons) . . . Why didn't the UN act against Israel in 1967? In Cyprus in 1974? In East Timor in 1975? Who put Pinochet in power? Who made Pol Pot possible? Who organised armed resistance to an elected government in Nicaragua? Answer: only commercial interests explain US foreign policy and in the Middle East that means oil. That's the meaning of 'stability' in the region. The US (and UK) supported Iraq in their invasion of Iran, they sold Iraq arms, they forgave the bombardment of an American ship, they turned a blind eye to the genocide of the Kurds; they helped to make and arm a monster. When the monster threatened stability (i.e. cheap oil) by invading Kuwait (a little dictatorship which treats migrant labour like slaves) the US tried to obliterate the monster. And there's no USSR to spoil the party. If the US and UK are really interested in stability why don't they settle the Palestinian question?

20th January   Queen Victoria once asked Disraeli if we had any permanent friends: 'We have no permanent friends, and no permanent enemies, we have only permanent interests.' Arthur Ransome to

Trotsky: 'The British make nothing out of India.' Trotsky: 'Then give up being so altruistic.' The Chief of US Forces confessed to a press conference that he had no TV set in his command bunker. Shock and amazement. He said he would get one. It's all a circle: life imitating art imitating life imitating art. 'We've got the special effects, all of them, but then so has *Starlight Express*,' an American said to Alan Bennett.

21st January At rehearsals Nadim Sawhalha [*actor, born in Jordan*] said, of the Gulf: 'We live in sorrowful times.' *White Chameleon* is starting to coalesce but I still find it hard to get a purchase on it, and I find Tom [*Wilkinson*] elusive. We haven't worked together since Nottingham and in some ways he's not changed at all: very talented, droll and very intelligent, but often seems slightly diffident – as if something more important was about to happen just round the corner. David Birkin and Saeed Jaffrey have a delightful relationship: David knows everyone's lines, and doesn't hesitate to prompt, but Saeed protects him from his own endearing smart-arsery. I went to bed early with a sleeping pill and I fell asleep during the news about the Gulf. 'It's not going to be as easy as we thought,' I heard a soldier say.

28th January I went to see Wally [*Shawn*] in *The Fever*, which we're doing with the Royal Court. I drove to Basildon – on the edge of Greater London – but it seemed much more remote than Birmingham. A small audience, who concentrated hard, and emerged silent, moved. There was a faint and alluring sense of religious ritual – Wally as evangelist performing his remarkable monologue about the Third World and us, capitalism and colonialism, with an unassailable sincerity, to natives eager for conversion.

29th January Appointment with neurologist and the results of the CAT scan. The good news: I don't have any sign of incipient Alzheimer's. The bad: I have a spot that might be the beginnings of Parkinson's. I'm assailed for a moment by panic and self-pity, then I feel completely stoical. I can't work out whether it's because I'm not really admitting that I might develop it, or because of strength of character. I think the latter is unlikely. But I read from an article about Parkinson's disease: 'For me, the disease started with a spasm in my left arm which soon became a tremor.' Exactly.

30th January The war's worse. An Iraqi friend said to Neal Ascherson: 'Must a whole nation be destroyed because Caliban recognises his own face in the mirror?' I have a feeling of real hopelessness, and bilious anger against the bellicosity of the Americans, mercenaries, bullies, self-righteous thugs. And the British mimicking them.

Cecil Day Lewis's poem is called for:

Where are the War Poets?
They who in folly or mere greed
Enslaved religion, markets, laws,
Borrow our language now and bid
Us to speak up in freedom's cause.

It is the logic of our times,
No subject for immortal verse –
That we who lived by honest dreams
Defend the bad against the worse.

31st January *White Chameleon* has gone into the theatre. It looks beautiful and is very delicately acted. When Tom gets hold of it and tells the story it packs a real punch. Christopher is very nervous: his first play for years, he's very exposed and very raw. And I'm very anxious about letting him down.

5th February We started previewing *White Chameleon* last night. It's full of resonance, nuance, atmosphere. It grows from the small and personal to the large and epic, but it does so elusively. There's a moment where the schoolmaster burns the boy's fez in the wastepaper basket and the boy watches and we watch, and then his older self steps out of the dark and watches over his shoulder – his past, his Egyptian childhood, Britain's history, smouldering away in real time – and he says: 'I was holding hands with grief.' It's as perfect a moment of theatre as I can remember and impossible to create in any other medium. Tom played it perfectly. Perhaps people will dismiss the very fastidiousness and elusiveness of the play and say it's lightweight and insignificant but it isn't: it's dense and poetic.

8th February I should be in Prague today. I woke up at 6 a.m. to go to the airport: there was an eerie silence as if London had stopped breathing. I looked out of the window: snow, still falling, as thick as I've ever seen here, softening the features of the houses, carpeting the streets and the cars. No traffic is moving and all flights have been cancelled. So I've had an odd day, walking and playing music and reading, and I've missed meeting Havel who was coming to *Lear*. I sat at home and read plays, including a wonderful play called *Angels in America* [*Tony Kushner*] about the American Right, McCarthyism, Mormonism, Marxism, the Millennium, homosexuality, AIDS, God and angels. I knew halfway down the first page – a virtuoso monologue by Roy Cohn having three phone conversations, one of them trying to book tickets for *Cats* – that I wanted to put it on. I'd like to direct it but I won't be free, so will ask Declan to do it.

9th February Christopher [*Hampton*] was on *Start the Week* on Monday to talk about his play, but in spite of his play being about Suez, he was asked not to discuss the Gulf War: 'We have another channel to do that.' *White Chameleon* is gradually gathering layers of resonance that make it (at least for me) a very powerful play about childhood and about growing up to the heartbeat of the British Empire: 'As for Ibrahim, I never found out what became of him, but all my life I've heard his faulty old heart, beating under the floorboards.' That central image – the legacy of the Empire – is as strong as any in the plays of Christopher's generation. The show started unevenly and then on Tuesday acquired its balance; Tom very strong. The two previews after seemed a bit glib in the first act.

13th February Press night of *White Chameleon*. Familiar nerve-wracking dream of standing naked in a courtroom. Genial smiles at critics, concealing resentment. A member of the audience overheard by David [*Hare*]: 'This is like Paul's childhood, only for Egypt read Chingford.' Very good performance and very nice party at Norma Heyman's: profusion of the newly Oscar nominated – Stephen [*Frears*], Jeremy Irons and Glenn Close. Glenn says she loved the pauses but was shocked by them, the way that things took the time they took.

14th February Bucharest via Vienna to put on *Richard III* and *King Lear*. Inflight mag (Austrian Airlines) describes a world tour of

twelve 'Mozart Girls' to publicise Vienna and the Bicentenary 'in their immaculate period costumes and Mozart make-up . . . The real sensation, though, was their appearance at a special Viennese evening in Abu Dhabi and Dubai.' I'll bet. Arrive at Bucharest in a blizzard. Greeted by a welcoming committee: Dan Jitianu, Marian Popescu, and Victor (again) from the Ministry – the Vicar of Bray, who I discovered later was the person who shopped Trixie Staicu [*a translator*] and sent her to prison for years. Ion is away in Prague at a conference. To the National Theatre, which is a crude parody of 1960s brutalism. The interpreter, Andrea, is a director; she speaks excellent English and is dogged and drily witty. A small, pixie-like woman, slightly retarded, walks around chanting 'Are you happy? I am happy' in English. Most of the stage crew live in the theatre. At least here they can get hot water. Outside they can get only cold, and often only for an hour a day. Cocteau wrote: 'I once asked Eisenstein – When did you think the Revolution had begun? The day when the taps and toilets no longer worked.' Some of their actors live in the theatre as well – there are some fully furnished dressing rooms. One of the crew (who had hidden in the theatre for seven days during the Revolution) said he wasn't frightened of being shot. He said being dead would have been better than what went before.

Talked to Andrez Pleszu after *Lear*. He's still Foreign Secretary but is very depressed and thinks that nothing has changed since the Revolution. At least we're able to talk about it which we couldn't have done before. He feels defeated. Recently he gave permission for the King to return to his family grave. His permission was countermanded by the Prime Minister but no one told him. I get to bed very late, quite drunk, falling in the deep snow on my way back to the hotel.

15th February   At the start of *Richard III* there was a gasp of recognition and applause as Ian appeared out of the smoke, a ghostly profile in a military greatcoat: Stalin. I was sitting in Ceauşescu's vast imperial loge at the back of the stalls when Gerry, who was operating the follow spot, fainted. I jumped up and grabbed the follow spot like Rambo manning a machine gun. Gerry recovered, but I encouraged him to stay sitting. At the end of the show, when the boar's head was ripped off the flag, there was a huge roar of approval, rhythmic clapping and shouts. Then I went with Roger Chapman to the

Athenée Palace for supper: caviar and Romanian champagne, the caviar paid for in dollars, the champagne in lei. The dollars were taken away and the change (in lei) returned on a plate, wrapped in a crisply laundered napkin.

16th February Gorbachev joke: A chicken farmer went to his village priest after ten of his hens had died. 'Give them aspirin,' said the priest. The farmer did, and ten more died. 'Give them castor oil,' said the priest. The farmer did, and ten more died. 'Give them penicillin,' said the priest. Ten more died and the farmer told the priest in despair that all his chickens had died. 'What a shame,' said the priest, 'I had so many more remedies to try.'

17th February Standing with David Bradley [*actor*] waiting for the lift. 'I think we've missed Sunday's one,' he says. One of the consequences of bringing the West to Romania is flocks of beggars on the streets, mostly small boys, mostly gypsies. I weave through them on the way to the theatre, handing out money as if I was handing out leaflets. I stayed backstage during *Richard III* and enjoyed watching the offstage world – actors larking around, or in silent concentration, or whispering, or laughing, or waiting for their entrance like athletes; then the transformation as they walk onstage, ordinary humans becoming giants. After the *Lear* performance a man hands a note to Brian Cox. It reads: 'Nobody can play Sir William Shakespeare's plays better than his English people. I've seen with your remarkable help that somewhere in England Sir W. Shakespeare is still alive. Thank you. Signed. A Simple Man.'

Dinner at Dan Jitianu's house. Generous hospitality and jokes: 'Mummy, at school they hit me, they spit at me, they throw mud at me. Why do I have to go?' 'Because you're forty-five years old and you're the headmaster.' Dan showed me a photograph of Ceauşescu, which originally showed only one ear, but there's a Romanian saying that to have one ear is to be mad, so another ear was painstakingly painted on the photograph.

18th February A conference this morning. Collection of about a hundred journalists, teachers, students and actors. 'What is the difference between Alexander the Great and Buddha?' I was asked. About 3,000 miles, I should have said. In the evening I went onstage

with Ian McK. at the end of the performance to make a speech. I
started with Andrea interpreting, but the audience chanted 'English!
English!', so I continued in English. I told them the production had
come to its spiritual home, that this sort of cultural exchange was the
only true diplomacy, and that we were overwhelmed by their
hospitality. They didn't want us to go, clapping rhythmically and
incessantly, but we walked offstage slowly, blinking back tears.
There was a party afterwards in Nicu Ceauşescu's house. The house
is spotted with bullet holes, which have been left as a reminder: LEST
WE FORGET. The house is decorated in 'tyrant's baroque' – swanky
drapes, gold braid, gold-plated taps, etc – and now houses the
Theatre Union. It was to have been called UTER, but that's the
Romanian for 'uterus' so it was christened UNITER. The actors from
the Bulandra Company are there, heartbreakingly generous. Ion
arrives at about twelve-thirty from Prague. He's very anxious about
the future for theatre in Romania because only 33 per cent of GNP
has been allocated to culture. I say that's about ten times the British
proportional allocation. He won't or can't see that things must
change in the theatre, where seat prices are fantastically low and
all the actors have guaranteed jobs for life. He can't contemplate any
actors being made redundant or any theatres ceasing to exist.

19th February   Going through passport control, the official hands
my passport back and asks for a cigarette. The plane is delayed for an
hour, then takes off, is diverted to Gatwick and I arrive back home at
4 p.m. I have to drive straight to Bristol to see *Long Day's Journey
Into Night*. It's extraordinarily difficult to concentrate. The actors
are very buttoned up, but the production is very 'finished'. Howard
[*Davies*] has staged it artfully, but it doesn't catch fire. It's fiendishly
difficult to capture O'Neill's incantatory repetitions and make them
add up to more than the sum of the parts. I see the same critics I saw a
week ago at *White Chameleon* and feel as if we're all trapped in the
same circle of hell. They've been grudging about the play, even if
complimentary about the production. Only one critic has mentioned
the beautiful design ('austere' – which it isn't) and none have
mentioned Jean's exquisite lighting. Perhaps they just don't notice.

20th February   I went to the Motley Exhibition and talked to a
rather jittery John Gielgud, anxious about being late for his appoint-

ment with Alvin Rakoff to discuss a small part in a TV film. Also talked to a wonderfully clear-headed Peggy Ashcroft. I wish I'd worked with her. She talked about Dan D. L. being a character actor, about the problems for good-looking young men playing the romantic roles. The Motley designs are utterly of their time; but most stage design dates very quickly: what is avant-garde today will look archaic tomorrow. Motley introduced the idea of simplicity and beauty and human values to stage design which had been suffocated with decorative excess. Percy [*Margaret*] Harris, who was one third of Motley, is a remarkable eighty-six. Jocelyn [*Herbert*] is several years her junior and refined their aesthetic.

21st February   Argument about the security at the theatre. When it snowed they wouldn't clear the snow because if they cleared it and someone slipped they were accountable, whereas if they didn't clear it and someone had an accident, it was an act of nature.

24th February   The war gets worse every minute. Neal Ascherson argues that Britain can't see anything odd about its attitude to war. Sending armies isn't seen as political failure. Offensive war is seen as something which *works*. Britain only looks solid and convincing in times of external strife. War without Britain – yes, possibly. But Britain without war?

26th February   Lunch at Maurice Saatchi's office: Norman Foster [*architect*] and some bankers. One banker, a chairman of several British companies and on the Board of Deutsche Bank, said that Britain would never progress while its educational system was so backward, and that meant the abolition of private education. Then he left, and another banker, Old Etonian, confidently dismissed his argument: 'Of course he was born in South Africa.'

28th February   The Gulf War ended today, and the announcement was followed by an avalanche of self-aggrandisement and myth-making. A British general said it was one of the greatest victories in the whole of British military history. The war revived those euphemisms from the Vietnam War: 'military capability', 'body count', 'friendly fire'. Was it worth it? The answer *must* be no. Surely if the UN means anything, if any force was sent it should have been from

the UN. Horrible crowing over the 'victory'. In the *Daily Mirror* an article by Joe Haines, once Wilson's press officer: 'Anti-war chorus must not be forgiven.' From Tony Harrison's new poem:

> Let them remember, all those who celebrate
> That their good news is someone else's bad.

1st March   American woman in the Olivier Theatre prior to performance of *Racing Demon*, waving her ticket: 'I want my money back. I refuse to see a play with no scenery.'

3rd March   Article in the *Independent on Sunday*: 'Is it OK not to go to the theatre any more?' I'm tempted to reply but remember the adage: never fight people who have a barrel of ink. This is the fourth such article that I can remember in the last six months: Edward Pearce, Gilbert Adair, Simon Hoggart and now Sebastian Faulks. Their charge: theatre is too exposed, too frail, too imperfect and often too bad. Faulks quotes Updike: 'I've never much enjoyed going to plays. The unreality of painted people standing on a platform saying things they've said to each other for months is more than I can overlook.' It's missing the point. It's the *re-creation* that animates the art and makes it unique. Who doesn't question the unreality of film? All art forms are unreal in some sense. They have their formal rules, their conventions, their partiality, novels as much as paintings. Woman to Matisse: 'Surely the arm of this woman is too long.' Matisse: 'That's not an arm, Madame, it's a picture.' I wish I could develop Picasso's sangfroid: 'Critics should mean as much to artists as ornithologists do to birds.'

4th March   John Keegan, the military correspondent of the *Daily Telegraph*, rails against the contemptible reporting of the BBC. He says that the Army gives better value for money than the BBC – as if they had the same objectives and provided an analogous service. TV could as well be provided by the Army: it offers us nothing but 'facts' of questionable reliability. We've had an unremitting diet of news throughout the Gulf War but an almost total absence of voices that questioned the wisdom and conduct of the war. Its morality and its philosophy remained unexamined, drowned in the wash of 'expert' voices discussing the efficacy of Scud missiles, Challenger tanks,

FI11S, and desert strategy, with all the enthusiasm of small boys deploying their tin toy soldiers. It was only when I saw a photograph of a dead Iraqi soldier in his armoured car, charred beyond recognition into a grinning skeletal death mask, and heard Tony read his poem about him, did I find a voice that echoed the outrage, confusion and despair that I felt about the whole event. This is what art does and journalism doesn't; balance is the enemy of art and it's the essential premise of news broadcasting, and that's precisely why it is so difficult for those who run television companies to allow the artists to flourish. David [Hare] was told recently by a BBC executive that they aren't looking for 'strongly authored' projects now. Which means the death of the single drama – one of the few things that makes the BBC 'distinctive' and justifies the licence fee.

15th March   There are largish flutterings in the dovecote of the stage-management department because I'm trying to make changes to the way it's run. My heart sinks at the task of sorting it out; like so much in the NT, they're locked in the late '60s. 'British institutions, however much they try to adapt, carry the imprint, seemingly for ever, of the genetic code from the era in which they were conceived,' says Peter Hennessy in the *Guardian*.

16th March   The NT has been nominated for twenty-eight awards in the Oliviers. Are we the only player in the game? Do we succeed by sheer quantity? I'm nominated for *Richard III* and *White Chameleon*, and of course I'll lose but I hope with grace.

28th March   My birthday. Quiet, but faintly uneasy day. A raging feeling of not quite LIVING. Or at least of constantly being about to start living. I feel explosive: I'm dangerously impatient. I want to do so much more than I have done. And do it *now* while I have the will and the energy.

8th April   Board meeting. Having played Cassandra for two years – predicting painful end-of-the-financial-year deficits each October – I'm now the bringer of good news: we've got a small surplus. Derek Mitchell points this out and says I should be more confident. It's always going to be like this.

14th April   Theatre conference in Birmingham organised by David Edgar. David's kept the true flame of theatre writing burning; I really admire his patience and persistence. And optimism. In a discussion about running theatres Max [*Stafford-Clark*] said that the Royal Court used to need a hit every three years. Now they need one every year. That's 50–55 per cent audiences, i.e. 200 people a night. At the NT we need 2,000 a night: that's 75 per cent. Michael Attenborough said the RSC was a 'writer's theatre' – the work was based on the work of one writer. He said they had appointed two women 'quite deliberately' to their 'central think tank'. A man said he'd been bet a bottle of vodka that he wouldn't ask me a question. What was the question? I asked. 'Why weren't you at the women's writing seminar last night?'

18th April   I had lunch with David Puttnam, who wants me to direct a film musical. Of what? He doesn't know, but wants to offer me money so that he can 'ask me to read a book without feeling guilty'. Oh brave new world, where you can be offered money to read a script. At this rate in the theatre I would be a millionaire several times over.

19th April   Martin Amis says in an article: 'Perhaps because of their addiction to form writers lag behind contemporary formlessness.' Theatre is always and inevitably unfashionable in that sense: you can't dispense with narrative and structure. And it has to start on time.

20th April   Nick [*Hytner*] and Howard [*Davies*] have dropped out of their productions, and *Arturo Ui* is looking dodgy because of the intransigence of the Brecht Estate. We've had to cancel the first preview of *Black Snow* [*Adaptation of a Bulgakov novel by Keith Dewhurst*] because they didn't finish the tech and there are continuing problems with the stage management. And I'm anxious about *Murmuring Judges*, which we're going to read next Monday.

21st April   Ian McKellen told me he joined the theatre for the boys. When I was growing up in Dorset you'd have been better off for meeting girls if you'd become a horse rather than an actor.

22nd April   A reading of *Murmuring Judges*, which I found inspiring. In the afternoon David [*Hare*] and Bob [*Crowley*] and I visit Clapham Police Station, which conforms very closely to what David's written. The Superintendent had Marilyn Monroe and the Queen on his office wall. Sample dialogue in the police station:

> SERGEANT: (to Portuguese suspect) There's a bogey in this passport.
> SUSPECT: *Cómo?*
> SERGEANT: Do you know what a bogey is?

25th April   A day on the theme of punishment and power. David and Bob and I went to lunch in the Great Hall at Middle Temple with Ben Hytner, Nick's dad. Much talk about the function of the judiciary and the system of advocacy. There's a distinct distaste for criminal law, or for any law that gets your hands dirty or, indeed, for going through a process that deprives people of their liberty. After lunch we go to Ben's chambers and talk to him and his pal, Stephen Sedley:

> BEN: It's not quite true that the whole legal profession is motivated by greed.
> STEPHEN: No, we know two or three who aren't.
> BEN: Yes, and two of them are sitting in this room.
> STEPHEN: Who's the third?

In the afternoon we go to Wandsworth Jail, where the warders are known as the Gestapo and they wear their caps with the brims hard down against the tips of their noses, so their eyes are unreadable. I think of Oscar Wilde: 'If this is the way Queen Victoria treats her prisoners she doesn't deserve any.' It's raining and the three of us are wearing macs. 'Oh look,' says a prisoner, 'cunts in coats.' It's hard to escape the conclusion that the system is the rich sentencing the poor. There's reform coming in slowly but, as the Deputy Governor says: 'It means there'll be more privileges to take away.' The smell of the prison – cabbage, piss, bleach, sweat, misery – stays with me the rest of the day even (or particularly) at the dinner in the evening at Lincoln's Inn. How often do the lawyers visit the prisons? Or the judges?

In the evening a dinner called a Grand Night which lived up (or down) to its name. It's the first time I've ever worn white tie and tails and I feel like a head waiter. I'm greeted by a genial man who says he has to partner me in to dinner. We have drinks in a panelled room, surrounded by portraits of lord chancellors from centuries ago. I meet the Treasurer who says he's delighted I'm running the NT without my hand in the till. It turns out he's a great theatre fan and that I've probably been invited in order that he can ask me for tickets for *Wind in the Willows*. My fellow dinner guests are Margaret and Denis Thatcher, the Nigerian Ambassador, Andreas Whittam-Smith [*Editor* Independent] and Miles Kington. We're led into dinner by our 'partners', our names announced as we enter the Hall, under the mocking gazes of a couple of hundred would-be lawyers who are obliged to dine here several times a term in order to qualify as barristers.

At my place (well down the table from Mrs T.) I'm faced by silver and glasses fanning out from my plate like a display of pikes in an armoury. The food is good, the wine is excellent and the conversation is mostly gossip. Someone lives down the road from Jeffrey Archer ('How did he get away with it?' they all cry) in Grantchester. Archer owed a builder money. The builder saw him sneak out of his drive to use the phone box (huge guffaws: 'Who was he phoning??'), so the builder parked his truck across the door of the phone box, trapping Archer, and went to the pub. 'Archer had to phone the police to get the builder to move his truck!' (Volcanic spasms of laughter.)

After three courses and two different wines, we retire to a long panelled room where I talk to Andreas Whittam-Smith. We watch Thatcher, who's alone, ignored, and who, devoid of her circle of power, looks old and pathetic. I suggest he goes to talk to her. 'You must be joking,' he says, 'she tried to put me in prison.' We go to the Library for pudding, dessert wines, port and cheese. I sit next to a man who is an expert in building law who tells me he's having trouble with his shirt studs (diamond, I think). 'My valet must have put them in wrong,' he says. 'Your valet?' I say, smirking. 'Do you mean your wife?' 'No,' he says tartly, 'my *valet*.'

After dinner, more drinks – whisky and champagne – in another panelled room, this one clad with portraits of more recent legal luminaries. I talk to a gaggle of High Court judges – including

Humphrey Potts and Peter Taylor, who I first met in the Milk Bar in Newcastle twenty years ago – about the Home Secretary, who they think is a buffoon. Then I walk – stagger – through Lincoln's Inn Fields, past dossers in the park staring like sans culottes at the aristos and wishing the same (deserved) fate on us, get a taxi in Holborn, and imagine the bottomless contempt of the Wandsworth prisoners for everyone at tonight's dinner.

28th April   I went to Alicante – it's the city where *The Changeling* is set – for the weekend to see the education dept production of *Tartuffe*. After the show I went with the British Council man and his wife to a bar in a converted nunnery (fifteenth-century). Huge church candles, roses, fruit, gross statues, two live lions in cages in the courtyard, and a lot of stiletto – heels not daggers. The place stank of rose petals and lion piss.

30th April   Bill [*Gaskill*] has done a hugely enjoyable production of *Black Snow*. It's all the things you expect of Bill – fastidious, dry, spare, unsentimental – the unexpected thing is the sheer fun of it. Peter [*Brook*] was slightly miffed because he didn't know that we were doing *Black Snow* and fears that it's straying on to his territory with his Meyerhold show.

1st May   To Paris to see Ariane Mnouchkine's production of *Iphigénie*, which I found very moving. As you enter the auditorium you pass pits, dug as if being excavated by archaeologists, full of life-sized figures from Ancient Greece – like Chinese funerary figures. Visceral rhythmic music and an eclectic selection of instruments; a very artful concoction of craft and showmanship.

2nd May   'Solti here!' Solti rang me to ask if I would direct *Falstaff* at Salzburg. I talked myself out of it; I said I didn't think my Italian was good enough.

5th May   I'm thinking about the lecture I said I'd do about the state of the theatre. It's all too easy to respond to 'theatre is rotten' articles with a knee-jerk 'Well, I like it' when much of the time the truth would be 'I am paid to like it.' The questions must be:

Why is theatre different; isn't all art in trouble?

How do we avoid the theatre being a subculture within a subculture?

Can art compete with the real world? It always looks so frail and equivocal.

Why is the British theatre so celebrated?

Why is theatre strong in Britain and films weak?

Why are the British good actors? Are the British always pretending to be someone else? Are we in love with ceremony, with dressing up?

How do we democratise our arts, how do we educate the disenfranchised?

How do we distribute the arts round the country?

Why do we listen to the media: are we drowning in an ocean of opinion?

Is class the fuel of British art?

12th May A week's rehearsal of *Napoli Milionaria* [*Eduardo di Filippo*]. I feel underprepared, but the actors seem confident. It's a little like O'Casey set in Naples, written in Neapolitan dialect, brilliantly transposed to Liverpool by Peter Tinniswood. The task is to make the production true to the original *and* to the translation. I want the actors to act – behave, move, gesture – like Italians so that with your fingers in your ears you'd believe that they were Neapolitan. To which end I've got a book of gestures, including many from Naples. Much vying over who does which gesture when; particularly prized is the vertical horn-sign – hand held up with forefinger and little finger extended vertically. Other fingers bent down by the thumb: cuckold, general insult, protection or curse.

14th May Simon Callow tells me of a conversation with Peggy Ramsay:

SIMON: I've just done a film with Vanessa Redgrave.
PEGGY: Oh yes, didn't I play her in a film?
SIMON: No, she played you.
PEGGY: How was she?
SIMON: Not very good. She was rather benign.
PEGGY: Oh no, quite wrong. Hadn't she ever met me?

15th May   *Long Day's Journey* has opened, much improved from Bristol. Strange, rambling, circular play; it's utterly uncompromising and pushes an audience to its limits. O'Neill spared himself nothing in the play, excavating his life, heart, soul – call it what you like. He didn't want the play to be performed or published until twenty-five years after his death. Matchless ending, unbearably sad: 'That was in the winter of the senior year. Then in the spring something happened to me. Yes, I remember. I fell in love with James Tyrone and was happy for a time.'

16th May   I hosted a lunch for the NT corporate contributors. I sat next to Vivien Duffield, who said that her man, Jocelyn Stevens, hoped to become Chairman of the BBC. 'It needs sorting out,' she said, 'it's so wildly left-wing.' Later I went to a dinner with David Mellor, whose purpose was unclear. Much talk of what he could do if/when the government lost the election. The cast included Graham Dowson [*businessman*], Grey Gowrie, advertising moguls, and a nice man who writes for David Frost. It seemed as if everyone (including myself) was attempting to play roles – the man of class, the man of wit, the man of power, etc. Dowson railed against the foolishness of the British film industry, who won't make films that we can sell in America. It was a very uncomfortably blokey evening that ended with dirty jokes, clockwise round the table. I dreaded that my turn would come. It didn't.

17th May   Ian [*McKellen*]'s the Cameron Mackintosh Professor of Drama and I went with him to St Catherine's, Oxford to take part in a talk about the theatre and the community with John McGrath and Philip Hedley. I fumbled and waffled at the beginning – over-confident and over-casual. I thought I could stand up, open my mouth and wisdom would tumble out, instead of a mouthful of dead lizards. I recovered a bit and cobbled together a defence of the theatre as an activity. 'School of eloquence,' said John McGrath, not entirely ironically. He and Philip *were* eloquent and passionate. I went back to London and caught the second half of *Timon of Athens* at ENO. It was bewilderingly inert, tuneless, morbid, with an inaudible libretto and a graceless, leaden production. The party afterwards was an assembly of the cultural aristocracy, which seemed to define the world of opera: self-important and irredeemably elitist.

3rd June   Rehearsals for *NM* have been good: warm, humane and funny, even if occasionally a bit strained, at least on my part. *All* actors are demanding and sometimes I give up. I lost my patience with Clare [*Higgins*] and Ian [*McKellen*] when I arrived for rehearsals and they were waiting for me to goad them into activity. 'I don't see why I should always be expected to get you going,' I said. 'I'll go to my office and come back when you're ready to work.' They were shocked and so was I, but we did good work after that. Ian is still unsure of the play and still doesn't know his lines. Like all stars he consumes the energy of everyone around him, particularly Clare. He dominates rehearsals often at the expense of other actors, but all strong actors radiate an energy that has an almost physical heat and they draw the heat like poultices from the actors around them. Being combative, impatient, irascible, and frustrating is often an implicit demand to be challenged and stimulated, to be given competition by their fellow actors.

4th June   Dinner with Al [*Clark*]. We talked about niche marketing: he'd been to a film market where he'd seen a poster for *Anal Arousal II*.

11th June   It's five o'clock in the morning. Clear, soft blue sky and amber light on the chimney pots. *The White Devil* [*John Webster*] has crept up on me like an iceberg to a liner, while I've been sitting diffidently on the bridge ignoring the approaching catastrophe. It's as bad as anything has been during my time: miscast, awkwardly staged and fraught with bad luck. It will damage the theatre, but not fatally, just a large hole in the Olivier that will need mending. Every time that this sort of thing happens I think how lucky I've been, how perilously chancy the theatre is. I take too much for granted and founder on hidden obstructions that could have been avoided.

13th June   *The White Devil* has taken its toll. We've had to reschedule in the autumn, bringing *Wind in the Willows* earlier and shortening the run of *W. Devil*. We need a hit in the Olivier at *all* times, one show that we can always count on. Actually we need one in each theatre. What commercial manager would accept the risk of always budgeting a production on an expectation of 75 per cent?

14th June   I've finished my lecture for the Hamlyn Trust. It's so difficult to write about art, it crumbles in your hands or comes out as 'artspeak'. Is there any point talking about theatre at all? I don't quite like the tone of voice of it. There's something a bit solemn and worthy and smart without being clever.

19th June   I've started the tech for *Napoli*. It's going very smoothly, in very good spirits. Everything else is in turmoil. Another thirty performances of *The White Devil* to go and no audience for it in 1,100-seat theatre. I'll need to take radical measures to avoid an epidemic of bad morale. What was I doing asking Philip [*Prowse*] to direct it? I've admired his work for years at the Citz, but it doesn't seem to transplant. I was looking for a bit of *his* success, in bad faith, mistrusting my own taste.

22nd June   Middle of the night after the first preview of *Napoli*. It went well, with a good response from the audience: really good ensemble work. I was exasperated by Ian when I went to his dressing room and he said curtly: 'It's fifteen minutes too long.' He was right, but I was angry. He'd had his confirmation from the audience and couldn't see that I needed it as well. He was responding to my excessive relief (and the fact that I'd been proved right) by excessive disengagement. He told Sue later that he'd upset me when I went round 'to be stroked' by him.

24th June   We went to lunch with the Palumbos. Beautiful house near Newbury. Some excellent paintings, mostly post-war. Jocelyn Stevens and Vivien Duffield were there. They talk about the difficulty of getting second gardeners. Peter says that Cecil Parkinson came to lunch shortly after the revelation of his illegitimate child, got pissed and sat on the sofa next to his wife talking about how he couldn't resist women: 'I've been a bad boy, a bad, bad boy . . .' Peter complains of David Mellor and Tim Renton [*Arts Minister*], and the government attitude to the arts. Says Major's friends are David Mellor, Robert Atkins (Minister of Sport) and Jeffrey Archer. This is bad news. Peter asks me what I feel about the Arts Council. I tell him.

25th June   Dad died exactly a year ago. I still think of him a great deal, more now than when he was alive. I was never prepared to

admit his influence and his power over me, or to confront him as a person when he was alive. He was so alien to anything that I thought *I* was, that I could never reconcile that with what *he* was. Somehow we didn't seem to belong; he despised or ignored everything that I thought was important. 'Shakespeare is balls,' he used to say, and he meant it. He was always calling a spade a spade. Or to be more precise, a bloody spade. Or to be more precise still, a fucking spade. And yet he wasn't an insensitive man, or without an impulse to gentler feelings. He would sometimes surprise me with his perceptions and his awareness of other people's cruelties. How exasperating to feel that I only got to know him within a few weeks of his death. It took the fear of death to make him approachable, and I still feel it was my fault as much as his.

26th June   Dinner with Mary and Iona and Peter Carrington, who told stories about Thatcher all confirming her irrationality. He arrived back once from a Foreign Ministers' conference, having negotiated a new settlement for Britain's contribution to the EEC. After negotiating for twenty-three hours without a break he went straight to Chequers. She stood waiting for him on the doorstep and as he got out of the car she screamed at him that he'd sold out.

28th June   *Napoli Milionaria* has opened. Enthusiastic reception, and I feel that my enthusiasm has been matched by the audience and the critics, barring Jack Tinker [*Daily Mail*] who couldn't understand why a play set in the Naples dockland written in Neapolitan dialect had been played with Liverpool accents, although Jack did seem to know the play was set in a port because he came to the first night wearing a sort of sailor suit.

29th June   I went to the High Court to research *Murmuring Judges*. I slipped into one courtroom and discovered that the Guinness appeal – Ernest Saunders – was being considered. His barrister was claiming to have medical evidence that Saunders was suffering from pre-senile dementia. He said that Saunders was unable to remember three numbers backwards, and couldn't even remember the name of the President of the US. None of that, I would have thought, convincing evidence of dementia, senile or otherwise, and having watched Mum for years I felt well qualified to adjudicate.

Saunders was listening, comprehending, and I thought: You lying bastards – client, barrister and doctor all in a (financially) well-oiled conspiracy. I strolled into another court and was unprepared for seeing Humphrey Potts in full regalia sitting on the Bench with two other judges. There's no satisfactory etiquette for acknowledging the unscheduled appearance of a friend in a Court of Appeal, but he bowed towards me almost imperceptibly and I smiled broadly.

30th June   Dinner with John Mortimer. John tells this story: a drunken father comes home and falls asleep on the stairs. His sons come back later, see their father asleep, get some chicken giblets from the fridge and put them in his flies. Then they go to bed. Some time later the wife comes downstairs, looking for her husband, and sees the dog bent over him, apparently eating his genitals. She screams, falls downstairs, breaks her arm, and sues her sons for damages.

1st July   PM to *NM*: John Major came to the theatre to see *Napoli*. His bodyguards sat behind him, dozing during the first act. They woke with a shock when Naples started to be bombed, dived on Major and pushed him under his seat. They looked rather bashful in the interval. It was just possible to see how Major had become Prime Minister: he's an affable, personable, amenable man, the bank manager of your dreams – understanding, forgiving, but tough and pragmatic. He asked about the theatre's finances. 'Oh,' I said, 'we're like Mr Micawber – poised between happiness and misery.' He looked behind me at the Ruskin Spear portrait of Ralph Richardson as Falstaff. 'How many times,' he said, 'must he have played that part?' (i.e. Micawber). I warmed to him when he said the thing he had over Mrs Thatcher was that he'd never anticipated being PM and it wouldn't be the end of the world for him if he ceased to be. 'This means,' he said, 'that I'm determined to do what I want to do, and there are many things I want to do after being PM.' I half believed him and found him refreshingly prepared to talk about his feelings. Ian [*McKellen*] collared him about homosexual law reform and Major said they should meet to discuss it. Mary [*Soames*] was baffled when he said that Norma liked to take the washing home and do the ironing over the weekend. 'I'm sure you know the feeling, Mary.' 'No, I don't,' said Mary. We were all baffled when Major said

he'd met the Archbishop of Canterbury. And? Pause. And? 'He's a very nice man.'

When Major left, Mary said we could all relax and sent Nicholas [*her son, Tory MP*] off to get more drink. As he left the room, she said: 'He's frightfully nice, but frightfully stupid.' Nicholas came straight back: 'Maasie, are you talking about me?' 'Yes, darling, and you know it's true.' When he came back, Ian propounded his thesis, only half facetiously, that all men are latently homosexual. Nicholas was unconvinced by this, and didn't rise to the bait. Instead he had a very good bantering debate with David [*Hare*] about the last trade union – the Army, and rather disproved his mother's assessment of him.

3rd July   The Lloyds Bank Theatre Challenge in the Olivier – for youth theatre groups. I had to make a speech at the beginning. I walked confidently onstage and tripped. It's clear, I said, why I don't get paid to appear on a stage. I talked about the fear I had of theatre becoming a completely marginal art form, enjoyed by its participants but devoid of spectators, like morris dancing or cricket. At the end Emma Freud castigated Tim Renton for the government's philistinism. He was very put out and complained to me about it afterwards.

4th July   I did my Hamlyn Lecture at the House of Commons. A baking hot day. I paced the flagstones nervously outside the Grand Committee Room, up and down the great Gothic expanse of Westminster Hall, where Charles I was sentenced to death and Churchill lay in state. It was bathos to arrive in the Committee Room: dispiriting decor but a fullish audience, all *parti pris* – but no MPs except for Mark Fisher. I saw John Mortimer at the back, Peter Nichols at the front, and worried about whether I'd included both in my litany of playwrights of the '60s. A frail, elfinold man sat near the front and smiled sweetly whenever I caught his eye. Sometimes he dozed, but I thought the weather might be partly to blame. Afterwards he told me he'd agreed with everything I said. 'Have you met Yehudi Menuhin?' said Mark Fisher. I spoke to a couple of journalists afterwards, who asked for the full text. I've become a pundit. 'Celebrity is a mask that eats into the face,' says John Updike. But so is status and authority. Dinner in the House of

Commons later with Mark Fisher. 'You know Neil Kinnock,' he said. 'Can you arrange a meeting with him for me?' Got quite pissed and very depressed about our parliamentary system: what a chaotic process.

5th July   Board meeting in the morning. Dismal financial projection, three months into the financial year and we're heavily down on box office. Then bitter meeting with Josette Simon over her experience with *The White Devil* and even more bitter argument with Lindsay Anderson over my reluctance to get him to direct any play that isn't written by David Storey. Then a run-through of Mustapha [*Matura*]'s play *The Coup* in the afternoon. Wonderfully well directed by Roger Michell, a very good company: Jeffrey Kissoon powerful and unexpectedly witty. I'd asked Mustapha if we should get a black director for the play. 'Just give me a good one,' he said. Then more rows in the theatre and a threat of a strike because we've made the deputy manager redundant in the costume department.

14th July   I'm just about to go on holiday. I wish I felt more tranquil about it. Stephen Wood phoned to give me some 'friendly advice'. He tells me that there's huge disquiet at the theatre over the redundancy. This is the downside of the theatre as family. According to Stephen there's a feeling that I have a blacklist of people who I want to get rid of at the theatre, a strategy for purging the old regime. If that's the feeling it can't be argued with; what makes it so depressing is that after three years it seems my credibility is alarmingly thin. I've received a petition signed by many members of the staff, suggesting that the wrong person has been sacked. The really depressing thing is that they may well be right.

16th July   I'm reading George Steiner's *Real Presences*: 'The dramatic critic par excellence is the actor and producer who, with and through the actor, tests and carries out the potentialities of meaning in the play . . . All serious art, music and literature is a *critical* act. It is so, firstly, in the sense of Matthew Arnold's phrase "a criticism of life". Be it realistic, fantastic, Utopian or satiric, the constraint of the artist is a counter-statement to the world.'

11th August   *Arturo Ui* is a success on account of Tony Sher's performance, a brilliant cameo from Michael Bryant, and a production by Di Trevis which keeps the ball in the air in the staging, even if it scores an own goal by stressing the historical parallels of Hitler et al. It's a slight play (like *Schweyck*) and doesn't land its punches, or those that it does land seem slight. But I love the theatricality of Brecht's plays. Of course much of his polemic has no force now, but his theatrical imagination I still find remarkable: there's nothing that he feels can't be put on a stage.

12th August   I'm nervous of starting rehearsals of *Murmuring Judges*. The play is much more difficult than *Racing Demon* and not as good. And the Olivier is always daunting. It'll be OK, I'm sure, but I'm scared. Saw Lord Goodman, looking as always like a Gerald Scarfe cartoon. We talk about *Murmuring Judges*. He says that somebody needs to act as a scourge of lawyers, 'a frightful lot, greedy, over-ambitious and self-serving'.

19th August   It's the dog days of summer. There's been a coup in the USSR. Gorbachev has been deposed, held in the Crimea, 'too ill to continue' in the words of the plotters. Yeltsin, the beery populist, stood up for democracy and defied the coup, barricading himself into the parliament. Incredibly, the parliament wasn't stormed. When the coup failed after three days, Ion (who's in London) said that he was convinced that the whole thing had been arranged by Gorbachev. But they could no more have designed a coup that was a bluff than they could one which was successful. There's likely to be a revolution in Russia and all the Soviet states. But for what? Freedom, of course. But a freedom to allow market forces to enter every area of their lives?

23rd August   Two weeks into rehearsals and it's proved to be as unnerving as I'd anticipated. The read-through on the first day was a classic encounter of the old and new: Keith Allen was on very best behaviour. He was astonished to see Michael Bryant listening to the Test Match on his earphones between his scenes. The play has a huge cast and is difficult to stage without becoming fussy, over-elaborate or *too* sparse, but Bob's design is a beautiful solution to linking the three worlds of judiciary, police and prison.

24th August   Alan [*Bennett*] rings me to say that Innes Lloyd [*producer all Alan Bennett's TV films*] has died. He was a charming, diffident, honest and decent man. He'd been politicised recently by Thatcher, whom he'd come to hate violently – a hatred all the stronger for emerging from such a quiet, undemonstrative and apparently apolitical man. Alan also said he'd had a card from Alec Guinness with two items from the paper: one was an announcement of Ronald Lacey [*actor*]'s Memorial Service; the other was an announcement that Vernon Dobtcheff [*actor*] would be unable to attend. Vernon's was the larger.

25th August   Reading letters from Namirovich-Danchenko when he was running the Moscow Art Theatre with Stanislavsky: 'Have I the strength to rescue our enterprise from the path it is following and which will surely lead to a shameful, ignominious fate? Am I still tenacious enough? Is it too late? Where are we going?' These letters have an eerie familiarity: discussions about 'accessibility', debates about an 'open' theatre, about the composition of the audience; balancing the repertoire, balancing the accounts; art versus the commercial, seriousness against trivia; coaxing plays from authors (in the case of the MAT, Chekhov, Gorki and Bulgakov amongst others) and performances from actors. And struggles with sponsors and patrons, pleas to playwrights, the frustrations and exasperations of trying to retain a company, the vortex of egos. The problem for any theatre is that it must always retain its contemporaneity while sowing the seeds of its own destruction. It must be topical, 'socially aware', and it must be fashionable. These are perishable virtues.

27th August   I saw Nick [*Hytner*]'s production of *Lear*. It's full of engaging ideas. Some of them restrict rather than liberate the play, but I found myself crying at the death of Cordelia and marvelling at the detail of John Wood's performance.

30th August   Meeting with Robert Lepage, who is elfin, impish, charming and inventive. He breathes a kind of innocent creativity. We talk about the production he'll do in the Olivier. I suggest *Le Roi S'amuse* or a Shakespeare. Then I had dinner with Lindsay Anderson and we made peace. He talked of the British film industry, of British Rail, of traffic, table manners, and the service in restaurants. He was

determined to find a common link in their Britishness – a diffidence, a lack of passion, a callousness. He's very British in sound – an Indian army colonel – but he's like a Pole in his temperament. When I tell him he's like a scientist looking for a unified field theory to link electro-magnetism, behaviour of atomic particles and gravity, he says: 'You mean like Forster, "only connect"?' Then he goes into a long riff about how awful Merchant-Ivory's films are. I feel sad that it's taken so long for me to be able to talk in this way to Lindsay – my fault as much as his, intimidated by his ferocity, unwilling to recognise his very thin skin.

31st August   Isabella di Filippo came to *Napoli*. She is a very attractive, late fiftyish blonde from the North. She had met Eduardo when she was a student and they'd fallen in love: a *coup de foudre*. She really liked the show, and said Eduardo would have approved. She was unnerved by how like him Ian McKellen was: his physique, his gestures, his timing, his presence.

6th September   Had a run-through of *Murmuring Judges*. The play's very entertaining. I felt frustrated by the actors and more exasperated by what wasn't happening than pleased with what was. I got impatient with David afterwards who told me in painful detail what was wrong: I knew, I knew, I knew. Then felt guilty for having been irritable.

7th September   They say everything goes in threes, well, deaths anyway. First Innes Lloyd, whose funeral I went to on Wednesday. A beautiful, clear, sunny day. The church was full of BBC folk and his contemporaries from the golf club. His family looked very touching and comely. A smiling vicar, radio-miked, pursued an ever-thinning metaphor – saying goodbye in the departure lounge, waiting for your gate number to be called. Then I heard that Peggy Ramsay had died. More than anyone's death, for my generation this is the end of an era. Who else had the authority, the wisdom, or the gall to tell writers the truth about their work?

8th September   At a meeting of the Sport and Arts Foundation I was told that my wife was on the phone, an emergency. Sue said that the hospital had just phoned and Mum was about to die: she was

having fits and had turned blue. I told Dickie Attenborough I had to go, and he grasped me in a bear hug. By the time I'd got back to the NT she was stable and the staff nurse said she'd 'stopped fitting'.

10th September   Peggy's funeral at Golders Green Crematorium. All her writers are there (except, I think, for a couple of dissidents) – John Arden, John McGrath, Nick Wright, Jack Rosenthal, Christopher [*Hampton*], David [*Hare*], Alan Plater, Alan Ayckbourn, Robert Bolt, Howard Brenton, Caryl Churchill, Tom Clarke, Peter Gill and more. The service was simple, no religion, just her favourite pieces, Vanessa read a piece of Virginia Woolf beautifully.

Peggy offered to help me in '68 or '69. 'Do you need money, dear?' she'd said. I was too gauche, too in awe of her, to accept her offer. But she used to pitch me ideas for plays or television: 'Read Paul Scott, it would make a wonderful TV,' she told me years before *Jewel in the Crown* was made. I once had lunch with her in the Café Royal. She'd invited Michael Codron, me, Tom Kilroy (whose play we'd just done) and Irving Wardle, who had given it a poor review. Irving was to be instructed in the error of his ways. She said that Brecht had never been good box office in this country. Irving pointed out that *Arturo Ui* (with Leonard Rossiter) was playing to packed houses in the West End. 'That's because Hitler's a fucking star,' said Peggy to the astonishment of our fellow lunchers. She once told me about recognising whether an actor is in character: 'Look at the feet, dear.' She completely lived Ruskin's axiom: 'Quality is never an accident.' When I took over the NT she said: 'Dear, I hope you'll have the courage to be unpopular.'

14th September   I seem to be fulfilling part of Peggy's hopes: the box office is terrible. But I'd disappoint her: I don't have the courage, and I'm paranoid and disheartened. Walt Whitman: 'To have great poets there must be great audiences too.'

16th September   I went to a meeting of a Labour Party Committee where we discussed how to get Kinnock over to the public: John McGrath, Hugh Hudson, Dickie Attenborough, myself, and party advisers (Philip Gould and David Hill). A strange discussion which intimately dissected his childhood (only child), his ambition, his determination, his isolation and his insecurity. I said it was like

an actor's problem. 'Yes,' said John, 'and how do we fix the script?'

21st September We had lunch at Chequers. The cast list included Andrew Lloyd Webber, Jeremy Isaacs, Michael Caine, Diana Rigg and the Chief Rabbi. I talked a bit to Chris Patten, who seemed much too nice to be a successful politician. He said Thatcher didn't like the countryside much because it was 'too untidy'. He said John Major was a great improvement because he was competent and likable.

23rd September Brigitte Bardot: 'I have given my youth and beauty to men. Now I will give my age and wisdom to animals.'

25th September Lu's birthday. Yeats' 'Prayer for his Daughter':

> She can, though every face should scowl
> And every windy quarter howl
> Or every bellows burst, be happy still.

27th September *Murmuring Judges* is coming together; it's thrilling when all its themes come together in a symphonic way. The police scenes are the most satisfying to play, perhaps because that's where David's sympathies lie – with the guys who turn up and shovel the shit, not with the ones who dish out the punishment.

29th September Meeting of the associates. We talk about regional theatre and the Young Vic; how should we help them out, and how can we? None of us knows what to do. On the one hand we want to help out but are afraid of imperialism; on the other hand, we just want to put our heads down and get on with running the NT. Part of the problem is that the NT is too big and the RSC has grown to match it. So instead of six separate companies in London with different identities we have just two, which dominate the scene and dictate its rules.

30th September It's the evening before the tech of *Murmuring Judges*. I'm nervous but excited. I'm worried sick about the miserably poor showing at the box office over the past few months. I don't see it

getting better for ages and I think we'll end the year about £1m. down. It's due to carelessness; bad luck but also carelessness.

5th October   *Murmuring Judges* has had its first preview. There's a unique thrill to the first performance of a new play: this play in some ways shocks the audience with the prejudices of the characters. We've got a huge amount of work to do, but I don't think it's self-delusion to be optimistic for its success, even if I did hear a lawyer coming out of the show saying: 'It's so fucking naive.' Hardly any less naive than the Head of the DPP who has resigned because he's been caught kerb-crawling. As the judge said when arrested: 'Oh thank God you've arrived, officer, I've been trying to get this woman out of my car.'

7th October   Tacky story in the *Evening Standard* today about Adrian Noble and Joanne Pearce [*actress, Noble's wife*]. Terry Hands rang Jim Hiley to protest. 'Why doesn't the National get attacked?' he said. 'Oh there are a couple of editors who think it's about time that they had a go at the NT.'

8th October   The Kabuki Theatre are at the NT. Ian [*McKellen*] and I visit the great actor, Tamasaburo, player of women's roles. He's young, early thirties, and has been an actor since he was a young child, apprenticed to the previous master of cross-dressing. He's a star of proportions unimaginable to us – Madonna and Danny La Rue combined with Simon Rattle, a living treasure, paid £20,000 a week. Ian asks him if he's seen any theatre in London. Yes, he says, he's seen *Hedda Gabler*. 'Did you enjoy it?' asks Ian. 'Too much –' and he makes a face like Munch's *The Scream*.

11th October   I've been very optimistic about the press for *Murmuring Judges*, but I was wrong. The reviews have all been bad so far, after a first night that I thought had gone well enough for the press to be more or less irrelevant.

12th October   One good notice, 'a stirring night', in the *Guardian*. I'd anticipated some of the things that could be said about the play but I had thought that, in spite of its occasional longueurs, its occasional plonking tone, its wit, its humanity and its passionate

intelligence just shone through and carried it. And the previews had been so good, the audiences so responsive. Why do journalists and novelists think that writing for the theatre is easy, and why if it's so easy do none of them ever manage it? Julie Burchill on writing plays: 'Drama is easy. It's writing without the difficult bits.'

14th October   Disappointed by the Kabuki. It's highly ritualised and that's attractive, but the sets are ungainly: they lack the supreme grace of the best Japanese art. Everything – acting, costumes, scenery – is as it was when it was lit by candlelight a century ago, and it's not flattered by bright stage light. I like Tamasaburo's performance, it's witty and delicate. All the actors belong to a 'house' and pass down the 'house name' from generation to generation (or adopt a talented child, like Tamasaburo). Aficionados call out the names of the actors in appreciation, like shouting '*olé*!' at a bullfight: here they'd cry 'Redgrave!' Norma Major was at the show; she's very nice, very shy, rather bruised. She wore a dress that looked like a ruched velvet curtain.

16th October   Now a few good notices for *MJ*. I suppose the Left liked the show, the Right hated it, and the liberals can't make up their minds. At least the audiences respond and the box office looks promising. The lawyers say how wonderful the police scenes are, the police say how wonderful the prison scenes are, and the prison people say how wonderful the law scenes are.

23rd October   I spoke to the entire company and staff today. Well, hardly the whole 900 of them, but a fair selection, say 250. I talked for a long time – about fifty minutes – and felt like Castro talking the nation into submission. There were only two questions at the end: one, from a bloke who'd just left his wife, about crèche facilities; the other was this: 'Why didn't the NT actors get to meet the Kabuki actors?' Answer: 'The Kabuki actors had no interest in meeting them.'

24th October   Tony [*Harrison*] did a poetry reading in the Lyttelton. He read brilliantly, including his two Gulf War poems. Dinner for friends, with Tony surrounded by admiring women and Trish [*Montemuro, stage-manager*] skilfully stage managing their appearances. After dinner Mary started talking about how her father made

them learn poetry by heart, and how on her anti-aircraft battery during the war she learned a new sonnet every night. She went to Paris after the Liberation and watched her father and De Gaulle walk down the Champs Élysées flanked by jubilant Parisians. She was with him when they drove from Brussels to Antwerp, the whole route lined with waving crowds. Then she went to Belsen – two months after the Allies had entered the camps. Huge mounds of earth, placards on top: 1,500 bodies, 2,000 bodies, 3,000 bodies . . .

3rd November   I went to Oxford to see the last night of *Richard III* in the huge, florid, forbidding, '30s barn of the Apollo Theatre, formerly the New. 2,000 seats, all occupied. The performance was crude and baroque and made me feel uncomfortable. In that huge, echoing hall the production seemed glib and flash. It wasn't always like this, but how else do you fill this space? The next day I went to see Gladys Mold near Oxford. She's eighty-nine now, never been abroad: 'It makes you old, that does.' The world goes too fast for her now, and she doesn't like it. She's not unhappy; she's been used to being alone most of her life.

6th November   Robert Maxwell has fallen overboard from his yacht. Did he fall, was he pushed? Mountains of newsprint about his life and death. His empire was crumbling and he was accused of being a Mossad agent. But it seemed like he would have weathered almost anything. A lot of latent (and not so latent) xenophobia and anti-Semitism has emerged: *Daily Mail*, 'The man who never understood England'; *Telegraph*, 'He took endless trouble to dress like an upper-class Englishman. Dark Savile Row suits and spotless white suits were often ruined, however, by overly large and flashy cufflinks.' I.e. he was Jewish. I remember Princess Margaret saying to me about David Aukin: 'He's not English, is he?'

12th November   Depressing *Evening Standard* Awards, hardly any reference to the NT. As I came out of the Savoy a TV reporter pushed a mike in front of my face. 'Well, Richard, an unhappy year for the National, eh?'

13th November   Student Day. From ten in the morning the theatre is teeming with young people, who show no sign of being intimidated

by a 'cultural institution'. We must find a way of perpetuating this: cheap tickets. We should do what the Citz have done – one price across all three houses. But how do we pay for it?

15th November The post's just arrived: an important-looking envelope with a crest on it. I've been offered a CBE. I felt flattered and then depressed at how easily pleased I was, given that I've always deplored the honours system. Alan [*Bennett*] told me a few years ago that Virginia Woolf had said when she was offered a Damehood: 'I never take presents from strange men.'

23rd November New York for a few days to publicise our tour of *Richard III* to the US. Spent a lot of time telling journalists why we weren't going to Broadway with the production. Because, I said, we've toured the UK, Europe, Japan, Egypt and Ireland for no better reason than sharing our work with other audiences, why should we suddenly acquire double standards and not tour here? The only point of going to Broadway is to make money. Sam Goldwyn summoned Shaw to Hollywood and spoke to him at length about his genius, the importance of his plays, etc. 'The problem with you, Mr Goldwyn,' said Shaw, 'is that you care only about art and I care only about money.'

25th November *The Madness of George III* has started previewing. It's the most uncharacteristic of Alan [*Bennett*]'s plays, the play most unlike his voice, but it's immensely entertaining and its only drawback is the difficulty in seeing what its real subject is: monarchy, medicine, power, public image/private face, madness? It's a discursive essay, brilliantly acted by Nigel Hawthorne, who burns very strongly at the centre. Alan's been in amazingly sociable and puckish form; he loves working with Nick [*Hytner*] and I sometimes feel like Ratty deserted by Mole for Badger.

29th November Peggy Ashcroft's Memorial Service in Westminster Abbey. I sat in the same place as for Olivier's, feeling slightly less inadequate on this occasion. It was a beautiful service, mainly for the music: Murray Perahia played the Andante from the Mozart C Maj. concerto, and it was utterly, heart-stoppingly perfect. I met him afterwards and was tongue-tied. He's without exception the musi-

cian I most admire. I listen over and over to his recordings. I saw him recently on TV talking about Mozart: 'Always something is new, always something is green.' The poetry at the service was fairly dire: actors orating. It's not their fault here, the acoustics are terrible, but actors usually do too much, they won't leave the words alone. But Gielgud recited Prospero's last speech exquisitely.

30th November   *Madness* has opened to pretty good notices. Nigel's performance is utterly winning, and the period politics, the ghastly doctors and the King Lear scene are hugely enjoyable.

2nd December   Roger [*Chapman*] came to see me today. He said he was worried about me burning out. I feel that I'm on a treadmill. I don't have the confidence not to feel that with each show I'm starting from zero and now I'm nervous of starting *Night of the Iguana* [*Tennessee Williams*]. I feel bad on every front but, as Rodin said, '*toujours travailler*'.

3rd December   David [*Hare*]'s in love with Nicole Farhi and very happy. Bob introduced them on the first night of *Murmuring Judges*. 'I hear she has a wonderful house,' said David. 'I'm sure you'll get to see it,' said Bob.

4th December   *Death and the Maiden* [*Ariel Dorfman*] at the Royal Court. It's powerfully and honestly played by Billy [*Paterson*] and Juliet Stevenson, but I don't believe it: it's a conceit, not action growing out of character.

5th December   Painful meeting with Howard [*Davies*]. He feels I take him for granted, a trusted director who fills slots, when (justly) like all of us he wants to be seen as unique and irreplaceable. Also, I recognise his symptoms all too well: encroaching middle-age and the agony of professional identity. I feel really sad that I may have lost a friend and I'm beginning to count the cost of being at the NT.

6th December   *The Sea* [*Edward Bond*] is in rehearsals. I was walking to the Studio along the side of the NT building when I saw Edward Bond coming towards me. He turned his head away, peering upwards as if riveted by a flying buttress. I knew that he wanted to

avoid talking to me – as Director of the NT I'm a sort of pond life to him – but I insisted on stopping him. And of course he was very civil and very enthusiastic about the cast and Sam [*Mendes, director*]: 'He's got something,' he said, pausing a long time, 'but I'm not sure what it is.' What it is is a very astute mind, a preternatural self-confidence and a willingness to learn by observing other people.

8th December   I had a letter from a cousin of Dad's: 'I was abroad when Snowy died and did not learn of it till later: my wish to commiserate with you was tempered by the fact that he was not an easy person to have as a father. But he was a real character; he did enrich our lives by his independence and his eccentricity, and I learned of his departure with regret.'

9th December   Piece in the *Evening Standard* about the salaries of those who run subsidised theatres: 'SOUR TASTE OF SALARY SOUP'. It's about the Royal Court – why they need two artistic directors. It asked: 'What does Richard Eyre get paid? . . . About £65,000 a year. If I am wrong Eyre should blame his policy (of not disclosing it) and not me. In any case, he deserves much more.' I agree.

10th December   I've just started rehearsing *Night of the Iguana* and I feel I've made a mistake. First of all I don't think the play is right for me, secondly I've cast it wrong, and thirdly I think we've made the wrong decisions about the staging – too flat, too formal. After the read-through Eileen [*Atkins*] said: 'It's such a relief to get that over. It doesn't get easier. It's a relief too not to have to look round the room and think who you're going to have an affair with on tour.' Maria [*St Just*] comes to rehearsals as if equipped for a long journey: large handbag, Harrods carrier bags, warm coat, trousers, jumper. She treats the stage management as servants to do her bidding – open doors, bring her coffee, take messages.

11th December   Second day of rehearsal and I feel better already. I've lost that feeling that I've set off on the wrong plane for the wrong continent with the wrong passengers. How can I change so quickly? We talk through the play, Maria sitting like the perfect pupil, pencil sharpened, butter-wouldn't-melt-in-her-mouth, forcing herself to

stay silent until asked a question. It's always a mistake to underestimate Maria, who's very intelligent about Tennessee's plays even if
she is utterly tactless and a ferocious snob. She silences Frankie
Barber by saying: 'Well, what *are* we going to do about your
breasts?' Eileen, Fred [*Molina*] and Robin [*Bailey*] raise their collective eyebrows, and Robin sings 'What are we going to do about
Maria?' just at the threshold of audibility.

12th December   Dinner with Mark and Joan [*Boyle*]. Talked to an
admirer of Mark's who has been back to an exhibition of theirs eight
times, drawn by the same picture: 'It's like going over the handlebars
of my bike and thinking – I want this to go on for ever.' Also there's a
barrister, now acting as a stipendiary magistrate. When it was time to
make his first judgement, he missed his cue. A silence. He was
prompted by the Clerk of the Court: 'The silence is yours, sir.'

14th December   A splenetic attack on me in the *Evening Standard*
by Ronald Harwood about *Murmuring Judges* and subsidised theatre, which he sees as a self-serving conspiracy. 'The Director of the
RNT, Richard Eyre, known as Thin Eyre, devoted almost an entire
lecture to a moan about his theatre's lack of funds . . .' I wonder if his
bile has anything to do with the fact that I rejected a play, well, two
plays, of his.

27th December   Simone Weil about the gift of compassion: 'Love
for our neighbour, being made of creative attention, is analogous to
genius . . . The love for our neighbour in all fullness means being able
to say to him: "What are you going through?" It is a recognition that
the sufferer exists, not only as a unit in a collection, or a specimen
from a social category labelled "unfortunate", but as a man exactly
as we are . . . The laws of necessity are as unexceptional as the laws
of gravitation. The human faculty of compassion opposes this order
and is therefore best thought of as being in some way supernatural.
To forget oneself briefly, to identify with a stranger to the point of
fully recognising him or her, is to defy necessity.'

29th December   Watching TV over Christmas reminded me of
how inadequate TV versions of opera and theatre performances are.
If you put a camera into a theatre you destroy the conceit that makes

theatre work. When you're in a theatre or opera house it doesn't seem absurd or alienating to see people behave in such an extravagantly extreme fashion – singing, stylised language, non-naturalistic settings. The distance from the stage and the audience's acceptance of the conventions of the medium make us believe in what we're watching; when we're alone at home, viewing the singers or actors in close-up, it seems silly.

1992

1st January Much congratulation at the theatre on my CBE, partly ironic, but partly not. It wrong-footed me all day – Roger Chapman brought in champagne to the planning meeting, the cast bowed to me *en masse* and called me 'The Commander'. My father would have loved it. And resented it. Shaw: 'Titles distinguish the mediocre, embarrass the superior, and are disgraced by the inferior.'

5th January I woke up dreaming that I was on a submarine. I start to think about the war and how much it looms in my life – which of course dates me for several reasons. For a start it's not even the *last* war. World War II, as the Americans say, as opposed to the Gulf, the Falklands, Vietnam, etc etc. I was talking to a group of American students a month or so ago and mentioned World War II. A hand went up. 'You talk about World War II. Does that imply that there was another one?' I have a fascination with battle, with extremes of behaviour and with the vicarious test of character. Then I listened to Billy Wilder on the radio: 'It's difficult to argue with a thousand people in a theatre, but maybe I get it wrong . . . It's hard to get an audience to listen any more . . .'

6th January I'm enthusiastic and optimistic about rehearsals of *Iguana* now. This is very highly wrought, very detailed, very highly charged stuff. It's in some ways Tennessee's best play, marred by bad construction (as with all his plays). I have a very good cast.

10th January Meeting with Trevor Nunn and David Edgar, who want to do a play about the New Europe, set in Eastern Europe – nationalism, old/new culture, refugees, with a cast of hundreds.

Literally. I struggle not to sound discouraging; isn't this what the NT should be doing? Also a visit from Donald Sinden. I was saddened by the spectacle of a large, big-hearted, genial man with a florid voice, in his late sixties, asking me for work.

15th January　First run-through of *Iguana*. The play reminded me of Mahler: agonised, romantic, sensual, lyrical, angry, neurotic, craving peace and wishing for silence. I felt completely exhausted when it was over, spent with feeling. If I can push it further and further it'll be very powerful in the theatre. At the first run-through the actors are always charged with a febrile nervous energy. Things that have never happened before occur effortlessly. It was unnerving to see Fred thrown about as if he was possessed. At the end of the run-through he was exhausted, etiolated, as if the 'spirit' of Shannon had left him. How can he repeat the experience without living it, i.e. how can he simulate it? Maria says they all move too much; she's right. Eileen needs to find more stillness, but if anyone can, she can. She's a zen actress – everything distilled to its essence.

16th January　Dinner with Salman, his first theatre visit since the fatwa. I watched him go into the theatre from the stage management box at the back of the theatre. No one recognised him, partly because he never caught anybody's eye, but also with his new-look beard and his new plump, bucolic look, he's not immediately identifiable as the haunted and hunted figure you'd expect. Dinner with David and Nicole. David and Salman argued over art – was it moral or was it all 'play' (or 'ludic' in the new critical jargon). They ended up agreeing, but it felt as if Salman had been waiting to exercise his debating muscles. David is about to start writing his third play of the trilogy, about the medical profession, provisional title: *Nil by Mouth*.

18th January　*Angels in America* started previewing last night. It was thrilling to see the response. It's a quite wonderful play which deserves to be a huge success. This is a test case for me. I've never felt so strongly that a play deserves to be recognised, partly because it's not from our world, but also because I've championed it. I had to twist Declan's arm to direct it, to work with a living writer, and he's done it beautifully, even if he's chafed at not being in absolute control.

21st January   We had another run of *Iguana* today, which I found strangely unsatisfing. Giles [*Croft*] said afterwards that he found the play a bit 'audience unfriendly'. There is something remorseless and unrelenting about it, but maybe that's because the actors started by trying too hard: they didn't let us in.

24th January   *Angels in America* has been a huge success, and no shouts about simulated buggery. It's an extraordinary play, hugely ambitious, that really does confront guilt, homosexuality, millennium fears, life's meaning and the lack of it. 'I understand justice, and I understand democracy – but not love,' says one of the characters. The critics have responded to the play, they have understood it and for once proved Rilke wrong: 'Works of art are an infinite solitariness, and nothing is less likely to bring us near to them than criticism. Only love can apprehend and hold them, and be just towards them.'

25th January   I woke dreaming of Eileen [*Atkins*], who was eerily calm. We had another run of *Iguana* yesterday. It's still getting away from me. I haven't got the first act right yet, so it starts to roll downhill out of control, or it feels inaccessible – too furious, too over-projected. The second half is better and almost clear now. I think we've just got enough time, but it's a cliff-hanger. I still think Eileen should go even further into stillness and repose. She has to embody her philosophy: on the one side of the kabuki-like stage her peace, on the other the raging disquiet and restlessness of Shannon.

27th January   Board meeting. I made a pre-emptive strike by telling the Board how stout and resolute they'd been over *Angels*. Later I had a row with Maria. She was complaining about the performance of one of the 'nobodies', by which she meant one of the actors playing a very small part. I told her she shouldn't speak of anyone like that. 'I know, Richard dear,' she says, 'but I can't help it.' This is her I-am-a-Russian-aristocrat defence, her most monstrous aspect. She maddens me – and knows it – by referring to any form of technician and the stage management as 'low-class people'.

30th January   Tech for *Iguana*. Maria tells me that she's too nervous to watch, but does so anyway. All went smoothly. Hopes are high. I talked to Jean Kalman about the difference between

European and British theatre. He talks about the coldness of lighting in Germany, as a metaphor for the 'distantation' of the actor from the audience. 'I like to work here,' he says, 'because I can use warm colours. In Germany I can only use blue.'

2nd February *Iguana* has started previewing. So far so good, and Eileen already remarkable.

3rd February I went on *Start the Week* to talk about Tennessee Williams, and J.F.K. and the monarchy. I said that monarchy is the English religion, and I had an argument with Brenda Maddox about Tennessee's plays, which she thinks are tosh. I told her she was immune to metaphor. Later, lunch for the Ian Charleson Awards. I had to introduce Prince Charles to everyone. As I introduced him to Declan, I told him that Declan had just done an all-male production of *As You Like It*:

> CHARLES: Really? No women at all?
> DECLAN: Well, no, they didn't have women in the theatre in Shakespeare's day.
> CHARLES: (stupefied) Really?

I sat next to Andrew Neil [*Editor* Sunday Times] who appeared not to know the name of his theatre critic and had clearly never met him. He – John Peter – made a speech which took us through the history of drama from the Aeschylus to the present day, which Prince Charles thought helpful and the rest of us thought just a spot superfluous.

6th February 12.30 a.m. after the first night of *Iguana*. I lost my nerve and spent most of the performance in my office watching a documentary about the Queen after forty years of her reign. It endorsed everything I've ever thought about the effect of the institution, and yet she seemed amiable, quite intelligent, bourgeois *and* upper class. She looked like a parody of a German eighteenth-century princess with her hair permed into a pomade and a face that Goya could have put into his portrait of the Spanish Royal Family. But the issue isn't her character, or any of the other royals. It's the principle of heredity. If you accept it, you have to accept luck

of the draw. I think the show went well. Everyone said so, but I don't trust it. As always, I fear the reviews. Lu's just been in to see me. She said she thought the show was great and: 'Dad, don't forget to go to sleep.'

8th February   The reviews have been good. I don't believe anybody actually *reads* reviews, the eye just goes to adjectives and adverbs that flash out in your face like leaflets pushed at you in the street. You flinch at 'disappointing' or 'dispiriting', 'uninspired' or 'incompetent'. This time there's only the caressing balm of 'excellent', 'finely judged', 'tender', 'steamy', 'moving', 'gripping', 'poetic', etc. But as always with a success, relief rather than triumph. High praise for Eileen and for the production. It's been well enough received for me to feel sanguine about taking a few months off from the theatre, or at least from directing, without feeling I have to prove myself.

9th February   I went to Leeds to see Trevor [*Griffiths*]' Gulf War play, which I found confused and confusing. The play didn't have the passionate clarity and muscle of his earlier work, but it was very good to see him again and made me feel very nostalgic for the heady days of *Comedians*.

11th February   Alan [*Bennett*] feels that *George III* is being neglected by not being played enough in the rep. It's a hit and given how difficult it is to write a play at all, let alone a successful one, his exasperation is understandable, but it's the price of having a play in repertoire in a subsidised theatre. No commercial manager would have put this play on: simply too expensive and too risky – even if now, because it's a hit, there seems to have been no risk at all.
      Interview with John Osborne:

INTERVIEWER: Was it love at first sight?
JOHN O: No.
HELEN O: (Giving him a sharp look) Yes.
JOHN O: I didn't hear the question.

12th February   I did a speech that was supposed to be about theatre in Europe at Lu's school for their Euro Week. I talked a lot but, as a teacher observed, was rather muted on the subject of Europe. Lu was

very nervous, but said afterwards that I'd got a good review from her pals. I was talking to Gorg about fathers turning up at school. She said that she had an indelible memory of Dad turning up at her confirmation by the Bishop of Bath and Wells. Dad sat at the back of the church but could be heard muttering: 'Fucking mumbo jumbo.'

14th February　Maria St J. rang protesting that the *Observer* called *Iguana* Tennessee's 'last great play'. She wants to write to 'that awful Donald Trelford' to complain. I'm confused: I thought it *was* his last great play and I thought Maria was a friend of Donald Trelford. She took me to dinner with him. Donald said, as if everyone knew, that the Archbishop of Canterbury couldn't stand Terry Waite.

16th February　Article in the *Independent on Sunday* on why people don't go to the theatre. We're playing to 90 per cent houses *consistently* – well, for a few months now. Who are these people who buy tickets? Not novelists or journalists, clearly. The new orthodoxy – from the arts editor – is that it's not smart to go to the theatre and if lots of people do go it's even less smart. But come to that, who reads the *Independent on Sunday*?

21st February　I woke from a dream in which Julia McKenzie was very angry with me for saying that she was only in three-fifths of the show, and the other two-fifths of it were fine. It was distressing. And Jonathan Pryce was rehearsing with Declan, rather churlishly taking notes of everything he didn't like.

22nd February　I keep thinking of Dad going away when I was, what? Nine. For three years. I got a postcard from him, I think from Port Said, of a large white ocean liner – P and O line – with a yellow funnel. He'd drawn a cross on the side of the ship: 'X MY CABIN'. I had a jigsaw puzzle of a P and O liner surrounded by dhows, traders in some eastern harbour, maybe Istanbul. I used to do the puzzle thinking: And this piece is my father, he's in there, in this cabin. He sent me postcards from Hong Kong, Tokyo, Singapore, and Sarawak. And occasionally a photograph of him on his destroyer: white shorts, bright sun, always smiling. While Mum stayed at home, not smiling so much, perhaps. Nabokov: 'I often think there should exist a special typographical sign for a smile – some sort of concave mark,

a supine round bracket, which I would now like to trace round your question.'

24th February   I've been reading Stephen Spender's Journals. He's an alternately engaging and exasperating man: quite self-aware, very conscious of his 'inferiority' set against Auden and Isaiah Berlin. He knows he's a second-rate poet and on the one hand one wants him to be less self-abasing, and on the other hand to be more self-confident but not less self-aware. I think he chose between perfection of the life and the art, and has chosen life: family, friends, conversation and conviviality. But can we choose or is the choice made for us? From his Journals: 'No one should want anything except to find his place in life, the centre of his potentiality to love and be loved . . . The problem of married people is *not* to become absorbed in each other; how, in a word, to trust one another in order to enter a strong and satisfying relationship with the outside world . . . Perhaps the American taste for violence is really the endeavour to discover a mystery . . . Perhaps I wrote poetry because in some way I was carrying on a dialogue with my father.' I love his account of blithely asking Jackie Onassis what she thought was her greatest achievement in life: 'After going through a rather difficult time, I consider myself comparatively sane. I am proud of that.'

26th February   Sean [*Mathias*]'s production of *Vanya* opened last night. I didn't think it was what it had been in the Studio – absolutely pure and unaffected. Now there's the clutter of scenery, fussy lighting and the burden of 'performance' as opposed to 'being'. So it was like looking at a stream to which a coloured dye had been added. But, nevertheless, it's as good a *Vanya* as I've seen, including Olivier's at Chichester. The Kinnocks were at *Vanya*. Neil was crowing about a three-point lead in the *Mail* opinion poll. He said that the story about John Major having an affair was about to break.

27th February   I'm on six-month sabbatical, or semi-sabbatical, to write. An eerie freedom. It's as if I've got tinnitus in my ears, a ringing to replace the noise of the meetings that I'm missing. Reading Updike's *Essays*. Updike: 'High art, we might say, is art which presumes knowledge of other art; popular culture is prepared to

deal with the untutored . . . a high art divorced from popular culture would be as sterile as Esperanto . . .'

28th February 'The first forty years give us the text; the next thirty give us the commentary,' said Schopenhauer. I have a restlessness, a lack of a sense of place. So I envy the life in small villages, in spite of all I know of the suffocating inward-looking meanness of spirit that can be generated. I envy the happiness of others, which seems to me a gift as great as the ability to draw or play a musical instrument. I envy the sense of belonging: to a village, to an ideal, to a family. And I regret the way I've discarded lives, or personae, like a snake shedding its skin. Childhood, school, university, work: they don't seem to have happened to the same person. I know no one from my childhood, and if I did they would have as much difficulty recognising me today as I would recognising the child that I was. I seem always to have been remaking myself. Now I'm anxious to stay still, to stop changing, to rest. Perhaps that's why I don't sleep; I'm too impatient, too unsure to settle, as if to rest were to become dormant, and to become dormant were a slow retreat to the fears of childhood.

1st March Mum's been moved from the NHS hospital to a private nursing home to 'free up the ward'. Went to Dorset with Gorg to see Mum in her new home. I didn't think she would survive the move, but she looked as well as she has for ages. We also went to see the nurses at the hospital who used to look after her, who still haven't been told what's happening to them or even if they've still got jobs. Of course after looking after her for six years they were the last people to be told.

3rd March Meeting with Stephen Daldry. I've recently seen two of his shows at the Gate; both of them were unmistakably directed, both were hugely inventive, and both were entirely different. He's a beguiling mixture of the watchful and the flirtatious, charming, manipulative, strategically blunt, selectively iconoclastic ('Oh he's no good at ALL . . .') and really ambitious for theatre and, I suppose, for himself. We talk about a number of possible plays. He wants to do *An Inspector Calls* which he's done at York. I'm extremely sceptical and ask him to justify it. He describes his production – political parable, exploding house, real rain – and I'm hooked.

4th March   Frank Rich describes me in the *NY Times* as 'the most successful and versatile producer in the world'. This improbable paragon spends his morning waiting in the service area of the garage for his car to be fixed where he reads a car mag. Car dealer slang: a soft-top = an innocent, a spanker = a good buy, a Cap'n Bob = a dodgy job, a good donkey = a good engine, a bidet = a rear window wiper, a Jeffrey = £2,000.

5th March   Went to Buckingham Palace to receive my CBE. It was pure Ruritania; the English really *are* in the grip of the religious passion of monarchy. How can it change? It can't if people like me go on accepting honours.

> HMQ: Is the National in an up or down phase? Theatres do go up and down, don't they?
> ME: Up, I think, Ma'am.

15th March   The election has started. The Labour Party so far are looking much more convincing than the Tories. And *The Recruiting Officer* has opened to modest reviews. Nick [*Hytner*] agreed to do it because we couldn't get the production of *Don Carlos* together. There's a bright superficiality about it; it's well packaged and intellectually respectable but, as Nick says, it's hollow. He said to his assistant: 'If I were Director of the NT, this is the sort of production I'd do all the time.'

25th March   Away from London and at the instigation of Liz Calder [*publisher, co-founder of Bloomsbury*], writing about my parents and grandparents. She wanted a book about the theatre but all I wanted to do was write about Dad, somehow to try to get in touch with him. Writing takes a lot of nerve, or arrogance, or a very thick skin. It's so hard not to imagine a reader. 'In the morning light one can write breezily,' says Updike, and I'm taking his advice, which is also David's: 'Sit down to write by nine in the morning.' And Tony's: 'Just *write*, don't be self-conscious, put something down.' I'm following his edict and trying not to be self-conscious. Thinking about my childhood, this from John Barrell: 'To attempt to write yourself away from what you fear is a risky business . . . or to be aware at last of the beast stamping on the distant shore, if only to be better at *not* confronting it.'

27th March Reading my grandfather's diaries. About pitching camp in a blizzard, the tedium of taking his clothes off to change into dry ones, ice sticking to his beard, breath icing, matches damp, tobacco sodden, pipe frozen, flask of tea frozen, fingers too as he takes off his mitts to undo his leggings – too frozen to undo but he has to undo them nonetheless – and he gets cramp as he's taking off one pair of his several pairs of long socks, he wraps himself in fur, climbs into his sleeping bag, hungry and desperate with tiredness and he's too cold to sleep. Incredible conditions about which he's amazingly laconic: 'These and many others all help to make sledging far from a picnic.' He talks of the 'monotonous discontent' engendered by enduring the endless polar night, bored by 'having to see one another's faces, encounter the few bad traits of character for weeks, months, and years' and by the 'unpalatable sameness of the food'. To relieve the monotony he gets up an entertainment ('as full of fun as possible, temperature −26°, easterly gale') for which he plays the piano and Captain Scott gets into drag: 'Scott was a really awfully pretty servant girl.'

4th April I was sitting waiting for the dress rehearsal of *Pygmalion* to start on Saturday night, a day late. The Olivier auditorium was almost empty, a desultory sprinkling of people, everyone's spirits dashed from not opening on time. Someone came into the auditorium and said there's a phone call for you and I knew – as you do – that Mum had died. And after years, years of waiting and expecting, nearly ten years, it was still a shock and I feel guilt and sorrow about not seeing her just before she died, not saying goodbye to her. But there never was a goodbye, I never knew the moment when she stopped being a person.

5th April I tell Alan [*Bennett*] that my mother has died. His mother has hung on, like her, for years. Alan says it's not that you decide to let go of life, but that life decides to let go of you, which is altogether more capricious. David [*Hare*] said that Peggy Ramsay had said to him: 'The only thing that prepares you for death is death.'

6th April I've been reading the second volume of John Osborne's autobiography. It's quite easy to understand him in the first half, in love with success, floating above his fear of mediocrity, his talent

acknowledged and his fame apparently infinite. It must have seemed
as if it'd go on for ever. Then he becomes psychopathic – he appears
to have no feelings and it becomes impossible to understand his
actions, or anything except for his bitter resentment at being cast out
of paradise: 'Talent is kept waiting at the tradesman's entrance of
power . . . What we remember is what we become. What we have
forgotten is more kindly and disturbs only our dreams. We become
resemblances of our past.'

13th April   Talked to Tony [*Harrison*] about Mum's death. He
said: 'You're the one in the red jacket now, the Thin Red Line, going
over the top.' I've felt an orphan for years. I'm looking at Mum's
photo now. I can see the edgy side of her, but I can see the energy and
the readiness to come forward and open her heart. And her intelligence, which Gorg can't concede because Mum treated her cruelly,
saw her as competition and edged her out. Gorg said to David
[*Hare*]: 'I don't think she loved me, but perhaps she loved Richard.
At least I think he thinks she did.'

14th April   The election's over, the party decorations have been
taken down, Labour has lost and Neil faces the end of his political
career. It's very sad, he's so very able, but in the end people don't
trust him. Is it because he's *too* like them, too matey, too easy to
understand? So now we have another five years of realising the
highest aspiration of man – to become very rich, and the disen-
franchisement of local government.

16th April   Mum's funeral was held in the village church. I hadn't
been inside it for nearly forty years and it was much smaller and less
bleak than I remembered, a beautiful Norman arch over the door.
The day was showery with bursts of bright spring sun. The undertaker complimented us on the quality of the programmes for the
service and the flowers, but stopped short at saying he approved of
our choice of coffin. Quite a surprising number of people turned up,
including a cousin of Mum's from Surrey. They all looked desperately old. There *were* people who were very fond of Mum, but not
very many, or at least her London friends had been driven away by
Dad's oppressive jollity which didn't allow for dissent. The nurses
who used to look after Mum were there; they had loved her, and I

was overwhelmed by their generosity. I gave an address, getting through by taking long, deep breaths. I wanted badly to do justice to her memory in front of witnesses. I ended with Blake. Gorg read a wonderful poem by Anne Ridler. Afterwards there was a small do at home, but most people wanted to get away. A bit too close to death.

27th April   The Olivier Awards. The NT had twenty-one nominations and only two awards. There seemed to be a hidden agenda, the commercial theatre putting us in our place. The show seemed more than usually tacky; an excerpt from *Moby Dick* looked like the end-of-term show of an amateur brothel for trainee transvestites.

3rd May   *Bourgeois Gentilhomme* is previewing and is getting better. Richard Jones' production is conceptually intact and unassailable, except that it absolutely fails to release the wit – and the tragedy – of the play, in spite of being full of invention and bravura. It's another of our failed attempts to make Molière come alive: too superficial, too far outside the culture, too satirical. Richard's a curious director – meticulously detailed planning, like putting together a mechanism. 'It's not quite there yet,' he said to me as if it still needed technical adjustment to fulfil the machine's design, irrespective of the audience and text. I can't seem to get Molière right at the NT. We never seem able to get Molière's blackness, and his seriousness and weight. The plays need actors with huge weight, literal and metaphorical – a Gambon or Depardieu – at the centre of them. Tim Spall is a marvellously detailed actor but not a colossus. From a life of Molière: 'Ballet is to comedy what death is to tragedy: the leap into the beyond, the following through of its momentum to its conclusion with no turning back, no artificial re-adjustment to the world of common sense.'

5th May   The reviews of *Bourgeois G* are very bad. Nick Wright says the one in the *Mail* is the worst he's ever read for an adaptation: 'I cannot believe that Eyre read this translation without vomiting.' Well, he did. I felt deep unease during the first night; it felt like being with a group of strangers in the cold room of a slaughter house. I saw Tim Spall, who was dashed but stoical about the reviews. 'How's the sausage factory going?' he asks. It never feels to me like a sausage factory. Quite the opposite: we spend hours at script meetings and at

planning meetings talking about what play to do and why and how. So it always seems so odd when a play appears to goes on without a sense of purpose.

10th May Lunch with Peter [*Brook*]. He loves to talk about theatre; his commitment to it and his enthusiasm for it is shaming. He endures, with considerable curiosity and warmth and generosity for other people's work, even if he did tell me about not seeing Peter Stein's production of *Pelléas* in order that he wouldn't have to express an opinion about it. He told me about going to Barbara Brecht's apartment in East Berlin. They had a sumptuous dinner and her husband, Ekkehard Schall [*Berliner Ensemble actor*] got drunker and more withdrawn as Barbara bemoaned the passing of the communist state and the decline of standards. 'And do you know what, Peter? The Yids are back. They're buying up apartments all around us.'

12th May I've finished the first third of my book. Liz Calder wants more about me being expelled from school; David [*Hare*] wants more about Alzheimer's and thinks I should write about being an actor. He asks: do I *really* believe some of the things I've written? He makes me conscious that meaning is everything, choice of adjectives and observations – the opposite of Robert Lowell's: 'When I'm having trouble with a line of poetry I sometimes find the problem is solved by inserting a not.' David infers from the book that I'm manic depressive. Lu said it made her cry, partly because it made her sad, partly because she was grateful that I was close to her. Sue was very encouraging, gave me her endorsement.

14th May Marlene Dietrich has died. I heard a story about her on the radio. She'd got her husband out of Germany and he'd become a chicken farmer in California. He lost his entire flock in a landslide. She said: 'I always told you, you should have stuck to ducks.'

15th May I sacked an old colleague. I didn't do the deed, and felt ashamed at having been persuaded by Jenny not to. I feel I've let him down; but then I feel he's let me down. He thought I'd betrayed him by not giving him sufficient warning. I did warn him but he ignored the warning, but I feel awful about the whole business. I should have

confronted this problem ages ago. 'One is always punished for being weak, not for being cruel,' said Baudelaire.

21st May   I rang Gorg to discover what she'd thought of the first third of my memoir and had to prise her objections out of her. It amounted to two things: my picture of Dad, necessarily biased, was one-sided and she was upset that it would be the only published version. And I'd underwritten her part in my childhood. I have, but out of tact, not spite. She protected me throughout my childhood; she was my champion, stood up for me against Dad – for which he resented me – and grieved for me, and with me, when I was sent off to school.

22nd May   To Charleston, Vanessa Bell and Duncan Grant's house, for a discussion about funding the arts. I saw the event advertised in the *Independent* with a thick black border, like an Italian notice of death: 'Britain's most successful producer' would be talking. I imagined I'd just have to answer questions, but when I got there I discovered it was me and Philip French and he'd prepared himself with a written thesis, and I improvised rather unhappily. The garden was lovely but I found the house cold and unsympathetic, and all the decent pictures had gone.

29th May   Keith Allen was off from *Murmuring Judges*. He'd double-booked himself and was doing a film. When I saw him he said: 'I think people seem to think it's my fault,' as if there might be some supernatural explanation of his thoughtlessness. Saw Lesley Sharpe, and we talked about acting and Ian McKellen, who she's just done *Vanya* with. I said I thought women found acting easier than men because they were used to role playing and being looked at. She said it was because they're closer to the creative process: they know about giving birth. Male actors often say 'This is no life for a grown-up' but I've never heard an actress say this.

I did a platform with Robert Lepage after a performance of *Needles and Opium*, which is dazzlingly enjoyable. He said that as a child he quickly grew bored of the toys but liked to play with the box. He emphasised the importance of 'play' in rehearsals: the ability of a child to be unselfconscious.

2nd June I saw Tom Clarke. He told me he'd started writing for TV after writing a couple of short stories and seeing a newspaper hoarding which read: 'RAB SLAMS SEX AND VIOLENCE ON TV'. That's for me, he thought. He looked terribly old but I loved his energy and enthusiasm: a film about Esterhazy, his frustration with his life, his loneliness, all encrusted with a dogged pride and a refusal to stoop to self-pity.

6th June New York for several days to open *Richard III*. It's a village – here everyone knows everyone in the only worlds I know anything about: theatre and publishing. They have one newspaper and all drink from the same well. There was a piece on me in the weekend edition of the *NY Times*. Everyone I met on Thursday had read the piece, having received their complimentary copy; it's considered a useful privilege, but it seems odd behaviour for a newspaper. What's in the paper? Dense, dogged, soggy and thorough news stories, but mostly domestic news, and odd 'savvy' articles about the culture you should acquire. Preferable however to the English Sundays where the whole tone is superior, knowing and world-weary. In Britain the assumption is that you know it all before you see it.

8th June *Richard III* opened well at BAM [*Brooklyn Academy of Music*], with a dinner afterwards organised by Tina Brown [*Editor Vanity Fair*] and Sonny Mehta [*publisher*] who, as an act of friendship, overcame a lifetime of prejudice against the theatre. I sat between Tina and Diane von Furstenberg [*fashion designer*]. Next to her sat Henry Kissinger. I tried to draw him out on the similarities of Richard's politics and Nixon's (or his own). He wouldn't be drawn beyond the fourteenth century. Mary [*Soames*]'s friend, Sarah Giles, said that she wouldn't speak to Kissinger because of Cambodia; Mary said she wouldn't speak to him because he sent Christmas cards with a photograph of himself and a printed signature.

10th June Talked to someone about brain surgery: it's the toughest of all surgery because it's so difficult and the operations are so long. There's a phenomenon known as 'poking': staff and fellow surgeons poke the surgeon with scalpels and draw blood in order to keep him on the spot. The surgeons must end up like German

students with duelling scars. Perhaps the practice should be introduced for theatre critics.

17th June Jim Cartwright's play [*The Rise and Fall of Little Voice*] has opened. It's a gallery of grotesques, knit together by the genuine idiosyncrasy and sincerity of Jim's writing. Alison Steadman is wonderful, but the tone of the show is uncertain. There's a sense of the middle classes being invited to laugh at the dispossessed.

18th June Tom has just sent me a new play, *Arcadia*, which is very Stoppardian – by which I mean original, witty, intelligent – but, perhaps less characteristically, is very passionate and moving. Beautiful writing: it juggles past and present – the early nineteenth century and today – Byron, chaos theory, mathematics, landscape gardening, and never seems ostentatiously clever. He wants me or Trevor [*Nunn*] to direct it.

19th June I had a message to ring David Mellor at the Department of National Heritage. I rang him (Puccini in the background): 'I'm trying to choose my eight records for *Desert Island Discs*,' he said. He wanted me to meet 'a friend of the family', an aspiring actress.

21st June Neil and Glenys came to lunch, partly for us to commiserate, partly to talk to David [*Hare*], who followed the election with the Labour Party for his new play. Neil said that the danger with the Tories was that beyond them there was infinity, they were in for ever. And he made a Nazi salute. Neil and Glenys's feelings are, unsurprisingly, unresolved. 'Come to me for the bile,' said Glenys to David. 'I have the feeling that you gave the loyalty to John Smith and it wasn't reciprocated,' says David. 'Hear, hear,' said Glenys.

23rd June Meeting with David Mellor. We have to transfer hastily to the House of Commons for him to vote, then we have a drink on the terrace. He says the Lottery will happen and encourages me to think of preparing a strategy for the redevelopment of the NT. He says it's the only possible way we'll secure the lease of our own building, and it's certainly the only way we'll ever be able to afford to renovate and re-equip it.

1st July Tom has decided that Trevor should direct his play. He says he should have said that he wanted Trevor to do it when he first spoke to me about it, instead of saying that it could be directed by either of us. He's promised Trevor a play for twenty years. I felt humiliated, but I'm not quite sure why. It's my fault for having jumped to the conclusion that since I was running the theatre I would have *droit de seigneur*. I saw a run of Robert [*Lepage*]'s production (*A Midsummer Night's Dream*). I was partly excited and partly terrified. If everyone comes up to the level of Jeffrey Kissoon's and Sally Dexter's performances the production will carry utter conviction. If not it'll be a muddy mess.

2nd July David tells me, apropos his politics play, that he's writing *Faust* or *Pygmalion*. Actually, I thought he was writing *Joan of Arc*. I've just finished the chapters about acting for my book. I get drunk – relief and exhaustion. I've said some of the things I wanted to, but not enough.

3rd July David Mellor's 'friend of the family' came to see me. She's a rangy, nervous, insecure drama student called Antonia de Sanchez, whose relationship to David was only semi-obscure.

9th July Robert's production of *A Midsummer Night's Dream* opened tonight. It really divided the audience: 'Where's the poetry?' or 'This is the best production of the *Dream* since Peter Brook's.' I felt very proud of it even though it isn't really achieved: there's so much to admire and enjoy. I met Steven Berkoff in the interval, walking out. 'It's a bloody travesty of the play,' said the guardian of the classical canon.

14th July The reviews have been violently mixed, but I don't feel apologetic. I always felt we were right to be doing what we were doing, and that, although the production was vulnerable, the freshness of the view of the play was invigorating. Some of the critics were militantly self-righteous: you *can't* do this. But the play is 'still there for somebody else to set the record straight', as Lindsay Anderson said to me after my production of *Hamlet* at the Royal Court. I've decided to do *Macbeth* in the Olivier, which may well turn out to be a terminal act of hubris.

15th July   I went to Chartwell [*Churchill's house*] with Mary. As we drove down we talked about the war, and her childhood, and her father. It's always hard with 'great' men not to be so blinded by their reputations and status that you can't believe that they lived and breathed, ate and drank. Their houses feel like mausoleums, but Mary gave the breath of life to her parents' house. In her father's study I sat in his chair, facing a photograph of her at the age of eighteen as she sat, still beautiful at the age of sixty-nine, on the other side of the desk. Churchill's presence was strong everywhere, strongest here in the study, where you could almost hear him pacing, dictating to a file of secretaries, exhausting one after another, irrepressible until the onslaught of depression, always the corollary of excessive appetite for work. His small bedroom was next door, his bed almost like a child's. In the pale-green dining room, with the comfortable chairs at the table, the easily accessible wine store and the large round table in the bow window looking out over the garden that he had landscaped himself, you could imagine him inexhaustibly dominating the conversation, fuelled by champagne and brandy.

Oddly, only in his studio, even though it was still filled with many of his paintings, did there seem less of the personality that dominated his family like Kafka's father did his: 'Often I picture a map of the world and you lying across it. And then it seems as if the only areas open to my life are those that are not covered by you or are out of your reach.' Mary's brother, Randolph, and her sister, Sarah, died of drink; Diana committed suicide. Mary, younger than all of them, seems to have been protected by the absorption of her parents in the war and by a remarkable governess. In her mother's bedroom – pale-blue walls, four-poster bed, vaulted ceiling – Mary talked of seeing her mother sitting at her dressing table with no make-up on, pouring tears, holding the letter from Sarah saying that she was marrying Vic Oliver [*bandleader and comedian*]. And Mary, at the age of thirteen, felt guilty because Sarah had confided in her. And downstairs in her mother's sitting room, she told me about the hardest thing she'd ever had to do: telling her parents about Diana's suicide. Diana had taken an overdose after being told by her ex-husband, Duncan Sandys (in a rare moment of thoughtfulness), that his new wife was expecting a baby. Mary thought, perhaps self-protectively, that Diana hadn't intended to go all the way. When she told her father about Diana's

death, he retreated into an unreachably distant silence and sat in his study, motionless, for the whole day.

She said her mother was slightly inaccessible, slightly cold, hard to know or to get close to. Very much a woman of her time and class. She wants to write another book to set the record straight about their marriage, which she says wasn't loveless. My impression is that it was very loving but not physical, and neither of them missed that. Or at least he didn't. But there's a possibility that she had an affair on a cruise.

16th July   A David Mellor lunch at the Admiralty: Alan Yentob [*Controller BBC2*], Margaret Matheson [*film producer*], William Rees-Mogg [*ex-Editor* The Times] and other folk who I didn't know. I sat next to the man who runs the British Motor Racing Federation, who couldn't be persuaded that any subsidy to the arts was justified, and if they were going to subsidise arts, why not motor racing. It was pointed out that there was no more heavily subsidised (by the manufacturers) activity on earth than motor racing. Mellor dilated at length about the Royal Opera House – the pros and cons, but mainly the cons. If they charged £130 a ticket, why couldn't they charge £200 and lower the other prices? William Rees-Mogg said: 'Let me start by explaining that in the nineteenth century opera was an activity where the rich watched the poor perform. It is now an activity where the rich watch the richer perform.'

After lunch I went with David Mellor to Bradford to see Ariane Mnouchkine's production of *Iphigénie*. He was on the phone in the car to someone called 'Ant', who I thought at first was his son Anthony, who'd been one of the princes in *Richard III*. I stopped myself saying 'Give him my regards' when it became clear that perhaps it wasn't his son but the girl he sent to see me called . . . Antonia. I thought *Iphigénie* was not as good as in Paris, but then nothing could match the atmosphere of the Cartoucherie. I went back on the plane with David Mellor. He said Douglas Hurd was a pompous, hypocritical, incompetent bastard. Why don't you speak your mind, David, I said. We talked a lot about music; he's utterly passionate and knowledgeable about it. He's a strange man – genuinely enthusiastic about the arts, and genuine in his desire to emancipate them; very vain, entertaining, self-important, gauche,

generous, awkward, dominating, and probably a very good politician.

19th July Jenny's rung me to say that David Mellor's affair with Antonia de Sanchez has been revealed. Huge spreads in the Sundays. He's in real trouble: the press want to do him because he wants to bring in a privacy bill to curb them. They'll fight very hard. But there's really no story – he's had an affair with an actress and their phone conversations have been tapped. His professional sin appears to have been being too knackered to make or to write a speech after a 'night of love' with her.

25th July The Mellor-drama has been growing throughout the week. He's fallen out with his in-laws: his father-in-law says he's a complete cad. He's fighting very hard to hold on to his job. He's not helped by his self-importance, but I suspect that he's gratified at being described as a 'lover'.

26th July Nick Hytner says I've been beatified: there's an article in the *Evening Standard* by Nick de Jongh which describes me as a 'brilliant impresario and canny diplomat'. What goes up, comes down. At the moment things are surprisingly quiet at the theatre: it bubbles, or stutters, along. At the moment I can only be anxious about not being anxious. Or complacent. After his success with *Dangerous Liaisons* Stephen Frears said guilessly to Michelle Pfeiffer: 'I just don't know what I'm going to do now. I've had so many offers.' 'I expect you'll make three flops in a row, like everyone else,' she said.

13th August *Street of Crocodiles* [*adapted from the stories of Bruno Schultz*] has opened. This is really good work, and the healthiest of collaborations between the NT and Théâtre de Complicité [*theatre collective*]. Isn't that what we should be: a facility, an enabling organisation as well as a producing one? I didn't know anything about Bruno Schultz, but he's an extraordinary voice – Polish/Jewish, partly real, partly surreal. This is brilliant 'theatre-making' – horrible neologism – a synthesis of the work of the company, but driven by Simon [*McBurney*]'s imagination.

24th August   Back from San Francisco where *RIII* was playing.
Peter Radmore [*head of lighting*] has died. I thought of him as the
conscience of the National Theatre: he believed passionately that it
should always aspire to and achieve excellence in all departments,
and that it should be a community united by common aims, that it
was worth more than the sum of its parts, and that it was an ideal
worth devoting his life to. He was exacting, and enthusiastic, and
sometimes even exasperating in pursuit of this ideal. When he lit *The
Beggar's Opera*, and I pointed out to him that an actor was unlit, he
said – with some justice – that the actor deserved to be unlit and
would remain so until he started to act better.

5th September   First preview of *An Inspector Calls*. Daldry was in
a lather of disappointment and frustration but it was a really
impressive preview, and the production, the whole all-singing, all-
dancing hyper-concept, is played with such honesty and such conviction that it really does make Stephen's case for the play as a
political parable, even if its political agenda only amounts to an
assertion of the importance of charity and compassion.

6th September   I'm away from the NT now, rehearsing *Suddenly
Last Summer* [*film of Tennessee Williams' play for BBC TV with
Maggie Smith, Natasha Richardson and Rob Lowe*]. Maggie is a
little daunting, but I like her very much. She's not well and often
bending under the strain. I wish I could have worked with her years
ago. Her biography has just been published. It reveals nothing of her.
I asked Maggie if she'd read it: she made a vinegary face. 'Good God,
no, I couldn't. I'm an ostrich, I can't bear publicity.' Rob Lowe told
me a story about Clint Eastwood. An anxious young actor went to
see Clint in his dressing room on the first day of a movie. They'd
never met before, and their characters were supposed to have a close
relationship. 'How should I play the scene?' asked the young actor.
'Let's not overthink this,' said Clint. 'We're going to hit a few marks
and say a few words.'

14th September   *An Inspector Calls* has opened, and it's a huge
success. The general consensus of the critics is that Stephen's debut is
as great a debut as Peter Brook's. I talk with Stephen about the
possibility of him working here more permanently, even running the

theatre with me. Severe problems with Tony [*Harrison*]'s *Square Rounds*. I'm unable to help him, and unsure that I could even if I was on the spot.

27th September   We finished shooting the film at twelve-thirty on Saturday night. At nine-thirty the next morning I was rung by Ken Pearce [*film editor*] to say there was a problem with the rushes. I had to go to Shepperton to look and there was fogging on the negative on intermittent frames. Incredibly bad luck, but incredibly good luck that nothing that really mattered was spoiled. It was a short, insanely tense but enjoyable shoot. The cast were entirely game and Maggie had only one bad day – the first. She was very raw and as the day got longer and the studio got hotter, the layers of protection came away from her and she became bitter and bilious and savage: 'This is like the Bridge on the fucking River Kwai,' she said. She wasn't joking. It got so hot – 120° F – that the fire alarm went off. Yet she still managed to act with extraordinary grace and power, and when you looked into her eyes in close-up, you could see into the character's soul.

28th September   The ideas in *Square Rounds* never really lift off, but there's something moving in the endeavour – the folly, the courage, the pain, the unshakable refusal to appease – that lifts it into a different order of event. Lindsay Anderson comes out rubbing his hands: a disaster but a disaster for the right reasons.

2nd October   A week back at the theatre. A lot of problems, not least the opening of *Square Rounds*. It's been a kind of noble disaster, and I couldn't help. Partly because of being away, and partly because I had made the mistake of urging Tony to do the play before the script was ready, and his pride (and my expediency) demanded that he didn't delay. A number of smaller problems including the *Carousel* budget (excessive), the prop shop (tumultuous), the children's show (disastrous) [Dragon *by Yevgeny Schvarts*] and the education department (vexed). It's really a matter of how to reconcile the aims of the department outside the NT – the work in schools, colleges, etc, which is all well achieved – with the internal artistic and institutional imperatives. In every theatre I've worked in there's been this problem: how to avoid a hierarchy of objectives. However hard you try,

education gets pushed aside in favour of putting the shows on the main stages. It's compounded by the fact that the educational work is, by definition, invisible, i.e. it's outside the building.

11th October   We gave Jessica Mitford and Bob Treuhaft a lift to the Mortimers' for lunch. Decca said that her brother-in-law, the Duke of Devonshire, owner of the largest estate and one of the largest houses in England, had once stood for parliament. Someone had asked him what area of politics he was interested in. 'Oh . . . er . . . housing,' he said. At lunch John told a courtroom story: a woman was giving evidence in a case in which she'd been sexually harassed, and she was too shy to say out loud what had been said to her. 'Write it down,' said the Judge. So she wrote it down. It read: 'Do you want a fuck?', and it was passed around the court, eventually ending up with a dozing juryman, who was sitting next to an attractive woman. The woman prodded the juryman awake and handed him the note. He read it, looked at her, smiled, folded the note and put it in his pocket. The Judge asked for the note to be returned to him. 'Merely private, my lord,' said the juryman.

25th October   Lunch with Peter Hall. As always I'm in awe of his energy, his resolve never to be cowed. He just keeps going. He talked about the importance of technique and the tension between form and content – a model for our age of confusion.

27th October   I gave the keynote speech at the Brighton Conference for Arts and Broadcasting. Most discussion of television and the arts is underwritten by an implicit (and sometimes explicit) snobbery: the belief that television is a medium that is inherently impregnable to artistic ambition or achievement. There's an uneasy partnership between the arts and broadcasting, which isn't disinterested on either side. We tend to view 'the media' as a promotional tool to be employed at the appropriate time to plug our work. It doesn't do much for the cause of the arts to treat broadcasting as our servant. Just as it doesn't help if TV treats the arts just as another exploitable commodity. Public service TV should put the best of the arts on television and give the arts in general a forum for discussion and promotion. And if government believes in providing money for theatre, opera, dance and music to flourish (which by their nature are

accessible only to small numbers of people), surely it's logical to oblige publicly funded TV to promote them. I knowingly pandered to the prejudices of my audience: i.e. exaggerating the decline of the BBC, presenting an apocalyptic future, etc, drugged by my own rhetoric. The BBC management were mightily pissed off, and those who wanted to misread what I'd said did so very successfully.

1st November   Giorgio Strehler's show *Le Baruffe Chiozzotte* [*Goldoni*] is in the Lyttelton. It's an excellent example of his work, but not the best: visually beautiful, limpid, minimalist, rhythmic, real. I went to see him just before he started his tech; he insisted on showing me the material that the cyclorama was made of, a very finely woven gauze. He reduced several of his company (men and women) – many of whom he's worked with for years – to tears during the technical. He's hyperactive, fuelled, it's said, by a huge infusion of cocaine. I did a platform with him. He talked via an interpreter for forty-five minutes without drawing breath, respond-ing to one question from me: could he describe the difference between the Italian and the British attitude to theatre? He was shocked, genuinely shocked, when I interrupted him and said we had to end. *Nobody* interrupts Giorgio, which is why a modest public utterance from him is about two hours.

2nd November   Kenneth Macmillan [*choreographer*] has died – only sixty-two. In rehearsal for *Carousel* and seemingly in his prime. I barely knew Kenneth, but warmed to him and miss him hugely. The loss of a working colleague is very shocking.

3rd November   I went to see Solti in his studio. He was flanked by two grand pianos and enough Gramophone Awards – dogs sitting by a gramophone horn – to make a decent pack of hounds. He sat with his back to me. 'Maestro,' said his secretary nervously, 'Mr Eyre is here to see you.' Silence. Perhaps thirty seconds pass. 'Maestro, Mr Eyre is here to see you.' Another ten seconds pass. I'm about to speak, to suggest that perhaps if the Maestro is too busy to see me I'll bugger off, but just as I am about to defect, with perfect timing he puts down his pen, turns to face me, and grins impishly: 'My dear boy, how nice of you to wait. Now sit. I loved your *Guysandolls*. Very open. Now, I have never conducted *Traviata*, you have never

produced it: together we will make our first *Traviata*.' We talked
about this and that. He forgot the name of someone, and said: 'I'm
sorry, I can only remember the name of my friends, the – er –
Alzheimer's.'

8th November   Franco Zeffirelli is here with his production of *Six
Characters*. I went to see him on the stage of the Lyttelton. He greeted
me with an extravagant whisky-flavoured kiss on the mouth.

9th November   Had a huge number of letters about my Brighton
speech. Almost all of them assume that I was speaking in support of
the BBC. I had a letter from Joan Bakewell, who told me I'd ignored a
Heart of the Matter about the Falkands War, Michael Jackson [*head
BBC arts*] told me I'd ignored *Moving Pictures*, Nigel Williams that
I'd ignored *Bookshelf*, Jeremy Isaacs that I was wrong about opera
on TV, and Will Wyatt sent me a framed page of the *Radio Times* for
October 27th to show how the BBC's output hadn't deteriorated,
and as a reminder never to criticise the BBC in public.

15th November   Mary rings to tell me that *Dragon* is a disaster.
I've already told her that, but she needs to tell me herself. 'Perhaps it
wouldn't have happened if you'd been around,' she says.

17th November   I read in the paper that Prince Charles believes in
the migration of souls, and was overheard saying to his mistress:
'When I come back, I'd like to return as your trousers.'

19th November   *Stages* has opened. Like all David Storey's work
it has a sort of sculptural solidity and beauty: like a Henry Moore.
But it seems stately, instead of disturbing. Not that I could ever
suggest that to Lindsay [*Anderson*] even though I've developed a
much warmer relationship with him, and I've got to like and
admire his stubborn determination not to be cowed. He now
regards me as an ally, fellow bulwark against the incoming tide
of what he describes as the 'obtuseness' of the critics – 'How could
anyone with half an eye or half an ear say that this is the same old
story of the working-class lad who has grown away from his
background . . .' How indeed?

24th November   Alternate horrors and excitement about doing *Macbeth*. I've got to make it fresh. There should be an injunction, like the warning about pulling the communication cord, against performing Shakespeare unless absolutely necessary. People should only do Shakespeare because they want to, not because they have to. At the moment I feel confident, but doing Shakespeare at all is like walking into a minefield, and doing it in the Olivier is walking into a firing range in a minefield. Some thoughts: a military world; the absence of children (Macbeth's); the presence of children (Banquo's and Macduff's); a young wife, a dead child; the darkness of Scotland – the light of England; the thin veneer of civilisation; fire (the Witches); water (the washing of hands); trees (the Wood); animals (horses, dogs, bats, crows, frogs, snakes, beetles, owls, housemartins, etc); the weather (storms, mists, fog, the seasons); the power of sleep; the lack of it. There are two worlds in the play: there's the world of blood, mud, battles, witches, thunderstorms, cannibalistic horses, and woods that appear to move, and there's the world of civilised society – good manners, hospitality, gifts, dinners, and ceremonies. In committing murder Macbeth tears away this veneer of civilisation and lets evil spread like a poisonous fog. Shakespeare shows us that evil isn't a force that comes from outside us, it's latent within us. All that the Witches do is tell Macbeth what will happen: it's his hand that holds the dagger. What frightens us in the play is that we feel that evil is within the grasp of all of us. We are made to realise that what makes all of us capable of doing evil is not its weirdness, but its banality. Macbeth's a professional soldier: his trade is killing people. He's very good at it, has no professional guilt, is a man of honour, and ambitious. Violently disappointed at not being appointed the successor to the King. He's in love, in lust: married to a young wife, newish wife. Marked out from his fellow soldiers. He kills for love. Desire dies after the murder. Lust for power, lust for success, has the same dynamic as sexual lust:

Naught's had, all's spent
When our desire is got without content.

30th November   I'm puzzling what to do about *Macbeth* when I get back latish from the theatre. I'm sitting at my desk reading *The Shifting Point* by Peter Brook when the phone rings. The sentence I'm

reading is 'We talk of "directing". The notion is vague and includes too much . . .' I answer the phone: it's Peter Brook. We talk about *Macbeth* and the problem of the Witches. 'It shouldn't be a pleasant adventure for them,' he says, 'there should be no personal satisfaction, like a Greek chorus.'

1st December   *Carousel* started previewing tonight. It went well, although the first half is a problem in the writing, paradoxically exacerbated by Nick [*Hytner*]'s brilliant *mise en scène* of the overture, which raises your expectations to unfulfillable heights. Although the production is very strong, pure and unaffected, and the design is exquisite, it doesn't quite sustain for the last quarter of the first half – not the production's fault: the score puts a great strain on the Billy, who is a very good actor, but not a very strong voice. The show is on the edge of mawkish, but stays this side of it – helped in particular by Joanna Riding, who is real in a way no other musical performer I've ever seen is. She stops it feeling like a musical that endorses wife beating. Princess Margaret came to see it, and after she met the cast, I walked her to the front door.

ME: I'm glad you enjoyed the show.
SHE: I didn't. I can't bear the piece.

2nd December   A gala for *Carousel*. I introduce John Major to people before the show, including Sue and Lu. 'That's a nice top, Sue,' he says, staring at Sue's breasts. At the dinner after the show I sat next to Norma Major, and we talked about opera and the demise of the corner shop. She made a point of not being ready to go home when John wanted to, 'to do the boxes'. I thought she was flexing her muscles.

3rd December   Long conversation with Cameron about *Carousel*. He's been admirably restrained, in spite of his obvious frustration at having to allow us to produce the show, but now his opinions spill out in a cataract of words. Much of what he has to say about the show is spot on; the rest is a matter of taste, particularly when it's the colour of the fishing boats that he takes exception to. The designer of most of Cameron's big musicals – John Napier – has designed *Trelawny*. We're having huge budget problems. Years of large

musicals may have expanded his imagination, but haven't taught him economy.

7th December   I'm having the horrors about *Macbeth*. No progress at all with the design. Bob's exhausted after *Carousel*, and it's difficult for him to get a purchase on a new show. Bob and Jean [*Kalman*] and I sat and stared at an empty model box, and all I could see was despair.

8th December   I had lunch with Ted Chapin, who's the Executor for the Rodgers and Hammerstein estate. He told me, I think knowingly, that *High Society* was the worst musical he'd ever seen, and he affected surprise when I said I'd written and directed it.

13th December   David and Nicole's wedding was very touching. There's something about love between mature people that's much more affecting than love between the young. With the young you're touched because they're innocent, or ignorant, and optimistic and untainted by pain and disappointment and failure. When you're old you know all that can go wrong and yet you go ahead with the full knowledge of what can happen. I made a speech and read a Chinese poem:

You and I
Have so much love,
That it
Burns like a fire,
In which we bake a lump of clay
Moulded into a figure of you
And a figure of me.
Then we take both of them,
And break them into pieces,
And mix the pieces with water,
And mould them into a figure of you,
And a figure of me.
I am in your clay.
You are in my clay.
In life we share a single quilt.
In death we will share one coffin.

14th December   *Carousel* is a huge success, for Nick, for Bob
[*Crowley*], and for the theatre, and buys us a bit of peace and quiet. I
had a dream about *Macbeth*: a head consumed by fire, a brain in
torment, witches within a circle of fire. Then I talked to Bob about it,
and we think that's what we should do: Macbeth is a man with his
brain on fire, the witches are like the flames. I've decided to play
Macbeth without an interval – one long (I hope not too long) arc.
When I said this at the Friday meeting Barry Rushmer [*head of
catering*] ruefully asked me if I was aware of the damage to bar sales.

20th December   New York for a Gala showing of *Suddenly Last
Summer* that Natasha organised for an AIDS charity in memory of
her dad [*Tony Richardson*]. More than usually like being on the
surface of the moon, surrounded by the Milky Way which included
as many stars as in heaven – well, a good few, including Jackie
Onassis. The faces of the gawpers pressed flat against the plate glass
ogling her looked like squid on a fishmonger's slab.

1993

1st January   I spent the weekend clearing out the house in Dorset. Every atom of the house contained memories over forty years that ought to be as indelible as my genes, yet I've rubbed so many of them away. I came across a small brown leather suitcase, full of elastic-banded bundles of letters, hundreds, perhaps thousands, of them, mostly on blue airmail paper: 'AIR MAIL LETTER CARD USE OF H.M. FORCES ONLY'. I recognised Dad's handwriting and tentatively took out some letters. I read only enough (about four or five letters) to blush at the invasion of their privacy. The letters, written while Dad was in Dover or on convoy, were all about sex – recollections of sex with Mum and descriptions of sex with other women – and the ones I read, the ones I could bear to read, were incredibly graphic and detailed and anecdotal and anatomical but not without love. They were mostly love of sex, but also genuine affection expressed in a litany of inventive endearments. My head reeled and once again the lesson was proved: never read anything that isn't for your eyes.

4th January   I had lunch with Scott Rudin [*American film producer*], who is eerily well informed; he's more reliable about what's on in British theatre than a listings magazine. He offered me a film in New York about political correctness in a university: very good script. I'm tempted but it would mean total defection from the NT.

11th January   We've done a co-production with Cambridge Theatre company of Marivaux's *Game of Love and Chance*. I've never seen a successful Marivaux production, not even in France, not even Patrice Chereau's production of *La Dispute*. Maybe I have a blind

spot. It's like Restoration plays: I understand why they're good but I never enjoy seeing them. This production had an excellent pedigree – adapted by Neil Bartlett and directed by Mike Alfreds – but it's less than the sum of its parts. I don't know how you'd make Marivaux work. But then I don't know how you'd make *The Way of the World* work.

14th January   I've been to Paris to see Peter [*Brook*]'s production of *Pelléas*, which was lucid, elegant and touching. I saw Peter the morning after. We talked about how *Pelléas* was achieved (with three casts), about not having scenery, about doing opera – not like a play, not like a musical pageant, but somewhere in between – about the need to start an opera with nothing, just the words: to improvise, then to act with the words, then to sing a capella, then with the piano. About Peter Hall's approach to Shakespeare – the impossibility of imposing form and having rules. 'That's death,' he said, 'you can't start knowing the text and the shape of it; you must begin with nothing, just the situation, the paraphrase, then add the words so that you know what is being expressed is the best way to say what you are thinking.' But to me this is circular – you can start at either end: what the character is thinking can only be extrapolated from the words and their meaning. And sometimes their sound. I told Peter I'd seen him on a French TV channel in New York interviewed by Bernard Pivot for the book programme, *Apostrophe*. He says he's now recognised in the street in Paris.

16th January   Tom Clarke's died. I miss him very much. I keep thinking of the speech he wrote – for a rather faded good-time girl – for the TV play of his that I did: 'I mean, say you go round thinking things are getting better, like people do. And say it looks as though things are getting better. Then, when you think they have got better you turn round and . . . well, it seems like they haven't after all.'

20th January   Letter from John Osborne saying he's delighted that we're going ahead with *Inadmissible Evidence*. 'I'm certain that you will be able to dispel the long shadow of Nicol [*Williamson*] . . .' Well, I'm not so certain. He says he's been gripped by an 'iron cast of gloom . . . last year was pretty well the worst I can remember – well, since the Adolf days,' afflicted by worries over health and money and

unable 'even to write the proverbial "fuck in a shutter" . . . I look forward to the enterprise.'

23rd January   I'm making advances with *Macbeth* now, and feel reasonably confident of what I'm doing with it. Bob and I have developed a language and a universe for the play that embraces the world of social occasions – dinners, ceremonies – and domestic detail: servants, drinks before bedtime, times of dinner, *and* the world of soldiery – slaughter, blood that won't wash off. And of course a wood that contains witches and bleeding soldiers; crows make wing to it, Banquo is killed in it, branches are cut off it. And it moves.

In Scotland you can ask in a pub for a 'Souness', meaning 'a half and then I'm off', after Graham Souness was sent off so many times last season.

25th January   I went to Vienna yesterday to see a Romanian soprano called Angela Georghiu in *Bohème*. The opera house was very neat, very Austrian, and markedly more friendly, less posh and more relaxed than Covent Garden. I sat near the front among a lot of experts who talked of balance and dynamics as if they could have conducted better. It was a twenty-year-old production by Zeffirelli: some rudimentary acting and some goodish singing. Angela G. was very affecting, particularly in the first act. She has an outstanding voice, a real innocence and an expressive strength. I had dinner with her afterwards. Like the Dalai Lama, she's absolutely certain of her destiny. Born in a peasant village in Moldavia, one of several children, her father a railway guard. No musical instruments in the house, just TV and radio. From the age of five she wanted to be an opera singer. 'I've always known I would sing,' she said. 'It's my destiny to play Violetta.' 'And is it your destiny to play her in this production?' I said. 'I can't tell you,' she said, with a grin that I took to mean yes.

26th January   I talked to Solti to enthuse about Georghiu but he was firmly on another tack: Julia Varady. She's forty, maybe forty-five, he said, but looks very young. He's a selective listener and has chosen to forget my condition that I'd only do the production with a young singer. Originally he'd suggested Kiri Te Kanawa and spoken

to her. 'I'm too old,' she said to him. 'I know many whores older than you,' he said.

27th January Tom's funeral, a very Clarkeish occasion in a decayed chapel in Kensal Green Cemetery, rain dripping through cracks in the roof. A humanist took the ceremony and made it more awkward and self-conscious than any vicar would have done. We were soaked, standing on thick clods of clay, a small group of us including Dennis Potter. It reminded me of the funeral in *The Third Man*. I know what Tom would have said about it, with a great guffaw: 'It's awful . . . awful.' And he'd have been right.

28th January Solti rang to say that Varady wasn't free, so we would go with Georghiu. I'm very pleased.

29th January I can't sleep: I'm worrying about *Macbeth* rehearsals. From the *Guardian*: 'Shakespeare was right to depict Macbeth as being unable to sleep because of guilt, anger and jealousy, psychiatrists said yesterday.' It also said that 15 per cent of people suffer from insomnia.

31st January I start rehearsing *Macbeth* tomorrow. Jim Carter [*actor*] told me of a man he'd met who'd shared a prison cell with a man who'd tried to kill his wife. He'd been married to her for years, had just built a house extension, and caught her in bed with his best friend. He stabbed her with three different kitchen knives, twenty wounds, and she still lived. 'Why didn't she die?' said his cell mate. 'Big woman, cheap knives,' was the answer.

7th February A week of *Macbeth* rehearsals. I felt well prepared and worked well. The cast are very game and friendly and intelligent. We talk a lot and work a lot around the subject of soldiering: Shakespeare's obsession: Richard III, Othello, Macbeth, Henry IV, Henry V, Benedick, Hamlet's dad and Fortinbras, Lear ('I have seen the day, with my good biting falchion/I would have made them skip') – all soldiers. Shakespeare was fascinated by the hunger to fill the vacuum left by battle, and by war as the defining male action. Macbeth is a full-time professional soldier; Lady M. is excluded from the action, wants to become the 'soldier', the 'man': 'Unsex me here . . .'

8th February   Good read-through of a draft of *The Absence of War*; felt very powerful, but there's still a missing scene in the second half.

12th February   *Trelawny* has started previewing. It's good but slow, but will pick up. I'm very fond of the play – perhaps fatally so – it's such an affectionate (sentimental?) view of life in the theatre that occasionally is spot on. Very few plays or films have any resemblance to the reality of theatre; only *Mephisto* and Charles [Wood]'s *Fill the Stage with Happy Hours* give a real sense of what it's like, a closed world, with its rules and ordinariness like any other.

13th February   Creeping anxiety over next year's budget. We're £1½ m. short after struggling for four months to balance it. We've been victims of over-confidence: spend, spend, spend. Our financial ecology is now as familiar to me as the passing of the seasons. I've learnt to accept the stomach-churning pattern of the box office – lurching down in the summer and climbing to a peak for the three months after Christmas. I've learnt to be sanguine about not knowing our grant until very late in the year. And I've learnt how difficult it is to control expenditure. Why? Inflation of materials and outside labour in the theatre world always seems to be above the RPI, and the inflation of the expectations of directors and designers likewise. It's partly the size of the auditoria, partly that if directors and designers see successful productions with lavish sets they expect parity: it's the National Theatre, after all. And the staff expect constant updating of technical facilities: it's the National Theatre, top of the range. And we (I) encourage this: it's the National Theatre, we're the best. We really should try to raise more money from sponsorship, corporate and private. We're locked into this head-banging cycle with the government over the annual grant, and are too dependent on it.

15th February   I've read articles in the last week saying the theatre is dead, that no painting has happened of any importance since 1914, that the British film industry has expired, that television has dwindled to a flicker, and that pop is 'an ageing, jaded, art form'. Oddly there are no obsequies for journalism. The phenomenon is partly due to the same journalists stirring the same pot week after week, partly to a millennial decline or spiral or vortex, and partly

that none of the arts *has* re-invented itself. Alan Bennett says: 'I don't think people should be made to go to the theatre if they don't want to. It makes it such hard work for the actors.'

19th February   Alan Bleasdale's *On the Ledge* in Nottingham. I don't think it'll survive the critics in London, but Alan's immensely game to make it work. The last half of the second half is a farce looking for a conclusion and the character at the centre of the play is still too faintly drawn. From the play: 'Who is Jeffrey Archer?', 'I've just heard the perfect description of ignorance is bliss.'

23rd February   I went to *Turandot*. Angela Georghiu was really good and I was very pleased that we'd cast her. It's a curious piece – a creaky, mechanistic plot, a musical idiom that relies on fortissimo effects, some exquisite melodies and their pounding repetition in unison by the chorus. It was wonderfully staged by Andrei Serban, robustly sung, blandly conducted and – with the exception of Angela – completely unmoving. I saw her afterwards; she was very excited about *Traviata* and didn't mind showing her enthusiasm.

28th February   *Macbeth* is going well. Alan [*Howard*] and Anastasia Hille are doing good work. The production makes sense, but the problem is to bring the performances to boiling point. Humanity, detail, passion, accuracy.

5th March   Went to Lovell's funeral [*cousin*], a Catholic one. The priest was over eighty and had considerable difficulty remembering Lovell's name, let alone getting through the liturgy. He was assisted by a substantial scattering of nuns for whom presumably this was a good afternoon out. Afterwards we went to the crematorium at Weymouth – dazzling sun over Ridgeway, the chalk downs, the sea. As we left the crematorium the priest said to me of Lovell's sister, Zoe: 'Well, she'll see a hundred, no doubt.' She asked my cousin Kitty who was the elderly man with the grey hair who had kissed her; she was told it was me. That cheered Kitty up immensely.

20th March   Jenny [*McIntosh*] saw a run-through yesterday [*of* Macbeth] and was very encouraging. I thought it was strong, carried

through, and yet there are still parts where Alan is sketching in what he's going to do.

21st March   From *The Diary of a Snail* by Günter Grass: 'I am a Social Democrat because to my mind socialism is worthless without democracy and because an unsocial democracy is no democracy at all . . .'

22nd March   Letter from Maria [*St Just*], who's been having treatment for very bad arthritis. It's not worked and she's in terrible pain: 'Maybe this is the punishment dealt out to me by the Good Lord for my forefathers whipping those serfs into submission and despair. Things do not seem much better now in Russia. Back with the knout!' She's very keen for me to do *Camino Real*, which she imagines being done almost like a musical or opera in the Olivier, a show filled with music, a theme for each character. 'How I wish I could whet your appetite, my dear Richard.'

23rd March   I'm apprehensive about the publication of *Utopia* and swamped by publicity for it. It's been approving – no anonymous quotes yet from 'a friend'.

25th March   *Macbeth* is about to start previewing. I can't tell if it's survived the move from the rehearsal room.

28th March   My fiftieth birthday. I had to meet Stephen Wood and walked down to the prompt corner of the Olivier to have my photograph taken with Bob Crowley on the set of *Macbeth*. When we got there he dragged me on to the stage and I saw maybe 300 people sitting in the stalls, who started singing 'Happy Birthday'. I was very touched, very embarrassed and completely speechless. 'We find words only for what is dead in our hearts,' said Nietzsche, right for once. *Macbeth* started previewing; it was clear and lucid but somehow inert: it seemed dangerously underpowered, just didn't accumulate enough critical mass to fill the theatre. We'll get there if Alan puts his foot on the gas.

30th March   Wonderful party, brilliantly stage-managed by Sue. I was very moved by being with all my friends. It was a very happy

day, thinly underscored by my anxiety about *Macbeth*. I confided to Ian McK. that I sensed catastrophe. Salman's security men sat upstairs in my study. When I came to tell them that Salman was ready to go I found them leafing through one of the women's volumes of *Spotlight*. I ended the evening sitting by the piano on the basement floor, while Imelda [*Staunton*] sang 'You are my sunshine' and Brian Glover whispered over and over in my ear: 'Stick to the writing, Richard . . .'

2nd April *Macbeth* opened last night. I watched the show with Bob on the TV in my office. We were both wreathed in gloom and when the red silk failed to drop properly, hanging like a giant limp handkerchief, we knew it was a metaphor for the half-cockedness of the event. Afterwards people said to me that it had gone very well, very tight, very clear, etc. I was grateful for their support but sceptical. Next day: platform for the publication of *Utopia*, followed by the novel experience of signing books. I was unprepared for the long line of supplicants who approached me with a mixture of kindness and awe, having paid £14.99 for the privilege.

4th April The notices for *Macbeth* were as bad as expected: the *Mail* – 'appalling, the best idea of the evening was not to have an interval', the *Telegraph* – 'this is as bad as Peter O'Toole's', *The Times* – 'awful', the *Sunday Telegraph* – 'awful', but on the other hand: the *Express* – 'exhilarating, a night to remember', the *Standard* – 'the star of the evening was the director', the *Guardian* – 'very good but needs more momentum', and others not so bad. I feel, as one always does, as if I've been tarred and feathered and don't dare to walk down a street for fear of being mocked.

10th April Maria [*St Just*] calls me to tell me that she'd enjoyed *Macbeth* and had chastised some unfortunate member of the public (possibly a critic) who'd been complaining about it. She says she's sent my book to her friend Marlon Brando (who I suspect was her lover light years ago) because of what I say about his reasons for giving up acting. She says she'll arrange for me to meet him: 'You can tell him to his face what a fool he is.'

12th April I've been away, slept a lot, ridden a lot and I don't feel my brain is on fire any more. But I'm apprehensive and insecure and dreading having to go to work. I have to take the only action possible, following Peter's example from his *Diaries* when he did *Macbeth*: 'The notices are as terrible as any I have had . . . After five minutes of blind anger I settled down and got on with the job. It's the only way.'

I've just finished Andrew Motion's Larkin biography. It's very well done, and very melancholy. The life of the writer as anchorite – or someone who appears to have made sacrifices to preserve the sanctity of 'the writer's life'. But in truth, as Alan Bennett says, it's just the life of a man: selfish, strategic, opportunistic and shamelessly exploitative of women. Charlie Parker embodied the perfect fantasy of the romantic artist: he worked very hard and in his saxophone he had the perfect means of exercising the male creative fantasy – inspiration, intoxication, fornication.

14th April *Arcadia* has opened. Trevor has a ferocious self-confidence which he successfully communicates to his actors, and it's beautifully played, has been very well received and will do fantastically well. Tom says critics are an anomaly in our world as they have no penalty for failure. Nobody chastises them if they do a bad job, nobody notices if they do a good job. And above all they hate to be criticised. Trevor Grove [*Editor* Sunday Telegraph] said to me: 'I think journalists are very self-critical. Much more so than actors.' I don't think so. I think people outside the theatre – all that 'luvvie' nonsense – consistently get actors wrong. As did Auden: 'The actors today really need the whip hand. They're so lazy. They haven't got an ounce of the pride in their profession that the less socially elevated musical comedy and music-hall people and acrobats have. The theatre has never been any good since actors became gentlemen . . . Empson pointed out that English theatre has declined since the abolition of sub-plots. I wonder why they went. Of course the influence of realistic stage design made sudden shifts of plot more difficult.' I think he's right about plots but quite wrong about actors' laziness, except maybe in the movies. Godard said in the '60s when Liz Taylor got $1m. for *Cleopatra*: 'Once you start offering actors these sums of money they won't want to work.'

17th April The earth hasn't stopped going round the sun and *Macbeth* has now settled down as a production – not the best, not the worst. I won't admit defeat. I think it's good, the cast is positive, the audiences enthusiastic. And I'm following Chekhov's dictum: 'If I'd have listened to my critics I'd have died drunk in the gutter.' I'm just about calm about the show now but I hate being pushed into a defensive position just when I'm feeling at my most tired and most raw. The production didn't lack nerve or boldness. I've had lots of letters – some from friends – saying how much they've enjoyed it, but is it because it's often easier to praise something which has been slated?

18th April Terrifying events in Yugoslavia. And we're helpless. Why don't we intervene as we did in Kuwait?

21st April *Utopia* has been warmly received in the few reviews it's had. Now if I were a journalist instead of a theatre director . . . I went to Manchester to do a reading at the Royal Exchange to about ninety people: large hammer to crack small nut. Next day I did a reading at Waterstone's in Charing Cross Road with Michael Billington, who's publishing a collection of twenty-one years of reviewing, called *One Night Stands* – never able to resist a pun; God alone knows how he would end a review of a play with the same title. All critics have to travel hopefully and there's been no more expectant traveller than Michael B: he's been 'hailing' new productions or being 'disappointed' with them for failing to 'yoke the public and private' for the last twenty years, while spraying the page with phrases like 'cardiganed deity' and 'mufflered priest' . . .

22nd April To the opera house to audition a tenor for *Traviata*. I arrived early and wandered round the shops in Covent Garden. I went to two bookshops, but neither had a copy of *Utopia* on display. I found Solti and entourage (assistant, secretary, wife) waiting at the stage door. I greeted him only slightly satirically: 'Maestro!' We go to the auditorium. I've never been there without an audience (I've seldom been there *with* an audience), and I'm like a child in a toyshop, dazzled by its beauty. In the auditorium were the casting director, Ted Downes and Jeremy Isaacs. Solti started the proceedings. A tenor walked on stage; he looked like Griff Rhys-Jones. A

pleasant voice, a complete absence of personality, and no dynamic. 'Don't worry about that, I take care of that,' says Solti. The tenor was charming, light and innocent. Solti wasn't convinced. Neither was I. Then we all consulted diaries like fashionable hostesses to arrange our next meeting – in May. 'Let's not spend two days then,' says Solti, 'I need to do some work on the score.' 'So do I,' I say.

29th April   To Bristol to do a debate on the theatre with Fiona Shaw, Benedict Nightingale, David Edgar and Jatinder Verma. I went for a walk in a park in Clifton with Fiona beforehand, both of us feeling like prisoners preparing for execution. She's very bright and droll and warm and admirable. The event lived down to expectations. An audience of about 300 plus. Someone shouted out 'Bullshit!' when I was bullshitting. The questions from the floor were a series of prepared assertions. Benedict said he hadn't seen anything good in the British theatre since he'd come back from the US. I got a cheap round by saying that I thought perhaps the problem was his apathy, not the theatre's lack of energy.

7th May   I went to Paris to see Peter [*Brook*]'s new show, *L'Homme Qui*, an adaptation of Oliver Sacks' book: beautifully acted, distilled, elegant. The show is a logical destination for Peter's work: its subject matter is how we think, feel and act, and it's as near to an 'authored' piece as he's ever done. *All* directors lean towards *auteur*ism, and the longer they go on, the more acute the leaning becomes. I had lunch with Peter. I feel like a surrogate son with him, always slightly anxious for his approval, always keen to know his opinion. He quoted Matisse, apropos what I can't remember – critics, perhaps. 'You can't work with hate. You can't create with hate in your heart.' We spoke of the change of climate in Britain: it's very competitive now in all the arts, as if there's a small patch of territory that we're fighting over and we're all afraid of being pushed off it. Like Borges' view of the Falklands War: two bald men fighting over a comb. But Tristan Tzara said that the politics of the art world are only a diminutive parody of the real power.

8th May   Salman and the Yentobs came to see *Macbeth* on Saturday night. They were polite about the show, but were suspiciously keen to say what they *hadn't* liked. Salman is very stoical. He's always cheerful when I see him and I suppose one of the more

depressing things for him must be the obligation to be jolly whenever he sees people for the brief periods that he does. The next day we saw him again, at lunch with Alan and Philippa [*Yentob*] – and Don Everly of the Everly Brothers, who is apparently the nice one, and doesn't get on with brother Phil.

9th May   BBC2 are running a *Richard Eyre Season* – six of the plays/films which I directed and/or produced for *Play for Today: The Imitation Game, Country, Comedians, Just a Boy's Game, Past Caring* and *The Insurance Man*. It's advertised as 'vintage drama'. 'A tonic' says the *Independent*. Certainly to me.

10th May   Meeting with Solti. Music gives you life, and Solti is the living evidence. 'Can I call you, Georg?' I ask. 'If I can call you Sir Richard.' We talk about sex and money and death, and Dumas *père et fils* and their knowledge of the world of the demi-monde. It's very hard to portray sex on stage and nudity is invariably not sexy. 'Although I had trouble concentrating with Peter's Rhinemaidens.' The music in the first act is not 'sexy', but how to portray a world which is soaked in sex in a way that is truthful and not crass? Verdi's audience would have recognised the world on stage. He says Verdi is uncritical of the society he portrays: 'It's a world where men buy sex. At home they have their wives, their hausfraus, large fat women, and they relax with their prostitutes.' I'm conscious of Solti's Hungarianness, also of his humility and his impatience with modern music. He says he only listens to three composers for pleasure now: Bach, Verdi and Mozart. 'Everyone else is too excessive.' But he wants to write a letter to Shostakovich ('No, I never met him') to say sorry for having thought of him as a collaborator with Stalin's regime. He was a difficult man, but a man of great humility. The letter would be like the letter that Von Bulow wrote to Verdi. He'd dismissed the Requiem initially and then after Wagner's death he listened to it again and thought it a great work. We talk of Visconti's production and of Visconti: 'a noble man, great humanity and wit, but not very musical. His black-and-white *Traviata* was too simple, too black-and-white. And with *Rosenkavalier* he was out of his depth.'

13th May   I had a meeting with Peter Katona at the ROH. He was rushed (a plumber) and snowed under by the endless cycles of revivals,

etc. We talked about casting; he said he liked musical *theatre*, the voice was important but the performance had to be dramatic and plausible. His life, he said, was endless compromise. He told me that Leo Nucci [*baritone*] wouldn't be free for all the rehearsals. I groaned: it's begun already. Nucci is essential to Solti: he'd come all the way from Italy for Solti's eightieth-birthday concert.

16th May   An interview with Gregory Motton [*playwright*]. He says: 'All theatre at the moment is shit. The RSC and the NT are run by mediocrities.' He says that David Hare and Howard Brenton's plays never changed a single vote.

17th May   There's an interview in the *Observer* today with Trevor Griffiths. He talks about critics being drunk, and about the BBC failing to recognise and celebrate him in their Fiftieth Anniversary – true and unjust. His TV plays really were the best of their time, not excluding Potter. He says: 'It's like capitalism's view of Stalinism . . . I personally don't give a shit except for what the work represents, a strand of practice and a terrain of struggle. It's as if you never existed.' But he does give a shit, notwithstanding the 'terrain of struggle'. Trevor says of writing his play about Danton: 'A terminally bleak experience. I went to a space inside me I shan't return to in a hurry. I might not come out next time.' David says all playwrights are ill: it's the effect of year after year living to please and pleasing to live. It disturbs the mind, fractures the ego.

20th May   Reading of *Johnny on the Spot* by Ben Hecht at the Studio. It's a possible answer to our holy grail: a comedy for the Olivier Theatre. Very good cast; very funny play. We talk about whether it would work on stage. It made *us* laugh a lot. Could it inflate the Olivier balloon? And if not, why aren't we doing *The Front Page*, which was Ben Hecht's triumph (with Charles McArthur). Vanity, I suppose; it couldn't be done better than Michael Blakemore's production.

21st May   Problems with *Inadmissible Evidence*. Di Trevis [*director*] rang me from the rehearsal room and asked me to come down. I went down to discover a bleak impasse. John [*Osborne*] thinks that it's all a disaster and has told them so. He's no longer there, and they

all sit looking like refugees from a landslide. We talk, I watch a scene, and I say I'll talk to John.

30th May   This week I had a sticky Board meeting (the *Trelawny* problems and the box office), I've tried to persuade Bill Gaskill to do *Man of Mode*, and I've been to New York for the day by Concorde courtesy of *The New Yorker*, for a lunch celebrating the New York theatre. I'd never been on Concorde, the world's most expensive cigar tube; you arrive before you leave. On the plane I sat next to a South African, who asked me if there were a lot of Negroes going into show business. The lunch was entertaining enough for me, but I can't imagine what *The New Yorker* got out of my presence. I talked to Arthur Miller, who said he felt fearful for Tony Kushner. Why? Because he can never follow that success, Arthur said. I had meetings, went to a press conference for *Madness* at which Nick Hytner told jokes about the monarchy, came back to London, had a finance meeting, and went to Hay-on-Wye to do a talk about *Macbeth* in a tent in a storm, introduced by Peter Florence [*director Hay Festival*] as a 'huge critical success'. I felt duty bound to put the audience straight.

3rd June   Explosive letter from John Osborne, who effectively feels he's been banned from rehearsals of his own play by Di Trevis and Trevor Eve: 'I have long suspected there is no place left for me in the theatre, but I frankly never realised that I was held in – or would be treated with – such fierce contempt. Your theatre's revival of my old play is a very bitter blow indeed.' I've written to John. I was thrilled that he was back in the theatre and it's become a nightmare. What do we do? We have three options: (a) don't do the play, (b) fire Trevor, (c) get John to come to rehearsals and tell Trevor he can't play the part. I should have been much more closely involved, but you can't ever know what's going on in a rehearsal room.

4th June   *Sweeney Todd* opening. I think it's Sondheim's best work, and Declan has done a flawless production, and of course it's right to have done it in the Cottesloe. When I first saw the show in 1982 I thought it was etiolated and over-extended in Drury Lane. I remember Peter Hall saying it was 'fag art' – meaning, I suppose, arch, overblown and mannered – but I can't see that at all: it's an

astringent, unsentimental, hard-edged, slightly self-mocking chamber piece. With *Sweeney Todd* he created an idiosyncratic masterpiece which lifts a scab of *grand guignol* horror and finds a psychological reality underneath.

7th June   Very sad, gentlemanly letter from John Osborne, which thanks me for my lack of recrimination, and: 'This will be the last presentation of my work in London during my lifetime and it is a melancholy way to say farewell to my profession. I still had fugitive hopes – a humiliating and bitter way to bow out. Everyone can go on acting in other plays, directing plays or running theatres but my options have run out. Still, better grievous respect than aggrieved acrimony.' I watched a run of the play this morning; the play is wonderful – impossible to separate from John's voice, passionate, eloquent, droll – and the production certainly doesn't earn John's abiding contempt, but it's not incandescent and, yes, it does lack some of the things that he bemoaned. I rang John with a report on the run, which I told him was convincing.

13th June   I'm back from France after five days with David and Nicole. Wonderful food, company and weather. I got back to news from Judy [*Daish, my agent*] that Bernie Simons [*solicitor and friend*] had died, and she asked if I'd speak at his funeral at Golders Green. It was utterly unbelievable that he could be dead, and the impossibility of it accounted for the mood of confused anger and bewilderment at the funeral. I met Bernie in the '70s through Brian Gibson [*film director*], who wanted me to produce a film based on a story Bernie had told him of one of his clients. Bernie's client was in prison in Dartmoor, and was keen for his story to be dramatised for TV. He'd asked Bernie to make sure that it was 'done proper'. The man had grown up in the East End, made a bit of dodgy money, bought a few terraced houses, borrowed a few hundred thousand pounds from a willing Bank of Scotland, bought a few more houses and a hotel in Hampshire, evicted a few tenants and then sat back to enjoy the life of the likely lad. He made two mistakes: the first was that he didn't understand that you had to pay interest on borrowed money, and the second was confronting Edward Heath when he complained about the service in the hotel with the words: 'Sod off, Sailor.' Bernie was seismic with laughter by this point: 'His defence was the best bit; he

said he couldn't possibly have defrauded the Bank of Scotland because he was officially registered educationally subnormal – he'd had an IQ test, and it was less than blood temperature.'

14th June I started rehearsals for *The Absence of War* [*David Hare*]. I felt confident, and scared only because I didn't feel scared. I kept thinking of what Jimmy Jewel said about an understudy who professed not to be nervous when he went on: 'You can't be any bloody good if you're not bloody nervous.'

15th June I've had another letter from John Osborne, steeped in pain and fury:

Thank you v. much for your report on the run-through of I.E. Oh, dear, 'convincing' is a pretty anodyne adjective. During my days in tatty rep it was applied – in weekly 'notices' written by some 16 yr. old cub – as a polite afterthought to actors playing the butler, gardener, or housemaid. 'Mr. O was convincing as the butler,' meaning he had remembered his lines and most of them were audible.

What I have feared most of all is (a) monotony of delivery and rigidity (b) lack of humour. If the character and the play don't emerge as funny the audience will quickly tire. It's the habitual mistake of actors playing J. PORTER. They stand up being fucking 'angry' all the time. The result is a bullying bore. When Eve insisted on doing one of his telephone arias like an aggrieved customer complaining to his bank manager about an overdraft rather than a man trying to escape from the pain of simply being alive. Those arias need a musical ear, variety, invention, spontaneity, and do need to be sung. One of the few notes that I was constrained to give Nicol was a generalised one, but similar to that I've indicated to other actors in other plays: Treat every other line as if it had just come upon you by surprise, as if it had just invented itself. That is the way, the only way in my opinion, to treat this complexity of text. It's my belief that it also applies to Shakespeare and others. Otherwise the result is glib, dead and predictable. Eve was 'acting' grief and bewilderment: HE NEVER LET THE TEXT DO THE WORK FOR HIM. Ah, well, that's my ten cents' worth. I didn't

think it would be resisted as the weird unfeeling heresy of a detestable DODO . . . As I think I said tediously to you before: there really is no place for the likes of myself any longer. Well, thanks for the reassurance.

Best wishes, in haste, John

I went to the first preview haunted by John's letter. Certainly Trevor wasn't Nicol, but he was truthful and witty, and not monotonous, and the production *doesn't* support John's view that his 'markings' and intentions have been ignored. Actually you can't fault the good faith of the enterprise, even if you could argue with its achievement.

16th June Simon Curtis [*TV producer/director*] tells me that the BBC have just done a production of some TV plays by Edward Bond. 'We're the only company in the world to make TV like that,' he says, 'and the only one to hide the fact.'

17th June The press have got hold of the story of the difficulties with *Inadmissible E.* John rails about the 'dwarves and pygmies' at the NT, and accuses me of political correctness in getting a woman to direct the play. Every director I asked (male or female) baulked at it except Di, and Trevor Eve took the greatest persuasion to agree to be in it. The show had its press night last night. I felt very gloomy about the event, but I admired Trevor for his sangfroid and determination and, actually, his performance.

18th June Postcard from John O., written on Thursday: 'I expected to be driven out by the prevailing despotism of mediocrity but not with such vindictive glee from within my own profession. Neither did I anticipate my work, my life, would be degraded by a shabby exercise in political correctness; that you dwarves should run squealing to the newspapers knowing that they would be only too eager to cast me as a kindless villain and, above all, that *you*, yourself, should behave with such utter and shameless DISHONOUR – J.O.' And on the top of the pc: 'FRIDAY: YOU SEEM TO HAVE GOT AWAY WITH IT. THEY DON'T KNOW ANY BETTER.' I wrote back to John, a letter at least as angry and intemperate as his.

22nd June   Dinner with Maggie [*Smith*]. I never quite know what to expect with her. Today she's wonderful company, very warm and friendly. She feels very alienated from today's theatre. I hope we can do *The Glass Menagerie* together but I'm not confident that she's convinced. She said she'd run into Joyce Hytner who'd said of *Carousel*: 'It's a wonderful production.' 'Well, you would think that,' said Maggie, 'you're his mother.'

3rd July   *Absence* goes well, although David rattled me with his anxiety over John Thaw. I think John's biding his time; David thinks I should 'move in'. An old discussion between us – when to intervene, how long to let the actor (and director) meander, when to put the foot down. And of course it's frustrating for the writer to have to stand by while we blunder round the territory trying to find its boundaries and its topography.

6th July   I'm very happy at the theatre as long as I can keep my mind closed to the nightmare of the declining box office. I think we'll lose about £400,000 in the next few months, and I feel embarrassed and depressed by it, even if I'm almost sure that, as in every other year, we'll end up in the black. Virginia Woolf on writing: '. . . accentuating all these difficulties and making them harder to bear is the world's notorious indifference. It does not ask people to write poems and novels and histories; it does not need them.' Or plays.

17th July   Just back from Gloucestershire, where we've seen a house that we want to buy with the money from selling Mum's house. We've been married twenty years (last Wednesday) and I feel no (only mild financial) anxiety about buying it and committing us to another twenty.

18th July   We went to the opening of *Sunset Boulevard* at the Adelphi. It was elephantine and literal and in thrall to Hollywood and showbiz – which is what it's supposed to be satirising, and it didn't really exploit the dream element of the story; it was as if the purpose was to pay homage to the film, which is certainly better than trying to traduce it. The audience was simmering with *schadenfreude*. I was asked afterwards by a *Telegraph* reporter if I thought the show would last as long as a Rodgers and Hammerstein show. I

said no and was told by Nick Hytner this morning that I was the bravest man in London. I felt churlish for accepting Lloyd Webber's hospitality, and about as brave as refusing to buy or read *The Times* or *Sunday Times* (which I do) to defy Murdoch. When Andrew asked me to direct *Sunset Boulevard* I read the script by a pool on a hillside in Tuscany and thought: Will this be such a success that I could have a house on the side of a hill in Tuscany? Then I thought: You can't do it – bad faith always breeds bad work. Andrew wanted me to open it at the NT. I'd have been lynched. Two songwriters watch a man fall off a roof of the Brill building. The man crashes through the awning, hits the sidewalk, brushes himself off and walks away. 'Isn't he lucky?' says one songwriter. 'You call that lucky?' says the other, '*Andrew Lloyd Webber* is lucky!'

21st July   Dinner for Yolande Bird's retirement. She covers the whole history of the NT and possesses all the secrets. I spoke after dinner about the death of liberal institutions which afterwards provoked a torrent of elegiac stuff about how the world of arts subsidy is over. I felt sceptical about this nostalgia, but it's true that the Arts Council is in chaos: Brian Rix has resigned from the drama panel, Price Waterhouse have condemned it as 'useless' and Anthony Everitt is talking about 'contracting the portfolio' and 'focusing their spending', which must be code for cuts for all.

12th August   I've been reading a biography of the physicist Richard Feynman: 'It's wrong to think that the task of physics is to find out how nature is, physics concerns only what we *say* about nature.'

15th August   I had dinner with Alan Howard and together we railed defensively about the fate of *Macbeth*. I still don't know what to think: was it bad work? Did it fail because of Alan's inaccessibility? At the moment I tell Alan I feel what Jed Harris said about directing *The Crucible*: 'I'll never do another play where a guy writes with a feather.'

20th August   I'm really enjoying *Absence*, in fact the whole Trilogy. In the proofs for the published version of the Trilogy David has credited me with 'literary advice'. I told David I felt a bit short-changed; he admitted that my relationship with it has been 'Siamese'.

25th August   An *Inspector Calls* has opened at the Aldwych. The houses were falling off in the Olivier, and Michael Codron gives it three months in the West End, but Peter Wilson, who's producing the show, is very confident. The play – or Stephen [*Daldry*]'s production – is now like a modern fable or cautionary tale.

26th August   A pc from Max [*Stafford-Clark*] in response to my *Guardian* piece [*about the Arts Council and loss of faith in our liberal institutions*]: 'The '80s have been like trench warfare fighting endlessly on the same miserable yards of territory and, of course, being pushed slowly backwards. It's the English inclination to celebrate defeats: Corunna, Dunkirk, but in truth "marketing" and "security" have been the only growth areas.'

27th August   We ran all three plays today in the rehearsal room starting at ten-thirty. The sun shone in brilliant slanting shafts across the room, occasionally hitting faces like a Renaissance annunciation. There was an unostentatious energy and concentration in the room that I've never quite experienced before. And no tension, at least no stress, in spite of our audience of one – Irene Worth [*actress*], who sat regally throughout, occasionally murmuring encouragement; she won't be in London when the plays are on. The subject matter of the plays came across very strongly: how do people combat evil? Why do the good always fight among themselves? How does a good person change people's lives for the better? Can an institution established for the common good avoid being devoured by its own internal struggles and contradictions? Is man a social animal interested in justice, in equality, in love?

28th August   Gave a speech at the Edinburgh TV Festival. TV drama is moving towards a system of values that mimics the movies. Paradoxically, it's been underwritten by a generation of producers and directors who have been educated in 'film culture' by watching old movies on TV. The position of the writer in British TV used to be a much more privileged one which owed much to its theatrical antecedents (not an unmixed blessing); it put the emphasis on content. The enemy of good TV is self-censorship and inertia, just as much as the implicit censorship imposed by the ratings war. No 'demand' for 'good' drama on TV can be proven; only with hindsight

can it be demonstrated that when imaginative risks have been taken audiences have responded and defied the bogus logic of 'market predictions' and the bollocks of 'focus groups'. The best films I've seen in the last two years were made for TV: Edgar Reitz' *Heimat II*, and Keislowski's *Ten Commandments*. They were both serials (of a sort), and both came from countries which haven't been colonised by American culture. Tony Garnett was on the panel: if TV drama can be re-invented he's the only person I know who can do it, but he misunderstood what I was saying, and construed it as an attack on TV. I read an interview with Ken Loach: 'What's interesting in broadcasting is that it's full of people who ask questions. But overall, often, it seems to me it's about reassurance, about not asking questions at the key time, in a way – to be extreme – it's about social control. The hypocrisy is to pretend that this isn't true.'

19th September   We've moved into the cottage in Gloucestershire. My first action was to grab a chain saw and scythe through a row of Leylandii that had been planted by the previous owners. They divided the house and the garden when their marriage went bad.

26th September   *Absence* has started previewing. It's been oddly calm. I've never seen a cast (and crew) at a first preview quite so relaxed. John Thaw, though nervous (first time on stage for years) was inspiringly steady and superb. The audience responded well to the play, but stopped short of rapture at the end. Is it the play, the production, or is it John's immaculately good taste? Or is it that the work isn't quite as good as we think?

29th September   Still previewing. John Mortimer introduces me to Roy Hattersley who's apparently reviewing the play for the *Mail*. Hattersley gives me the impression that we needn't hope for a good notice there. There's good feedback from the show. People take from it what they want: some think it's an indictment of the Left, some apolitical, some satirical, and some see the themes of the play.

3rd October   Yesterday was the most extraordinary day I've spent at the National Theatre, not least because, as Wally Shawn said, it was so moving to see an institution working at full stretch, which acted as a metaphor for the aspiration of *every* institution – i.e. that

the sum should be greater than the parts. The performance began at ten-thirty in the morning and ended twelve hours later. I wish I had been more able to enjoy it but I felt overwhelmed: ludicrously tired and even more ludicrously tense, standing in rictus all day at the back of the auditorium, willing everything to go right. It did, but before I was able to relax and enjoy the day, it was over, and I was having to jump aside to avoid the buffalo charge of self-advertising critics running for the exits as if their trousers were on fire. Then I went backstage and Robin Bailey [*actor*] told me his wife had just died, and I never quite got to the moment of ecstatic exhilaration that I'd been promising myself for four months.

4th October   The reviews are very good for the event and mealy-mouthed about the writing of *Absence*, including Roy Hattersley who pisses on it. I think it's a classic journalistic confusion between documentary and art, between simile and metaphor. They say they need more 'distance' from events and at the same time want the theatre to be concerned with contemporary events.

6th October   Russia has been on the edge of civil war – a coup, or something like it. I saw Ion recently who thinks it's play-acting – as in the Gorbachev coup, a device to get Western aid. If so it's been grotesquely mishandled and hundreds have died. I think sometimes Ion's cynicism gets the better of him, but he thinks I'm naive.

10th October   The Trilogy is a genuine hit, in spite of the reviews which have been mean-spirited for the writing, as if they think it's an act of hubris to write and to present these plays – 'this "so-called" Trilogy', says one. Well, it's hard to deny that three plays are a trilogy.

11th October   The Tory Party Conference is about to start. Glorious Steve Bell cartoon of a Tory couple at breakfast:

MAN: What are you going to do when *Margaret* comes on to the platform?
WOMAN: Well . . . I'm going to *jibber*, and then I'm going to *whoop* and *shriek!* What about *you*, dear?
MAN: I'm simply going to *BARK LIKE A DOG!*

15th October   Bob and Jean and I meet with Solti, wary of his cautiousness and conservatism in staging. We argue amiably about the Prologue – I want a projection of Violetta as a child, then the live adult appearing through the scrim. I explain the idea of the set – the staircase, the vortex, where the chorus will be, where the soloists will be. He's animated and seems to go with it, but doesn't like the colours. 'It must be light. Not too much red. Champagne.' There is no red on the set. Then to the second act, our bare arctic-blue country house, rented, beyond the means of Alfredo, full of 'shopping' – paintings, furniture, fabric samples. And Alfredo's father, Mediterranean man, coming into this Northern world. He looks carefully at a model of Violetta, a tiny black-and-white cut-out. 'Why is she wearing a hat?' A large, elegant stove in the corner of the room. Solti likes the stove, and the set. 'I can buy that.' He buys the third scene as well, and he buys the notion of an instant scene change. He buys the last act and we pack up, discussing dates for our next meeting. He has his calendar – 'SIR GEORG SOLTI SCHEDULE 1991–2000'. He shows it to Bob, says 'An impertinence', and then: 'You must make the costumes very beautiful.' To me he says: 'Beautiful costumes, beautiful sets, what do you need to do?'

16th October   *Machinal* [*Sophie Treadwell*] has opened. Fiona [*Shaw*] gives a remarkable performance, and it's an extravagant and fearless piece of staging, although the play doesn't feel *quite* up to the production, which I'm not sure is fair. Stephen [*Daldry*] works in impenetrably good faith and for all his self-advertisement, at heart he wants to give his audience a good time. Kathleen Tynan loves the play and Fiona's performance but says: 'Does Stephen prefer sets to actors? Can't he be expressionistic and imaginative without overwhelming the thing with set? The designers are taking over with an arrogant vengeance. Don't you agree?' I don't. I see it all as a way of making the theatre expressive and using all the tools at your disposal. The important thing is always to hold on to the humanity and the human scale of things – which is what I think Stephen and Ian [*McNeil*] *have* done: in fact the production is about the 'machine' attempting to crush the 'human'.

18th October   We went to Wales for a weekend with the Birts [*John Birt, Director-General BBC*]. Long, virtuous walks organised

with military flair by John, even if we did lose our way and find ourselves running for our lives from a wild white horse. Sue committed the solecism of asking for her Mars Bar and soft drink before the appointed stopping place. John has huge enthusiasm and energy and an appealing clarity (or simplicity) about his vision for the BBC. He's thoroughly (to a fault?) unsentimental, and sees the need to carve his way through the culture of Utopianism – what he calls 'old fartism'. Getting some grip on budgets – or allowing programme makers to do so – wouldn't be a bad start. John's knowledgeable and very perceptive about the programmes that he talks about, but seems oddly unwilling to become at all interventionist when it comes to improving the programmes that he thinks are poor.

24th October   David's furious at the failure of the critics to meet his own estimation of *Absence*, underwritten by his feeling that they have a personal agenda. He's written to me saying he wants the word 'masterwork' in the brochure. This presents difficulties because it was said by a columnist not a critic but perhaps I'm being over-fastidious. He says I owe him this favour because he 'has filled my largest theatre'.

29th October   I drove to the Sherman Theatre in Cardiff to see *Ghosts* which Sean Mathias has directed. I always feel embarrassed that people are so grateful that I've come out of London to see anything. I don't see nearly enough. And we don't tour nearly enough. So much for putting the small 'n' into National. Sian Phillips was very good, but the play is only intermittently convincing. But Sean had made something of it, and I think he's the man for *Les Parents Terribles*.

2nd November   Boston to see *George III*. Roger [*Chapman*] had arranged a tea party for the company in a hotel on the waterfront. Nigel Hawthorne took great delight in presiding over a Boston tea party where the tea stayed in the teapot. The show was bright and sped along, possibly at a pace that was slightly ahead of the audience.

4th November   New York. I saw Tony Kushner and talked about commissioning a new play, talked to Jack Viertel [*dramaturg*] about an adaptation of *Pal Joey*, saw part of *The Kentucky Cycle*, which

was dull but very well-meaning, talked to André Bishop [*artistic director Lincoln Center Theater*] about doing *Racing Demon*, and saw Natasha [*Richardson*], who chastised me for calling her dad an opportunist in a review of his book. 'How would you feel,' she said, 'if Lucy had to read that sort of thing about you?'

8th November   I stayed for a few days in the cottage: at first no furniture, sleeping (or not) in a sleeping bag on an air bed on an uncarpeted floor. The air bed had a puncture and I spent a frozen night: frozen but exhilarated. Pottered around the house interrupted by phone calls about Robin Bailey, who's had a breakdown after his wife's death.

19th November   Meeting with Katie Mitchell – a gifted, bright, young and idealistic director. She wants to run a company like Ariane Mnouchkine and she looked slightly dashed when I said that Ariane took years to establish herself and still works herself to the bone: she directs the plays, runs the theatre, oversees the catering and tears the tickets. Katie's generation seem less willing to go out into the wilderness and start their own companies. And we voraciously draw them into the big companies.

20th November   *Perestroika* [*the second play of Tony Kushner's* Angels in America] has opened in the Cottesloe. I love the scale and the wild ambition of the whole enterprise. It's a defiant affirmation for an age of doubt and despair, crawling towards the Millennium unarmed with God or ideology. Declan has done a really good production, but has found it difficult working with Tony – albeit at a distance – feeling tyrannised by Tony's notes. I show him some of David [*Hare*]'s. It's inevitable that writers will have strong views about how their work is performed; why would one wish it other-wise? This, from Tennessee Williams, should be the director's credo: 'Just as it is important for a playwright to forget certain vanities in the interest of the total creation of the stage, so must the director.' And: 'The playwright has two alternatives. Either he must stage the play himself or he must find one particular director who has the very unusual combination of actively creative imagination plus a true longing or even just a true willingness to devote his own gifts to the faithful projection of someone else's vision. This is a thing of rarity.'

24th November   I've been in a steady decline since the Trilogy: constant feelings of panic, insecurity, inadequacy. One small incident can start a descent into despair. I'm like water, everything moves me. I've recognised all my working life a pattern of exhilaration leading up to a first night, followed by depression – the withdrawal of adrenalin. Working on the Trilogy has amplified that cycle. Now I've committed myself to a year of work that engenders nothing but overwhelming anxiety: I haven't chosen the right plays to do next year – for myself or the theatre – and I don't seem able to escape. But I have to clam up at the theatre. Don't give the game away. 'Think of it always, speak of it never,' is what Clemenceau is supposed to have said about Alsace-Lorraine. In his Diaries Peter quotes George Devine: "When you feel the walls coming in on you, get out." I can't resign now because it would be defeat. But I want to . . . I am in an extraordinarily emotional state. I keep losing control.' Is it that Peter and I are temperamentally similar, or is this state of mind endemic to running the NT? Ingmar Bergman said he'd been depressed most of his life, and he'd always thought that it was just his nature. Then he stopped running the Royal Dramaten Theatre and his depression lifted.

29th November   Talk with Stephen Daldry about whether he'll take over the Royal Court, about whether we could run the NT together, and about whether he'd succeed me. I talked to Jenny about wanting to pull out of *Johnny on the Spot* and *Sweet Bird of Youth*. She convinced me that this was a familiar pattern: anxiety, doubt, panic, joy, depression.

1st December   To Munich to see a creakily maladroit production of *La Traviata*. The production would describe itself as expressionistic, but that's just a way of saying that it has no architectural or emotional logic and consistently ignores the musical notations, the stage directions and the meaning of the libretto. The tenor, who looks like a plump car salesman, has to sing '*Di miei bollenti spiriti*' sitting in a swing. His father is younger than him, and plays Germont as coarse, crass and exploitative. Somebody said to me of a German director that he directed opera like he was invading Poland; this was more like the Channel Islands. Seeing the production does point out how difficult it is to reconcile the 'naturalistic' with the 'expressionistic' that the opera embraces.

3rd December   Went to the cinema with Lu: *In The Line Of Fire*. Clint cries! On the way home we saw a tree that had been cut down. Someone had put a card on the tree: 'THEY CUT ME DOWN THE BASTARDS, signed TREE.'

4th December   Back in Glos for the weekend. I used to despise people who said they were 'going off for the weekend'. Now I'm the person I warned myself against. I'm yearning for peace, silence, seclusion. My problem is simply that, like David's leader in *Absence*, I don't believe sufficiently in myself. I'm Director of one of the best-known (and best) theatres in the world, applauded for running the theatre and for directing plays, and I ache with self-doubt.

5th December   Today we took Lu to Oxford for an interview at New College. I felt fearful for her, and for the loss of her to adulthood.

6th December   Reading Joseph Brodsky: 'The word was "treach-ery". A wonderful word that. It creaks like a board laid over a chasm. Onomatopoeically it beats ethics. It has all the euphony of a taboo. For the ultimate boundary of a tribe is its language.' Also: 'The upsurge of spy novels in our time is a by-product of modernism's emphasis on texture, which left literature in all European languages absolutely plotless.'

7th December   Reading of Nigel Williams' adaptation of *Lord of the Flies* with a group of very bright children, but only one of them has a real, unarguable gift for acting. Howard's turned it down, and so have Deborah and Declan, and I was considering directing it, but all my doubts about it were confirmed. I don't see how it's possible to stage what Nigel has written, and I don't think it's possible to adapt the book. It certainly wouldn't work with some sort of distancing device – like adults to play the children.

8th December   We show the model to Solti, and to Valerie [*his wife*] in a tiny model room at the ROH. He doesn't quite get it, but Valerie acts as his eyes. The characters on the model are black-and-white cut-outs, which he imagines are how the costumes are going to be. Valerie explains about 'penny plain'. Georg says: 'But the costumes, they must be beautiful.'

10th December   Martin Sherman, coming out of a show about cottaging at the Royal Court: 'Don't you sometimes think we should all get back in the closet?'

18th December   Better today, less panic. Things that I'm sad about: the weather, Bosnia, unemployment, homelessness, lack of hope, lack of purpose, grey hair, too much knowledge, too little wisdom, too little interest from the public in the arts, too much talk, British politics, Ireland, debt, death.

20th December   There's a new climate of journalistic hostility to the arts. The question is more and more: why them? Why are they (the arts) a special case? Liberal newspapers are beginning to ask whether the arts should be subsidised. The arts have *always* been subsidised by public or private patronage. I'm always wary of arguments for funding the arts based on the grounds of cost-effectiveness, or as tourist attractions, or as investments, or as commodities that can be marketed, exploited and profited from. It's always hard, though, when you pit the demands of the arts against the demands of the homeless.

21st December   I went to Nottingham to do a talk to an adult education institute. I came on hot and strong about the National Health Service being dissipated, the BBC being diluted, British Rail being parcelled out, the GLC being abolished, the network of repertory theatres being diminished by the body that is supposed to protect them, and the education system being dismantled, leaving it to councils like Nottinghamshire to fight rearguard actions. A woman Tory councillor walked out calling me a prat, but at the end a woman was in tears, moved, she said, by what I'd said. Several people said I'd given them the best Christmas present they could hope for and I felt a fraud just spinning in and out and stirring up their fears.

23rd December   I've been reading William Styron's book about depression. He talks about its indescribability and of 'despair beyond despair'. At the moment I can read this with academic detachment but within a few days I may be back in the whirlpool and he'd be addressing a fellow sufferer, who'd be feeling something like this

(from Virginia Woolf's Diary): '. . . I'm screwed up into a ball; can't get into step; can't make things dance; feel awfully detached; see youth; feel old; no, that's not quite it: wonder how a year or two is to be endured. Think, yet people do live; can't imagine what goes on behind faces. All is surface hard; myself only an organ that takes blows, one after another . . . the inane pointlessness of all this existence; hatred of my own brainlessness, and indecision; the old treadmill feeling of going on and on and on, for no reason . . . worst of all is this dejected bitterness. And my eyes hurt; and my hand trembles.'

31st December   New Year's Eve. The butterscotch-yellow sun is glinting through the only remaining fir, a Chinese juniper. There are layers of clouds the colour of a dying bruise, and I'm feeling moderately at ease with things. For how long? I've got the very gravest fears about next year in the theatre. I don't see where the successes will be, and my own plans seem to be a shambles. I'm going to do two plays set in Louisiana, both imperfect, one which teeters on the edge of melodrama, and one a farce that will seem absurdly foolish if the audience doesn't laugh. Why am I doing it? To fill the Olivier. Why aren't I doing *Front Page*? Because it seems lame to turn the clock back. Every step I've planned for next year, including ending the year with *La Traviata*, seems maladroit.

1994

3rd January   Getting ready to go back to London, half listening to *Start the Week*. They're talking about the danger of 'the big idea', and of the need for 'an art of despair', meaning writers who can deal with the real misery of today. But what would happen to a Dostoyevsky today if one were to appear? He'd be made to do book-signing tours, go on *Start the Week*, and talk about 'the art of despair'. We're all victims of knowing too much, of marketing, and of public relations. Actually, I feel more in need of 'an art of joy'.

6th January   Back in London. It's five-fifteen in the morning and I can't sleep. The odd desolate chirp of a bird. I'm full of panic about doing *Johnny*. I know it's the wrong thing to be doing. Nothing about it feels right – wrong play, wrong theatre, wrong actors. I spoke to Tom [*Stoppard*] yesterday about it, and he confirmed all my worries. He didn't say so but I know he thinks the play is a stinker. 'Why aren't you doing *Born Yesterday*?' Well, yes, why not? I predict disaster but it's too late to cancel, and I don't know how to minimise the damage.

7th January   Bill [*Dudley*] and I walk around the Olivier stage talking about stage reality, how disconcerting (sometimes wonderfully so) it is to see the elements of fire and water on stage. Bill says: 'Water on stage is like an animal, it can only be itself.'

10th January   Monday morning. I'm trying to gear myself up to go to the NT. It's going to be a bad year, in a wilting theatre. I want my life back – from reading plays, from propagandising for the theatre,

from funding problems, from the moaning, from the sniping, from under the constant cloak of anxiety.

11th January   I'm listening to Schumann's *Fantasie* – heartrending balm. He was in appalling pain when he wrote it: 'Often at night I would implore God: "Grant me at least one night of tranquility in which my mind would not give way." ' I feel caught between needing balm in order to assuage pain and providing the pain in order to apply the balm. I'm a Catholic in everything but religion – I believe in guilt, suffering as the cost of happiness, failure as the cost of success. It's a Newtonian emotional universe – action and re-action are equal and opposite. It's all mounted up: anxiety about the future (and present) of the NT, frustration and pain over *Macbeth*, fear of failure with the Trilogy, anger over my feeling of futility, and guilt about my sense of worthlessness. Where is the 'I' in directing? Nothing on stage is visible as the authorial self – not the actors, not the sets, the lighting or the writing. At least a conductor is there waving his arms about, even if there is more show than is necessary. Of course I'm exaggerating but don't trust myself in any situation. I keep dreaming of dying.

12th January   I've started a course of an anti-depressant, Prozac. I feel mildly, very mildly, elated, not free of anxiety but free of the panic that normally accompanies it. I feel as if my brain has a number of compartments, like dog traps, out of which wild things emerge – insects, spiders, frogs, snakes, and wolves, surrounded by a gnawing cold damp wind that permeates everything. The drug has closed these traps, and I feel that sand, or snow, is piling up outside them. I don't feel quite clear-headed. I'm not happy, just not in pain.

14th January   Been reading Cocteau's Journals: 'What is style? For many people a complicated way of saying very simple things.' I remember this from Arthur Miller's autobiography: 'Jed had style, which is always suspicious, especially when it is not only a form or entertainment but is also a weapon.'

20th January   Lunch with Maria [*St Just*] at Gerald Road. She's really ill, muted, without her usual bite, and submits without a fight when I say I don't want to do *Camino Real*. She's been having treatment, gold in her bloodstream – 'Nothing but the MOST

expensive' – but it hasn't worked. Her energy is dimmed; she picks at her food and talks about death. She's enthusiastic about me doing *Sweet Bird*, but I think is too hard on the play, which I love and she thinks is second-rate. Her devotion's divided between *Streetcar* and *Camino*; she finds *Sweet Bird* uncomfortably revealing. I told Maria I'd always suspected that the Broadway edition of the play was Kazan's version not Tennessee's, and I'd had my suspicions confirmed when I'd read an article by an American academic saying that there were several drafts of the play before the Broadway production and one which came after its opening. Maria said she'd rout out all the drafts from the University of Texas, who appear to live in terror of her. 'We'll have such fun,' she said, 'sorting out the best.' 'What do you think Tennessee would think?' I said. Maria said that when she protested to him about a Moscow production which gave *Streetcar* a happy ending, he'd said: 'They're right, Maria, Blanche would have conned her way out of that mental home in a fortnight, and she'd have married Mitch.' When I left her she held me a long time and I was sure this was a last goodbye.

21st January   I feel tired without feeling sleepy, tranquil without feeling contented. I'm insulated and it's better than the heaving sickening drowning sense of despair that overtakes me without the pills. I've got all the symptoms of manic depression, and the artistic temperament without the redeeming genius. I'm forced daily to confront my own limitations in public.

23rd January   From Douglas Dunn: 'Only a garden can teach gardening' – only a theatre can teach theatre, and only directing a play can teach you how to direct a play.

25th January   Mary [*Soames*] and Jenny [*McIntosh*] and Maggie [*Whitlum, NT general manager*] and I went to the Royal Fine Arts Commission to explain our plans for the redevelopment of the NT. Norman St John-Stevas upset Mary by referring to her as 'real royalty, unlike our middle-class monarch', which is a bit rich coming from such an indefatigable palace crawler.

28th January   I'm on a plane coming back from New York after two days away auditioning. The actors are better prepared than their

British counterparts. I know now what running the NT is like: grieving. But because I'm often elated and exhilarated, rather than sad or ill or wasted, it's also like being in love. Either way, it's a cladding like a second skin that can't be shed.

29th January *Skriker* [*Caryl Churchill*] has opened. It's an extra-ordinary, unclassifiable piece, and I think it's been about half realised.

30th January Bucharest, principally for Ion's theatre awards ceremony – the Uniter Gala. Bucharest seems very run down, but not beaten like before. It's insular and on the margins and one of the peace dividends is being patronised (in both senses) by visiting Brits like myself and Neil Wallace [*Scottish impresario*]. We sniff round Romanian theatre because it appears to offer everything that our theatre doesn't: the exotic, the mysterious, the incomprehensible, the socially significant. The Gala was amiably disorganised, and lasted from sixish to twoish, prompting Neil to say that he'd never been to an awards ceremony which lasted two days. I gave an award to Gina Patriche, who is the Judi Dench, Maggie Smith and Peggy Ashcroft of Romania. I saw her first over twenty years ago. She was Signoret-sexy, now she's sadly depleted, dying of cancer, with a few months to live, but still beautiful and leonine. Ion invited me onstage, then announced the award to Gina. So she had to stand in the stalls being applauded for ages before the audience would let her up onstage. I gave a speech and then she thanked me, thanked everyone, and ended by reciting Prospero's last speech in English: 'Our revels now are ended . . .' Most of the audience seemed able to speak English, and most, like Ion and me, stood weeping as she pronounced her own epitaph.

31st January In Craiova (where I went fifteen years ago to see the Brancusi sculptures in the park), a three-and-a-half-hour train journey to see Silvia Purcarete's production of *Titus Andronicus*, which was very modish and untouchable (and untouching). A sort of unappealing directorial swagger, full of imagistic ostentation, but now and again a brilliant device – as in a shadow execution.

1st February I was searched at Heathrow. They found the beautiful first edition of *Our Mutual Friend* that Christopher Hampton

had given me, fat and leather-bound. 'What's this?' they said. 'A book,' I said. They looked very doubtful; to them it was a perfectly plausible cocaine container. 'Open it, please, sir.' I did so and riffled through the gold-edged pages to their evident dissatisfaction.

2nd February   I went to Newcastle to do a lecture in C.P. Taylor's memory. Cecil died over twelve years ago. I felt ashamed that I was asked to direct one of his earliest plays, *Bread and Butter*, and I turned it down for a worthless alternative. Later I got to know his work and him (a bit), and both were tenacious, and compassionate, and witty, and unfashionable. He was obsessed by the gap between our ideals and what we end up with. I wonder what he would have made of what we've created in the years since his death. He wrote of ideals that are now tarnished by their constant invocation in the politicians' litany of insincerity: 'region', 'community', 'family', 'society'. I saw Tony [*Harrison*] afterwards, and when we were walking down the street two young people came up to me and thanked me, said my lecture was a revelation and an inspiration. I looked at Tony and laughed. 'Don't knock it,' he said.

8th February   Went to a party for London Arts, where John Major made a witty, well-informed, noteless speech for fifteen minutes, about his enthusiasm for the arts and the need to support them. Eyebrows arched in question marks: why doesn't his government do so more generously? He revealed his total faith in the Lottery as the saviour.

10th February   Prozac: the advantages – mild euphoria, tranquillity, fatalism, energy, optimism, suppression of appetite, loss of panic, anxiety and fear; the disadvantages – can't sleep well without temazepam, can't drink (is this an advantage?), gives false confidence, provides insulation, is an artificial cure, destroys creative ambition. It's like the Dickens short story, 'The Haunted Man': a life without pain is one without pleasure. From an article about Prozac: 'I think the first impact of Prozac was that it built up an index of answers in my mind to the terrifying questions anxiety provokes, and slowly I began to feel more confident.'

12th February   Brian Ridley [*chief lighting technician*] has died after not many months of a wasting cancer. His death has blighted

and blasted the technical staff. None of us can accept the suddenness and the injustice of someone dying so young. And Brian was one of those technicians who made you calmer and more confident. When I was last at the Bulandra Theatre I was shown the lighting board by the chief electrician – an antique Strand Grand Master, all handles and brass like a railway signal box – 'How is my friend, Brian?' he asked me. 'Not well,' I said. He looked crestfallen. 'Tell him from me,' he said, 'to get well.'

13th February   I was walking over Waterloo Bridge, and I saw a police launch circling a bloated body floating face up in the river, and it reminded me of the opening of *Our Mutual Friend*. It seemed like an omen, that Christopher and I should and would make the film of it. I've just finished the novel – I haven't read it since I studied it, although I've been championing it for years and we've talked for years about the film. I remembered the book as richer and more vivid and darker and more pessimistic. It seemed to be full of holes and loose ends with some really wonderful passages in between. This is London: 'Such a bleak, shrill city, combining the qualities of a smoking home and a scolding wife; such a gritty city; such a hopeless city, with no rent in the leaden canopy of its sky; such a beleaguered city, invested by the great Marsh Forces of Essex and Kent.'

15th February   Grey Gowrie has replaced Peter Palumbo as Chairman of the Arts Council, which must give a resounding message when it comes to the arts – it's a toffs' game. I don't know how we begin to change people's perception of the arts, but the more we fail to break down the class barriers, the less case there is for continuing subsidy. Education, of course, but from primary level. And we've got to stop imagining that the 'choice' of going to the theatre – or to the opera, or to an art gallery – is a 'choice' that's been offered to most people in this country. Most young people *aren't* taken to the theatre by their parents or their schools or their colleges. And a lot of people feel that theatre-going isn't for them – they don't feel comfortable in the buildings, and if they feel anything at all about the theatre they feel disenfranchised from it.

17th February   I've been rehearsing *Johnny on the Spot* for two weeks. It will be enjoyable, inconsequential, and people will say

'Well, it's not *Front Page*' and of course they'll be right. I *think* it can
work as farce, or as 'political farce' as we consolingly call it, if it can
move too quickly for the audience to be able to catch their breath.
But it takes too long to get going. If the audience don't take to it it'll
seem absurd and charmless, and will leave a huge yawning hole in the
Olivier's box office. As (almost) always, of course, I'm having fun in
rehearsals.

18th February   Christopher Hitchens: 'Can it be that faced with
the ghastly alliance between Fleet Street populism and enervated
royalism, the British public has finally done what the Spencer girl
cannot do, and started to grow up?' I won't hold my breath.

20th February   Maria's died. At first I felt, shamefully, a little relief
that I wouldn't have to tussle all the way over *Sweet Bird*, but with
every day since I miss her more and more: her scathing wit, her
unpredictability and her unerring instinct – about Tennessee's work
she was never wrong. Yes, she could be a monster: wilful, imperious,
capricious, bullying, haughty, devilish even, but, if she gave you her
trust and you returned it, she was an indelibly loyal friend and an
affectionate companion. The several drafts of *Sweet Bird* (five of
them) arrived from the University of Texas yesterday. In a letter
Tennessee W. said it was about 'the betrayal of people's hearts by the
subtle progress of a corruption that is both personal and social . . .
the native power-drive of the individual and the false values with
their accent on being "top dogs" . . . that defeats the possible true
and pure and compassionately loving relations between people.'
Territorial imperative with a whiff of Marxism. He told his agent:
'If you can get half a million for it (as a film script), I will eat my
Olivetti.'

21st February   Dinner tonight with Peter Brook. He points out
that mercifully political correctness hasn't hit France, which is gender
blind – or specific but blind – in its language. We talked about
directors, the need for innocence married to the need for discovery.
He's very dismissive of some of the young English tigers.

22nd February   I met Leo Nucci at the Savoy. An amiable,
straightforward man: 'I am a singer.' He prefaces every remotely

contentious idea with 'That's my idea.' He has no truck with
conceptual productions. We talk about discovering the opera
through the libretto: 'Verdi was first a dramatist, then a composer.
That's my idea.' Nucci has an eerie resemblance to Ken Dodd when
he smiles, the teeth. We talk about Germont's attitude to Violetta:
'She is a woman; he is attracted to her. That's my idea.' The next
night I went to see *Rigoletto*. It's a terrible production, really quite
embarrassing. The soprano, a Korean, sounds like a Japanese nightclub singer; Nucci is strong and rather wooden, without great vocal
variety. We had dinner afterwards: Nucci, the tenor and the tenor's
wife, and their very young baby, who was perfectly behaved. As for
the adults – they bitched about bad productions, bad conductors,
and swapped the names of cities like bus stops. Much talk of how
much money the Big Four tenors make and how much some directors
get. They talk like actors, but are less showy, less ostentatious, less
glamorous, more workmanlike. After dinner Nucci says on the
pavement: 'It's a strange life, it all depends on what you do on
the evening, there's no continuity.' And he walks off into the night
with his sports bag, like a golf pro. Tomorrow Vienna to do *Lucia*.

23rd February   Maria's funeral. I went with Mary to the Russian
church in Knightsbridge. The church was lit solely by candles, and
we had to add to the illumination by buying a candle. We all held our
candles, the light giving everyone a tender glow, making us an instant
congregation. Liz McCann came up beside me and started talking
about New York theatre in a theatrical whisper. I evaded Liz and
walked to Maria's open coffin, candle in hand. She looked small and
peaceful and ready to open her eyes and say something vinegary that
I'd smile at and feel the better for. The priests entered and they
started to chant the service, after dashing incense to all corners and
circling the coffin. Then, quite unexpectedly, ravishingly beautiful
Russian harmonies emerged from the choir in the gallery above us.
The service made me ache for the absence of ritual in our own lives.
At the end of the service the family (and Franco Zeffirelli) kissed
Maria and kissed the coffin. Then a straggle of men and women in
thick overcoats, but mostly women in scuffed wool-lined ankle boots
and headscarves, went up to the coffin to pay homage. They looked
like Soviet refugees or exiles from Maria's domestic staff. Then they
started to sing and I realised it was the choir. Our candles had burned

low and we knew the service couldn't last longer than our candles. We filed out, embracing the daughters on the way out, rite of passage discharged.

In the evening John Lahr came to see me to talk about Maria for an article he's writing. He wanted me to corroborate his thesis that Maria had an unhealthy stranglehold on Tennessee Williams' estate. I was reluctant to do so (a) because I'm not sure it was true, and (b) because having just kissed her corpse I'm unwilling and unable to say anything uncharitable about her. And (c) I really liked her.

27th February   I talked to a journalist who's doing a piece about Stephen Daldry. She asks me if Stephen might take over from me when I leave, whenever that might be. I say I don't know, maybe it'll be '96. This is apparently news, because a journo rings Stephen Wood to ask if it's true. I don't know. Some days I doubt if I can last another six months; others I want to go on for ever. I'll stop when I fear boredom.

28th February   Front-page story in the *Guardian*, and a piece on the *Today* programme about me leaving the NT. Reports much exaggerated but I had to do a bit of therapy at the theatre. Later the *Standard* did a story headlined: 'IT'S NOT CURTAINS FOR ME YET, SAYS NATIONAL CHIEF'.

6th March   The last night of *George III*. Like most last nights it was played a bit monumentally, as if everyone was saying their lines for the last time, which of course they were, but Nigel as always was very touching. And Alan [*Bennett*] afterwards was very warm and very generous.

7th March   I need to decide about a director for *Oh, What a Lovely War!* for the Olivier – if, *if*, we can gets the rights. I feel much happier, more equable – Prozac, of course. There's a loss of edge, of that anxiety and danger that seems to fuel me, but it's a small loss for not being immobilised by self-doubt. I read a clinical description of depression and felt like I was answering one of those magazine questionnaires. You should have at least four of the following symptoms:

significant weight loss or gain (neither)
insomnia (yes)
loss of energy (no)
feelings of worthlessness (yes)
diminished ability to think (often)
recurrent thoughts of suicide (yes)

Depression should have a blacker name: 'melancholia' is better, a shrinking of the spirit.

8th March Rehearsals continue to be fun, and I love constructing the mechanics of farce. We laugh a lot, but laughter in rehearsals isn't always a good sign with a comedy.

10th March I had a letter from Dad's cousin, who says there's £34 in a marriage settlement of 1873 of my great-grand-parents. He tells a story about visiting my grandfather, who molested Charles's fiancée in the gooseberry patch, then showed him his bedroom, which had a sort of animal skin on the floor. 'Viceroy, best damn pony I ever had.' He also remembers Dad slipping off the sofa, pissed, and Mum saying: 'Bloody fool, I warned him not to do that.'

11th March *The Birthday Party* is a good production, but un-evenly cast. Sam [*Mendes*] reminds me of how people describe the young Peter Hall: boundless energy, puppyish charm, great cap-ability, daunting self-confidence, canny strategist. Perhaps it's an act, but if it is it's a remarkably complete one.

16th March I saw Complicité's new show, *Lucie Cabrol*, at Riverside. It's excellent work, slightly too ostentatious perhaps, but really achieved and unmistakably its own thing. Also Terry Johnson's play *Dead Funny*, which is funny and touching, even if occasionally you have a sense of the diagram of people's emotional lives instead of the reality of them.

20th March The last *Absence*. I was very sorry to see it go, and I still can't see it through the eyes of its detractors.

21st March   I went out to dinner with Ian McKellen. Ian and I talked about whether he might succeed me if and when I decide to go. I don't think he can quite bear the prospect. He's tempted, but I think horrified by seeing at close quarters what it involves – a total loss of liberty, sacrifice of freelance acting life, gathering anxiety as well as respect. We saw Neil [Kinnock] in the restaurant, who was very cheery. Glenys wasn't there. 'Out campaigning,' he said. Sad for him, good for her.

22nd March   *The Birthday Party* has opened well, Harold seems fairly pleased, and I'm gearing up for the opening of *Johnny*. People who have seen the run-throughs have enjoyed it, some extravagantly. But that's a world away from the Olivier and an audience of 1,200.

25th March   *Johnny* starts previewing today. I've just had a letter from the Editor of *Burke's Peerage* (!?) complaining about accents in British productions of American plays and ending up quoting a reviewer in 1942 saying that *Johnny on the Spot* well deserved the short shrift that the public and the critics allotted it. That's encouraging. We've decided to do *Oh, What a Lovely War!*. I love this show and wonder only if it's right for us here, now. Do people under the age of forty have any connection to the First War?

27th March   Previews are OK but only OK, and that won't be enough for the critics, and this one *needs* them. Tom [Stoppard] thinks we've done the play well but still believes that the play isn't good enough. There are few laughs in the first thirty minutes – after that it's fine, and by the end the audience have a grudging affection for the play. But it's not enough.

1st April   Came down to Glos last night with Lu and a friend, trying to hold on to the last hours of happiness with *Johnny*, which has been fun in spite of all anxieties. I knew at the party afterwards, when I asked someone if they'd enjoyed it and they smiled ruefully and said no, that we hadn't pulled it off.

2nd April   It's hailing now, thick white stair-rods and mothballs settling on the lawn. Reviews predictably terrible. Ben Hecht's book describes the opening of *Johnny* on Broadway. The day after the

opening he looked at the unanimously bad reviews, put his head on his wife's shoulder and wept. When I read that, I had a precise premonition that it would be the same for me. It's a huge public embarrassment. Later: the sun's come out and everything is washed with a clear golden light.

3rd April   The news from the front line is so bad that I can't even bring myself to speak to Stephen at first. Uniformly and universally bad. This is probably the worst failure I've had at the NT – and I could foresee it. I saw it clearly when I was in New York and I tried to get out of it, but everyone persuaded me to go on. I suppose because they believed I could bring it off. Well, I couldn't and didn't. Still – *en avant!* as Maria (and Tennessee) used to say.

5th April   David [*Hare*] consolingly (and generously) says that *Johnny* is the victim of zeitgeist – wrong play at wrong time. He says the reviews are respectful, much more in sorrow than in anger, no one crowing for my blood. Jonathan Lynn says he had the same response when he did *Three Men and a Horse*, which then won Best Comedy Award. Well, that won't happen. I speak to Stephen Wood, who says we have two and a half good reviews.

8th April   Solitude, calm, optimism. It's a glorious morning, a clear bright lemony sun which makes me feel light-hearted. I have breakfast, put out nuts for the birds, then work on *Traviata*. Verdi: '*La Traviata* requires a singer with an elegant figure, who is young and sings passionately.' Now afternoon and the rain is sheeting down like thin muslin. After rain the landscape looks laundered.

20th April   Joan Littlewood has refused us the rights of *O WAL W*. I sent her a card on her eightieth birthday. I got a pc back: 'Thanks for your card, Richard. I really don't know what you're up to. Whatever it is you'd do better to bomb that building. *I* had to put up with an *old* slum in London, yours need never have been. JL'

22nd April   *Les Parents Terribles* has started previewing and enjoyably louche. It's good, really good. We've had to delay the press night because Sheila Gish is ill, but it'll be more than fine – Jude

Law shines with an irresistible innocence and guileless sexuality, and Sean [*Mathias*] has cooked the whole thing very adroitly.

23rd April   I've hated the last week in the theatre. I can't work properly as a director, I feel hemmed in on all sides. I went to a meeting at the Royal Opera House (the opera house!!!) and felt liberated simply because I had no responsibility other than for the production. At the NT I feel oppressed by the building, the administration, the expectations, and I find it so difficult to concentrate on the work. I envy the monocular vision of freelance directors. Bergman on a fellow director: 'He was well-read, reckless and manically vain – a combination not to be despised in a theatre director.'

24th April   I talked to Mary today about the problems with Lasdun, his opposition to any change. She's very worried about it becoming public: 'We'll be set on at cocktail parties and while we're at the ribbon counter at Harvey Nichols.'

25th April   Meeting with the Board to discuss funding the redevelopment. We have to grasp the opportunity to renovate, refurbish the building – even to rectify inherent defects. The money is there (from the Lottery) if we can get it. If we don't do it now the building *will* decay and be unusable (unlicensable) within ten years. It's not at the expense of the art – except that it's going to take a monumental amount of energy to push the plan uphill. Then the start of rehearsals for *Sweet Bird*. I wish I hadn't just done another play set in Louisiana, but I don't feel cowed. Rather the opposite: the sheer abandon and bravura of the writing is inspiring. And I've got the cast for it.

26th April   I went to see *My Night with Reg* [*Kevin Elyot*] at the Royal Court which flirts with, but avoids, all the dangers of the 'gay' play. It's very touching and well observed, on the edge of sentimentality, underscored by the dignifying tragedy of AIDS, which can easily be used just to sanction bad art – like Oliver Stone using Barber's Adagio in *Platoon*. The danger is of making compassion a form of entertainment. This was beautifully acted and directed (by Roger Michell). There was a long scene with two naked men which made me think how ridiculously unprotected men are without their clothes. Such odd dangly bits.

29th April Denys Lasdun continues to abuse me in print, calling me a 'barbarian', saying I want to turn the NT into a supermarket – this because we want to move the bookshop *out* of the foyer where it was arbitrarily plonked in the '70s without any reference to Lasdun, restore the foyer as it was, and re-site it. I think of sending this to Denys: 'In the seventeenth century the cultivated Roger North found the stupendous Romanesque pillars of Durham Cathedral evidence of the work of an "extraordinarily high-spirited barbarian".'

30th April In the past two weeks I've been accused in the press of doing too many new plays and neglecting the seventeenth/eighteenth century and foreign plays, *and* of not doing enough for new writing.

1st May Glos, glorious weather. Exhilarating break, all the more so for being a retreat from the theatre. But how could I live without the theatre: I wouldn't be able to define (or afford) my leisure.

3rd May Peter Brook arrived with *The Man Who*, and I'm keen that we don't let him down, that he doesn't perceive this as a play-factory. To me it's never not a theatre, it's just an impossibly large one, or three.

9th May Irene Worth did her Edith Wharton platform. I was very pleased I'd asked her to do it. 'My heart is full,' she said to me and thanked me for letting her be part of the theatre. Her show had brilliant passages, none more so than a wonderfully moving and erotic account of discovering happiness in sex late in life. She ended with the story of a seventy-five-year-old goldfish which she illustrated with fluttering hands encrusted with gold rings.

10th May *The Man Who* has opened hugely successfully. I asked Peter if everything was all right with his visit, if he'd been properly looked after. 'Yes,' he said, 'everything's fine. The only thing that depresses me is the thought that you have to run this giant organisation.' We talked of many things, including making mistakes with the press. He said he'd lost two good friends that way. He once said in an interview that Orson Welles – 'a very dear friend' – had taken on the impossible with Shakespeare by directing and acting the leading part and had a noble failure. Welles never forgave him. 'Like all fat men

he was very touchy. Paranoid.' And Peter lost another friend when he
was asked why so many writers were driven by left-wing ideology,
and said it was impossible to think of a writer who was driven by
right-wing ideology, unless you counted religion in which case,
Graham Greene. Greene was livid and wouldn't speak to Peter
again. We spoke of the appetite of the media for showbiz stories.
He said the reason he'd left was not because he anticipated being
vilified, but he realised that if he'd stayed his turn would have come.
He said that in the late '60s there was none of this media attention.
We talked about opera, the need to make singers act with detail and
speed. How slow a piece of music is compared to thought and
speech.

12th May   We had a really enjoyable dinner in an empty Mezzanine to celebrate Jean Kalman's marriage to Kyoko – Peter Brook,
Deborah Warner, Billy Paterson and Hildegard Bechtler, Fiona Shaw
and Bob Crowley. We started singing folk songs – Fiona and Billy in
the Gaelic, mine half-Gaelic, Hildegard a German child's song and
Kyoko a Japanese lullaby with beautiful, strange, heart-stopping
intervals.

15th May   Sunday in the country. I never knew such greens
existed: black- and orange-green of the yews, verdigris of the Chinese
juniper, pale lime, luminous green green rowan, olive-green oak, and
the wild confusion of messy curling curving cotton-wool leafy
shapes. Ian McK. is staying, and last night in the sitting room he
performed the one-man show that he's doing in New York. I felt
overwhelmed as I sat alone a few feet away from him and he turned
on his astonishing virtuosity to its full force.

16th May   In the past two days *Sweet Bird* has become intractable,
the show we're doing with Complicité has become very precarious
(contract impasse), I might have to cancel *The Children's Hour*
(budget impasse) and *Pericles* (incipient catastrophe), and the
box-office prospects look grim. But the reviews for *Les Parents
Terribles* are excellent.

17th May   We've turned a corner: rehearsals are good today. The
play is better than I thought and Clare Higgins and Rob Knepper are

remarkable. Dinner with Peter Brook. I'm fascinated by the way in which he's able to be a working director and yet at the same time remain above the struggle – or appear to.

21st May   *Pericles* has opened in the Olivier. Phyllida [*Lloyd*]'s done a production that's a brave folly, and it's been disastrously and punitively received, perceived as flashy and self-regarding. We've managed to recover the Complicité show and *The Children's Hour* [*Lillian Hellman*], but at what price? I think we could be in for a box-office loss of £1.5m., giving us a deficit of – what, £500K. I *know* that every year I predict a box-office haemorrhage at this time of year, and every year so far we've arrived at the end of the financial year on an even keel, but this year I just can't see it. But we have hope of generous sponsorship from Carol Shorenstein Hays. Roger Chapman told me that her mother has just died leaving her half of California. 'Associate yourself with quality,' she said to Carol on her deathbed.

27th May   Really gripping run-through of *Sweet Bird*. I try to keep a sceptical distance from it. The real difficulty is trying to keep both parts of the Rob [*Knepper*] and the Clare [*Higgins*] equation together. When they're really doing it together they're fantastic, but sometimes Clare, however remarkable, insulates herself from him and he goes into freefall.

31st May   Feeling better for having faced the possible net loss at the end of the year of £300K. I don't know where the hits are going to come from. I feel stoical – or is it indifference? I find myself looking for plays for actors: I'm trying to get Tony Sher to play Iago and Fiona Shaw to be in *The Relapse*. But who to direct?

1st June   We take Lu to Heathrow to see her off on her round-the-world trip, trying (unsuccessfully) for an air of diffidence. We stand at the bottom of an escalator, straining to look cheerful, watching her disappear into the unknown.

3rd June   *Rutherford and Son* [*Githa Sowerby*] has opened. It's very fastidiously directed by Katie [*Mitchell*]. Bob Peck is wonderful, and so is Brid Brennan. There's an admirable (or enviable) refusal in

Katie to appease the audience which results in the show being slightly underlit and occasionally celebrating the beauty of silence at the expense of momentum, even if the self-celebrating austerity has lessened during previews.

12th June   I spoke to Lu in the Pacific this morning. She's in paradise or on Paradise Island, staying in a hut on the beach. The operator said: 'Call for Mister Eyre from Miss Lucy.' Sue told the operator I was in the shower, the operator told Lu I was in the toilet. Lu sounded great. I miss her but am very happy that she's very happy.

16th June   *Sweet Bird* opens tonight. Michael Codron says it's going to be a hit. I wish we didn't have to deal in that hit/miss currency, but it's in the nature of *any* theatre whose economy is so dependent on box office. And however much any of us disguise it, we're all creatures of the theatre's Darwinian universe.

17th June   Sue couldn't be at the first night of *Sweet Bird*, as she's filming *Pride and Prejudice*, and her absence made me feel unlucky, but I had a good-luck charm in my pocket: a pearl tie pin that was given to me by Charles Bowen when he saw my film of *Suddenly Last Summer*. He'd directed the premiere on Broadway, and had been given it by Tennessee Williams. It went well – Clare magnificent, but at the end the flaming torches refused to light, so the final image of the lynch mob was at half cock.

23rd June   I spoke at a Music and Arts Department Seminar at the BBC about TV and the theatre. They were all young – well mainly under thirty-five and knew very little about the theatre, but they weren't dismissive, in fact very good-natured, but it's just not their culture.

24th June   It looks certain that Tony Blair will become Leader of the Labour Party. Poor Neil: John Smith died just when Fleet Street wanted him to. Mary told a story at the F and GP about her brother Randolph going to Althorp and commenting on some beautiful chairs. When he left the room Lord Spencer said: 'Who was the feller who talked about my things?'

26th June   All's well with *Sweet Bird*. On the Peter Hall index of buying grace with a success, about six months this time. Denys Lasdun told me that his building was being insulted, vandalised and mutilated. He said that our plan to remove the walkway – which is self-evidently (and provably) an afterthought since it *entirely* blocks the view of the river from the Lyttelton circle level – was like removing a pediment of St Paul's.

27th June   Dinner organised by David Puttnam to persuade Gordon Brown of the need to subsidise the arts if/when they get in. Melvyn Bragg, Stephen Daldry and myself. It's all very cordial, the wine flows freely, Gordon's very enthusiastic, and Stephen comes back home with me for a drink. We grab a cab (his bike in the back), go home and after we've shared most of a bottle of brandy and reformed the *entire* British theatre and government, he weaves off, defying gravity.

28th June   Meeting with Solti to discuss the score. He says he hasn't done his homework, which makes me feel better, even though I have. He opens his score for Act 1 and the bindings crack. He talks about the beauty of the unmarked score, untouched, virgin. We talk about the Prelude; he's worried that I'll distract from the music. He plays it through on the piano, me propping up the score and turning the pages. He talks about fathers and daughters, about his vertigo, the EEC, the rise of China, and, of course, the score. Also about the 'mediocracy' of the English music scene. 'Only Simon Rattle is a musician of the really first rank.' He hopes he can get the ROH orchestra to play well. 'We must follow Verdi's markings. As a young man I thought I knew better.'

9th July   It's hot, sticky, torrid, then thunderous and threatening. We went to Glenys's fiftieth birthday party, which was very jolly. Met Tony Blair, who seems like an amiable, intelligent young academic until he smiles – then he's a politician. He says we've met before. I know we haven't and I say so. But he says that I came to his school when he was in the sixth-form at Fettes and I was at the Lyceum Theatre. His class had come to see *The Crucible*, which he'd loved. Apparently I'd talked about the theatre, and I'd shaken hands with him and made him want to be an actor. He talked of the

impression that the play had made on him, said it had woken him up
to the latent tyranny of a repressive society and the dangers incurred
in dissent. I wish I could say that I'd spotted the future leader of the
Labour Party among the desks of the sixth-form at Fettes School.

13th July I've been to New York for four days. I saw *Passion*
[*Stephen Sondheim*], which belied its title, and Stephen's production
of *An Inspector Calls* which, to my surprise, really engaged the
audience, who were confronted by a polemic against the free market
and social Darwinism. In fact they took to it with rapture. David
Hare's theory is that all successful plays on B'way are left-wing – it
acts as a covert poultice for liberal sympathies. Also saw Nick
[*Hytner*]'s *Carousel* at the Lincoln Center Theater, which is still
dazzling but with less heart and no Joanna Riding. I went to Sardi's
bar with Bob [*Crowley*]:

> BARMAN: Aren't you in the theatre?
> BOB: (certain of his fame after winning the Tony Award) Yes, I
> am.
> BARMAN: I know – you're Elton John.
> BOB: (shocked) Well, at least my hair's my own.

Bob heard an exchange on the night of the Tony Awards between
Stephen Daldry and Diana Rigg. Diana: 'God, I need a drink.'
Stephen gave her one. 'And a fag.' He gave her one. 'And some
lipstick.' He gave her his. 'Sorry, wrong colour,' said Diana. The next
day I was in a bookshop and an assistant came up to me. 'You're a
star on TV, aren't you?' My denial merely reassured him.

16th July Glos. I've not taken Prozac for two weeks, and I feel I've
never been happier. I feel suspended in a bubble of true peace. On his
deathbed John Steinbeck was asked by his wife when he had been
happiest. Write it down, he said. Both wrote down the same thing:
'Somerset contentment 1959'. I've been weeding, mowing, watering,
dead-heading and now I see the point of gardening – putting your
signature on a little patch of earth.

20th July Lunch with Jonathan Miller to talk opera. Jonathan's
directed fifty operas. His advice is that there's no mystery about

opera – just go with the sound and make sure the singers aren't facing upstage. He talks a great deal about conductors and their sense of music – invariably learnt as a child and insulated from any other medium, like life or art or books. He says opera can sometimes be a glorious combination of music and movement – skittering, whirling in unison, they sing at you, and what's more you get paid for it. I always enjoy hearing Jonathan talk. Once in Nottingham he came to dinner and as he was leaving I asked him something about blood circulation; for an hour he explained the history and science of the circulation of blood. He knows more or less everything about more or less everything. I once saw him on TV explaining why you could fart on a plane because the frequency of the engine coincided with the frequency of the average fart. Boulez on opera: 'I've always been troubled by the basic convention – why should these people be singing? It amazes me how easily most people accept that strange idea – it seems as oddly ritualised as Kabuki and Noh seem to other people.'

29th July   The first preview of *Broken Glass*. It went well, the audience applauding long after the lights went up. The acting was excellent (Ken Stott, Henry Goodman particularly), the play cumulatively good, but an awkward setting that forces clumsy scene changes where seamlessness is called for. For once, with a play of Miller's, the struggle is about the difficulty and the possibility of a woman taking control of her own life, 'that moment when, in my eyes, a man differentiates himself from every other man, that moment when out of a sky full of stars he fixes on one star', he says in his autobiography.

30th July   *Le Cid* has opened well. It made a substantial leap from the first preview, which was forthright but slightly dull. Usually Corneille seems like something one *ought* to admire but can't, but Jonathan [*Kent*]'s done it with immense conviction and elegance. Cocteau: 'Invisibility seems to me a sine qua non of elegance. Elegance ceases to exist once it is noticed.'

3rd August   Sue is filming *P and P* and I'm staying with John and Penny [*Mortimer*] in Italy and reading Cyril Connolly: 'Who would not rather than the best of reviewers be the worst of novelists?' We

went to visit the best of novelists near Arezzo: Muriel Spark. I thought she'd be spiky but she was generous even about C.P. Snow, Jeanette Winterson and Silvio Berlusconi. She has an impish smile and, although pale and in pain, a great deal of energy. She's writing a new novel about unemployment. She claims that snakes are dropped from helicopters in order to keep down the mouse population in Italy. We don't believe her, although it's the reverse of the (true) story of a man who was swimming in the sea being scooped up by a helicopter in a giant bucket and dropped into a forest fire.

5th August Went to Grossetto to see the Soltis. We arrived and Valerie said Georg was down on the beach. He was walking in the sea, the waves above his knees, wholly absorbed, silently conducting the Tchaikovsky he's about to do in Salzburg. He has a big bruise from playing tennis, which he does every day. At lunch Valerie tells me about Pavarotti coming to the house and cooking a meal: he brought his own cooking pot and used a litre of olive oil, a litre of wine and a kilo of parmesan. Georg says that Pavarotti couldn't read music when they first worked together: he'd mark the score with coloured arrows – red for up, green for down. I talk to a musicologist from Bologna who says the libretto of La Traviata is a mechanism like a watch and mustn't be tampered with, and to the widow of Calvino, who is v. nice and v. Anglophile. I tell the plot of La Traviata to Claudia Solti, daughter who wants to be an actress, who has never seen or heard it.

6th August Two views of conservatism – Harry Truman: 'When there is a choice between conservatives and those in pragmatic approximation thereto, the voters will always opt for the real thing.' And Nancy Mitford: 'You know, being a conservative is much more restful . . . whereas communism seems to eat up all one's life and energy.' Conservatism is a product of frivolity, of refusing to be committed to anything.

7th August Back from Italy. We have to make next year a year of startling plays, productions and performances. I've got to give more discipline and order to my work. That's the key. Inspiration isn't the fire, it's the breath. I'm reading a biography of Constable, who opposed the setting up of the National Gallery: 'There will be an end

of the art in poor old England . . . the manufacturers of pictures are then made the criterion of perfection instead of nature.' Also: 'The art of seeing nature is a thing almost as much to be acquired as the art of reading Egyptian hieroglyphs.'

24th August   I saw Robert Lepage's show [7 Streams of the River Ota] in Edinburgh. It's in its early stages, some of it uncharacteristically clumsy but intermittently touching and inventive. I sat behind Victor Spinetti [*actor*] who said that he'd tried to persuade Joan Littlewood not to be so stupid about preventing the NT from doing *Oh What a Lovely War!*. He told her: 'It would be so good if Jane (i.e. Jane Eyre, i.e. me) was going to direct it.' 'But he's not,' said Joan. I got the bus back into town with a clutch of London critics all discussing their hotels and expenses.

30th August   I read *Utopia* for the radio today. I found it very difficult – all the awkwardness of being an actor and few of the skills. I found it hard to characterise, hard not to render it all as a dispassionate, slightly acerbic, slightly melancholic persona, but the director, Michael Earley, made me see more in it, or at least made me give more *to* it. Virginia Woolf: 'The truth is that writing is the profound pleasure, and being read is the superficial.' And reading it aloud is a bit of both.

5th September   Heard this of an actress friend of a friend. Her boyfriend (a photographer) was in Prague with her when she heard her brother had died. She went home leaving him with her credit cards. When the statement came she saw a charge for £2,000. What's this? she said. Two days of my time, said the photographer.

6th September   Lunch with Maggie Smith. She was in good health, fairly benign, quite blunt about her career prospects. She's about to do *Three Tall Women* [*Edward Albee*] with Anastasia Hille. 'I didn't do her any favours casting Anastasia in *Macbeth*,' I said. 'No,' said Maggie, 'you certainly didn't.'

9th September   Call from Charles Kaye [*Solti's assistant*] about Solti having 'certain concerns'. I talk to Solti later: he tells me that the Prelude is a 'masterpiece' and he wants *nothing* to happen during it. I

say let's look at the projection – Violetta as a child, sold from her Normandy farm at the age of thirteen – we have in mind: is it that difficult to listen and look?

12th September   Lunch with Walter Hays, the father of Carol Shorenstein Hays. He tells me that whatever his daughter may have given me to expect she will not be able (allowed?) to give money on a not-for-profit basis to a Britsh institution. I feel like a suitor being warned off by the horsewhip.

14th September   First night of *Tosca* at ENO. It's very bitty, with no fluency, a ragbag of styles. The atmosphere is a bit like a bullfight – will he/she get gored. Dennis Marks [*Director ENO*] comes on stage to tell us that the tenor has an 'allergy' and craves our indulgence. We don't give it. I talk to Frank Johnson who Anna Ford says 'knows everything about opera'. The audience is full of people who know everything about opera. It's like a pub after a football match.

16th September   George Fenton tells me about doing a session with the LPO. He shouted at them to be quiet, then apologised to the recording engineer. 'Don't worry,' he said, 'Solti was in here earlier in the week and when they were playing fortissimo he was shouting above the orchestra: 'Play, you bastards, play!'

18th September   Lunch with Grey Gowrie. He's slightly dishevelled, slightly distracted, dandyish and dilettante-ish, and rather bored already by the Arts Council. He said that it was an irony of the '80s that the quality he most associated with Mrs Thatcher was thrift. He spoke of 'unionist' thrift, of Calvinistic virtue in N. Ireland as a result of the Troubles. He advised me not to expect any extra money from the Arts Council and thought it should act more like a charitable foundation than a welfare agency.

23rd September   *The Children's Hour* has opened. Hugely successful on Broadway in 1934, it was banned in Britain because of the lesbianism of the two schoolmistresses, which actually turns out to be a false accusation. The British theatre was ossified for decades by censorship, but I'm not sure if the case for revival is made, even

though it's very well acted – by Harriet Walter, Clare Higgins and Emily Watson. *Two Weeks with the Queen* [*Mary Morris; adapted from a novel by Morris Gleitzman*] has also opened. It's really charming; one of the very few examples of 'plays for young people' which is genuinely funny, about something, doesn't patronise and genuinely appeals to 'young people'. Of course it's Australian.

25th September To Johannesburg. The view of a city from the air is often the most reliable: London is neat, green, quaint, almost fetishistically cultivated; Johannesburg is dominated by Brobding-nagian dust mounds from the gold mines that gave the city its reason to exist, which loom over the strips of concrete tower-blocks, the matchbox shanties scattered by a careless giant, and the fat mansions with their emerald necklaces of swimming pools. I was met at the airport by John Kani [*actor*] and Barney Simon [*director*]. Barney took me on an impromptu tour of the city. We passed a middle-class suburb which reminded me of Golders Green. Johannesburg is one of the world's wealthiest cities, but its wealth is concealed behind high walls and hedges in suburbs. Barney points out a water tower from which snipers tried to kill Joe Slovo, who's now Minister of Housing. We stopped outside Slovo's heavily fortified house. B. told stories about him, his Stalinism now redeemed by the new government, his pragmatism and his new young wife.

We go to Yeoville, a mixed-race suburb, quite Haight-Ashbury. Of course *real* integration is going to depend on introducing an equi-table economy and J'burg isn't the most conducive atmosphere for that. The poverty is more visible: in the townships, the shacks on the edge of the city, and the tower blocks in the centre. 'It's not a graceful landscape,' says Barney, 'but I love it; it's a landscape of people.' Romania after the Revolution wasn't unlike Johannesburg; the institutional oppression had been removed, but what remained was poverty, resentment, and endemic violence. 'Don't put your hand out of the window,' Barney said to me in the car. 'You'll get your hand cut off at the wrist to get your watch.'

We go to the Market Theatre. All theatres should be like the Market – born out of a particular time and context, out of need, the need to find a place to perform, and the urgent need of a group of actors, writers, and directors to express feelings about the world as they saw it. The theatre is in the old fruit market, a perfectly shaped

auction room, and an ideal metaphor: a place of exchange, meetings, noise, celebration, commerce, activity. In the p.m. we watch Ian McK.'s one-man show there. It's touching and eloquent and gives an exhortation to tolerance and acceptance of common humanity. In the evening we go to an awards ceremony; in between awards there's a sketch about Martina Navratilova being a lesbian. This goes down quite well with the audience, and makes a mockery of all the buoyant assertions of tolerance of Ian's show in the afternoon. John Kani and Winston Ntshone [*actor*] got lifetime achievement awards – the first awards they've received in South Africa. The inference drawn from this was confirmed when a production of *Buddy* was given an award over a show Barney has directed called *Josi Josi*, which had more wit, imagination, truth, and skill than even the *real* Buddy Holly. Actually the award show is better than the Olivier Awards, which don't have gumboot dancers or Peter Dirk Uys, who is S. Africa's Dame Edna. 'Hypocrisy,' he says, 'is the Vaseline of political intercourse.'

26th September   Johannesburg is a Gold Rush town built in 1886 by migrant workers who were cleared from their area after they had served their function. The Dutch settlers lost control of the town in the Boer War to the British, whose mark remains as a mocking irony in the names of the city's districts: Westcliff, Hyde Park, Mayfair, Brixton, Waverley, Sandhurst, Sandown, Hurlingham, Kensington. The Afrikaans accent is very pervasive, as is the mindset – pinched, mean, sharp, percussive – like a knife across a stone. Apartheid is the legacy that's most clearly, and probably indelibly, stamped on the city: genocide by degree. In the Museum of Africa at the back of the Market Theatre is a mock-up of part of a typical hut used to house workers in the gold mines: concrete coops, with bunks barely long enough to stretch out, punctuated by small portholes. It reminds me of Dachau.

27th September   I notice Samantha Fox is doing cabaret in the city but I don't imagine we share the same audience, which includes Nadine Gordimer, who mistook me after Ian's show for Ian. I give my lecture at the Market – about directing plays and directing theatres, about the temptation to look at theatres at other times or in other countries with envy. I've stared, as sick with envious lust as a teenager, at the theatre created by La Mama Company in New

York, and the Moscow Art Theatre, and Ariane Mnouchkine's Théâtre du Soleil, and Giorgio Strehler's Piccolo Theatre, and the Berliner Ensemble in the early '60s, and Peter Brook's Bouffe du Nord in Paris, and the Bulandra Company of Bucharest, and the Cinoherni Theatre of Prague, and the Kantor Company from Cracow – and the Market Theatre from Johannesburg. But I've always known that it's as futile to imagine that I could re-create those pieces of work as it was for me to have imagined that I could end up in the arms of Brigitte Bardot. It's not a matter of whether I have the talent or not to do those things: it's a matter of time and place and context. Whatever else we do in the theatre, we have to try to show ourselves to ourselves, not borrow our identity from other people's lives. We can dress up in the clothes of other people, we can pillage the plays of other languages, but we must always do it in our own voices, not mimicking either the people we would like to be, or the people we feel we *ought* to be. A Sowetan: 'Shakespeare is sawdust for us in Soweto.'

28th September I'm on a flight from J'burg to put on *Racing Demon* in Los Angeles – another city with a short history, built around a gold mine (Hollywood) – and it could be a sister to Johannesburg: its architecture, its insulated suburbs, its violence, its extreme wealth, its extreme poverty, and its de facto racial segregation. I'm reading Alan [*Bennett*]'s Diaries. He's elegant and eloquent and funny and never, ever, dull. His persona is quite studied – mild curmudgeon, generous only in spite of himself, a bit arch and wholly self-aware. *Not* 'nice' (as he reminds us) but indignantly decent.

3rd October As always I'm jet-lagged and watching TV in the early morning. From a movie set on Easter Island: 'I'm busy, I've got chicken entrails to read.' And contestant in a beauty contest: 'It's very important to have the right self-identity,' and Nelson Mandela at the UN in New York, who pledged himself to rid South Africa of racism, sexism, poverty and famine, and I wished that he could live for ever.

4th October Party last night for us at Lew Wasserman's, Crown Prince of Hollywood. He (or his wife) is a friend of Lois Sieff [*NT Board member*]. Handsome (not vulgar) Bauhaus house, some very

good paintings – inc. Matisse. Michael Bryant was very excited to
meet Suzanne Pleshette; I was very excited to meet Kirk Douglas,
who didn't want to talk about his films, just his novels. At dinner I
talked to Lew W. about his life; at least half of what he told me must
be true. He talked about his days as a music agent – at one stage he
managed over 2,000 bands and spent the evenings in New York or
Chicago going from club to club to hear his clients. I had visions of a
world of Legs Diamond and Meyer Lansky and said: 'You must have
met a lot of criminals in your work.' 'Richard,' he said, absolutely
straight-faced, 'I have never met with a criminal in my life.'

7th October   Plane from LA. The first night was fun, buzzy if
bemused audience and an excellent performance. I don't think I felt
as foreign doing a workshop with directors from the townships in
South Africa as I did sitting through my production of an English
play about four South London vicars in a theatre on the edge of
Hollywood Boulevard.

9th October   I drove to Oxford to see Lu. She was pleased to see
me but slightly embarrassed at the excess of parental visits. We had a
meal; she told me she wanted to be a writer, although not of fiction.

10th October   I'm trying to plan the theatre as far ahead as
possible, and my own life. I think that I can do another three years
at the NT without becoming stale and diffident, letting people down
or getting found out. I want to do David [*Hare*]'s new play, Tom
[*Stoppard*]'s new play, di Filippo's *La Grande Magia*, the *Le Roi
S'amuse* with Tony [*Harrison*] and maybe another Tennessee Williams. And before I leave, the play I *have* to do is *Lear*. I've asked Ian
Holm if he'd play it. I think he's ready for it; he hasn't said yes and he
hasn't said no, but I'm hopeful. He says how do you play an eighty-
year-old man with manic energy? I say: meet Georg Solti.

12th October   Mary says (of something Jocelyn Stevens said he'd
do): 'Never believe a proposal made in the 400 Club – unless it's
followed up by a phone call in the morning.' She says that it must be
like running from fresh water to salt for me to direct opera – or was it
the other way round?

16th October   David's finished his play and promises it for next w/end. He's thrilled and says he cried when he finished it. Is this a good sign?

17th October   Two days of working with Solti. He's very tired from his Tokyo trip. He talked about the pollution, the cost of bringing the Chicago Symphony Orchestra, his $3,000-a-day hotel room, and the nobility of *Traviata*. We went right through the score, at the end of which he said to me: 'Well, we'll make something of this. After all, we're both talented fellows.'

18th October   I did a platform for the paperback of my book last night, quizzed by Allison Pearson, who was attractive and matily acerbic. A long queue for signing, most of whom said please don't leave the National. Alan Bennett said that someone had once asked him to sign: 'To Clare. Sorry about last night. It won't happen again.' Allison confirmed my feelings that her generation (thirties) aren't interested in the theatre: *too* fragile, too vulnerable, too unreliable. Have we lost our audience for ever? Going to the theatre just seems irrelevant to a whole generation, who'd as soon get their feet scorched by walking on burning coals.

19th October   I start rehearsals for *La Traviata* tomorrow. Karen [*Stone, assistant director*] called to say that Frank Lopardo [*tenor*] had had an accident on the way to the airport and hurt his back but would be on his way tomorrow. Is it starting – what Declan calls the turning-up-at-rehearsals-as-if-you're-shopping-at-Harrods syndrome?

20th October   Rehearsals start. Angela [*Georghiu*] is fifteen minutes late, but charming on arrival. I have lunch with her in the canteen. She says that Nucci's acting is the worst she's ever seen. Nucci isn't present but the other baritone is good if absurdly young. I tell them they're not going to sing for a few days and we talk through the score – like a play. The only awkwardness in the day is Angela's discovery that she is supposed to sing the whole score, no cuts. Nobody has told her, not Nicholas Payne [*Director of Opera, ROH*], nor Jeremy Isaacs, nor Peter Katona [*casting director*], nor Solti. 'Why should I sing all the verses of '*Fors'e lui*' just because Verdi has

written them? Nobody else ever sang them.' I'm amazed at the cavalier attitude of singers in cutting the score to suit them.

21st October   I'm in the ROH canteen at lunchtime. A chorus member who looks like my auntie if I had one comes up to me: 'We're very annoyed with you for not having us in Act 1.' Terry Edwards tells me that one disenfranchised chorus member had said: 'I've been singing in Act 1 of *Traviata* since 1942.'

22nd October   I rang Hayden Phillips [*Permanent Secretary Department National Heritage*] to ask (not that it's anything to do with me, etc etc) if there are plans afoot for replacing Mary as Chairman when she retires. Hayden confesses that it's slipped his notice and have I any suggestions. I suggest Christopher Hogg [*Chairman Reuters and Courtaulds*]. Good idea, he says. Any more?

23rd October   We rehearse the Brindisi, then the First Act duet, then '*Fors'e lui*', which Angela sings without the second verse. I tell her what Solti has said: that there's a nice way to proceed and a nasty way. I say if she goes, I go. We're in a nuclear state, I say. We must negotiate, not make a pre-emptive strike. A pause. We do it, OK, says Angela.

25th October   The chorus have been having costume fittings and are pleased with them, which makes my life easier. Bob [*Crowley*] told one of them – who looked like a prison warder – you look so attractive, so much shape. No one's ever said that to me, she said. I like the chorus: they're amiable, quite generous and willing to work.

30th October   Ten days in and I've blocked the big scenes. The singers have no rehearsal method. The whole time I feel as if I'm holding back an express train – the music – in order to be able to introduce some detail. The singers aren't recalcitrant, they just have no empirical process. It's random, at the mercy of the dictatorship of the music. It's all about timing, about the moments between the notes – the pauses, the fermatas, the orchestral breaks. I heard Barry Tuckwell, the horn player, on the radio talking about how few conductors understand the psychology of orchestral players, and how when accompanying a soloist it's all about anticipating the

'bottom of the beat'. There's a row between Frank and Angela. Frank started *'Di miei bollenti spiriti'* and stopped to query the tempo, Angela said he should sing what he wanted. Phillippe [*deputy conductor*] said it was what Solti wanted, Frank said it was none of her business. Tears from A. and sulkiness from F. But we ran the act, and the next day I got the two of them together and said they must make up their quarrel. They did and hugged a lot, which they seemed to enjoy. Angela's febrile, a hot, even feverish, little bird. Intelligent and instinctively shrewd but childlike and very vulnerable. The stakes are absurdly high for her.

31st October   Morning with the chorus, Act II. One of them asks how big the bets are in the gambling. I say about £4,000. 'Or a day's work for a tenor,' says a wag in the chorus. Then back to the NT for a Board meeting where we speculate about the future of the theatre – small and large 'T'. I feel as if I'm repeating myself.

4th November   We ran the first act for the first time. When we reached *'Fors'e lui'* Angela looked at me defiantly. Don't make me do this, her look said. I nodded: do it. When she started the aria the chorus stopped rustling and whispering, and there was an absolute purity of concentration, unbroken even by the movement of the chorus shuffling from the back of the room to the front where they could see her more clearly. We watched breathlessly, awed as she climbed, like an unroped climber on a vertical rock face, from note to note, phrase to phrase, verse to verse. When she finished there was a silence, followed by an earthquake of applause, and as the applause went on and on and on, Angela stood motionless, saturated by tears and astonished at her own genius. I've never had such a moment in a rehearsal room.

5th November   I'm spinning three wheels at the moment – the theatre, *Traviata*, and preparing for the film of *Absence*. I'm worried about my stamina. I'm also worried about the start of the National Lottery. It's just a further Treasury tax; if you play it you'll now be taxed three times. It's a massive monument to the government's bad faith. They don't have the courage to subsidise the arts properly, so they hide behind the Lottery. In the long run the arts will suffer because it'll be assumed that we're all on the gravy train, and

although there'll be money for capital expenditure there won't be any
revenue money until it's too late.

6th November   I read David's play [Skylight] last night and found
it very affecting. It has its heart on its sleeve, and deals with things
that matter: i.e. how you live your life. And it's funny. David's wildly
anxious about it, about how or why or whether it should go on at the
NT. Of course I can only argue that it should.

Reading David Sylvester's interviews with Francis Bacon: 'Do you
think there's any point talking about art at all? It's always a
fascinating subject because people reveal themselves talking about
art . . . Pavlova was right when somebody asked her what she meant
when she was dancing . . . and she said: "Well, if I could tell you, I
wouldn't dance it."'

7th November   Solti joins rehearsals today. Music all day in the
chorus room. Nucci also joins from the Met, jet-lagged. Solti says
he's tired and out of practice; he hasn't worked for ten days. He picks
on each singer in turn and examines a bar, almost at random.

8th November   Solti and I work together in the rehearsal room –
'collaborators', he says – on the second verse of the cabaletta at the
end of Act II scene 1, trying to make something live out of essentially
dramatically inert material.

Alice's Adventures Under Ground [Christopher Hampton] opened
tonight. It's elusive, so nearly something but not quite there. Christopher needed to take it further as did Martha [*Clarke, director and
choreographer*]. For such a wonderfully expressive and inventive
choreographer she's been strangely restrained. Is it the restraint of
changing from dance to theatre? I know *exactly* the feeling going
from theatre to opera: you're never quite sure-footed, never quite
confident of the syntax of the new medium.

9th November   We run the whole show for Solti without the
chorus. He's late, in a bad temper, bangs out a tempo on the piano
for the accompanist, stops the singers in the first act for a moment,
then settles down. I have to restrain him in the gambling scene when
the girls get the wrong accents with their heels in the gypsy dance. He
conducts with his hands – long elegant strong fingers with a slight

upcurve when the whole palm is extended, like a bird's wing, a kestrel perhaps. At the end of Act III he's in tears. Well, we all are, but he keeps saying: 'I can't speak, I can't speak. How can I conduct this?'

10th November First stage and piano rehearsal. Panic. An oceanic divide between the stage and the first seats of the stalls. The set looks good. We run '*Fors'e lui*' and Solti wants to change the staging. And I don't. So we fuck about for a while in an unsatisfactory fashion. Then I go to lunch with Adrian Noble, who is as cheery and optimistic as ever. In the afternoon break I sit with Solti in the stalls. He calls Angela over. 'My dear, you must be very careful of your career. I have seen many young singers destroy themselves by singing too much, and singing the wrong roles. You must not do that.' Angela nods agreement.

11th November Sitzprobe in p.m. I'm unprepared and overcome by the ravishing sound of the Prelude, in spite of Solti's commentary: 'Tempo, tempo,' during the waltz theme, 'More, more, break your wrists and break my heart,' to the cellos. We talk afterwards about the balance between the orchestra and the singers. 'Sometimes the sound is more important than the meaning, but not often.' He tells me the story of a performance of *La Traviata* in Catania. The Dottore was a local man and was drunk. He was booed when he came on in the third act. On his second entrance he was booed again, so he threw up his hands and left.

12th November Music session in Haitink's bare, desolate and apparently seldom occupied room. Detailed text work, examination of the meaning of the letter in Act III, the timing of it, the naturalism of it. Of Angela's final aria, Solti says: 'You are singing some sort of Romanian rhapsody. Romanian rhapsodies are very beautiful. Also Hungarian. But it's not what Verdi wrote.' I envy the accuracy of a musical text. I tell Solti of an essay I've just read by Alfred Brendel in *NYRB*: 'There are performers who want to go against the composer – to hate their father,' said Brendel. 'Exactly,' says Solti.

16th November First stage and orchestra rehearsal. Chaos. It's a ridiculous and hopelessly clumsy system of rehearsal – getting in the

orchestra at this stage, mounting a large musical without finishing the technical rehearsal. We don't finish Act III because the musicians stop in mid-bar at one-thirty. The singers apologise to me, though God knows it's not their fault. Remember Peter Brook on opera: 'People say it's the greatest of the performing arts because it combines theatre, dance, and music, but you don't call soup great cuisine because you put everything into it.'

17th November   Saw *Three Tall Women*. It's a rather reedy affair, a strange trio in a play that never quite coalesces. We went to the Ivy after the show, which was the full celebrity fairground. A waiter brought a note over to me from Ian McKellen. It said: 'Richard – now's your chance to ask Linda McCartney's husband to either write (a) the music for *Grande Magia* or (b) an extra song for *Little Night Music*, Ian. PS I'm *so* excited by all these famous people.' And sure enough I *was* sitting next to Linda McCartney, and (via Peter Blake [*painter*]) we *did* get talking, and I perjured myself on the subject of organic gardening but didn't ask Paul to write any music or give any money to the NT. Later I talked with Jeremy King [*proprietor the Ivy*] about the NT's restaurant. He says we need somebody (somebody like him really) who cares as much about what's on the tables in the restaurant as I do about what's on the stages.

19th November   Frustration through the week with *La Traviata*. Nothing is ever properly finished. Only the music gets the time for attention to detail. Today a run-through with piano. Angela gets a faceful of snow from *The Sleeping Beauty*, which was playing last night, then in Act II the curtain doesn't work, then the cueing of the follow spots is up the spout, and I feel sick with frustration. After that Solti, Bob and I meet the Friends of the ROH. Someone asks Georg what his favourite piece of music is. 'That is a question for an amateur. For a professional it's always the piece you're doing at the time.' Asked how he works on a score he says: 'Very slowly. Bar by bar.'

21st November   First dress rehearsal. Georg is in a bad temper because three of his best players have sent deps. He's distracted and conducts the first act very slowly. It's all a bit lifeless and dispiriting.

And the lighting isn't right, and Georg rehearses the orchestra at the end of Act II, so we don't have time to do the whole of Act III. I feel very pissed off with the musos, who Bob heard bitching Solti in the coffee bar – he's too old, he can't hack it, etc etc. And they don't play well today.

22nd November   Public dress rehearsal, or 'General' as they all camply call it. I feel exasperated by the haphazard nature of rehearsals, and the casual regard for everything but the music, and at the way in which we're expected to mount this production with wilful optimism in place of proper rehearsal time. It's the ethos of the amateur. Most operas demand the stage resources of huge musicals and we've been given less stage rehearsal time than you'd get for a two-hander in a single set in the theatre. Opera joke: (Goetz Freidrich) Why did Germany lose the war? Too little rehearsal time. I sit at the front of the circle, or, being the ROH, 'the Grand Tier'. Solti acknowledges applause with an 'Oh don't be so soppy' wave and starts. The orchestra play like different creatures from yesterday. Angela and Frank are a bit tentative at first, but then they both get in their stride. The principals give 25 per cent more than I've ever seen, the chorus 50 per cent. The end is intensely moving, not least because I get to see the lighting cues for the first time. Afterwards I meet Nicholas Payne on the stairs. 'How did you think it went?' I say. 'Fine,' he says, 'we were fifteen seconds short of three and a half hours so we don't have to pay overtime.' I see Solti, who is thrilled about everything but the length of the interval. 'But,' he says, 'we must not jubilate too soon.'

23rd November   Harold's done *Landscape* in the Cottesloe with Ian Holm and Penelope Wilton. It's mesmerising. Somehow the audience know that the author expects them to give undiluted concentration to the event, and thank God, they give it. I hope that Ian's got a taste for the stage now.

2nd December   The first night of *La Traviata* passed in a (champagne-assisted) glow of tense excitement. I loved it. I went on stage at the end for a curtain call and had no sense, nor did I care, whether the audience were booing or cheering. Georg drew me to him, said: 'I'm so happy,' and held my arm up like a boxer. Sue and Lu said that my

call was rather over-enthusiastic, standing in the centre with Solti as if I'd been doing the singing. The reviews have been mixed, but I don't care. *The Times* says that Solti makes four/four time sound like a waltz. Georg says: 'I am so angry I'll never conduct an opera in this country again.' A pause. 'Now, Richard, what are we going to do together next?'

6th December We had a press conference today, the point of which was to announce the new season, and to say – why did I think it wasn't news? – that I'd be leaving the NT in three years' time, towards the end of '97. But the press had got the story yesterday and printed it this morning. Jenny [*McIntosh*] was furious with me because she hadn't wanted me to say when I was going to leave and because that'll be the story rather than the season, and she doesn't want me to leave anyway. I *was* thoughtless and selfish, but I couldn't help myself: I had to give some shape to my life, give an end to my time at the NT, see light at the end of the tunnel, deliver myself from the sense that the planning, scheduling, nurturing, caretaking would go on for ever. I apologised to Jenny and she, as always, was very gracious, but I went into the press conference feeling chastened.

8th December I've been reviewed well in the papers and will probably never be in higher esteem. Is it a case of what Tennessee Williams said to an actor in one of his plays: 'They can't wait for me to die so that they can commemorate me'?

9th December We went to the opening of *Oliver* [*Lionel Bart*] at the Palladium last night which was lumpish, long, and loud. Consider yerself one of the famerly. No thanks. After the show I had to go to the ROH to catch the end of *Traviata* which was being televised live for BBC2. It seemed weird at first after being bullied for three hours by *Oliver* – the orchestra was so quiet, the unamplified singers so vulnerable. After the show Angela thanked me over and over and Georg wanted to discuss our next project. Tony Hopkins and Placido Domingo were backstage at the end of the curtain calls: an interesting problem for Georg – who did he greet first? He solved it by shaking hands with both of them at once. There's a passionate mutual admiration between Tony and Georg. Tony tells me he'd like to do some theatre, but that way sadness lies. He told a journalist

a couple of years ago that he had been asked by me to do *Night of the Iguana* and was going to do it. I rang his agent as soon as I read it in the paper. No, he'd changed his mind.

11th December   I've been reading Cocteau's Diaries again. A good story of a lunch in his house in the South of France with three of his friends: as the lunch drew to its close Cocteau became aware of the anxiety of his guests to get to their own rooms in order to write up their account of the lunchtime conversation. He says of the world of the arts: 'It strikes me that this world of honours, decorations, pictures in the papers, is on the whole the real world and ours is a kind of family attached to a wreck, drifting I know not where.'

14th December   A salvo from Noel Annan in *The Times* about the plan to remove the walkway: 'It is indeed like removing the lower jaw from someone's face. One is reminded of Dean Swift: "Last week I saw a woman flayed, and you will hardly believe how much it altered her appearance for the worse."' My, how they must have chortled at the Athenaeum.

15th December   Noel Annan has appeared on Channel 4 News fulminating about the removal of the walkway. To my intense satisfaction he stood on a balcony that he said 'the vandals' were going to remove. He pointed to a part of the building that no one has ever had any intention of altering in any way, shape, or form, making it transparently clear that he didn't know what he was talking about. But this is the problem: no one will *look* at the building in detail.

17th December   We've cast Lia Williams in David's play [*Skylight*], and we've got almost all the locations for the *Absence* film. Last night I had to plead with the Japanese managing director of an electronics firm to use his factory for filming. There's mayhem over our redevelopment plans, and abuse in every direction from Denys Lasdun. I'm worried about the box office as always.

21st December   'A huge awareness of mortality gives you a zest for life,' says Tony Harrison apropos my announced resignation. I feel rueful about it now, although it *has* given me a new lease of life, a new enthusiasm. But it was selfish to say I was leaving and everyone

seems to think that my time is coming to an end imminently. Tony and I talk about doing *Le Roi S'amuse* with Ian [*McKellen*] as the Jester. I feel sad and guilty that we've not done a Greek play together – but there's the rest of our lives.

26th December   John Osborne's died. He was sixty-five. The last time I had anything to do with him was exactly a year ago, when he wrote to me. He'd written the letter on Christmas Eve, so I imagine that it was a sort of stock-taking, auditing his life and work. I imagined John in his large house in Shropshire: lonely, bitter, ill and unhappy, drowning in disappointment. There was an entirely admirable lack of careerism about him, a real undiluted passion for theatre. He really *did* believe in George Devine's notion that the theatre had to be a religion, a way of life. And no wonder he felt out of tune with our opportunistic times. The letter he sent me was gracious, not recriminatory, above all terribly sad. I can't say that I really loved any of his plays except for *Inadmissible Evidence* but I admired the way that he insisted on making people *feel*, the way he goaded people – audiences and others – into feeling, not into action or thought or love, just into feeling that the most important thing was to be ALIVE, however painful and tormenting. That was his extraordinary, singular gift. That and his love of language and his intensely musical prose. John was very English in his cultivated eccentricity, his love of landscape and of liturgy, and he had enough self-knowledge to know that his prejudices and his passions were incurable. His life was in his anger and the anger in his life: anger was an existential force. He aspired, in a way, to the aristocracy – in the sense that he wanted to disdain opinion, and he wanted the licence to behave badly. He loved the role of the Edwardian cad who was almost-a-gent, but he was a patrician in all matters relating to his art. He was very English in that he was defined by the uniquely English form of inertia that he railed against, and when he lost his audience he was left alone like Lear raging on the heath.

28th December   I was asked by the *FT* to write an obituary of John O., but I didn't think I could do justice to the confusion of my admiration of him set against my feelings about his work. I was reading his collection of occasional writings a few months back; there's some indignantly scathing polemic, but often they're surpris-

ing in their precise intelligence and their objectivity. These pieces are continents away from the work of a manic ranter, except when a visceral snobbery emerges: pop culture, institutional life, social workers, 'youth' – but then he's not afraid of displaying his prejudices. It's odd that it was *Look Back in Anger* that achieved the seismic breakthrough in British theatre in 1956. However abrasive and excoriating, far from looking back in anger, it looks back with a fierce, despairing nostalgia. There was a wonderful speech in his sequel to *Look Back* [Déjà Vu]: 'Anger . . . is mourning the unknown, the loss of what went before without you, it's the love another time but not this might have sprung on you.' Of course, *Look Back* is saturated with the pain of marriage: impossible to do, impossible to do without.

29th December   Talked to Jenny for a while and felt a slight sinking of the spirits about next year, in spite of her optimism. We've stumbled this year – not a single success in the Olivier – *Pericles, The Seagull, Devil's Disciple*, the catastrophe of *Johnny* – thank God for *Wind in the Willows*; some real success in the Lyttelton with *Birthday Party, Sweet Bird, Parents Terribles* and *Broken Glass*, and in the Cottesloe only *Le Cid* and *Rutherford* stand out. It's so hard to get a strategy that can accommodate the financial exigencies of the three theatres, feed the huge appetite of the monster, and do really good work. I watched Peter struggle with the same equation and try to find a solution: one company in each theatre, five companies over three theatres, or ad hocery. I'd like much more continuity, a semi-permanent company, but how to achieve it, do new plays, work with outside companies? And all the time the duty to the audience. Jean Renoir: 'The public is lazy; to indulge their laziness is to hold the key to success. Maurice Chevalier told me that he never started his act with a new song. He sandwiched it between established favourites . . . The golden rule with a "commercial" film is that it must never surprise the public except physically . . . Don't forget that the public is twelve years old.'

30th December   Like Toad I long for the life of the open road, but at the same time I need to be part of a group, and, of course, usually at the centre of it. I'll miss running the NT because I like the role of paterfamilias. And I'll miss the companionship – and yes, the fun of

it. But I *know* it's right to leave. 'Happy is he who has renounced the world before the world has renounced him.' Tamburlaine.

31st December   I looked for the letter from John Osborne, not as I thought written on Christmas Eve, but on Boxing Day morning: 'I've just picked up your Christmas card, rather cold to the touch of the A.M. Shropshire wight if not its sentiment. I was oddly touched by it. I surely don't know why, simply, I suppose, as a courteous gesture from a remote but generous spirit . . .' He wrote without bile about the events of the past year: 'As my old friend, Tony Richardson, used to say: But what did you *EXPECT*? Indeed . . .' He wrote about Arnold Wesker's being 'fucking WELSH', about 'HARE D. and STOPPARD T.' being not quite happy with their 'acclaimed and lucrative lot', of enjoying reading my book, recommending a '*hilarious*' biography of David Merrick, and writing for the *Spectator*: 'Oddly enough, only journalists, who have been my lifetime's adversaries, seem to have grasped that I STILL can write with more GRASP and FLIGHT than most people . . .'

1995

2nd January   Back in London. Postcard from Michael Gambon:

I hear that the no-smoking crowd are now operating at the National. Surely that sort of mentality doesn't belong in a theatre, it isn't a place where you impose rules on people, it's a dirty radical place where an actor can work with a fag in his hand, a place where someone like me or you if you felt the need can piss down the staircase, surely these people who worry about what they eat and change their underpants every day should join IBM or SHELL. Screaming at night from the stage about the plight of mankind and the world would be ridiculed in a building where you can't smoke. The stage is like a war game and some wounded people have to smoke, love Mike. Happy New Year.

Exactly.

7th January   On the train to Manchester I read in the *Independent* that I was tipped to run the BBC. Would I do it? Could I do it? No to both, I think. It's an alien world of multichannel, ratings and focus groups and there's no room for the old vision. It will end up the way I predicted three years ago – a management with a solely editorial function who eternally second-guess the audience. The programme-makers will be freelance.

8th January   Hard time pulling *Absolute Hell* [*Rodney Ackland*] back from the brink of cancellation. Anthony Page wanted to cancel because another actor had turned it down and he was ready to

throw in the towel if he couldn't get the right cast. Half of me (the freelance director) entirely sympathises, the other half (the pragmatic producer) accepts it as the inevitable chaff and bran of putting on sixteen shows a year. 'How can you do this and retain your sanity?' says Anthony. He's a creative worrier, always vexed by something slipping away from him, and yet quite sanguine about things beyond his control. Good director, understands actors, and good at caressing with one hand and goading with the other. I'm also struggling to get Deborah [*Warner*] and Fiona [*Shaw*] in the starting gate for *Richard II*.

10th January   I talked this morning to Rupert Christiansen about *La Traviata*. He thought I was too respectful, and said that people thought that I'd been bullied by Solti. It's a half-truth; I was in awe of the project and cautious because of being on new territory but I have no regrets. It was very good work. A woman said to Philip Larkin of an early poem: 'I don't think that poem of yours is very good.' Larkin: 'Neither do I, but it was the best I could do at the time.'

14th January   Julian Belfrage [*actors' agent*] has died. 'And a very good morning to *you*, sir,' he'll be saying at the gates of heaven. He was a brilliant agent and really cared about actors but always gave the impression that a race track was more attractive to him than an auditorium. And often it is. And Kathleen Tynan's died too. I hadn't seen her for a long time; she'd retreated when she became ill, not wanting people to know, which was courageous but sad, because I never said any sort of farewell. She was always distant, emotionally recessed and painfully self-doubting. I miss them both. A letter from Helen Osborne in the *Guardian* chastising Arnold Wesker for a piece he wrote about John ends up: 'Finally, only Arnold and I know that he would not have dreamt or dared of publishing such a piece if John were alive. Cowardice is as unappealing as humourlessness. I hope you paid him handsomely for it.'

15th January   I'm about to start filming *Absence of War*. Had a charming letter from Neil [*Kinnock*] about filming *Absence* of which he said: 'Better you do it than anyone else. But *I* wouldn't be thrilled if you had Pavarotti singing the lead . . .' I'm excited, apprehensive, secure, but uncertain if I can deliver what I want from it. About

filming: the director has to decide where to come in on a scene, whose eyes you're seeing it from, and when to shift the point of view.

16th January   I'm at the theatre early mornings and late evenings. I'm disconcerted by standing outside the theatre and seeing its frailty – it's so unavoidably dependent on the will of the audience and the actors to make it work. 'The theatre is carried by the strength of the actors. When the actors are strong, that's when the theatre thrives,' says Bergman. But so often it doesn't. Mary said to me: 'Going to the theatre should be like going to church.' 'Mmmm?' I went. 'You have to put something in if you want to get something back,' she said.

20th January   Day off after a night shoot, and back at the theatre. Meeting with Hayden Phillips to try to twist Christopher Hogg's arm into becoming Chairman of the Board. Chris Hogg listens very carefully, asks several questions, but doesn't commit himself. He's very careful, fastidious (and sparing) with words.

27th January   We had a reading of *Skylight*. Out loud it seems flat and uninflected, when it's the precise opposite on the page. Neither Mike Gambon or Lia Williams are good sight-readers, so it didn't teach us much.

2nd February   Day off from filming. I work with Anthony Ward [*designer*] on *La Grande Magia*, or at least we read the play together, swapping parts line for line. Neither of us feels self-conscious about it, and even though it's faltering and absurd, it's the best way of getting to know a play. Then, with Jenny, to a meeting with the Arts Council with Mary Allen [*Secretary-General*], who has a way of making us feel that we've been fitted in between much more pressing and prestigious assignments. So nothing is settled and it's business as usual with the Arts Council living down to expectations. I simply don't know whether Mary can or *will* sort out the Arts Council. I won't hold my breath.

4th February   *Dealer's Choice* [*Patrick Marber*] has started previewing. It's a marvellously enjoyable piece of work, not at all like a first play. Patrick's emerged from TV, one of a group of really gifted writers and performers, inc. the great Steve Coogan [*Alan Partridge*]

whose Saturday morning radio show I used to stop the car to listen to. Patrick's spent years looking at and thinking about theatre, but his TV training shows (virtuously) in his avoidance of long speeches. His mum (who I encounter round every corner: 'Hello, I'm Mrs Marber') took him to the NT regularly as a child, and he was an usher here. He's exacting almost to a fault and is frustrated that the actors are never quite accurate enough for him. He finds it hard to trust them.

14th February   I've finished the film, and would like to go down a burrow rather than charge back to the theatre. *Dealer's Choice* has been very well (and deservedly) received. Among others things it's a satisfying vindication of the policy of encouraging new writers in the NT Studio – the play emerged out of giving Patrick two weeks at the Studio with a group of actors. It's also evidence that there are young writers who don't see the theatre as an outdated medium.

26th February   *What the Butler Saw* [*Joe Orton*] has started previewing. It's unsteady as yet, but the play shines through, entirely its own eccentric thing – farcical but breaking all the rules of farce. It was years ahead of its time and was disastrously badly done when it had its first performance. I'd love to see Ralph Richardson in it now, or at least *a* R.R., but at the time he looked humiliatingly confused. It looks as though I'll have to cancel *La Grande Magia* because I can't cast it. It should be Ian [*McKellen*], but he's hanging on for the film of *Richard III* and without him I've lost my will to do it.

28th February   Christopher Hogg has been appointed Chairman of the Board. I saw Tom who said: 'I see Miriam [*Stoppard*]'s boyfriend has been appointed – that's almost as good for her as doing it herself.'

1st March   The new Secretary of State for the DNH [*Department National Heritage*], Stephen Dorrell, visited the theatre. He's the fifth minister in six years: Luce, Mellor, Renton, Brooke. It's transparently clear that he's never been inside it before and had only the faintest notion of its location. And that he has only the trace of an interest in any of the arts. He seemed diffident, well briefed, determined (to do what?), and pleasant. I said this to one of his civil

servants. 'Mmmm,' he said, 'mmmm. Just watch him – he's got his own agenda.' I imagine that his agenda is to diminish funding to the big companies, because he kept talking about *risk* rather than continuity – which was what I wanted him to take on board. I find myself missing the courteous, whiggish literacy of Peter Brooke. I remember a meeting where Cameron, Philip Hedley and I went to evangelise for increasing funding for the theatre. Cameron made a passionate and eloquent defence of publicly funded theatre, backed up with astonishing figures of the net profit (in foreign earnings) to the government from their 'investment'. Brooke listened carefully to all of us and then delivered a brilliant précis of our arguments. Nothing changed, of course.

2nd March   I saw Stephen Dorrell again, when he came to an ABSA [*Association of Business Sponsorship for the Arts*] breakfast at the theatre. He cut a *pear*-shaped cake to celebrate the *pair*ing scheme: business and the arts, and this embarrassing leaden pun wasn't the most depressing thing about the occasion. I find the effort of maintaining eager geniality on these occasions really wearying. We really do please to live, and live to please.

3rd March   I saw Dorrell *again* at a do at Downing Street to celebrate the arts in London, rubbing shoulders with cultural titans like Joan Collins, Bob Monkhouse, and Shirley Bassey. Major made a goodish impromptu speech, which possessed many un-expected virtues: passion, wit, and eloquence being three of them. Not for the first time did I wonder what it is about the practice of politics that renders so many people who are lively in private so inert on television and in Parliament. I stood next to Judi Dench who was seething silently at the gap between the obvious good intentions of the speaker and the lamentable effects of his policies. He said that the arts were necessary to a civilised society, etc etc, and that the Lottery would transform arts funding. Judi and I collared him later, and told him that this wouldn't happen because of the legislation. 'Don't you realise,' we chorused, 'that the Lottery funds aren't for art, but for buildings?' 'That'll change in two years' time,' he said. 'Oh,' I said. 'Why don't you say this publicly?' 'I can't (Treasury perhaps), but trust me, Richard.' Then he was kidnapped by Shirley Bassey.

4th March   A run of *Women of Troy* [*Euripides*]. If wishing could make it so this would be wonderful. It's a monument to good intentions, but there isn't a language there – either verbal or visual – and with the exception of Rosemary [*Harris*] they just haven't got the firepower for the Olivier.

5th March   New York for two days for casting of *Racing Demon*. Some excellent actors, very courteous, bright and wildly enthusiastic, parts in straight plays here being like bread in a famine. I saw the end of *Arcadia* in the Vivian Beaumont. It's suffering from the intractable acoustics of the auditorium. Why don't architects care about acoustics? It's like designing a car without wheels.

6th March   The Charleson Awards. I sat next to Alec Guinness who I found quite hard going. He's very vigilant, dry, restless and uneasy in my company (and me in his). I was never able to get beyond the stage of fandom, even though we have a mutual friend in Alan Bennett. He was just off to the National Gallery to meet Alan. He said how much he'd liked *Racing Demon*, and would I keep him in mind for the future. In his brief speech to Toby Stephens, who'd won the award, he made some jokes about Toby being able to use his cheque to take refuge in Singapore or Bruges (*pace* Stephen Fry's defection to Bruges) but, he said, 'actors are tough old birds'. He was very philosophical about the actor's life: you have to be resilient and stoical, he said. The actors like these awards because they're made a fuss off, instead of being trampled underfoot by agents, publicists, producers and journalists.

Hugh Whitemore told me that John Le Carré had gone to stay with Alec Guinness. Leave your shoes out, said Guinness. Le Carré dutifully went to bed, leaving his shoes outside the door, puzzled because he wasn't aware of the presence of any staff. He got up for a glass of water in the night: there was Guinness at the kitchen table polishing Le Carré's shoes.

8th March   Lauren Bacall and Dirk Bogarde did a platform together for her autobiography. They asked me to introduce it. 'At the age of fifteen I was in love with both of them,' I said. They hadn't wanted to rehearse before and were very nervous. They're both natural monologists so were uncomfortable sharing the stage

and the anecdotes. Also because they had chosen to perch on high bar stools, which made them look like ageing nightclub singers. Afterwards Betty gave me a signed copy of her autobiography: 'Thanks for the intro, Richard.'

10th March A sign of the times. A note from our milkman: 'PETER HORLICK, YOUR FRANCHISE MILKMAN. I am self-employed as a Franchise Milkman in effect operating my own business with full backing of Express Dairy resources.'

12th March David and I don't agree how *Skylight* should look. He wants it 'painterly', and John [*Gunter*] and I want everything stripped to the bone. But he's lived with it much longer than I have: it's his vision and voice, not mine. Bergman: 'When I begin working on a play for the stage, I first consider these questions: why did the playwright write this play, and why did it turn out like this.' Claude Bernard: 'Art is I; science is we.'

13th March First rehearsals of *Skylight*. As always at the beginning of rehearsals I'm absurdly anxious but I conceal it all behind extravagant cheeriness. But it was a good day, I felt excited about the play and the cast and by the end of rehearsals my equilibrium was restored. Then the troubles of the rest of the theatre: *Trojan Women* very vulnerable, *La Grande Magia* extremely precarious.

19th March I'd sent Paul Scofield *John Gabriel Borkman* [*Ibsen*] and had a postcard this morning saying that he was keen to do it: 'Yes, I think Borkman is a splendid thought . . . I don't suppose Vanessa and Eileen are available but they seem to me a wonderful pair.'

20th March Rehearsals are enjoyable, the rest is not: *Women of Troy* is a catastrophe, *The Blue Ball* hasn't worked. Paul Godfrey's a talented writer and I really liked his play about Britten. We commissioned this one about the space project – a great subject but the writing doesn't rise to it. *La Grande Magia* is on then off then on then off and I can't face doing it but I expect I will do it and dread it.

22nd March I saw Nick's film of *George III*, which he's done really well and should be very popular. It's restless – possibly too

much so – but has a hugely engaging energy. And Nigel [*Hawthorne*] is brilliant. I've just finished an excellent Anglo-Irish memoir recommended to me by Max [*Stafford-Clark*], about a young English tutor falling in love with his young pupil: 'All vivid memories are attached to shocks of pain or pleasure. You can sit by a clock all afternoon and not hear it tick until a telegram announcing death arrives; then you remember the clock's rhythm all your life. This is what makes it impossible for me to give a truthful picture of my relationship with Phoebe. I remember only the intensities.'

30th March   Rehearsals of *Skylight* are still the sustaining joy. Outside that, what I endure is the possible cancellation of *La Grande Magia*, the opening of *The Blue Ball*, the continuing haemorrhaging of the box office in the Olivier, the mountainous problems of the redevelopment and the sense that the entire exercise might be pointless. What to do? Go on, of course, and know that things will get better. Herman Mankiewitz: 'Idiocy is all right in its own way, but you can't make it a foundation for a career.'

9th April   Things are better: *Under Milk Wood is* very good and popular, the reviews for *The Blue Ball* are not as bad as they might have been, the redevelopment plans have been approved by Lambeth, Clare Higgins won an Olivier award for *Sweet Bird*, rehearsals have gone well, and the sun is shining. The Olivier Awards were worse – if imaginable – than usual. The high (or low depending on your perspective) point was when Tony Slattery in his warm-up did a riff on theatre critics. I was standing backstage alongside a nervous Anthea Turner, who had just asked me if it would be a difficult audience, when Tony Slattery called Nick de Jongh a 'cunt', got a huge laugh and a round. 'Follow that,' I said and understandably she looked terrified.

12th April   I heard on the radio about an advertising campaign by the Church for Easter. They'd decided not to use the cross as a logo: 'It carries too much cultural baggage.'

14th April   I've been asked to become a governor of the BBC. I don't know whether to accept; I've mixed feelings about the BBC. It's changed so much and I'm out of sympathy with so much of what's

changed, and the 'internal market' has been a catastrophe – however virtuous the attempt to draw the attention of BBC staff to real costs. Producer Choice and the Independent Production Quota have had the effect of making the existing staff feel second-rate, inducing low morale and pushing up the rate of defection. During the pre-production of *Absence* we had to negotiate with the BBC to use one of their studios. Only by threats of exposure did we manage to secure a studio at the TV Centre for less than we could have rented a studio from outside the BBC.

16th April   Fairly ghastly week at the theatre which ended OK. I began to panic about the Lyttelton box office and finding a show to replace *La Grande Magia* if I don't do it. Time is desperately short. I had a hard week on *Skylight* – Gambon is suffering from what the Germans call '*Textangst*', i.e. trouble remembering lines, and David's angst is also about lines: has he written the right ones? There's another German word which describes what I'm trying for: '*Werktreu*' – faithful to the work.

17th April   I was asked by Vanessa [*Redgrave*] to go to the Riverside to welcome the National Theatre of Sarajevo. I went. She wasn't there but Corin [*Redgrave*] was in charge. The company weren't performing, as a protest, because Sarajevo was under siege again. The director was off doing a radio interview, so I waited, and the audience waited, and twenty minutes after the announced starting time the director turned up. Then the whole company, and Corin and I, trooped on stage in single file. Corin stood to address the audience but the director stopped him and asked if his speech could be translated for his actors. Pause. 'Well, we don't have a translator.' To the audience: 'Is there anyone in the audience who speaks Serbo-Croat?' Pause. Then a volunteer appeared. Corin spoke, each sentence repeated in Serbo-Croat; I spoke, with the same routine, and then I retreated in embarrassment.

18th April   I'm disappointed by the reviews for *Under Milk Wood*, which have been mean-spirited. I *know* it's a radio play but it's a marvellously realised evening in a theatre perfectly suited to its form and it's been immaculately staged by Roger [*Michell*] and Bill [*Dudley*]. I think (hope) it'll do well in spite of the critics. Karl

Kraus: 'Journalists write because they have something to say, and they have something to say because they write.'

20th April Sam Mendes and Jonathan Kent have both told me not to be so feeble about directing *La Grande Magia*, so I've just decided to commit myself to doing it without having a clue who's going to be in it. It's a beautiful play, one of Nick Wright's essential ninety-nine plays – 'a metaphysical comedy about grief' – but without the central performance, the Eduardo di Filippo part, extraordinarily difficult to bring off.

30th April We've started previews of *Skylight*. The last two weeks have been very tough – dealing with David's anxiety, with Mike's ferociously aggressive pessimism, sustaining Lia's confidence, and trying to conceal my own nervousness. We survived – a wonderful first preview and two good performances since – both Lia and Mike magnificent. It's a very good play and David's pleased with the production: 'The production is wonderful, Richard, it's wonderfully directed,' he says.

1st May I've cast Alan Howard in *La Grande Magia*, and hope we don't repeat the stumble on our last outing.

10th May I'm in New York to cast *Racing Demon*. I watched a morning (8.30 a.m.) talk show: a large fat black woman talked about having inter-racial fantasies and three hunky white guys in boxer shorts walked on so that she could choose which one to fuck. All US TV is showbiz – the news is like a talk show, the talk shows are news, it's all knowing and manipulative but guileless. I was in a cab with a driver called Albert Einstein; a talk show was on the radio – jokes about paedophilia. I read an article which says that a private in the German army was executed in 1944 for spreading rumours about Hitler pissing in a goat's mouth when he was a little boy and having his cock bitten by the goat. If the man had lived he'd have been a guest on the talk show. But then so would the goat.

14th May Stephen Wood's had a heart attack, out of the blue. He's forty-five, no history of heart trouble, eats badly but doesn't drink much, swims occasionally, walks a bit. So why?

15th May *Skylight* has gone as well as we could have hoped, and the whole has been applauded by the press, which could be evidence that the critics are always right and really do give a fair account of good and bad work, except that I know that this isn't true and that it's always something of a lottery. Princess Mgt came to the show. When she was asked by Mike if she'd found it depressing she said: 'It was a bit like one's own life.'

16th May Stephen Wood's making progress: they unblocked two arteries, an insertion of a clip to keep one open, inflation of the other. I'm listening to the Berlioz *Requiem*. It's a titanic piece by a titanic man. Unrecognised in his lifetime, tormented by failure in love, by lack of understanding, by prejudice and by stupidity. And this wonderful music, written as if were fully formed in his head: the orchestra as a single instrument. 'The luck of having talent is not enough; one must also have the talent for luck,' said Berlioz. I've had a very heartening letter from Doris Lessing, whom I admire hugely. She loves the theatre and the NT. She'd read my book and was worried that it ended on a melancholic note: 'I do know a book has an inner logic and yours might have demanded an elegiac note . . . But towards the end you sound discouraged. Is it possible that our perennial nay-sayers the critics and journalists have got you down?'

19th May Lia [*Williams*] rang to tell me she met someone – a city type – who'd seen *Skylight* and said her character was the most repellent he'd ever seen. 'Kyra,' he said, 'means "old woman". I've got a boat called Kyra.' She seemed very buoyant in spite of the abuse.

20th May The village plant sale. Cars parked up the hill, the car-park full, a sense of restless anticipation in the queue waiting for the doors to open. When the doors open it's like the Blitz, women fighting for a place in the shelters, using sharp elbows like knives on a chariot wheel. Sue pushes forward with no hesitation. I stand in the middle of the room, inert with amazement, scrutinised severely by the womenfolk, sympathetically by the menfolk. Sue spots a posh woman with the complexion of a pickled walnut making off with some unpaid-for plants, defying a prole who politely questions her about whether she's paid. A hippyesque girl in harlequin trousers

sails through the room looking lofty; a clutch of padded-jacketed country Sloanes dominate the centre of the scrum and the rest skirt the edges deferring to them.

22nd May I started rehearsing *La Grande Magia*. The play is charming, magical, mysterious, very un-English, and has real poetic resonance, but it'll be very difficult to realise its potential. I'm pleased to be working again with Alan, who is quirky and thoughtful and sometimes very recessed, but never diffident, even if he's sometimes off on his own planet.

24th May *Absolute Hell* has started previewing. I'm not sure that it quite lives up to the 'lost masterpiece' claims that I've been making for it, but it's got huge ambition and wit and political muscle and some sense of vision. It's a *tour de force* technically and balances a huge number of characters with astonishing virtuosity. It was way ahead of its time – rejected by managements, savaged by the critics, ignored by the public. It was written in 1952 – i.e. four years before *Look Back in Anger*. Of course, it's a huge cast and had to be done in a club performance because of censorship. Anthony Page has cast and directed it extremely well, and Judi is outstanding even by her standards. Harold Hobson buried the play on its first outing (as *The Pink Room*) in 1952: 'The audience at Hammersmith had the impression of being present, if not at the death of a talent, at least at its very serious illness.'

26th May An actress has gone mad, walking through traffic, and been sectioned. A friend of a friend has hanged himself, preparing the noose while his four-year-old son watched. Both incidents make art seem tame and absurd for wanting to give meaning to the meaningless. Wilde: 'It often happens that the real tragedies of life occur in such an inarticulate manner that they hurt one by their crude violence, their absolute incoherence, their absurd want of meaning, their entire lack of style.'

27th May *Richard II* has started previewing; it's long, partly because so many of them speak so slowly (and think so slowly), but it will be very good. It's very well designed. Fiona will be excellent, but at the moment her casting seems a commercial whim

rather than a device central to the revelation of the play. I saw Germaine at the end of the show. 'How did you find it?' I asked. 'Why do they speak so slowly?' she said. 'Don't they know it's in verse?'

28th May   I had a letter from Neil [*Kinnock*]'s assistant about *Absence*, still angry because she thinks it traduces Neil. She says he was NOT overpowered by his advisers; all decisions taken in his name were taken by him. And all his speeches were on paper so that he had a written record – to have proof for the press of what he'd said. And he wrote all his speeches himself. Losing the election was not because of the power exerted by outsiders; that, she says, was the view of only one person – who collaborated closely with David. She says (and at least I agree with this) that Neil would have made a great Prime Minister.

29th May   Read a very good lecture that Alan [*Bennett*] gave at the National Gallery. The *Independent* had printed it the day of the lecture, ruining his jokes, and it made him insane with anger. He told me he said to the Editor's secretary, 'You deserve to close, you're like a – a – a bucket shop.' Then he said to me; 'And I don't even know what a bucket shop is.'

30th May   I've been reading *Borkman* again. It's a strange, elusive, violent play, full of lovelessness and bitterness, but also about the need for love. I can see why Paul is keen to play the part; also why Eileen would rather play Ella than Mrs Borkman. But she'll do Mrs B. if Vanessa will do Ella.

3rd June   John Osborne's Memorial Service. Exquisitely English: it wasn't a paradox that the scourge of the English bourgeoisie should aspire to an English apotheosis – he just hated what was rancid in it. Maggie Smith read from *Pilgrim's Progress* brilliantly '. . . so he passed over and all the trumpets sounded for him on the other side.' David's address was powerful; he said John had broken the great taboo about making your hates as public as your loves, and had invoked the distaste of the media for a combination of passion and intellect. I ran into Ned Sherrin on the way out of the church. Ned had been to *Absolute Hell*. When he was leaving a man in front of

him had said: 'Well, if this is the sort of stuff that Richard Eyre puts on I'm glad he's leaving.' In the evening I had to make a speech at an opening of an exhibition of post-war British theatre architecture in the Lyttelton foyer. I made a feeble speech about the exhibition being a memorial to an epoch of public-funded theatre, but I should have burned effigies of the architects responsible for some of the calamities.

4th June   Tony [*Harrison*]'s back from Carnuntun where he had a triumph with his latest piece in the Roman amphitheatre. It certainly succeeded in *épate*-ing the bourgeoisie: a lion bit through a cable, a lion tamer was mauled, two bears escaped, there was a near riot, a large choir *and* Barrie Rutter.

6th June   I've finished a marvellous novel: *Ladder of Years* by Anne Tyler: 'When my first wife was dying . . . I used to sit by her bed and I thought, This is her true face. It was all hollowed and sharpened. In her youth she'd been very pretty, but now I saw that in completed form, the final, finished version she'd been aiming at from the start . . . Attractive young people I saw on the street looked so . . . temporary . . . Didn't they understand where they were headed?'

11th June   Much more optimistic about *La Grande Magia*. Alan has started to be clear and incisive, and Bernie [*Cribbins*] has stopped trying to make the character likable. We've all worked very hard on the detail and it's started to pay off. Tony [*Harrison*]'s keen to get going on the Hugo [*Le Roi S'amuse*]. Said we should call it *The Prince's Play*. He said that there was an 1877 version called *The Fool's Revenge* which Queen Victoria saw and was not amused – 'a most immoral, improper piece'. He's thinking about Dan Leno, who wanted to play Richard III.

14th June   I've been asked (and agreed) to be the Cameron Mackintosh Professor of Drama at Oxford in 1997. You can't fault Cameron's generosity – not just to us – he really does back his enthusiasms.

15th June   We went to a concert at Hampton Court: hideously garish floodlighting, a stage like the set for the National Lottery

draw, an out-of-tune orchestra (conducted by Menuhin) and hideous acoustics in an exquisite Tudor courtyard. Jocelyn Stevens went to sleep in the first half during Beethoven's Pastoral and Vivien Duffield did the same in the second. I met Sir Michael Rose, who'd been Commander of UN troops in Bosnia. He said the war was run by gangsters on each side, threatening, blackmailing, bribing. When he created the safe passage of trucks into Sarajevo, the trucks were full of TV sets, VCRs, drink and fags. Vivien had an argument with the General's wife and told her to get fucked. As Jimmy Wheeler would have said, a very entertaining evening.

29th June   I saw the revival of *La Traviata*. Not having rehearsed it I was surprised at how fresh it was – and how good Carol Vaness was. I saw Solti afterwards, holding court with a queue of admirers waiting to see him. It was like the circle round the Kaaba in Mecca. He asked me to do Gounod's *Faust*, which I don't know. Opera joke: How many sopranos does it take to change a light bulb? One to change the bulb and four to tell her she won't reach it.

1st July   Box office is bad, except for *Skylight, Richard II* and *Absolute Hell. Under Milk Wood*, which I was counting on, just hasn't been a draw. It's crazy, we'd be better off closing the Olivier in the summer. I'm constantly engaged in propaganda on the theatre's behalf but now I feel that the much advertised party just isn't taking place. I ran into Jeremy Isaacs who says that the ROH always does badly in the summer. He says only *La Traviata* will sell out.

2nd July   *La Grande Magia* progresses. I think it's rather beautiful and could be very affecting on stage, but I can't tell if it's too elusive, too insubstantial, too diaphanous, too illusory. It could just crumble.

3rd July   I saw Andre Agassi interviewed on TV. Asked if he was affected by British newspapers, he said: 'Well, every newspaper you pick up here, all those big ones, is like a tabloid back home.' I've just read a new play by Wally Shawn [*The Designated Mourner*]. It's a dramatic meditation about the death of culture, a dense and haunting lament. I asked David [*Hare*] to direct it; he immediately wanted dates, contracts, actors, etc.

4th July Barney Simon has died. He was the unofficial voice of South Africa for us; through him we got a glimpse of its new face long before it became a political reality. Soon after his operation Sue Higginson [*director NT Studio*] said to Barney: 'Is there anything we can do for you?' 'Yes,' he said, 'just go on being my friends.' I half remember a Thom Gunn poem, where a man is dying: 'What can I do for you?' 'Remember me,' he said.

5th July Alan Bennett has withdrawn *Habeas Corpus*, which we were planning to do in the Lyttelton with Matthew Francis directing. I'm upset as we'd got far down the line with planning it. Alan's work is all about unrealised hope and defeated expectations, so at least it seems thematically appropriate for this to happen. Perhaps he's right, perhaps it would have been the wrong theatre for it. He's very apologetic. Matthew Francis says that Alan's action reminds him of Arthur Donnithorne in *Adam Bede*: 'Ruin a young lady's life, say sorry, and send a box of candies.'

7th July I'd started the technical of *La Grande Magia* when I got a message that Sue had been taken into hospital with a burst appendix – peritonitis. She came very near to death and I'm terrified at how near and how hopelessly I would have coped. She's very brave and stoical, and more than anything upset by the fact that the locum wouldn't come out to see her. Now she has a long vertical scar, no navel, but no poison. Both Lu and I are very shaken. It's very disturbing going to and from the hospital and the theatre and trying to open the show when my mind's in the hospital.

9th July Early morning visit to the hospital on the way to work. Sue looks terribly pale, agonisingly vulnerable, and I feel over-whelmed by what might have happened. I've started previewing *La Grande Magia*. It looks beautiful, is very detailed, quite unex-pected and quite touching.

16th July Sue still in hospital, better day by day. Lu and I feel bereft, still shocked by how perilously close she was to death. Both of us are intolerant of illness – unless it's our own, but this is something altogether different.

17th July   *La Grande Magia* has opened successfully, press almost unanimously good. Meeting with Chris Hogg about the redevelopment. Can we deliver the deadline? Are the team stable? Can we get a government loan to bridge fund-raising? A fax from Isabella di Filippo: 'Richard *carissimo* . . . Since I saw your NAPOLI I know that, theatrically, your heart is Eduardo's heart twin, and this, even more than success, seems to me a miracle. Thank you, dear Richard, with *un grande abbraccio per tutti*, your Isabella.'

19th July   Sue is out of hospital. Huge relief. Kierkegaard: 'Life is understood backwards but must be lived forwards.'

20th July   Lu told me about a party given by an Oxford friend. There were two groups at the party – his pals from the college and his pals from the Oxford Union. The Oxford Union lot were sitting around listening to digitally re-mastered CDs of Churchill's greatest speeches.

21st July   Last night was Mary's leaving party. I remember reading a newspaper profile of Mary before I'd met her. It said: 'She is a great giver, the heart comes pouring out and when it reaches you it is warm.' No one who's ever met her could doubt that. She gave herself to the NT without reserve. In spite of her lineage, she's not a natural politician or administrator, and she's had to work very hard at the job to succeed. And she did. Her taste was always infallible, in people as well as plays, even if she was always tentative about asserting it. And she's had an unerring ear, nose, and eye for the bogus. Her loyalty's never wavered even when worried by hostile criticism or bad box office, or provoked by controversy. I'm going to miss her gossip, guidance, champagne, 7.45 a.m. phone calls, enthusiasm, wisdom and friendship. I said much of this and more at the party and Mary replied: 'You go too far – but then you often do, dear Richard.' I went to dinner with her and Lois. They were both desperate to know why Fiona Shaw didn't shave her armpits for *Richard II*.

23rd July   I feel rushed in both directions, behind with everything. I'm not coping well with looking after Sue at home and looking after the theatre. I met Janet Holmes à Court who's a striking and intelligent woman. We talk about Murdoch, who's now become

an American of convenience. 'Rupert Murdoch is an Australian as Attila was a Hun,' says Janet.

24th July   I talked to David about the idea of writing a play with Howard [*Brenton*] about Jeffrey Archer, whose life is an extravagant work of fiction. When I met Archer he asked me if we were doing *Wind in the Willows* again. 'Yes, we are.' 'And have you cast Toad?' 'Not yet,' I said. 'I should play it. You see, I *am* Mr Toad!' I sat next to his wife at dinner, the 'fragrant' Mary. Actually she's about as fragrant as ammonia. 'I'm reading a book by Richard Fineman about quantum theory,' I said. 'It's Feynman and it's about chaos theory,' she replied tartly.

29th July   It's six o'clock on Saturday morning and I'm sitting at my desk in Glos. There's a mist which blankets the valley, and the sun is starting to irradiate the mist with an expectant glow; it's all promise – of a glittering perfect English day. I had a letter from Mary which thanks me for all the interest and colour and new ways of looking at things and people that have come into her life via the NT. She quotes a Spender poem:

> What is precious, is never to forget
> The essential delight of the blood drawn from ageless springs
> Breaking through rocks in worlds before our earth.
> Never to deny its pleasure in the morning simple light
> Nor its grave evening demand for love.
> Never to allow gradually the traffic to smother
> With noise and fog the flowering of the Spirit.

30th July   *Volpone* is going to be very successful; Matthew [*Warchus*] has done a bold, cocky, stylish production – very well designed by Richard Hudson, and Michael Gambon occupies the stage of the Olivier as if he was standing in front of the fireplace in his own house. So now we have *Skylight, Absolute Hell, La Grande Magia, Richard II* and *What the Butler Saw* and *Merry Wives* – and *Under Milk Wood*, which should be pulling in the audiences.

31st July   I heard Steve Jones on the radio talking about the 'odour of sanctity'. If you're fasting the body starts to consume muscle

tissue, producing acetone which smells sweetly on the breath. I remember a Czech friend describing being searched by the secret police; after they'd gone she became aware of a vile acrid smell – herself – 'the smell of fear'.

1st August   Mary's last Board meeting, Chris Hogg's first. We confront the fact that we have to raise £7.5 m. for the redevelopment, as *well* as continuing to raise money for running the theatre. Even if we have to restore our building rather than just let it disintegrate, it's a poisoned chalice, this Lottery money.

2nd August   The ROH has got £58 m. from the National Lottery. Cartoon in paper: 'How can you be sure you'll make money from the National Lottery?' 'I'll open an opera house.' Column by Miles Kington about the reluctance of the British to give money for the arts. He has the Director of the ROH going into the streets with tins marked 'National Liver Week', having tried and failed with 'British Opera Week', 'Help the Tone Deaf' and 'Fight Philistinism'. 'The British taste for opera is all to do with that masochistic streak which makes us prefer French and Italian food to our own, Japanese cars to our own and American films to our own. So we go on pouring millions into the support of dead German and Italian opera composers. Extraordinary. If I weren't the Director of the ROH I'd kick up an almighty fuss. I'd demand that the money be poured into the British version of opera, one that we do supremely well and never get a penny of subsidy for . . . Pantomime.'

4th August   I saw Gambon and asked him to go to the West End with *Skylight*. I told him his performance was very rare and he has a *duty* to perform it. He looked sheepish.

6th August   Letter from James Cairncross [*actor*]: 'I attended an Equity conference at the Tron. The stage had been cleared but the backcloth remained in situ. It represented a galvanised iron wall, mercifully graffiti-free, but stained and dirty, ragged holes here and there, broken drainpipes and iron guttering. And just as I was wondering what drab, politically correct drama of death, deprivation, debt and casual sex would be played out in front of it nightly, the Chairman said, "I believe we are sitting on the set of *Midsummer Night's Dream*." '

15th August   An utterly mournful cartoon: three male dogs read-
ing magazines – the first magazine is called *Bitches*, the caption
'SAD'; the second magazine is called *Guest's Legs*, the caption
'SADDER'; the third, *Table Legs*, the caption 'SADDEST'.

20th August   We've been in the country for three weeks while Sue
recuperates. Glorious weather, and not many intrusions from the NT
– barring the business plan, the Lottery application, the casting, and
fixing the repertoire. But it's been lovely and I've been happy: this
wife, this child, this life, this house, this valley, these stars, this moon,
and reading *Lear* together by candlelight. Only one copy, so we
huddled together. I was struck by the domesticity of the play – it's a
play about family, about fathers and their children, about children
and their fathers. Two fathers in the play – one with three daughters,
the other with two sons – both receive a brutal education in parental
love, both are made to 'see' through blindness. I began to realise why
I had shied away from the play until now: I didn't know enough
about the subject matter, but with the death of my parents I was no
longer a child, I was an orphan, a grown-up and a parent myself. My
sympathies have shifted with time. I'm no longer prepared to judge:
everyone's to blame, everyone can be forgiven.

22nd August   It's wonderful *not* to be reading plays (apart from
Lear). I've read: a biography of Tom Paine – 'After the sermon I went
into the garden, and as I was going down the garden steps I revolted
at the recollection of what I had heard, and thought to myself that it
was making God Almighty act like a passionate man that killed his
son when he could not revenge himself in any other way'; *Dan Leno
and the Limehouse Golem* by Peter Ackroyd – bit over-elaborate, but
ingenious and thought-provoking; *What a Carve Up!* by Jonathan
Coe – witty, satirical, almost touching, underpinned by a Swiftian
rage for what's happening to the country. *Kenneth Williams'* Diaries
have a morbid fascination, partly because of his own compellingly
ghastly persona and self-hatred, but also his ostentatious honesty, as
if he was thinking: This is my revenge, you'll read this when I'm dead
and then you'll be sorry. As he says, he's a lifetime suicidalist. A
biography of Jeffrey Archer – good plot, just doesn't quite develop
beyond the story, i.e. it's journalism. A thriller by James Lee Burke –
bit maudlin but cracking line in over-heated prose and local colour;

The Intellectuals and the Masses by John Carey forces me to ask how genuine my feeling for democracy is, how much I take refuge in the inherent elitism of art as a self-vindicating position; do I admire the audience that I'm interested in reaching? *Continental Drift* by Russell Banks – a melancholy but unsour novel of the American Dream fused with an odyssey of a Haitian immigrant; and *Captain Corelli's Mandolin* by Louis de Bernières – very unexpected, very inventive, un-English, utterly delightful, engaging and, however artful, gives the impression of having written itself.

And Sunday papers: all 'STYLE CULTURE FASHION', full of windy opinion, gossip that they don't bother to pretend is true, empty speculation about politics ('BLAIR UNDER ATTACK' – from *one* back-bench MP), earnest moralising on Bosnia, and postmodern cynicism where nothing matters more than anything else. It's all like standing in the saloon bar of a pub smelling of stale beer and cigarette smoke. Except for a wonderful piece by David Thomson about films: 'Movies have made us more melodramatic and less stoic, more fickle and impatient, less abiding . . . At some point in the mid '70s – with the success of *Rocky* and *Star Wars* – the business of film began to give up complex experiences, unsettling subject matter and artistic voices . . . Film is another state – call it dream or coma – but it is not the same as being awake or ourselves.'

Also from the papers: the film producer David Begelman committed suicide yesterday. He'd been convicted of fraud, run a couple of studios, started CMA, been done for embezzlement and left a note which read: 'My real name is David Begelman.' And Brian Appleyard saying that when he was an arts correspondent in the '80s he had the impression from talking to a succession of the arts mandarins that they thought the consensus was over, that people didn't think 'art' was necessarily a good thing, that all the propaganda was empty posturing.

23rd August   Baking hot. Neil and Glenys have been to stay. I told Neil that Lu had given up politics on her course. 'Bloody good thing. Total waste of time.' But we talk a lot about politics. Neil's more interested in vision than strategy. 'No one these days,' he says, 'takes the time to talk about ideas.' He's very generous about Blair, but fears that he has no object apart from election and that his supporters are going to be disappointed. He says at the European Commission

at least he's achieved something, he's saved lives with rear-seat-belt legislation. We get drunk and Neil lies on a bench looking up at the night sky. 'Look at the bloody stars,' he says.

24th August Letter from Tom [*Stoppard*]. He'd hoped to write the Housman play this summer. He's written the first couple of pages – 'which would normally mean that I'm over the hump'. But he's not despairing: 'The summer's achievement . . . is to recognise the unwritten play.'

26th August I went to the Edinburgh Festival with Sue for an orgy of self-promotion: a Book Festival appearance, signings, a TV interview, a 'Masterclass' (a hard word to say without irony), and a lunchtime-radio chat show with Ned Sherrin. I'm not sure I like the Festival now – too much 'enterprise' and opportunism, but I suppose it was always like that and I used to love it. We stayed in Leith on the edge of the old port, which was the haunt of sailors, tarts, drunks and poverty when I lived in Edinburgh, and is now colonised by estate agents. We saw *Don Carlos*, which was wanly acted and looked like a Harvey Nichols carrier bag. I did the Book Festival with Simon Callow, who's written a marvellous book about Orson Welles. A cartoon of the two of us appeared next day in the *Scotsman*: it made Simon look like Edith Sitwell and me like Tam Dalyell. I was told that I'd been attacked the day before at the Book Festival by Steven Berkoff, snarled at by the pit bull. On the chat show I was flirted with (on air) by a funny San Francisco gay comic: 'Britain is the only Third World country where you can drink the water.'

27th August I spoke to John Mortimer who'd met Jean Marais in Italy. He told John that he'd said to Cocteau: 'I want to do three things in a play – I want to be silent in the first act, I want to cry with joy in the second, and I want to come down a long staircase in the third.' Cocteau wrote *The Eagle Has Two Heads* for him. John also told me about an American waiting to go into a play at the Royal Court that had been slammed. 'Don't go and see it, it's awful.' 'Oh, I don't mind, just so long as it's not about the Irish poor.'

28th August People say theatre is dead; they say the same thing about painting. What's wrong with painting is that the work is all

mediated through critics and arts bureaucrats and gallery owners, and the public never gets to see most of the work. The agenda is set by the 'experts', not the artists.

1st September   Gambon has agreed under duress to go to the West End, as long as Broadway is guaranteed. He's angry with himself, and with us for making him go on playing a part that he finds so difficult. I had a rehearsal – words and notes. We came across a disputed passage. 'I don't feel it,' he said, 'I just do it mechanically.' I think the problem is that, like most actors, he prefers to hide behind a beard and a wig, rather than reveal his self to the audience. Why should he show in public what he doesn't want to show in private? And every time he does the play he has to do it as if for the first time. I went to the first half of the show; it was fine, funny and moving. I ran into Mike coming offstage, raging: fucking play, fucking part, etc. I was angry and I told him so. He apologised, said he hated to upset me, loved me, but what to do . . .?

2nd September   I spoke to Eileen Atkins who's just had surgery for breast cancer. She's stoical and defiantly buoyant, fed up with the deluge of advice she's receiving from friends, neighbours and any-body she encounters. 'If anybody else tells me what I should be eating, I'll stuff it down their throats.' When she was in hospital in NY, the management were trying to get the head of the hospital to persuade her to go back into the play. The doctor wanted her to do it to prove his genius. 'What?' she said, 'I could go on with a drip and a catheter?' I asked her if Vanessa had gone to Bosnia. 'No,' she said, 'Arundel.'

3rd September   I've decided to do *Guys and Dolls* next year – the solution to the summer rep. I'm apprehensive that it will be seen as a distress signal, a flag flown at half mast. We'll have to (a) clearly present the reasons for doing it and (b) do it better than before. But why should I apologise? It's the best musical *ever*.

4th September   Saw *The Steward of Christendom* [*Stephen Barry*] at the Royal Court. Donal McCann was very very good, almost flawless, but, like a musician who insisted on staying in only one key, he modulated far too late in the second act. The play wanted to be

about everything, and ended up being about fathers and sons – enough to be going on with, without pulling in Irish history, the First World War, Michael Collins, mental hospitals and sectarianism. 'Oh, here's a foreign person.' 'Foreign? I'm from Cork.'

5th September   I went to a lecture by Robert Wilson. 'For me, my responsibility as an artist is to ask questions.' He gave an entertaining, intermittently (I dozed through some of it) compulsive account of his work. 'I hate naturalism,' he said, but then said one should contradict oneself. He's the authentic American avant-garde – elusive, almost inaccessible, determinedly opposed to the oppressive populist tradition. There *is* no middle road in the US. In the course of a two-hour lecture he credited no writer – except for his brain-damaged friend Christopher – and no designer, although all his work is done with collaborators. He presented himself as the undiluted *auteur*. He studied business as a young man and it shows, but that's part of his allure as operator, artist-on-the-make without a response to society or politics. His imagery is musical; it's conceived and composed and 'played' with the appeal not to observable truth in behaviour but to dream, illusion and sensation. 'I make silent operas – images which are composed in structured space and time.' However, it's all ferociously (and pretentiously) dependent on the 'painted word' – literary references, anecdotes, codes that exist *outside* the work and require the complicity of the knowing spectator, the membership of the club.

He's endearingly passionate in his anger that drama schools teach nothing. 'They don't teach you how to *stand*. Or to *sit*.' And he cites Jessye Norman as a paradigm, who *always* knew how to sit and stand. Which of course is a paradox, because for years he only ever used amateurs on stage. I read a quote from Patti Smith the other day: 'I am an American artist and I have no guilt.' But Bob Wilson's a humane man, fascinated by the ways that we think and feel and act *beyond* reason and speech. Bob Wilson's epigraph: 'I have a feeling something's going on.'

10th September   'The world of the happy is quite different from the world of the unhappy,' said Wittgenstein, and you don't have to go far for proof. I rang Ian McEwan last night from Box, about six-thirty, and he said: 'I'll come over.' So he came from Oxford, and he

looked worn out, but defiant. He's got his divorce and had spent eight days in court arguing over custody of the children, and has won, but feels humiliated and angry.

12th September   There's an epidemic of literary biographies. It's the desire to level, to make art an equation, to diminish the mystical, rob the writer of mystery, make him/her 'accessible', clubbable, explainable; writing becomes another profession and writers satisfyingly *more* vulnerable to weaknesses. Auden: 'Biographies of writers, whether written by others or themselves, are always superfluous and usually in bad taste. A writer is a maker, not a man of action . . . no knowledge of the raw materials will explain the peculiar flavour of the verbal dishes he invites the public to taste: his private life is, or should be, of no concern to anybody but himself, his family and his friends.'

16th September   George Raistrick [*actor in* La Grande Magia] has died. I told the cast the next day and they were stoical, as actors always are. Yes, the show did go on – what else could have happened? And everyone felt George's absence and grieved for him in their way. Bernie Cribbins was defiantly buoyant, pushing down the grief, almost belligerently defying it to hurt him. But on Thursday, as he approached the part of the play where the daughter of George's character has a fatal heart attack, he broke down – dried on stage utterly and irrecoverably. He stopped the show, the curtain came in; then the show started again and the act stumbled to a conclusion. Poor George: he was mild, generous, funny and talented. I remember a story of Bergman's: he was in a church with his father, a retired pastor. The pastor turned up, ill, said he couldn't give communion. B.'s father went into the vestry, told the pastor that he would do it, put on vestments and hobbled out. The lesson: 'Irrespective of anything that happens to you in life, you hold communion.' Bergman writes a lot about actors. I love them as he does, unsentimentally.

17th September   Lunch at the Mortimers'. I talked to Robert Harris about *Enigma*, his book and the code. 'Writing a novel without plot,' he said, 'is like having a car and growing flowers in it.' I sat next to Barbara Castle. She was keen to know where I

stood politically: 'Are you a right-wing spy?' She said she wouldn't
speak on a platform with Blair but would always do it for Neil – 'I'd
say *I* can be irresponsible, but *you* can only say what you're told to.'
She reserves her contempt for Callaghan and Tony Benn – both
completely self-serving opportunists in her eyes.

22nd September   Gala of *A Little Night Music*. Sue and I sat next
to Steve Sondheim, who said, after Judi had sung 'Send in the
Clowns': 'That's what you write them for.' Michael Oliver [*NT
board member*] told me that a banker had come up to him and said: 'I
suppose you have to put on this sort of thing for people from
Guildford.' A journalist said that it was the kind of show that
you take your parents to.

23rd September   The next day I got my notes on the show from
Cameron, as always very precise and lucid: he's right about the
staging in the first half and that Judi carries the show. Steve
Sondheim told me that Cameron thinks that *Martin Guerre* will
be a combination of *Tosca* and *West Side Story*.

24th September   Meetings with department after department
about how to change the face of the NT, how to broaden the
audience, about the future, about the need (and the modus operandi)
of fund-raising. Then a meeting with Sean [*Mathias*] and Steve
[*Sondheim*] about *A Little Night Music*.

25th September   Board meeting. I didn't give my usual report but I
described how the planning works, which is like three-dimensional
chess in the dark if you don't understand it (and often if you do). It
filled the Board with horror and awe. Here's the equation: three
theatres, three shows in repertoire in each theatre. If you want to play
your successes and nurse your failures you need total freedom of
manoeuvre, but if you cast an actor in two shows you restrict your
freedom of programming, and if you cast one in another auditorium
you're scuppered. As you are if you want to tour a show. Or have an
unusually complex set. Or stage a musical. You have to guess at the
number of performances for each show, i.e. predict your successes, or
worse, your failures. And if you want to transfer a show to the West
End you have to anticipate getting an option on the actors. And the

freedom to change the repertoire according to demand is restricted by the three-month print deadline of the brochure. If you shorten that you diminish the advance booking and therefore prejudice your cash flow. So it goes . . .

29th September   New York: rehearsing for *Racing Demon* at the Lincoln Center Theater. It's a very bright and enthusiastic cast, none of the listlessness that sometimes infects the early days of rehearsals.

1st October   Dinner with Ian Holm, who's making a film with Sidney Lumet. We talk almost entirely of *Lear*; about love of family, of children, of failing to express it, of fathers, and of kings. Of parental tyranny, different only in scale from the political variety. We talk of old age, and we talk of madness. 'That's the easy bit,' said Ian.

2nd October   Monday, day off. I'm buying CDs voraciously. I was in HMV carrying a copy of *Emma*. 'Great book,' said the guy at the till. 'And they're going to film it, God forbid.'

3rd October   The OJ verdict came. *No one* seems to think he's innocent; it's just a question of how you react to it – the divide between jubilation and despair is entirely racial. Jurors are now giving interviews, being pursued by the press with offers of up to $100,000. I saw OJ's daughter interviewed, who said they'd been very prayerful during the trial, and his mother said she'd kept the faith. His son read a statement about how his small children (Nicole's) were going to be brought up properly, and the father of the dead man said that the country had lost today. In the *NY Times* there's a piece saying that the whites will riot against the blacks in the way they always do – vote to withdraw aid for unemployment, medical care and housing. A third of young blacks in their twenties are in jail or under law-enforcement supervision.

4th October   The Pope's here in New York. They're selling baseball caps with the inscription: 'JESUS CHRIST IT'S THE REAL THING'. *The Village Voice* had a front cover: 'IS THE POPE A CATHOLIC?'

16th October   I've established a daily routine. The first three hours of the day I answer faxes from the NT and make phone calls, and

then my mind's clear for the day. Rehearsals continue well, and I'm very well looked after at the theatre. It's very curious to have a social life after rehearsals end in the evening – something that I haven't really had for years. The Pope has been and gone. A New Yorker says to the Pope: 'There was these three Polacks . . .' and is stopped by a Monsignor. 'Don't you know who you're talking to?' 'Oh, sorry, there *were* these three Polacks.'

22nd October   *The Way of the World* has opened. I think it's the first time that I've missed an opening since I started running the theatre. It's a fiendishly difficult play. The word is that parts of it work, parts don't, and that Geraldine [*McEwen*]'s performance is brilliant. Phyllida [*Lloyd*]'s gone for modern dress, but I can't guess from the reviews what it looks like. So I just try to remember the model and people it with my imagination.

25th October   There's a homeless man who sleeps down the street from the hotel, who I pass every morning and empty the coins in my pocket for. It's like paying a toll. He's often shaving with an electric razor.

26th October   *Racing Demon* has started previewing. It's mostly fine, and, thanks to Bob [*Crowley*]'s design and Wendall [*Harrington*]'s projections it looks excellent. It's not yet (four performances) taken the audience along with it from end to end. I suspect the audiences may be fed up with the Brits on Broadway. I remember John Lahr's review of Ralph Fiennes' Hamlet: 'The definition of genius is anyone from England.' Also, as Robbie Baitz says, NY isn't supportive of theatre that is about anything other than emotion and family. And the episodic form of the play is hard for an audience who want a straightforward narrative. Robbie says that NY theatre is 'faggy', meaning 'not serious'. Maybe it needs an audience prepared to take it seriously.

27th October   Ted Chapin [*head Rodgers and Hammerstein Estate*] told me that when Rodgers and Hammerstein produced *Annie Get Your Gun* they had meetings in which Irving Berlin would say: 'I've got a great song, it'll be a huge success, it's got the same chord sequence as White Christmas.' And they'd have to say: 'But the character couldn't *sing* that.'

2nd November   *Racing Demon* is going OK. A Jewish couple sat behind me – he was wearing a yarmulke and told his wife everything about every line in a penetrating whisper. A play about the Church of England seemed as remote from her as the courtship rituals of the Yoruba tribe. The audience are held by the play, but they don't know what it's *for*. I talked to Brian Murray about his character. He asked me what I had meant by saying Harry was a good priest. 'I've spent thirty years trying to be a good actor and fifteen trying to be a good person,' he says.

4th November   A sign on a door, not a hairdresser's, down 56th St: 'COMPLIMENTARY BLOWDRY'. What does it mean? Alan Bennett's story of walking in the Village in summer and hearing from an open window: 'For Chrissake, it's a figure of speech! You don't blow, you suck!'

5th November   Reading in Richard Avedon's apartment of Wally Shawn's play. It feels like the nineteenth century – a salon, populated by well-connected, well-read liberal intellectuals who have gathered to listen to the reading of a play which addresses the subject of the extinction of their universe: the death of culture. I'm eyed with curiosity because there's a piece about me in today's *NY Times*. The play was read by a poet, Mark Shand, an actress, Julianne Moore, and Mike Nichols, who I hadn't seen since *Comedians* in 1976. Mike's acquired a few pounds, but seems no older. The reading is mesmerising, extraordinarily potent. I can't imagine it being better done, or how it could be more powerful than this in a theatre, with all the baggage of 'performance'. I think Mike should do it at the NT and I tell him.

6th November   David and I were photographed by Avedon. He made us both nervous, but it was all over in ten minutes. We emerged feeling the earth should have moved but it didn't even shimmer. David coped better – more confidence in himself, and he always smiles in photos. I don't or can't. Bad teeth. So I'm a fatal combination of vanity and shyness and end up looking coy.

8th November   Back at the NT. *Mother Courage* has opened. Jonathan [*Kent*]'s made a defiant attempt to demystify the play with

a production that's unashamedly romantic and wholeheartedly theatrical. There are gains and losses: romanticism tips into senti- mentality (the *Les Misérables* music) and the set is often destructively decorative. But David [*Hare*]'s version is clear and unclogged and gets away from the pall of Eric Bentley – that English that isn't quite English. Diana [*Rigg*]'s performance is a triumph of the will; she certainly doesn't sentimentalise. The young audience are held by the narrative. It's not as strong as the *Galileo* – also David's translation – at the Almeida, but then the play's not as easy, although better. Also it doesn't have a mountainous performance from Richard Griffiths.

9th November   I saw Stephen Daldry who says he doesn't want to run the NT. Neither does Nick Hytner. I feel very disappointed. Daldry doesn't want to run the refurbished Royal Court either when it re-opens.

11th November   Isabella di Filippo came to *La Grande Magia*. She was full of praise, but questions David Ross's performance as the Policeman. I've encouraged him to take it to extremes, to play it farcically, a nightmare of a policeman, but Isabella says: 'It's a change of style, perhaps too expressionistic, but Eduardo was not expressionist, he was Sicilian.' She praised Alan Howard and Bernie Cribbins. I told her that Bernie was a comic actor. 'Eduardo always said it was possible for a comic actor to play tragedy, but not the other way round.'

12th November   I went to the BBC for a meeting with Duke Hussey about joining the BBC Board. I inadvertently stepped in front of a man at the reception desk. 'Do you always barge in front of people? I suppose because you're Director of the National Theatre you think you can get away with it.' 'I don't know what you're talking about.' 'Oh, pleeeeease,' he said with a Kenneth Williams-like sneer, and flounced off. I went to see 'Dukie', though didn't have the courage to call this extremely tall patrician by a name suited to a Labrador dog. 'Want a cup of tea?' he said. 'Yes, please.' 'Milk and sugar?' 'No sugar.' 'One milk and a Michelle, please Jean.' '?' 'Oh, I call it a Michelle after a secretary I had – said to be very keen on large strong black Indians.' For all that, he's one of those people who take a constant delight in belying his image: he's smart.

13th November   Back in New York. To the Sunday matinee; it's one of those inert audiences and a listless performance, but being in New York just directing makes me want to concentrate on it to the exclusion of everything else. 'Steven Spielberg is fortunate in that what he loves is then loved by so many people in the world. He is both successful and sincere,' says Fellini. 'An artist must express himself doing what he loves in his own style, without compromise. Those who want only to please cannot aspire to being artists. A little compromise here, and at what point is the soul lost? Chip, chip, crack. Being an artist, to my way of thinking, has less to do with external judgements of whether what you do is good or bad than whether you did it to please yourself, or only to please others . . . Success takes you away from life. It robs you of that contact that gave you the success.' And Wilde on the same subject: 'The moment that an artist takes notice of what other people want, and tries to supply the demand, he ceases to be an artist and becomes a dull or an amusing craftsman, an honest or dishonest tradesman.'

14th November   I had dinner with Ian Holm and we talked about *Lear*. 'I have two thoughts about the storm,' he said. 'Oh so do I,' said I. 'You speak,' he said. 'Real rain is the first thought,' I said. Ian nodded. 'And the second?' I said. 'He must be naked,' said Ian. And I nodded; anything less than the 'unaccommodated man' would be dishonest. I tell Ian what Alan Parker said of Ken Loach: 'I ask how he gets such reality, such honesty. Ken always says: "It's not to do with the How, it's to do with the Why."'

15th November   I gave notes and rehearsed on Tuesday after-noon. Then the performance got very sharp and my spirits revived with the show. Tina Brown gave a dinner in my honour. I felt shamed and moved by their generosity: is it conceivable that we'd turn out in London for an American director to honour an American arts institution? Or that the editor of a British magazine would host the evening? John Lahr made a fulsome speech. Normally you'd have to die to hear such things – and then, of course, wouldn't.

17th November   Lunch with Tony Kushner, who's teaching a playwriting course at NYU. He's giving them instruction in ideology, on the grounds that they should know what it is that they're

condemning or demonising. So he makes them read Marx and Althusser. Meeting with George Wolfe [*Director, NY Public Theater*]. He hates nostalgia, particularly in the American theatre, says it's a race thing. 'After all,' he says, 'why should I be nostalgic about something I would have been excluded from?'

22nd November   The opening went well. I was very touched by a present the cast gave me: a plaster cast of a '30s-ish racing car driven by a devil with a dog collar. I've really enjoyed working with them. For the first time in about twenty years I sat in the auditorium for the performance and enjoyed it. We decanted to the Tavern on the Green to celebrate, where I talked to Mike Nichols about Hollywood and bad faith and disaster and success. He said working with Ariel Dorfman had made him feel what it was like to be a woman: he'd abuse him one day, then kiss him on the next and ask for forgiveness.

23rd November   Back from New York. A woman in the check-in queue at JFK (a fashion editor) said she liked to go to the Chelsea Arts Club because there were 'so few poofs around'. Non PC is edging its way back. I heard several people on the radio in the taxi from Heathrow saying they liked male talk shows that allowed them to 'express their feelings about fancying women and liking football'.

24th November   I refereed a meeting between Stanley Spencer's daughters, Pam Gems, and Tim Hatley [*designer*]. They were elfin creatures of sixty-five and seventy, who painstakingly went through Pam's script [*Stanley*] page by page for two and a half hours. It was obviously extremely painful for them to have to talk about their father objectively as if he were (and he is) public property. They kept objecting to things on the grounds that 'people wouldn't have said that sort of thing in those days'. 'Well, I'm sixty-seven,' said Pam, 'and I can tell you that they *did*.' At the end we thought we had their support and could possibly copy some of the paintings to which they have the rights.

26th November   I've agreed to join the BBC Board, so I went to a meeting of the BBC Advisory Council. Quite depressing – not the Council, who were extremely clear and articulate, Jane Asher in particular, nor the governors who seemed surprisingly unwilling to

be complacent, but the BBC managers who seemed ineffably complacent. The question that remained unresolved was this: what is
their aim? Is it to 'maximise the market position' or is it to be a public
service broadcaster? Are they prepared to be good before being
popular? What do they mean by 'distinctive programming'? Are they
interested in developing the 'market' rather than the audience?

I couldn't stay for the discussion about the Diana *Panorama*, but I
watched the programme later and was astonished. I found it shocking in that one is used to seeing members of the Royal Family being
endlessly insincere, emotionally recessed, manipulative and arrogant.
Diana: 'You see yourself as a good product that sits on the shelf and
sells well', 'I was a fat, chubby twenty-year-old', 'He was a proud
man, I made him feel low', 'Fortunately I had two boys', 'We didn't
want to disappoint the public', 'I'm as thick as a plank . . . Prince
Charles is a great thinker', 'I was outside the net, not inside the
family', 'The enemy . . . my husband's department', of a photographer, 'Look up, Di! If I get my picture my children can go to a better
school', 'I can give love . . . someone's got to go out and love people'.
It reminded me of a Mafia confession, with the Family behind the
scene muttering: What do we do with her? With the giant caveat that
one should never judge a marriage, Diana seemed the humane,
injured party and a victim of monarchical politics and he seemed
the complacent oppressor. The ITV documentary on Charles was
like an old-style palace-creeping brown-nosing BBC film, which
made Charles seem self-serving and immature. But maybe it was
just that she was the better actress. It was clearly in the public interest
to show the documentary, and it revealed that the interests of the
monarchy and the public are (and always have been) completely
incompatible.

27th November A meeting with Michael Palliser [*NT Board
member*] to discuss my successor, or at least the method of choosing
him/her. Thelma [*Holt, producer*] has made a fuss about not being
consulted as drama panel chairman – a tactical error on their part. In
the evening an ABSA do where I met Virginia Bottomley, the sixth
minister I've had to deal with in my time at the NT. She asked me to
come and see her. 'How's it going?' 'The National Theatre?' 'No, the
BBC Governors.' 'Oh . . .' 'I had a job to get you on. There was a lot
of resistance from Downing Street.'

28th November I gave a lecture about directing at the Royal Geographical Society. I spoke in the same (un-redecorated) lecture hall that my grandfather lectured in when he came back from the Antarctic. Sarah Hawkins, the organiser, asked me if I thought Paul Scofield would do a talk. I said I doubted it. The *Guardian* printed excerpts of my lecture – which is now the third time that material's been printed, if you count my book and the *Sunday Times*. This is the Grub Street life; I long to write something new. I remember Brian Wenham [*ex-Controller BBC2*] saying to me: 'Journalism's a brothel, and once you've patronised it you keep going back.'

29th November At the *Evening Standard* Awards Mike Gambon won an award for *Volpone* and *Skylight*. His speech: 'Fuck me, I'm off for a piss.'

30th November I saw a run-through of *Rosencrantz and Guildenstern Are Dead*, which was very encouraging – Simon Russell-Beale and Adrian Scarborough a beguiling combination. I haven't seen the play for many years, but seeing it again it seemed extraordinarily fresh and prescient, anticipating *Blackadder, Fry and Laurie* and *Fawlty Towers*. Or they caught up with it. Or copied it. In the afternoon we read David's Oscar Wilde film script. It's hugely enjoyable: a love story which the studio has said would be much more commercial if the young man changed sex.

1st December I had a pc from Bill Gaskill this morning. I have been to and fro with him for almost a year about him wanting to do *Luther* [*John Osborne*], but I've never been sufficiently convinced to push the button. You think the play's going to be great; then you read it and it isn't. Just some great patches. I apologised to Bill, whose card wasn't recriminatory, but he did say, characteristically: 'There are several plays in your repertoire that I am very fond of in productions that I couldn't bear to see.'

2nd December We went to Glos for the first time in months. I woke up this morning knowing that I *had* to write something. But what? It was something about 'knowledge' and 'compassion', but for the life of me I can't make the connection. I've been wondering whether I'll die here. I'm reading Tony's first draft of *Le Roi* – it's

full of wit and energy, and the flabby patches are the fault of the original and I hope can be treated. It's got to be very hard-edged in production, very violent. I've also been reading *Borkman*, of which the same is true – it's incredibly tormented, full of crazed passion and frustrated love. Also read a Nabokov play and a Chikamatsu play.

3rd December   Bob [*Crowley*] sent me this, it's Martha Graham to Agnes de Mille: 'There is a vitality, a life force, a quickening that is translated through you into action and, because there is only one of you in all time, this expression is unique and if you block it it will not exist through any other medium and it will be lost, the world will not have it. It is not your business to determine how good it is, nor how it compares with other expressions. It is your business to keep it yours clearly and directly – to keep the channel open. You do not have to believe in yourself or your work, you have to keep open and aware the urges that motivate you – keep the channel open. No artist is pleased. There is no satisfaction whatsoever at any time. There is only a queer divine satisfaction, a blessed unrest that keeps us marching and makes us more alive than the others.'

4th December   Jimmy Jewel died yesterday. I'm about to write a tribute to him – largely in response to a piece in the *Guardian*, which seems to be saying that his life was justified by the fact that he'd appeared in *Comedians*, and telling some bollocks of a story about him threatening to walk out of the dress rehearsal 'as the penny finally dropped about the nature of the play'. He was perfectly aware of the nature of the play – as we knew only too well, given that he'd withdrawn from the production two days before we started rehearsals. It's a tribute to his professionalism – and to his courage and tenacity – that he did turn up for the first day of rehearsals. Jimmy could be maudlin, sentimental, irascible, and intolerant, but he could also be generous, loyal, and in his diffident way, loving. He always expected the best of people, and was always shocked by the worst. He worshipped Sid Field, and must have told me thirty times what Val Parnell had said when he was told of Field's death at the Palladium. 'Uh huh,' said Parnell, 'uh huh. What's the understudy like?'

6th December I'm worrying about my commitment to the BBC. I feel strongly that some of what has been done at the BBC is wrong in principle and wrong in execution, and much is right in principle and wrong in execution. I don't know how I can make any difference. From a BBC Year Book of 1930: 'Think of your favourite occupation. Don't you like a change sometimes? Give the wireless a rest now and then.' Now that's what I call marketing.

8th December Sarah Hawkins has sent me a copy of a letter that Paul Scofield wrote to her explaining why he didn't want to speak in public about acting:

> I have found that an actor's work has life and interest only in its execution. It seems to wither away in discussion, and become emptily theoretical and insubstantial. It has no rules (except perhaps audibility). With every play and every playwright the actor starts from scratch, as if he or she knows nothing and proceeds to learn afresh every time – growing with the relationships of the characters and the insights of the writer. When the play has finished its run he's empty until the next time. And it's the emptiness which is, I find, apparent in any discussion of theatre work.

10th December I've found the trial of Rosemary West very disturbing. The evidence has been so unsettling that even the tabloids have felt unable to publish the details and it hasn't been a fit of propriety on their part. It was this: that it was impossible to reconcile her literally unthinkable cruelty with her palpable humanity. A court reporter wrote: 'Her testimony so stilled the court that journalists hesitated to turn the pages of their notebooks. When she looked at Rose, her daughter, it was with such gentle yearning that it capsized all who saw it.' By any definition of behaviour the Wests' actions were evil and insane: they were 'mad', and yet within their family there existed a sort of family life. One of the daughters said of her father: 'It was the only kind of love I knew from him, and I never complained.' No amount of reportage or analysis can help me to understand these relationships. Only if I make a huge imaginative leap, by putting myself in the position of the child – or the father – only through empathy – through drama or through fiction – can I

begin to grasp these all *too* human paradoxes: the banality of evil but also the complexity of it. Trying to investigate evil is to encounter Heisenberg's uncertainty principle: it's like trying to investigate the works of a watch with your thumb; it gets in the way. I read this by the novelist Gregory Maguire: 'You figure out one side of it – the human side, say – and the eternal side goes into the shadow . . . What does a dragon in its shell look like? Well, no one can ever tell, for as soon as you break the shell to see, the dragon is no longer *in* its shell . . . It is in the nature of evil to be *secret*.'

11th December   I went to Irving Wardle's farewell lunch. He's been fired from the *Independent on Sunday*, because they have to pay him too much, or he writes too well, or he takes theatre too seriously. He'd asked me to make a speech, and I felt like I was declaring the end of an era. Irving made a very funny speech about the things he wouldn't miss, which included deciphering the plots of the Jacobeans and seeing plays by Steven Berkoff and Howard Barker.

13th December   Jimmy Jewel's funeral. I talked to the widow of Dickie Henderson, who was a pal of Jimmy's. We talked about Jimmy's hypochondria. Val Parnell came to Blackpool when Jewel and Warriss were playing there. 'I'm feeling a bit funny,' said Jimmy. 'Better get on stage before it wears off,' said Val.

15th December   I had a phone call from a chinless voice that said: 'It's Sir Simon C . . . (indecipherable) from Buckingham Palace. Her Majesty would like to have lunch with you next year. Will you be free?'

17th December   Stephen Wood has told me he's resigning, because he's been offered the job of Alan A.'s administrator in Scarborough. I'll really miss him. It's a perfect job for him, come just at the right time – when he's really uncomfortable with changes I want/need to make. I have no doubts: like it or not, we have to be more on the front foot about raising money through sponsorship, and Stephen's uncomfortable with this. But we can no more resist it than stop the sun from rising. He told me with an undisguised shiver of *schadenfreude* that there was a lot of unrest on the fifth floor. He gave me this quote, years ago, by David Gower when he was England Captain:

'Any captain goes into a match fully versed on the basics; the crucial part is the fine-tuning from moment to moment. Making the swift decisions on the field is the easy part; the tough part is explaining your decisions afterwards. And 98 per cent of the pressure you get, having to explain yourself, comes from the media.'

18th December   I'm struggling to get Peter Hall to agree to do the *Oedipus* plays (struggle over fee) and Isabelle Huppert to do *Mary Stuart* (struggle over expenses). Today I saw a small girl holding her father's hand walking down Long Acre. 'Daddy let me look, I want to look.' They stood together looking at a building site, and I envied them beyond description.

19th December   Nick Wright says that Lindsay Anderson's diaries can't be published because they're full of hot sex with famous people. It sounds wildly improbable.

20th December   Party at the BBC, utterly Trollopian, talk all of hierarchy and appointment. Hussey is definitely the Archbishop. He spots me as I come in the room, draws me aside and we sit uncomfortably on a sofa as the tide of the party ebbs and flows noisily around us. 'You know John Birt,' he says. I nod. 'Could you see if you could get him to talk to me, you know, have a word with him?' Apparently they haven't spoken in public or private for eighteen months. When I tell John he says, 'It's a waste of time talking to him.'

21st December   Increasing speculation about who's going to succeed me. There's a campaign by Nick de Jongh about the 'disastrous' decision to have an appointments committee without 'a Trevor Nunn, a Terry Hands or a Peter Hall on it'. There are six people who *could* take over: Nick [*Hytner*], Stephen [*Daldry*], Sam [*Mendes*], Jonathan [*Kent*], Ian [*McDiarmid*], Ian [*McKellen*]. Both Nick and Ian McK. have told me they don't want to do it. Stephen's too restless – and has told me he doesn't want to do it. Sam's too young – or *he* thinks he is, but I'm going to start wooing him and try to persuade him that he must do the job. I don't think the Board would take Jonathan and Ian as a pair. A few letters of application have come in, one a letter that says: 'I want to be the new Richard

Eyre. I have no experience of running a theatre, or anything. But I have a safari suit.'

22nd December   I had a meeting with Virginia Bottomley at the DNH. The staff party was going on and I could hear the sounds of revelry down the dismal corridors. I waited for her for about twenty minutes in a waiting room, reading a catalogue for a Paula Reago exhibition. She came into the room, threw herself down on a sofa, tucked her legs under her and said; 'What would you like to talk about?' She's sexy in a Julie Andrews fashion, which can't have been a help in getting her colleagues to take her seriously. I told her a bit about the NT but she's not a listener, and she was indiscreet (to charm me?) about all her predecessors at the DNH, particularly Mellor, who she described as a show-off. She spoke fondly of Major and of 'Hezza', and angrily of Waldegrave, who she'd fought bitterly to prevent a cut of £70m. She had an image that she repeated to me over and over: it's not good to be perpetually hungry, she said of arts funding: 'in a famine you think of nothing but food'. But she seemed to think it was up to Grey Gowrie to sort it all out, to unlock the taps of the Lottery. She's determined to make the DNH of some importance, to 'make her mark' there. She identified strongly with John Birt, who she sees as a Messianic moderniser, who has achieved what she was trying to achieve at the Health Ministry. I refrain from saying that I hope he won't have quite such disastrous consequences for the BBC. She says she's obsessional. I believe it, but she's on the treadmill for *what*?

23rd December   I met another politician – Michael Howard – at the V & A. Like all the people one demonises, he's quite plausible in person. What do politicians do at the end of their lives, tot up the score? Say they've 'made their mark'? Perhaps that's what we all do. We don't say: 'I've lived a good life, given happiness, been unselfish, been loving, tried to leave the world a better place.' I read this about Albert Speer, a bit drunk near the end of his life: 'He simply said he had not done badly: "After all I *was* Hitler's architect; I *was* his Minister of Armaments and Production; I *did* serve twenty years in Spandau and coming out *did* make another good career. Not bad after all, was it?"'

24th December   David gave me a poem about Shakespeare by Louis MacNeice which ends:

> O master pedlar with your confidence tricks
> Brooches, pomanders, broadsheets and what-have-you,
> Who hawk such entertainment but rook your client
> And leave him brooding, why should we forgive you.
> Did we not know that, though more self-reliant
> Than we, you too were born and grew up in a fix.

26th December   Glorious iridescent sun, frost, peace. I felt my usual blend of relief, joy, weariness, misanthropy and gregariousness over Christmas. Alan Bennett has done three films for TV about Westminster Abbey. He's brilliant and they're wholly compelling, but he's in danger of self-parody, of his modesty becoming a form of pride, backing diffidently into the limelight to castigate those who hungered for 'fame', 'wealth' and 'power'. Also saw a brilliant documentary about Elvis's diet and how to cook squirrel. 'Elvis suffered his terminal event on the commode.'

27th December   I've been reading *When Did You Last See Your Father?* by Blake Morrison. It's a more or less definitive account of the rite of passage of losing a father. If I'd read it before, I'd never have written my book. It's unnervingly honest – only towards the end do you realise that the book had to be written as an exorcism. 'Now I am an adult. Now I don't pretend to judge. Now I see him in the mirror when I dress, feel myself becoming him, fear that I'm inheriting all the faults he would have wanted to save me from.' I hate the way I patronised my father, which I did out of fear and anger in my book. He was an original man, and a bold one, genuinely anarchic, even if it was restrained (or bolstered) by his class. He was a kind of poet – however coarse, crude and blunt – he made metaphors, he had his own voice, his own way of seeing the world.

28th December   I had a vivid dream about directing a Greek chorus in a production of *Christmas Carol*. They couldn't be persuaded to work together, but insisted on fighting for their individuality. I became hoarse trying to persuade them, while Sue sat in a corner talking to a secretary. I had to shout to get everyone's

attention. Again and again and again. Then I woke up angry about Rupert Christiansen having said in a profile of me: 'He hates conflict . . .' How could I possibly run the NT if I hated conflict? And I remembered this article had been headlined: 'HE WALKS AWAY FROM A JOB THAT MOST PEOPLE WOULD DIE FOR'. And I'd thought it should have read: 'HE DIES FROM A JOB MOST PEOPLE WOULD WALK AWAY FROM'.

29th December   The cold spell continues. Said on the news that Britain was the coldest place in the *world* – except for the Arctic and Antarctica. Seems improbable. I've been reading *Imperium* by Ryzard Kapuskinski: 'You can know real cold by the bright, shining mist that hangs in the air. When a person walks, a corridor forms in the mist.' Also: 'Power is seriousness. In an encounter with power, a smile is tactless, it demonstrates a lack of respect.' The book's epigraph is from Simone Weil: 'The present is something that binds us. We create the future in our imagination. Only the past is pure reality.'

30th December   It's raining and the rain is freezing on the ground, so the whole terrace and roads and pebbles and backyard are clear, solid ice. I had to drive Lu to Stroud. We skated down Scar Hill, just missing a parked car and a dry stone wall, reached the bottom and were told by an excited policeman that the road to Stroud was impassable, there'd been an accident. 'A fatal,' he said, his eyes glowing. We slithered up the hill and got to Stroud. On the way back I passed the wrecks of the cars, squashed beyond recognition. I almost got to the house but stopped 50 yards short; with the help of ash and salt and carpet and newspaper managed to make it.

31st December   Sue says that New Year's Eve makes her anxious, a cold hand round the heart. I hate the way that you're forced to audit the past year and measure up the possibilities for the next one. Making New Year resolutions is like going to confession – a meaningless ritual intended to show piety and to assuage guilt at doing nothing positive to improve your life.

1996

1st January An article in the *Guardian*, a reprint of a piece by the theatre critic, Philip Hope-Wallace, written in 1961: 'A nation gets the theatre it deserves. A nation which spends £20 million on Christmas cards but cannot 'afford' a national theatre gets ten years of *The Mousetrap*, four years of *My Fair Lady*, a revival of *Salad Days* . . . To look back over the years is often to groan in memory.'

3rd January I'm working on *Borkman* and reading Michael Meyer's biography of Ibsen. Of a performance of *The Master Builder*, a friend of Ibsen's said: 'The play is good enough, big enough. The actors were too small.' Ibsen thought that *Borkman* was about the conflict between love and the desire for power; it seems to me nakedly autobiographical. Everything in his life – wife, son, happiness – had been subsumed in his desire to write and achieve status through his writing. And his vanity: he used to have a mirror in the bottom of his top hat, and use it frequently to comb his beard. When he was seventy-six he was heard to cry out in his sleep: 'I'm writing! And it's going splendidly!' He said to a writer who had criticised him in a lecture: 'At least you read the stage directions.'

4th January Nick Starr [*head of planning*] came down to Glos today. We walked and then worked, and after four hours I felt as if we had control over the future of the theatre – at least for the next year. I liked Nick's observation: 'There used to be three categories of traveller in youth hostels: men, women and cyclists.'

5th January It's a lilac dawn, the first for a week, dispelled when I switch on my desk light. Today there's a Lottery pay-out of £40m.,

and it's reckoned that nine out of ten people will play this weekend. I feel wholly detached from it and depressed by the craven eagerness to embrace the absolute worst of contemporary life. It's a tax on poverty. Or on stupidity. And it's disastrous for the arts. I think what will happen is this: the public (and some newspapers), unable to distinguish between capital grants and revenue, will become ever more confused and resentful of arts organisations ('toffs in tutus'), who continue to demand more money from the government, while receiving huge sums from the Lottery. Legislation governing the Lottery will change. The grant from the DNH to the Arts Council will diminish when revenue as well as capital grants are made from the Lottery. The Arts Council will find itself rich in cash to distribute to hungry arts organisations but will have been so busy lobbying for change in the Lottery legislation that it won't have developed a strategy for distributing the largesse. The Chancellor, becoming exasperated by the sight of so much cash sluicing away beyond his sieve, will increase the proportion of tax obtained from the Lottery. The government will start to siphon off cash from the Lottery to help fund Education and Health (which is what's happened in several Australian states). The novelty of the Lottery will wear off, and the income will diminish. The Treasury will demand a higher percentage of tax, rather than see their portion of the cake shrink; the government will give priority to Lottery spending on Education, Health, Sport and Charities. (Recent tabloid headline: 'IT'S TUTU MUCH IT STINKS, IT'S A SLAP IN THE FACE OF HONEST DECENT HARD-WORKING LOTTERY PLAYING JOE PUBLIC WHO WANT TO GIVE THE MONEY TO CURE CANCER). The arts will receive no further funding, either from the Lottery or from the DNH, and arts organisations will turn to business and private sponsorship for revenue support. The patrons will shrug and say: 'We've given you what you asked for when you wanted matching funds for your grand capital schemes which were funded by the Lottery in the mid-'90s. We have no more to give.' New, or refurbished, theatres will have to raise their box-office prices to unacceptable levels or reduce their costs – fewer actors, fewer staff, no new plays (royalties), no Shakespeare (too large casts), no sets, no audience, and then once a week on the Olivier stage a lavish set will be unveiled, two machines will be wheeled onstage, pastel-coloured bouncing balls will be reverently handled by men in blue blazers and

white gloves, and once again Anthea Turner will unite the nation in its epiphany.

6th January   The ROH have just announced that they'll be shedding a hundred jobs front of house. How can they do that and keep going? What do these people *do*?

In 1868 Cézanne was asked what was his greatest aspiration. Certainty, he said. And that's his quality: a heroic and invariable one, it's the most alluring thing about his paintings. Yes, you think, that *is* what it looks like. Roger Fry said he'd turned sensationalism into the business of realising one's senses. If one was asked for the characteristic that distinguished the twentieth century you'd have to say: *un*certainty.

7th January   I listened to a recording of a piano roll made by Rachmaninov of a Chopin waltz. He plays it with great regularity and no romanticism. Rather academic. These days *everyone* is a romantic – feeling above everything. Just tell us you're ALIVE.

8th January   I went to a meeting of the succession cttee. There have been six proper applications for the job and enquiries from some improbable directions. I said it seemed inevitable to me, given that Nick's ruled himself out, that Sam or Stephen would be the best candidates – even if they hadn't applied. But I said that neither Sam nor Stephen had given me an indication that they would want the job. Tom [*Stoppard*] says he's talked to Trevor [*Nunn*], who might be interested.

9th January   I had dinner with Chris Hogg in the boardroom at Reuters. He's an oddly contained, engaging and piercingly intelligent man and I always feel faintly inadequate in spite of his continuous flattery of me. We have a '76 claret (can't remember what) and all the kind of food that makes my stomach go crazy but I can't resist and wouldn't have the social confidence to turn it down even if I could. He opened a notebook and took meticulous notes throughout dinner.

11th January   Duke Hussey rang me to say he was retiring and Christopher Bland was taking over. Apropos his departure he quoted

Harold Wilson: 'When I leave the bridge I will not come back and spit on the deck.' To which Dukie added: 'Unlike Margaret Thatcher.' He said he was retiring because he's had enough: 'I've been round the course, over the jumps, had the odd fall – there's no reason to want to do it again.'

12th January   Foreign Office joke: they call Thatcher Daggers. After Dagenham on the tube line – two stops past Barking.

13th January   I spoke to Tom about why Trevor might want to run the NT. He wants a knighthood, he said. 'Why haven't you been offered one?' I said. He quoted Cato the Elder. 'I would like the world to say why didn't they put up a statue to him, rather than why *did* they put up a statue to him.' Alan [*Bennett*] told me that when Francis Bacon was offered an OM, he turned it down. 'It's so ageing,' he said.

14th January   I went to Paris on the train; it's painless travel, like dreaming. I saw a matinee of Peter [*Brook*]'s show *Qui Est Là*, which is charming, childlike, enjoyable, but elusive. This is the show that's been distilled from all that work on Meyerhold, and Stravinsky, and Brecht and Gordon Craig et al. It's like a revue – a few anthologised pieces, some scenes from *Hamlet*, and a perverse lack of authorial voice, when the whole thing only made sense if you thought of it as an autobiographical piece – Peter and his Orchestra – to all of whom French is a second language. *Le Monde*, calling Peter a '*vache sacré*', had said the actors made the show incomprehensible; perhaps that's why I find I'm able to follow their French. I saw Peter afterwards, friendly and avuncular.

In the evening I went to Bobigny to see *Richard II*. The production's now very clear and Fiona's really good. I'm still undecided as to whether she really does illuminate the character's sexual ambiguity, or whether she annuls it. I had a long talk with Ariel Goldberg, who runs the theatre. They have pots of money, and expected an audience of about 6,000 over the run. Most of the audience for the first night were invited. I began to see why people are so enraged by the liberal consensus: of course he's a socialist, they give huge subsidies and Ariel and his colleagues (like me) live very comfortable lives as cultural commissars, presiding over our bourgeois fiefdoms.

15th January   I spoke to Ian [*McKellen*] about running the NT. He said: 'I don't think I'm up to it . . . I couldn't. I just couldn't.'

16th January   Mitterrand has died. He'd arranged everything about his own death, the timing of it, the instructions for his funeral and memorial service. He's very quotable. On Thatcher: 'One does not assuage one's own misfortune with the troubles of others, but they help.' And to Thatcher: 'You must know the distinction between Corneille and Racine. The latter describes people as they are, the former as they should be. In politics it is better to follow the example of Racine.' Of the Left: 'There is nothing worse than socialists who dream of being praised as good economists by men of the Right. They may end up forgetting they are of the Left.' 'I feel myself a social democrat, which is to say I never attempt a reform if I think it will fail.' 'I am a follower of Epictetus: I influence what I can. What I cannot influence I leave alone. Allow me to find that more effective than tilting at windmills.' 'Mourning for others is a way of mourning for yourself. Those who die take away a part of you.'

17th January   It's starting to look probable that Trevor could be interested in my job. Ironically the unrest in the theatre is at the thought that one of the younger people might be appointed; they're frightened of someone coming in with a determination to change everything. Whatever anybody says nobody is ever really up for change.

18th January   Lunch at the Arts Council with Grey Gowrie. Grey 'ventilates' his opinions, never answering the questions that he's asked, mellifluously ducking the opportunity to tell us what the fuck is happening with next year's grant and the Lottery legislation. Mary Allen acts as if she is running Grey, but it's possibly the other way round.

19th January   To Cardiff for a BBC Board of Governors meeting. BOG is an unfortunate acronym. I feel uncomfortable pretending to be a 'suit man', a New Manager, and wonder how long it takes for it to stick. It's mostly a very good Board but when we discuss religion and ethnic programming one governor is keen to point out that they are practising Christians, and that although blacks are a jolly good

thing, let's not go too far in acknowledging it. He asks if the statistics for ethnic population are reliable. 'Do they have radios?'

20th January   I heard David [*Hare*] on the radio with Michael Berkeley this morning. He described opera as a ludicrous activity, the acting terrible and all his director friends running off like lemmings to direct it. He was asked if he'd been influenced by me. 'Rather the other way round,' he replied tartly.

21st January   Glos. Sunday. A great orange ball of sun is coming up from behind the hill, and two vapour trails are scoring the clear pinky-blue sky. I'm thinking about the evidence that I have to present to the Parliamentary Select Committee on funding the arts. Believing in the virtue of funding the arts is like believing in the value of democracy – i.e. we fund the entire membership of the House of Commons even though hordes of MPs have no power and little influence. In strictly utilitarian terms you'd have to say that paying for back-bench MPs is as pointless a self-indulgence as funding the arts. But perhaps this isn't the wisest tack to take with the Committee, even if close to the truth of most ministers' beliefs.

22nd January   Our language has become like hobson-jobson. We absorbed 'juggernaut', 'chicanery', 'curry', 'ginger', 'sugar', 'toddy', 'pyjamas', 'pundit', 'nirvana' into our language. Now we've taken on 'grand', 'baseline', 'first base', 'ball-park figure', 'rain check' – they're terms from baseball, which isn't even played by amateurs here. And 'no way', 'momentarily', 'at this time', 'business-wise', 'level playing-field', 'dissing', 'hookers', 'hackers', 'high fives'. I suppose the language changed at about the same time as we lined our high streets with McDonalds, Burger King, Nachos, Baskins-Robbins, Kentucky Fried Chicken, Planet Hollywood, Tower Records, Warner Cinemas, Calvin Klein, Ralph Lauren, Donna Karan, Tommy Hilfiger, Levis, Gap, Nike, Coke, Buds, Becks and became the unofficial 51st State of the Union.

26th January   I'm reading *Sabbath's Theater* by Philip Roth. The character rages at life, Lear-like. Is there anything that a man can't or won't do, it asks, like Saint-Exupéry's: 'That which I have done no animal would do.' We're infinitely treacherous, promiscuous, sexu-

ally obsessed, disloyal, childish – and yet capable of love of a sort. It's a very brave book to have written and – just – comes off. David gave it to me for the *Demon* in NY: 'For his splendid production, in the profound hope that the author's fears will not be fulfilled – that these will be the last days of sense, beauty and proportion in the British theatre.'

28th January   Just come back from a weekend in Paris. I saw two productions – *Phèdre* at the Comédie Française and *Tartuffe* at the Cartoucherie. The *Phèdre* distilled everything bad about French theatre even if the auditorium is beautiful and it was full; but the performance was inert, affected, boring, long and snobby. *Tartuffe* was the exact opposite, but raggedly acted and too long. Beautiful day – bright sun, snow in the Tuileries Gardens. They do things here with such conviction and confidence: we do some feeble 'Millennium' projects, funded by the Lottery and requiring private matching funds to get going.

29th January   Last night an associates' meeting, which was a bit rancid: a long and unsatisfactory discussion about who should be consulted about my successor. Then a long and very frustrating discussion about the appointment of a head of public affairs and a campaign director to raise money. I explained that we needed to co-ordinate our press, marketing and box office *and* needed to raise money for the redevelopment, and if we *didn't* do the redevelopment the theatre would crumble within ten years and we'd lose our licence long before, let alone our public. But few seemed to buy this argument or feel there was any urgency to change ANYTHING. David said we were destroying the 'cottage industry' by introducing '80s-style management – as if we'd been got at, like Stepford wives. It's perfectly possible to improve 'management' without becoming a creature of 'New Management' but my associates weren't having any of it. The meeting ended with Nick Hytner suggesting that the associates go into self-destruct before my successor was appointed. Mitterrand was asked what quality is most necessary in a leader and he said: 'I'd like to say sincerity, but I'm afraid I must say indifference.'

30th January   I talked to Sam [*Mendes*] who'd heard rumours about Trevor for Director. 'Well, you're the only person who could

compete with him,' I said. 'Maybe I should do it,' he said. But his heart wasn't in it.

31st January   Robert Fox's (third) marriage party. Michael White [*producer*] says: 'It's very grown-up.' 'Grown-up?' I say. 'Well, I never go out with anyone older than my daughter.' 'How old's your daughter?' 'Twenty-six,' says Michael. Max Rayne corners me. 'Is the rumour true?' 'About what?' 'Trevor Nunn.' 'A disaster,' he says.

1st February   There's a documentary on TV on the ROH – *The House* – which is philistine, mean-spirited, meretricious but mesmerising. It's a long suicide note, and I can't understand why Jeremy allowed the cameras in: access or vanity?

2nd February   Michael Palliser rang me to say that the succession cttee have decided to go 'helter-skelter for Trevor'. They want to offer next week and send him to meet the Board the week after. Michael wants me to speak to Sam, Jonathan and Stephen Daldry, but I feel uneasy about doing this. *Stanley* opened very successfully. Very well directed by John Caird and designed by Tim Hatley – without the aid of any Stanley Spencer paintings, since the daughters refused us. Very well acted – with Tony Sher better than I've ever seen him, totally unmannered, very moving. He's completely subsumed his personality in Stanley Spencer, who he admires – loves – without reservation.

3rd February   Leaving party for Stephen [*Wood*]. A big crowd, lots of journos, a strong feeling of end of era. Stephen got Ian McK. and Judi to get the crowd doing 'Oooh Aaaah Cantona'. Why? No one knew why but no one cared. I made a speech thanking Stephen for his loyalty and enthusiasm and his honesty – rare characteristics in his profession. There were a lot of rumblings about Trevor. I thought he would be welcomed: he's a very good director and he's run a theatre immensely successfully and how many people can say that?

4th February   Talked to Sam. He's in turmoil. I think he wants to be asked to do the job, but doesn't want to do it.

5th February   It's a grey, frosty, still day, the greyest January for years. There's an acknowledged clinical condition now: SAD – seasonal affective disorder. Joseph Brodsky died last week: a pure poet, and wonderful prose writer in English, and expert on SADness. 'Ah, the good old suggestive power of language! Ah, this legendary ability of words to imply more than reality can provide!' Brodsky was put on trial for holding 'a world-view damaging to the State' and for 'decadence and modernism'.

COURT: What is your work?
BRODSKY: I write poems, I translate, I believe –
COURT: There will be no more 'I believe'. Stand straight! Who put you in the ranks of the poets?
BRODSKY: Nobody. Who put me in the ranks of mankind?
COURT: Did you study for this?
BRODSKY: I didn't think this was a matter of education.
COURT: How's that?
BRODSKY: I thought . . . Well, I thought it came from God.

His father was asked who were worse, the Nazis or the Communists. 'As for myself, I'd rather be burned at the stake at once than die a slow death and discover a meaning in the process.'

6th February   I talked to Jenny about Trevor, who has offered himself. She asks me what Peter Hall will think. I say he'll approve, he'll be generous, but he'll also probably be jealous – that Trevor has somehow timed things very well, *not* being freelance at his age. David is upset about the 'moral' implications, and also because he might lose a home. Sam is just upset. And Stephen is vacillating: 'I oscillate between wanting the job and not.' Both he and Sam would like to be offered the job and to decline it. There are two bona fide applications that the Board *have* to consider: Ruth McKenzie and Jude Kelly. Jonathan can't/won't do it and wants to propose a plan to me.

7th February   Stella Hall [*NT Board member*] tells me that Stephen has asked her why I hadn't tried harder to persuade him. He longs to be courted, but not to do the job. I thought I *had* tried to persuade him and that he had said no. Jonathan's been to see me to

say that Sam's ambition is not to run the NT but the RSC, and why couldn't Jenny run the NT? Jenny has written to the Board asking not to be considered as a candidate. I think people imagine that in some way the job is in my gift, but the *one* power that boards have – and they certainly want to exercise it – is to choose the Director. Chris is keeping a level head, talking to all parties.

8th February   Very good interview with John Smith's wife: 'Poor John: the life you lead at that level of politics is actually not very nice. You're putting into one day what should take you three days. It's not human, in terms of the sheer demands it puts on the body and the mind. You're just living a timetable . . . I was always very anxious not to let anybody down . . . You take on the whole cloak of responsibility and nobody's told you how to do it.' The interviewer asks her if she wants to read back what she's said, in case she feels she's said too much. 'No, it's all right. You can use all that. Because it's true.'

Dinner with Chris Hogg. He talks about Trevor with the fervour of a man who has just fallen in love, which has the effect of making me feel like the dull and faithful wife.

9th February   I had another conversation with Stephen Daldry in which he suggested that I hadn't been sufficiently ardent in my pursuit of him. It's clear that he wanted to be heavily courted by the Board – but in order that he could refuse. How was I to know that 'no' didn't mean 'no'? And why didn't he let me tell the Board to approach him?

I started (and finished) the tech for *Skylight* at Wyndham's. The front of the theatre is spattered with praise; it's an odd sensation to be opening a show when you can't get into the auditorium without being told it's a huge success. The actors were delightful and Mike played the last scene beautifully as if for the first time. We go for a drink afterwards and he says his father used to say: 'All men marry their mothers.' It's maybe truer than Wilde's 'All women become like their mothers. That is their tragedy. No man does. That is his.'

11th February   There was another IRA bomb in London yesterday, breaking the cease-fire and demonstrating that the IRA are an entirely autonomous force; they're locked into the politics of the

1920s, unable and unwilling to break the time warp. Their political thinking is based on the Johnny Rotten premise: 'History is just the winners telling the losers how bad the losers are.'

12th February   Lovely letter from Stephen Wood, thanking me, ends: 'Your next eighteen months are going to be difficult, Richard. Colleagues and mates will start to move as the new director and team start forming and planning – focus will start to switch. You'll have to be very patient and count to ten endlessly and take strength from your mates.'

15th February   Lunch at Buckingham Palace. My fellow guests include the Head of the Fire Service, the Chief Medical Officer, the Police Commissioner and Patricia Routledge. We stand around talking to the equerries and ladies in waiting, then conversation stops. In the silence we hear the light tapping of dog paws on parquet. Enter the corgis followed by HMQ and Prince Philip. She is *exactly* like Pru Scales's performance in Alan's play – the same mixture of charm, belligerence and bashfulness, and an endearing habit of giggling: an absolutely conventional and very well-briefed upper-class woman. I sat next to her at lunch. She asked me about the BBC and said that Dukie had been in a very difficult position over her 'daughter-in-law's behaviour'. 'Frightful thing to do.' Apropos what she watched on TV, we talked about racing and horses, and she became very animated. We also talked about the difficulties of the restoration of historic buildings. I said it was awful that they were trying to sell off the Naval College at Greenwich. She agreed and said it had all started with Mrs Thatcher. She said they were selling off *Britannia*: 'I feel rather miffed. They're selling it with the contents, and it's my stuff.' I asked her if she remembered Harold Macmillan's speech in the House of Lords about selling off the family silver. 'But of course he didn't have any,' she said, 'it was his wife's, she was a Devonshire.' I said I thought he was using a figure of speech. We talked about theatre and opera. She talked about going to Covent Garden with her mother and sister to see *The Ring* when the ROH opened after the war, with the giant Kirsten Flagstad crushing a tiny tenor, then putting a piece of chiffon over her face which kept blowing up because she was out of breath. 'Margaret and I couldn't stop giggling and Mummy was frightfully cross.' They'd also seen

another opera in which someone lost something in a forest. 'The Marriage of Figaro? The Magic Flute?' 'That's it. A flute. Yes, it was hilarious.' She had a cup hook under the table on which she hung her handbag. At the cheese course she took an oatmeal biscuit out of a silver box and fed it to the dogs. After lunch Prince Philip tells me that he stopped going to the theatre in the '60s. 'All that frightful kitchen-sink stuff. What are you doing now?' 'The Prince's Play.'

17th February   Run-through of *The Ends of the Earth* [*David Lan*]. It's wonderfully well acted by Samantha Bond, Michael Sheen and Tom Mannion, and I found it powerful and very bleak. It requires a lot of the audience and I doubt that they'll give it. David Lan's written this for the programme: 'Oliver Sacks . . . was asking about how I got into what I was doing. I told him about the conjuring and he said, "Oh, you've abandoned one magic for another." I suppose what you do with art is take an experience of one kind and magic it into experience of a different kind. The whole notion of style in the theatre is the particular way in which you conceal or disguise what it is that you've actually done . . .'

18th February   The Olivier Awards lived down to expectation – the tone set by Cliff Richard. David won for *Skylight* and made half a speech, drew breath and found the band coming in before he'd had time to thank anyone. Judi won two awards, Simon Russell-Beale one, and Anthony Ward one for costumes – not for his *Grande Magia* set. I was up against Anthony Page and Sam and Des McAnuff who'd directed *Tommy*. He won. Lia and Diana Rigg, fellow losers, felt glum. Diana said, 'I'm off to the Ivy.' And went. 'But I'm your host,' said David plaintively.

24th February   Tomorrow I start rehearsals for *The Prince's Play*. I *might* be able to pull it off, but it depends entirely on whether Ken Stott can give a huge performance, and if the Olivier can be warmed up. It really ought to be in the Cottesloe.

25th February   Shit hitting fan over Trevor's rumoured appointment. (I remember a *Guardian* cartoon when Tommy Docherty was thumped by a fan: 'THE FAN HITS THE SHIT'.) Divided press: an editorial in the *Independent* says it needs someone who is hungry and

wants to make their reputation through their work at the NT. The *Standard* says Trevor's a good idea – the best, but says Trevor's biggest drawback is that he can't keep his mouth shut. I'm sure there'll be bile in all directions but I'm equally sure that in the circumstances TN is the only choice.

26th February   Stephen [*Daldry*] apologises for giving me a hard time. 'I love you too much to lose everything,' he said.

27th February   *Variety* says that in London 'Eyre is in the spring . . . the National has been the theatrical capital of the English-speaking world.' I come across this in a book about Glenn Gould: 'Fame and popularity are signs of shamelessness.' I don't know who wrote this:

> The hall of fame is high and wide
> The waiting room is full
> And some go through the door marked PUSH
> And some through the door marked PULL.

28th February   I heard Alistair Cooke say on the radio that the British press have lost the art of reporting. They used to separate reportage and opinion. Now it's blurred into one. Today there was a piece in the *Guardian* by Michael Billington about Trevor. It says that the NT will become the RSC, and that Sam and Stephen haven't been 'sounded out'. I go nuclear and call Billington and tell him that it's irresponsible to write such stuff. Did he check with them? 'It's second-hand,' he says. 'I didn't have time to ring them, I had to write it yesterday afternoon.' I say it's like playing Fantasy Football League, putting his dream players on the pitch. Why doesn't he check whether his fantasies could be realised – if they even *want* to be? I tell him he has no idea what it's like to run the NT. 'But there must be some rewards,' he says. 'Of course,' I say, 'but as many terrors.' He ends by saying: 'I don't know why you're worrying, the paper'll be wrapping chips tomorrow.'

I spent the rest of the morning in a lather through a series of meetings – Jenny, Maggie and Anthony, then Michael Morris [*impresario*], then Maggie alone, and then rehearsal: improvisations on behaviour of and to monarchy, then text work till six, then talk to

Jenny, then meet an Australian actress with David who's going to be in *Skylight* in Sydney, then spend two hours with Trevor, who is understandably developing cold feet about the NT. If the consensus looks like being a majority against him, he'll withdraw. Back home I talk to Tom, who is rattled by it all. He talks about writing an article, but of course that's like saying that Trevor has the job and needs to be defended.

1st March   David says there are three qualities required from the Director of the NT – to plan a repertoire of seventeen shows a year, to run the building, and to be spokesman for the British theatre. He says that Trevor can do the first two. I think he'll prove that he can do all three. That's if he doesn't back out.

2nd March   I'm reading Claire Tomalin's book about Mrs Jordan: brilliant. 'It is astonishing how good acting refines the mind of an audience.' And good writing.

3rd March   Favourable piece in the *Observer* by Coveney, endorsing Trevor's nomination. He indicts Deborah and Nick for not being willing to take on responsibility, says that Sam will run the RSC, that Stephen is 'flighty', and that Trevor Nunn is the man to continue the work – that's if you believe the work is worth doing, which Coveney doesn't. He thinks that the best thing that could happen in the Millennium is that the NT building crumbles into dust. I've occasionally had the same thought.

5th March   Today Trevor was appointed. I held a company meeting to tell them the news and looking out over the stalls of the Olivier felt for a moment an overwhelming sadness about saying goodbye to all that. I stopped for a moment, fearful of tears, but finished without embarrassment. I went to my office; Trevor and Chris Hogg and Michael Palliser came in. Then we went to the press conference, and I listened to Trevor, defended him, listened more and then went to rehearsals, which was a wonderful purgative. I worked till six, then went to the Gate to do a talk about 'national' theatre with Ion. Then to a dinner given by the head of visiting arts, then home. Bob [*Crowley*] rang to say he knew what I was going through and how sad he was and everyone was that I

was leaving and how much I was loved and did I realise it? Then I did feel tearful.

6th March Read this, by Edmund Burke: 'To love the little platoon we belong to in society, is the first principle – the germ as it were – of public affections.'

7th March Rehearsals go well for *The Prince's Play*. Tony's writing is terrific; so is Ken [*Stott*]. If only this can work as I imagine it. Shaw: 'I dream what might be and ask myself why not?'

8th March David said that when he told Wally who was going to take over the NT, Wally said: 'Oh but that's like Tina Brown taking over *The New Yorker*.' Robert says that's what he should be called: Tina – There Is No Alternative. The press have been very good over Trevor's appointment, although they still give the impression that Sam and Stephen were turned down for the job, rather than not prepared to do it. A long piece in the *Standard* extols my virtues, but refers to my 'blokishness', whatever that may mean. I had a fax from Trevor which thanked me for being 'amazingly generous and large-spirited', which made me feel guilty about having had the odd small-spirited thought.

9th March Good press for Trevor in the *Observer* and the *Sunday Times* and *Variety*: RUNNING OUT OF EYRE, NATIONAL NABS NUNN. Alan Bennett was quoted 'I am only sorry that R.E. can't go on for another ten years . . .' I think, for only a second, and why *couldn't* I? I'm feeling liberated now, and if I hadn't got the whole fund-raising and redevelopment hanging over me would be feeling fancy-free. Lasdun is continuing to make threats, and we have to finesse the final stage by meeting the Arts Council. We're very near but could fall at the last fence.

12th March Late in the office after rehearsals and meetings. I'm reading BBC papers, bored by them and sated with administration. I was rung by a journalist who asked tentatively if I would write Peter Hall's obituary. Yesterday I saw Ken Macdonald [*actor*] in the corridor, who told me that Peter had had a heart attack. 'It's the jam tart,' he said. I rang Peter; it turned out he'd had a gastric problem and hiatus hernia.

14th March   Dinner for Dukie's retirement at the National Portrait Gallery. I spent the evening facing Handel and Dr Johnson, who presided over a dinner which ended with speeches: Dukie said the BBC lacks what makes armies and football teams win – morale. Bill Jordan [*trade unionist*] said we should never forget that any organisation has a stronger loyalty to itself than the people it serves, which should be inscribed in every office at the BBC (and the NT for that matter). It's a feature of institutions that the permanent staff resent those for whom the institution exists. I've been drenched in leaks from BBC staff, all telling me that it's being torn apart, losing its 'distinctiveness'; they talk of a lack of debate, of a culture of secrecy, of paranoia.

15th March   First preview of *Mary Stuart* [*Schiller*]. Howard [*Davies*]'s done a handsome, sumptuous and mannered production. Anna Massey is hesitant, then very strong, but with a disconcerting habit of dropping out vocally. It's nerves; she'll be brilliant. Isabelle Huppert is brave, hugely energised and charismatic, but gulps her lines, letting her voice race ahead of her comprehension. The audience strain to stay with her and most give up. In the interval I see a man ostentatiously writing in a programme. I catch his eye. He comes up to me. 'I'm from *The Times*. This could be good if you replace Miss Huppert. The voice is unacceptable.' I resist the temptation to boot him in the balls.

16th March   Saturday. I rehearse in the morning, then have lunch with Peter Brook and Marie-Hélène. Peter's been to see *Skylight*, which he enjoyed, and *Trainspotting* which he didn't. We talk of *Qui Est Là*, of the English attitude to it (my attitude to it?) – of seeing Hamlet played by an African: two images superimposed, the colonial consciousness, and the 'myth' of Hamlet – about the only surviving folk myth for a middle-class English person.

17th March   Excellent piece by James Fenton in *NYRB* about the transience of theatre: that's certainly what attracts me – it's in the present tense, it's live, it's unreproducible. It's ephemeral: it lives on only in the memory, melting away after the event. I *like* seeing the set broken up after a last night, the costumes and props being put in store to be re-used in other shows. I *like* not being able to have

retrospectives, not being able to archive productions. At best a production of a performance can only achieve immortality as myth. James quotes Jonathan [*Pryce*] when we did *Hamlet*. Asked why he didn't want to go on playing the part in the West End after the Royal Court: 'You see . . . it's already legendary.'

18th March   Dinner with Chris Hogg. He says he's not motivated by money or power or fame but only by making organisations fulfil their potential. In that sense he's a selfless visionary, and perhaps the *Mail* was right to say that he would make the best Prime Minister. He's quite emotionally recessed, wholly without deviousness, slightly severe: a grown-up. He makes me feel like a different generation, although he's only a few years older.

19th March   I've recently seen an excellent first play by Martin McDonagh, about rural life in the Aran Islands: *The Beauty Queen of Lenane*. Our playwright in residence at the Studio, he's never lived anywhere but the Elephant and Castle, even if his family all came from Ireland. Also saw *The Changing Room*, which lacked the resonance and poetry of the original production – partly their fault, but much more not – just the passage of time. David Storey wrote about a tribal life of loyalties, bonds, and affections, about community – when that wasn't simply a politicians' buzz word – and Lindsay Anderson garlanded the rugby players with his adoration for male beauty and the 'working man', the North, for the honest combat of sport and for the nobility of manual labour. It now seems as distant as the pre-Raphaelite movement.

20th March   Another fund-raiser. This time it's Jaguar Cars: a dinner, a speech. They're not cynical, their enthusiasm is genuine. I feel like a house-manager, or a performer wearing my suit and tie and my performance – or is it wearing me? I got home very late and read David [*Hare*]'s new play: *Amy's View*. It's elegiac, mournful, droll and mature. It's got an old-fashioned structure – four acts, passage of years – but uses its structure to serve its meanings, and also to make its case for theatre as a medium that endures as the main character endures. The end doesn't seem right yet, and the young man's character seemed undigested – David willing the character to a position in the second act that doesn't seem there yet.

24th March   *Mary Stuart* opened, a good performance. Isabelle much more comprehensible, and as spellbinding as in the rehearsal room. The whole play could have been cut by half an hour – after all it's historical romance – but it was never boring, and Anna and Isabelle were formidable. The reviews were mostly bad and some were racist. Isabelle's offence is being French and a film star. Nick de Jongh mocks her accent by pointing out that Isabelle makes the word 'peace' sound like 'piss'. But the Sundays are good for the production and for Isabelle and Anna. Howard's very depressed by the response, but he's done a really good job.

25th March   David's rehearsing *The Designated Mourner* in New York. He's very low about it: he can't get Wally to cut and Mike [*Nichols*] to learn his lines.

27th March   Dinner with Cameron and Bob [*Crowley*] to talk about *My Fair Lady*, which Cameron is keen for us to do, and we're keen to do it. In fact it's just about the only old musical that I would like to do. 'You understand class,' Cameron said. We didn't get far with talking about the show – just that Tony Hopkins was the only actor who could play Higgins, but we talked about his new show: *Martin Guerre*. He said it had radio-controlled scenery which would revolutionise stage design. Bob and I had the same vision at the same moment: a transmission failure resulting in trucks careering round the stage like daleks, and he kicked me under the table as he struggled for a response. Cameron talked about Trevor – not ungenerously. He said Trevor had written to him not long ago saying that he'd given up the theatre. Also that, at the first night of a musical version of *Jekyll and Hyde* in Bromley, the video camera focused on the conductor slipped and focused accidentally on Trevor and Imogen in the auditorium, and throughout the show the cast had to watch them rather than the conductor.

30th March   Saturday morning in the theatre, an eerie quiet, sitting at my desk looking over the river at Somerset House, feeling a sense of purpose, a *point* to it all. I'll miss this.

1st April   Today *Designated Mourner* and *War and Peace* started rehearsals, so I had two goes at my address to the troops on the first

day: 'The NT isn't an institution, it's a theatre ... etc etc.' Mike
Nichols was extremely nervous. 'This is worse than the first day of
school,' he said. What courage – at the age of sixty-five to act in a
play where he has to speak for about seventy-five minutes, not
having been on a stage for fifteen years.

2nd April   *The Prince's Play* is fine – for half of the play it's entirely
gripping, but in the second half the remorselessness seems to eva-
porate. Can it hold? I feel so odd – tired, disembodied, light-headed:
the fund-raising project is starting to get me down. It's the constant
repetition of 'Who do you know who is rich?' I'm even starting to
pity the rich. Why *should* anyone sponsor a 'national' theatre – any
more than they should sponsor the BBC?

6th April   A respectable run-through. We're marking time because
Ken still hasn't quite learned his lines. He's marvellously good, but at
the moment he's struggling for assurance, and the part needs *total*
control. With every day I admire Ken more – as an actor and as a
person. I wish I'd worked with him before.

8th April   Sunday. We visited a Norman church which, like so
many, had been renovated to its disadvantage in the 1850s. The
Tudor rood screen became the Vicar's rose pergola. The vandalism,
the confidence, the tyranny of taste. It was reinstalled by a subse-
quent vicar in the 1880s.

11th April   Start of the tech. In the Olivier it's always like launch-
ing an aircraft carrier. I'm hopeful about the production but can't
escape the feeling that whenever we come to the end of the show I
never feel the exhilaration that I ought to. Maybe it's the play. After
the tech went with Bob to a dinner at Tom [*Stoppard*]'s for Mike
Nichols. Simon Callow blurted out to me that he'd had his photograph taken for a book for my leaving – 'Oh, I suppose I shouldn't
have told you that.' Then to disguise his gaffe he talked without
drawing breath and told me a story of Maggie [*Smith*] in *La Machine
Infernale*. She wasn't well and was giving everyone a hard time. She
had to take a day or two off to get better and returned to find that
Lambert Wilson had fallen off the stage, while trying to act better in
order to impress her on her return, and had broken his wrist. 'Oh

well,' said Maggie, 'that's another one less to be slapped.' Mike
Nichols told me about meeting Thatcher, who was boring him to
death. In a brave attempt to change the subject he said: 'We have a
friend in common: John Le Carré. He says you're a very sexy lady.'
Thatcher, tartly: 'Well, I'm not.'

14th April I've had a pc from Andrei Serban: 'How can a har-
monious labour of love we all shared during rehearsals vanish just
like a precious bowl that slips through your hands and breaks
although you didn't do any wrong moves? It's a strange paradox,
our crazy profession.' His production *The Ends of the Earth* got vile
reviews, but I liked David's play and Andrei's staging, and the sense
of a consistent world that he'd brought to the play.

15th April We've had three previews of *The Prince's Play*. I think
– and so does Bob – that we've done something remarkable, but the
response I get from colleagues – or at least those who have seen it – is
lukewarm. I sat in a management meeting yesterday morning with
twelve other people. Only two of them had seen the show.

16th April Mike Nichols told me a Toscanini story (that I'd heard
about Klemperer): orchestral musician is dressed down by Toscanini
during a session. At the end of the session he comes up to Toscanini
and spits in his face. 'Is no time for apologies,' says the Maestro.

17th April The patrons and corpies seemed to enjoy *The Prince's
Play* but with a touch of bafflement. The pros' response is good.
Roger Chapman tells me he thinks the show is wonderful, as exciting
a work as we've ever done, but he foresees press resistance.

18th April Last preview. The audience doesn't quite get it. Good-
will, attention, respect, admiration even, but it's not enough. They
cough a bit – always a sure sign of disaffection, and when they're not
coughing they don't quite enter into it: too much talk, too much
verse, too remorseless, too melodramatic.

19th April First night. I'm sitting in my office after the interval. I
watched the first half on my TV, then went into the foyer. I
encountered Messrs Peter and Tinker [*critics*] running for the bar

as if they were fleeing a mortar attack. Then went to the party. Yes, they liked it but, as always, one is disappointed with anything less than rapture. Mike Kustow says that the picture of Britain is Tony's and mine in equal parts. I fear rejection, but then I always do. There'll be no solace on this one but I've had my first drink for eight and a half weeks: one glass of champagne.

22nd April   Victor Hugo said: 'I find I love my play all the more now that it is a failure,' and I'm starting to agree with him. I was right about the reviews, except for the *Independent*, which gives it an unreserved rave. The rest don't seem to get it. All very good for Ken, mostly for the production, but it's Victor Hugo they don't buy. It will be tough, doing bad business for forty-five performances. I've seldom had such warm response from friends, but Chris Hogg's response was more typical: 'This is exactly what the NT should be doing, but rather as a public duty than as a pleasure.'

23rd April   Preview of *The Designated Mourner*. It's a remarkable piece of writing and David's orchestrated it cleverly; Mike is charismatic but a little vague, a little inaccessible. It's very elegantly presented, maybe too much so, a danger of the painted word. After the show I came out of the stage door to be greeted by a Japanese man in a beret who had a copy of *Vanity Fair*, and wanted me to sign my picture in it, plus programmes of *The Prince's Play*. 'Did you enjoy it?' I asked. 'Yes, but not as much as *Way of the World*.'

24th April   *The Designated Mourner* has opened. On the first night it had lost the opaqueness that it had on Monday; most of this had to do with Mike's performance which was wholly in focus: he was mesmerising, making it seem as if he was inventing his lines, as if there was no gap between him and the script even though he was glancing at the little autocue in front of him. Afterwards we drank champagne in the corridor, Mike hugely relieved and jovial, calling David 'Dave', me 'Rich' and Trevor 'Trev'.

27th April   I had a meeting with David Puttnam about making theatre accessible to broadcasting. He said he's been shocked at the hostility of the public to the arts – and by the arrogance of the arts world. He thinks it *has* to be a condition of funding that a high

proportion of publicly funded performances are broadcast. I have such mixed feelings about putting the theatre on TV. But we shouldn't underestimate the effects that our educational system and our class system have had on disenfranchising millions of people from a culture that should be their birthright, and we shouldn't underestimate the importance of TV and radio as a means of helping to rectify this. Our work *is* inaccessible to large numbers of people, and we MUST do something about this, or die. The bigger problem, from my point of view, is that if you just squirt a camera at a stage (the cheap option) it will always look clumsy and undernourished compared to TV drama. It can't ever be regarded as anything but a wholesale dilution of the theatrical original. In trying to achieve this bogus 'access', we'd only succeed in making thousands more people doubt that a visit to the theatre was worth making. But maybe if it was a *live event*, a sort of outside broadcast, then it could work. But would the TV companies take it, and would the unions ever agree? David talked about his 'obligations' to the film industry. I don't know that I have 'obligations' to the British theatre, except to try to keep the NT alive.

28th April   Jenny [*McIntosh*] is being lured to the ROH. Or at least they've invited her to meet them for an interview, and I know they're very serious. As with all big news, I knew the second before she said it, when she walked into my office: 'I can't resist it,' she said. 'I've got to find out if I can do it.'

2nd May   Headline in *Stage*: 'WEST END SLUMP CAUSED BY BSE'. I've never thought of using *that* excuse. Dinner last night with Virginia Bottomley. She has a way of half listening to you, then turning away when she thinks a response is expected. 'People must give the public what they want,' she said often.

3rd May   I've made a bad mistake, inspired by sentimentality and blinded by ego. I should have given the Board the absolute minimum time to find a replacement for me, let them find one, then have left. Now I'm confronting the fact that Nick Starr is leaving, and Jenny wants the job at the opera house; so that's my left and my right arms gone.

4th May   I can't do *Amy's View* until next year, so it should be done this autumn without me, rather than make David wait a year for it to be put on. And I think I should leave the NT after I do *Lear* in March of next year. I feel like the character in the beginning of Updike's novel *In the Beauty of the Lilies*: one day the Presbyterian minister, sitting in his study before lunch, surrounded by books of theology, decides it's a fraud: God doesn't exist. I've lost sight of what I'm doing at the theatre and why. It seems like a giant hot-air balloon that I have to keep puffing to keep afloat a few inches above the ground. I'm writing a piece for the *FT* and I talked to Analeena MacAfee [*FT arts editor*] about theatre. She said maybe one in ten shows is OK. I told Lu this; she said it was a bit harsh – maybe one in six. For the audience it's the terror of being trapped, being voluntarily kidnapped, with the consoling possibility of the Stockholm syndrome – falling in love with your captor.

5th May   Bob [*Crowley*] and I talk about *Lear*. He's been through a bad time but has emerged stronger and more confident, as all works of moral instruction would have us believe. His father has got Alzheimer's and has been living with Bob's sister, who's been strained to breaking point by his behaviour. She broke down one morning, crying: 'What am I going to do with him?' Her five-year-old daughter, from behind her: 'Kill him.' Bob told me that at Kenneth Macmillan's Memorial Service Lynn Seymour [*dancer*] went wearing a top hat and carrying a dog. She was stopped at the door and told she couldn't bring her dog in. 'God is dog spelt backwards,' she said and swept past an astonished vicar.

10th May   Reading *Lear* in the garden. A sky of almost unbroken blue and an inconceivable variety of green lit by the sun as if from within. The painter, Boucher, said of nature that it was 'too green and too badly lit'.

13th May   I saw *Anastasia* [*Kenneth Macmillan*] with new designs by Bob. The first act cleverly – and satirically – used classical ballet to characterise the Russian court, the medium being the means of characterising the society; the second act was enjoyable but commonplace, and the third act was as fresh and expressive as it must have

been twenty years ago. Dinner with Bob and Deborah [*Macmillan*] afterwards. Deborah says the opera house needs blowing up.

14th May Lunch with Paul Scofield. We're both nervous but gradually become at ease with each other. He's very straightforward, very *un*complicated, but full of mystery and allure and like everyone else I fall in love with him. He said that when we met at Nottingham twenty years ago he was going through a bad time: he'd discovered that he didn't like the Athol Fugard play that he was doing, and his father had just died. I don't want to talk about it, he said to Athol, and then felt peeved because no one talked about it. We talked about *Borkman*. 'It's important to talk around it, but in the end it all has to be in the play,' he says. I told him what Munch had said about the play: 'There is no point in painting winter after Ibsen has done that in *John Gabriel Borkman*.'

16th May Dinner with Mike Nichols. We talk about directing – what it is, and how to do it. When he started directing films he says he looked at Bergman films to see how to work with actors, and at George Stevens for staging. He said it took about ten years for actors, good ones, that is, to learn to act on film. We talk about needing to appear to think and feel slow on screen, about Elizabeth Taylor being a Martian ('all stars are'), about how we fancied Rita Hayworth and Ava Gardner. Gardner wanted to be in *The Graduate* but she'd become Norma Desmond. Her secretary called Mike and got him to pretend that he was interested and had asked for a meeting. Mike said that Orson Welles was wonderful in private and a pig on the set. And we talk about how in the 'movies' you can't be an 'artist' – whatever Sidney Lumet might say. Mike Nichols has read my book, and said he enjoyed it more than Bergman's. 'Don't they have editors in Sweden?' he said.

17th May I've had an overdose of clamouring egos this week. Nothing that I wouldn't do myself if I were in their position, but it was hard to satisfy their need for attention: Simon McBurney, Sean Mathias, Deborah Warner, and David Hare. But I think at least that Simon will do *Caucasian Chalk Circle*, and I think we *will* make the Olivier a theatre-in-the-round. Then George Wolfe comes to see me. We talk about the play that we've both commissioned from Tony

Kushner [*Henry Box Brown*] and when/if he'll deliver. George has had a huge success on B'way with *Bring In Da Noise*; he tells me that the *NY Times* says he's a genius, and I think he agrees. Of *The Prince's Play* he says little apart from: 'Wow, you flew a whole house!' Whenever I'm with George at the NT I'm conscious of the '6osness of the building and the whiteness of the audience. I went to *P Play* in the evening. A thinnish house, and the Olivier always has a way of looking half empty rather than half full. I hadn't fallen out of love with it. David Hockney was there; he said it was the best thing he'd seen for ages: 'the colours, the staging, the verse, wonderful.'

19th May   I talked to Lu, who's doing an essay on 'The Meaning of Meaning', or similar subject. She talks it *all* out, which I really admire; I can't keep up with her. Tomorrow the assault on Mount Borkman.

20th May   Board meeting then start of rehearsals for *Borkman*. I was nervous, partly because I don't want to let them down, partly because I had got another attack of the meaninglessness of it all. Who's it all for? The AUDIENCE, of course. Who are they? Where do they come from? Where's the new public? A good read-through; Nick [*Wright*]'s version really clear and idiomatic, not a touch of Meyer-ism. The three stars behave immaculately, but all of them are demanding in their ways – talent demands and deserves attention and sometimes those with less talent make more fuss as a compensation for having been thrown out of paradise. Paul really went for it at the read-through, Vanessa followed and Eileen ruefully said to me later: 'Paul showed us where to go.' Vanessa has instincts that are strongly articulated and I sometimes have difficulty explaining ideas to her – or she to me. She said at the end of the day that she thought that it should be done in a later period – but not in modern dress. I feel, not for the first time, that I can't run the NT and direct a play at the same time.

21st May   I went to a dinner at Gray's Inn, given by the lawyers of the inn to celebrate the NT. It's black tie, not white, I'm told, because it's in honour of the NT. They've dressed down for the theatricals. Justice Heather Steele told me she was disappointed that decorations weren't being worn. Justice Rose Heilbron told me that she doesn't approve of women calling themselves 'Ms'. Another judge told me

that I'd got it wrong in *Murmuring Judges* – 'It's much more ludicrous than you showed on stage.' It's true: we have to make our way into dinner led by a beadle banging on the floor with a stick and announcing our names. Three-course dinner, then port and cheese in the library. I sat next to a very nice, quite drunk and quite openly gay Law Lord who pressed the port – a Taylor '47 – on me. 'It's the *only* year since the '34.' He was approached by a camp black waiter, who leaned over and said: 'If you want to go to Leo's party you'll have to ask nicely.' The Law Lord smiled at me benignly, placing a hand on my knee. 'Richard, dear Richard – may I call you Richard? Dear, dear Richard, when they ask you to join the House of Lords I beg of you not to refuse.' I asked John Mortimer about him the next day. John says that when my new pal was a circuit judge, he used to have Paddington Bear on the bench beside him and in his official car. He berated his butler once for having stuffed Paddington into a suitcase.

25th May *Borkman* is as difficult a play to direct as I've ever done. Not because it's difficult to stage – which it is – climbing up a mountain in the last act – but because of its emotional temperature. It starts with two twin sisters confronting each other in an icy silence. But it's an ice that burns, blisters when you touch it. And the *whole* play – continuous action over two hours – is maintained at this extraordinary pressure and temperature: liquid nitrogen. Eileen appears to meander, until suddenly she knows what she's doing with a line and then the line becomes illuminated without any penumbra by pure crystalline intelligence. Vanessa is pure instinct that she rationalises, sometimes with great eloquence, sometimes confusingly. She works very hard, she thinks very hard, and she's recklessly bold. Paul isn't instinctive – or at least is, but he wants to test his instinct. They all admire and respect each other in a very touching way. I talked to Paul about Ralph Richardson. 'He'd have been very good in this part. He had iron in his soul; he was ruthless.' He admired him but clearly didn't like him. He said he couldn't and wouldn't play with other actors. He had his own rhythm and would stick to it, forcing the actors to match his tune. We didn't talk of Olivier, who'd also played the part, and who I know Paul didn't like and suffered under. I loved Paul's simplicity and his lack of guile, which is not, of course, to say he is simple.

27th May   Flaubert said that when the talk turned to literary topics he felt like a former convict listening to a conversation about prison reform. I find myself shying away from conversations about the theatre. I feel that I'm regarded as the curator of a museum of ancient crafts, preciously defending a social ritual that seems as silly to some people as morris dancing does to me. But it's too easy for me to lose faith: I'm like a sceptical vicar who has to deliver sermons about faith to convince himself. Or in my case on the indispensability of theatre and the necessity of funding it.

2nd June   Paul doesn't talk of himself, doesn't use his life as analogy in any way. He's very clear, very thoughtful, and very energetic; he doesn't spare himself, doesn't keep his powder dry. He's intensely practical, and self-mocking. 'I'll just pull a face,' he said to Vanessa when deciding to cut a line and do the line with a look. When Erhart says: 'I don't want to *work*!' Paul said to me: 'Oh, we can all sympathise with that.' Eileen is, as always, clear-cut when she knows what she's doing and unaffectedly vague when she doesn't. Consequently what is in focus stands out very clearly, and like a careful painter she fills in the rest. Vanessa thinks hard, and remorselessly methodically – up to a point. Then beyond that point she'll follow a whim on the instant, speeding down cul-de-sacs, backtracking, then she's ready to pursue another route. It would be fatal to deter her from going on any of these journeys: in *Orpheus Descending* she changed her accent to Italian in a moment, in *Heartbreak House* she became a mulatto overnight. With her I sometimes feel that I'm driving a horse-drawn plough which is veering across the field, cutting across the furrows, and I'm struggling to pull it back. She's very insistent on the correct Norwegian pronunciation of 'Borkman' – the first 'o' needing to be spoken as if you had an apple in your mouth, and the 'r' purred like a tiger. They're always a pleasure to direct because they're so skilful, so game, and because you always see results. I was talking to Paul about Solti when we were rehearsing the scene where Foldal comes into the room. I said that Solti had kept me waiting like Borkman. 'Camp,' said Paul.

3rd June   Good piece in *The New Yorker* by Michael Blakemore: 'I sometimes wonder if American show business – particularly movies and musicals – isn't, with the greatest technical virtuosity, flawless

pacing, dazzling displays of a star personality, vanishing rapidly up its own arse, then easing itself out again as money.'

4th June   Rehearsals are very hard now. I can never relax with Paul and Vanessa. I have to be very patient, not let anyone see my frustration. I'm still not sure if they trust me. Eileen is a real friend; I'm safe with her and she's safe with me. Peter Brook was using the rehearsal room next door to audition singers for *Don Giovanni*. He came in to see Eileen and Vanessa but missed Paul. He told me it was thrilling, 'so full of promise'. Eileen said it was exasperating that he still looked sexy.

8th June   Went to Irene Worth's eightieth birthday party at Spencer House – very grand, very good food, very good wine, beautiful evening, drinks on the terrace, marred only by clowns 'entertaining' us: one left a plastic dog turd. I watched a waiter brush it away with a finely tuned gesture of contempt. I sat next to Irene at dinner. I told her I'd seen Peter Brook, and what Eileen had said. 'He's *never* been sexy,' said Irene, 'and what's he doing *Don Giovanni* for? Why doesn't he do some decent plays with good actors?' We talked about *JGB*. She said she'd written a line in for Ella about wanting Borkman's child. I said I thought Vanessa needed no encouragement to start rewriting. She said that Gunhild was the better part (Eileen was thrilled when I told her).

9th June   Francis Bacon: 'I think most people who have religious beliefs, who have a fear of God, are much more interesting than people who live a hedonistic and drifting life. On the other hand, I can't help admiring but despising them, living by a total falseness, which I think they are living by their religious views. But, after all, the only thing that makes anybody interesting is their dedication, and when there was religion they could at least be dedicated to their religion, which was something. But I think that, if you can find a person totally without belief, totally dedicated to futility, then you will find the more exciting person.'

12th June   Went to *Don Carlos* at the ROH last week, a well-sung, quite well-staged but thinly designed production by Luc Bondy. I sat behind Isaiah Berlin who clapped like a sea-lion at the end, then

turned to me and said: 'Great masterpiece, very well performed.' We had dinner with him recently, and he spilled out seamless reminiscences of Akhmatova, Churchill, Kennedy and of his Oxford neighbour Robert Maxwell, as if he'd found the secret of circular breathing. As always at Covent Garden I marvelled at the oddness of the occasion: the disengaged audience, the ritualised curtain calls, the footmen, the money, the money, the money. Jeremy Isaacs said the ROH was woefully underfunded. Well, in a sense yes, compared to La Scala, but relative to anything else in the British arts firmament, no. Gillian Widdecombe [writer, Jeremy Isaacs' wife] told me that Alan Yentob [Controller BBC1] had rung Jeremy to ask if Jeremy's job was still going. I told Gillian that I hadn't realised that Alan knew much about opera. Neither did Jeremy, she said. I said I thought that Jenny would get the job. She asked if I was going to write my memoirs. Don't think so, I said, why don't you do yours? She said she'd once had a boyfriend who offered her a choice between a Porsche and a box of chocolates. She took the car.

16th June   Heartening run-through on Friday. Just before we started Michael Bryant was talking about playing Brand and how every night before he went on he felt terror. 'Terror, that's the word,' said Paul. I said to Paul at the end of the run: this is thrilling, and he clasped my hand between his and said: 'Oh thank you, thank you.'

17th June   Dinner with Peter Shaffer, who has an idea for a play about Tchaikovsky and his brother. It's like Amadeus – the genius and the not-genius – but this contains a debate about homosexuality: to come out or not, against nature or not, art instead of children. I won't be at the NT when he's written it, so I suggested that Trevor should direct it. Then I thought: Why am I giving away this gift? Peter and I talked about Paul Scofield. The last time he'd seen him play Salieri [in Amadeus] he'd gone to Paul's dressing room and praised him to the skies. 'It was a gift for you,' said Paul. Peter went on praising him and Paul thanked him and gently closed the door on him. 'I could no more have re-entered that room than take wing,' said Peter.

19th June   Boozy dinner for our 'arts committee' – a small group of interested parties who meet to lobby the shadow government about

arts funding: Melvyn Bragg, Matthew Evans [*Chairman Faber & Faber*], Stephen Daldry and Jack Cunningham. Melvyn parodies his *Start the Week* manner: 'Let him have his say . . .' 'If we can move on to another topic . . .' 'I haven't spoken . . .' Jack Cunningham is a fruity (very conservative) politician, all ego and anecdote. He's quite raw and quite a loose cannon. He talked about 'the Mormons' in Tony Blair's office, and about seeing his dad arrested, his mum grilled by police, the desire of the London 'Establishment' to destroy his family, and his desire for revenge. Also about being brought up in a pit village by his gran, when his dad was in prison, and his gran being evicted by the National Coal Board: 'So don't tell me about socialism. That's what evicted my gran.' He talked like a politician about the arts – 'I used to go to the RSC, I go to the ballet, I go to the opera, of course I don't get much time to read much . . .' He never once mentioned the NT, the Royal Court, broadcasting or publishing. When Stephen and I left we stood on the pavement in Charlotte Street and Stephen said: 'Do you think we'd be better off voting Tory?'

20th June   Good atmosphere at rehearsals. Paul said yesterday in a scene '. . . the ceiling would crush me – like a . . .' long pause '. . . tomato,' then he started to giggle. He's very charming and quietly intelligent. Also very well-read. Eileen thought she'd got another cancer but the results came through in the afternoon and we all hugged her and she was radiant with relief.

21st June   Jenny is going to be offered the ROH job. Why would anyone take it? But how can she refuse it?

22nd June   Run-through of *JGB* yesterday. I was overwhelmed by it, the power of the play, the unhappiness of it. I found it impossible to talk coherently after the run, so I sat the actors down, said I couldn't be articulate about what they'd done, and sent them home. They seemed a bit bemused, a bit grateful, and, I think, a bit disappointed. I feel about Ibsen now as Solti did about Shostakovich. I asked him what he regretted most: 'Not being able to say sorry to Shostakovich for having underrated him and thought of him as a lackey of the state.' I feel I've seriously underrated Ibsen from time to time.

24th June Jenny's been offered the job at the ROH. Chris Hogg said we should be philosophical: we can't stand in her way, although Trevor tried very hard to discourage her.

26th June Our co-production with Shared Experience [*independent touring company*] of *War and Peace* has opened. It's gloriously enjoyable and I have no regrets about encouraging them to go for Tolstoy rather than a nineteenth-century English novel. I don't see the argument that novels shouldn't be dramatised; it's fine to take material from *anywhere*, and it's liberating to see plays with such a preposterously large canvas.

27th June Dinner with Vanessa and Natasha and Liam Neeson. After dinner I said I'd give Vanessa a lift home. We tried to get a taxi, failed, and found ourselves walking to the NT to get my car. Vanessa was talking all the way – about *Borkman* and acting and Sarajevo and love and marriage – and as we walked over Waterloo Bridge she paused for a moment, took off her high heels, and walked barefoot the rest of the way, still talking. When we got in the car, she talked awhile, then went quiet and I took over. Then I noticed she was fast asleep, lolling against the window, her face extraordinarily young and untroubled and beautiful. When we reached Hammersmith Broadway I nudged her awake, to find out where she lived. She said she'd say when we were coming up to her road, but she fell asleep again. After three attempts – each time she dropped asleep – we found the road. She got out, still barefoot, waved like a teenager and went in, probably for hours of phone calls to oppressed corners of the globe.

1st July I saw Stephen Daldry, who's doing a show about actors' bodies. He was complaining that the actors wouldn't pull down their foreskins when talking about them, or show the audience how the muscles in their sphincters worked.

3rd July The ROH have made the announcement of Jenny's appointment without consulting me (having promised to do so), so I couldn't arrange a proper way of telling the staff. One newspaper said she was off to 'brighter lights'.

6th July First preview of *JGB* went well. Paul said to me before the show: 'When we have time I'll tell you how thrilling this has been, but it's too late now.' He said to Sian Phillips afterwards: 'It went as it should have gone.' And it did. The audience rose to Paul, and to them all. The house lights went on and still they were applauding. It's good work, but we've still got work to do, and then the hurdle of the critics.

8th July Glos. The garden's stuffed full, overblown, blowsy: the last of irises, pansies, petunias, poppies, roses, honeysuckle, cistus, marigolds, nasturtiums, and the mallow and buddleia spreading like spiders' webs. In the *Independent* a story about Equity asking for a better minimum for actors who work in the regions where they get a pittance and nominal living allowance. 'MONEY – THAT'S WHAT THEY WANT. The great luvvie rebellion of 1996.' This paper feels it necessary to tell its readers that Hemingway was 'an American novelist'. It's no better in the *Observer*. Bitchy headline in the Arts Section: Q: Why do people hate Andrew Lloyd Webber on sight? A: It saves time.

10th July Patrick Young [*staff director ROH*] rings me to say that *Traviata* went well. Roberto Alagna [*tenor*] turned up for two hours' rehearsal. He said he'd sung the part 170 times, so didn't need any rehearsal. He familiarised himself with the furniture and the entrances, and that was enough. And he got marvellous reviews.

11th July Morning before first night. As always I feel exasperated by how desperately I want this show to be acclaimed. As Garrison Keillor says, all of us are secretly only satisfied with: 'Hail, Sun God, rise and lead thy people,' however much we claim to be indifferent to critics. Last night was the best performance: a telegram from Harold [*Pinter*] to say how much he'd liked it.

12th July Very good reviews for *JGB*, except for a toxic piece by Frederic Raphael in the *New Statesman* shovelling shit on the NT ('a sepulchre of good intentions'), on the production and the actors. Nick de Jongh says Vanessa is playing in a different style, and that I've been influenced by Bergman. That, at least, is true.

16th July   Letter from Tom about his Housman play: 'Seventeen pages. Very slow despite dogged application . . . It's turning into a dream play with lots of characters (but doubling up somewhat). It's a slow business because there's not much story to tell me what to do next, so I have to be clever every page and a half to stop it sitting down and talking about itself . . .'

19th July   I went to the French Embassy for a meeting about the French Theatre Season, then lunch. I met Mme Pompidou: 'Your theatre is the best in the world and your press is the worst.'

21st July   At Chris Hogg's sixtieth birthday party I saw Peter Taylor [*Lord Chief Justice*], who is dying of brain cancer. We talked for a longish time, and then a friend of Nicole's asked who I'd been talking to. I told him, and he said: 'I could tell from the way people were talking to him that he was dying.'

24th July   I started the week on the radio with *Soapbox*, the successor to *Start the Week*, chaired by Andrew Neil. My 'soapbox' issue was the habit of sneering at 'luvvies'. It used to mean actors, but now it's anyone connected with the arts. Does this matter? Well, in the catalogue of things to get upset about, not a lot. But it doesn't say much for the way we view our artists in this country that we talk about them with a reflexive sneer, and that New Labour – the party that plans to emancipate our souls – let it be known that they didn't want to be tainted with any 'luvvies' helping to elect them. The initiators and most frequent users of 'luvvie' are of course journalists, whose self-contempt is so acute that they describe themselves as 'hacks'. I wonder why they dislike themselves so much? I can't have been too successful making my point because Bruce Kent, who was on the rather more elevated soapbox of campaigning against arms sales, thought that I was just objecting to actors calling each other 'darling'.

25th July   Simon Sainsbury came to see me about the redevelopment. I told him why we were doing what we were doing, he asked a few questions, then said he would talk to his trust and would leave me alone because he was sure that I had much more pressing things to do. If only fund-raising were this easy, and if only all rich people were as charming and generous as Simon.

26th July   BBC meeting. The World Service row simmers on. It's the focus of the old dissent – staffed by émigrés from repressive regimes, Utopian, Reithian – all the anger of the past four years crystallised and focused on John Birt. There's a tidal wave of disapproval. I wasn't party to the discussion about the changes, which puts me in an even more ridiculous position. Much of the row is the defence of self-interest, and all the pain – justified or not – has been distilled into the one area that is unarguably underwritten by the Reithian ideology. We've got some way to go before our TV becomes as bad as Germany's and Italy's. They have TV programmes in which you can get divorced and the settlement is made through a general knowledge quiz, which saves on court time and lawyers' fees. There's a craving for ritual, which is what they get in a TV show and don't get in some small civil court. Which is why more people are asking to be married in church.

27th July   Terrifying documentary on C4 of a Russian prison camp for young offenders. Incredible scenes of cruelty and suffering. 'Human beings can bear anything . . . It's not so bad. You can't get run over. You get three meals a day . . .' Then CUT TO COMMERCIAL BREAK – ads about fast cars, port, chocolates – BACK TO RUSSIA. 'We get the same sun here but it's not the same sun as outside prison.' We were shown incredible ingenuity of self-destruction to achieve a stay in the hospital – injection with petrol, stabbing with nails . . . A boy is fucked by twelve men for a packet of fags, bread and soap. 'Be a good boy,' they said to him.

28th July   I heard the blind pianist George Shearing on the radio say that he started in a band whose theme song was 'I Dream of Seeing Sunlight in the Dawn'.

1st August   There's an article by Trevor [*Nunn*] in the *Evening Standard* bemoaning the state of the West End – the litter and the theatre, and propagandising (well) for the theatre as the medium of live debate. I remember reading an article by Trevor a few years ago about populism, which asked: 'Is what is popular by definition trivial?' and enlisted Matthew Arnold, Thomas Heywood, and Thomas Aquinas to arrive at a rather ambiguous conclusion: 'Surely the only thing that is not permissible these days is to lose

the audience.' I wasn't running a theatre then, so didn't sympathise.

3rd August   Had haemorrhoidectomy – probably more difficult to spell than to do. I've cut them off and stapled you, said the doc. He told me that the operation used to take at least five days in hospital and three weeks' recovery. 'We've had two or three VIPs from your line of country in here,' he said. 'Seems to be an occupational disorder.' The sister in the morning spoke to me as if I was eight. 'You must keep your bottom clean – I know it's difficult for a chap like you.'

5th August   Two days of intermittent agony, and last night – after an ill-advised curry – total agony. I prayed for morphine. Worked with Bob on *Lear*, and we started to see a shape, some sort of language. Bob told me a story which involved Maggie Smith waiting for ages in Joe Allen's in New York, being asked finally by a waitress what sort of drink she wanted: 'The sort you can pour down your throat.'

6th August   Been reading David Sylvester's book on Modern Art; he says: '. . . I made a resolve that my career as a critic was to be dedicated . . . to establishing that Matisse was a greater artist than Picasso' – or chocolate was better than marshmallow. Picasso told a friend that Giacometti's work was becoming increasingly monotonous and repetitive. The friend defended Giacometti, talking of his intense desire to 'find a new solution to the problem of figuration'. 'There isn't a solution,' said Picasso. 'There never is a solution. That's as it should be.' He should have told David Sylvester.

7th August   I've been asked to direct Tony Blair's party political broadcast for TV. I don't think I can do it while I'm running the NT, so I suggest Molly Dineen [*documentary film director*], and I say I'll produce it. So I'm reading a biography of him: *The Moderniser*. I end up with great respect for his ambition, his determination and his management capabilities. To expect more would be to imagine someone who couldn't be a politician. He argues that everything needs to change for a chance of winning the election. But do you stop believing what you believe in order to get elected? If you change only

to get elected aren't you in bad faith? I'm also reading *The Blair Revolution* by Peter Mandelson. There isn't a single mention of the arts, heritage, leisure, sport or broadcasting in the whole book. It's the Bible of 'New Labour'.

8th August   Mike Gambon's playing in a film Nick Roeg's doing about Samson and Delilah. Nick said: 'I cast him as King of the Philistines. Perfect casting.' Mike's cover is very good; he's actually very sensitive, highly musical, plays classical guitar and loves ballet.

15th August   Flight to Edinburgh. I got a lift from the airport with John Drummond [*ex-head Radio 3, Proms and Edinburgh Festival*], who's always good value. He dropped names like hailstones all the way into town. A little *schadenfreude* about cancelled performances and tenors and conductors ('Poor Brian'), and we drifted on to the subject of why there were so few conductors emerging. I said that perhaps it was the same problem with directors: no one serves an apprenticeship. John said that Peter Diamand had told him that there were ninety top conducting posts in the world, and only twelve conductors capable of filling them. George Steiner had made a speech here, according to the papers, advocating the end of the Festival. But reading his speech I can see he *didn't* say that. What he said was that all artistic forms have their epoch and there may come a time when 'a revered and outwardly successful structure starts to outlive its own vision and necessity'. Which is exactly what I feel about the NT. Even the Moscow Art Theatre (or the collaboration of Stanislavsky and Namirovich-Danchenko) lasted only seven years: seven productive years – and thirty-four of bitter bickering and bad work. Peter Hall told me years ago that he'd had eight good years at the RSC. The thing is for government to have the courage – and the will – to keep theatres going even if the work is poor precisely because things *can* change: everything in the world follows a wave pattern – what goes down must come up. But, as Flaubert said: 'Have you ever noticed how *all* authority is stupid concerning art? Our wonderful governments imagine that they only have to order work to be done, and it will be forthcoming. They set up prizes, encouragements, academies, and they forget only one thing, one little thing, without which nothing can live: the *atmosphere*.'

16th August I loved walking around Edinburgh. Every corner, every street, had a memory and I kept seeing people I knew, and having my heart tugged by the past – when I was so entirely ignorant and innocent, struggling to acquire knowledge and trying so hard to appear confident and knowing. I did three talks, pretentiously described as 'workshops'.

19th August New Orleans weather – sweaty thighs, heavy, humid, hot and dangerous. Reading a collection of essays by Janet Malcolm; excellent essay on the New York art scene, describing a doyenne of the scene who says: 'My greatest love is conceptual art. I may be more interested in thinking than in art . . . maybe I just hate art when the only thing going for it is that it's beautiful.'

20th August I sat through a meeting with three dissident members of the costume department yesterday, listening to complaints of harassment, victimisation, bitterness, bile – and I wondered if I have the appetite for all this. I'm treading water, acting as a counsellor.

27th August Meeting with John Birt. He's *utterly* certain that he's right about the changes he's made and won't take my point about the manner of making them or that the effect on the staff is to drain them of morale and the will to improve. No one – in any position – relishes being told about their inadequacies without being reassured about their virtues. John talks of getting rid of 'old fartism' but doesn't seem to be replacing it with any vision apart from efficient management. There's nothing I can see that makes the whole greater than the sum of the parts. John believes – and I don't doubt him – that he's doing it all for the long-term health of the BBC, but to me it seems as if he's obsessed with process and systems at the expense of the only thing that justifies the BBC's existence: its programmes. Afterwards I'm forced to confront my own conscience: I should have dealt with so many things at the NT and I haven't done it – partly cowardice, partly complacency.

28th August Bernie Jacobs [*of the Shubert organisation*] has died. He'd said: 'Of all the things in the world I think the least about it's what happens after you die. Dead is dead.' Sam Cohn [*agent*] described dealing with Bernie as 'the worst migraine of your life'.

Bernie said: 'I don't like Sam.' Bernie on the phone to Baron de Rothschild: 'I can't give you tickets. I'm in the business of selling tickets.' He puts down the phone, then: 'What is he? Just a man with a "de" in the front of his name.'

31st August   I went to Dorset to do a reading/talk in the Dorchester Museum, a place drenched in memories of unhappy hours staring at Roman coins. I paced nervously round the library, before I went into the gallery to confront about 150 people, many of them faces from my childhood, the past rolling towards me like a spring tide. I made the mistake, part vanity, part compulsion, of reading too much about my childhood, my Dorset. I felt a desperate need to close the circle; my head was full of whirling memories, my heart overloaded with feeling. I signed books afterwards and my past life trailed in front of me. The next day I drove over Eggardon to Maiden Newton, up our lane, and found I barely recognised the house that I'd known for nearly fifty years. In our garden stood five or six new houses; our house, spruce and redecorated, remained barely recognisable, surrounded by neo-Georgian tidiness, the past neatly plastered over.

1st September   I spoke to Peter Brook who's trying to get Paul [*Scofield*] for his film, but Paul's saying no. Peter came to *JGB* and told me that it was fastidiously good. Praise from Peter is praise beyond price. I sat next to a woman at the Royal Court on Thursday who said to her boyfriend: 'I saw *JGB* last night.' Boyfriend (coolly): 'Oh yes.' 'It was . . .' A long pause during which I died twice. '. . . fantastic.'

3rd September   I went with Peter Brook to backstage at the Theatre Royal, Drury Lane, where there's a large space behind the theatre scene dock which is a possible site for a London 'Bouffe du Nord' space. Peter was excited by the space, and not for the first time I envied his absolute commitment to the theatre. We talked about Paul: he says that of course Paul is attracted to the character of Borkman because it's one of the secret 'Pauls' – true to himself, and to nothing else. He said that there's a lot of him in the character – proud, lonely and obsessed. We talked about the part that Peter wants him to play in his film, but I didn't tell Peter that Paul had mentioned it to me: 'It's a dreadful part but he won't take no for an

answer.' Peter had arranged a meeting with Mike Gambon, who was at the stage door waiting for him. Mike told Linda [*stage door keeper*] that he was meeting Peter. 'Oh,' said Linda, 'that'll be for the part that Paul Scofield's turned down.' I told Paul this, who was entranced by the idea of Linda's omniscience and Peter's machinations: 'I love him, but he's very slippery.'

6th September   New York for *Skylight*. I got a call from Jenny to say that Vanessa is going to be off *again* tonight – after two performances off, and Paul is refusing to perform with the understudy. Actually I think it's got little to do with the understudy and a lot to do with Paul being furious with Vanessa, who is filming during the day even though she has flu. I spoke to Paul and Eileen, and couldn't resolve it. Jenny feels stuck in the middle and I feel guilty.

9th September   I'm helpless in the face of the *Borkman* problems, struggling to get the rights of *Lady in the Dark* from the Jesuitical Weill Estate, worrying about whether *Oedipus* is OK in Greece, about casting *Lear*, about replacing Jenny, and about *Skylight*. Plus jet-lag.

13th September   I'm lying in bed watching a re-run of the Oprah Winfrey show with Bette Midler, Goldie Hawn, Diane Keaton and Ivana Trump: a festival of self-regard, arrogance and plastic surgery.

16th September   Walk across Central Park – roller-bladers, musicians, picnickers, and a group of émigrés from Assam singing and dancing. Then went to the new Eric Rohmer film – shapeless, apparently artless and inconsequential but extraordinarily alluring: just *people*. Shots take the time they take, people cross roads, are bored, are repetitive; the sound is bad, the focus is off, the camera operation is haphazard, and yet you're held – it seems real, the people exist and, in the end, that's the only criterion. Went to Thelma Schoonmaker's [*Martin Scorsese's editor*] cutting room. Scorsese's offices are Citizen Kane-ish, in an ex-bank: every scrap of paper, every note, still, drawing, telephone message to do with his films is preserved. He's surrounded by devotees, who apply themselves to cataloguing and storing every item: a progress towards canonisation.

21st September *Skylight* opened quite painlessly. Nick Hytner asked Martin McDonagh what he thought of it. Martin: 'Well, I didn't write it so it's crap.' When I asked Martin why he started to write plays he said: 'I wanted to write the sort of plays that I would want to see if I went to the theatre.' At the party I was taken upstairs, as if to snort cocaine or see a porn movie, to read the NY *Times* review, which was good: 'Theatre doesn't get much better than this.' So, total relief and David made a speech thanking me in an entirely fulsome way, and I was (mercifully) stopped from replying and then, drunk and content, Sue and I got a lift to the hotel with a severely sober Robert Fox.

26th September Back at the NT – mountains of letters, casting for *Lear*, interviews for Jenny's job, anxiety about raising matching funds, confusion about working with Trevor, and a steady drip of petty complaints about Vanessa's missed performance in *Borkman*. Eileen told me that Vanessa had had a letter from a headmaster asking if she really did exist. He'd brought a party to *Antony and Cleopatra* and she was off. And the same with *JGB*. Eileen asked Vanessa if she was going to take up the headmaster's offer of going to talk to the boys to prove her existence. 'God no,' said Vanessa, 'I'm just going to ignore it.'

27th September I finally caught up with the Oedipus plays in the Olivier which have a stately grandeur but don't touch the heart. And oddly for a production of Peter [*Hall*]'s the force of the language seems diminished: none of the wild visceral energy that Tony's translation gave to the *Oresteia*. My real problem is with the masks; they rob everything of energy, giving everything the same weight – unexpressive and monotonous – robbing theatre of the very things that animate it: the human face and the human voice.

28th September BBC Board meeting: it's very difficult to cut through the corporate self-regard and cockiness. But the same would possibly be true of me at the NT from the Board perspective.

29th September Furious rainstorm throughout the day. I've been trying to work, to write a lecture about the 'new direction of theatre'. You can't theorise about it, only *do* it. I did a platform with Robert

Lepage last week where we spoke about the future of theatre. He was more worried about the future of film, which he regarded as much less robust. He saw an inevitable convergence of theatre and film, the two media becoming interdependent. He said this (or something like it): 'In the next four or five years we'll be amazed how theatre and film will have to live together, because film cannot continue in the form it is, in the way it's presented. People want direct life, three-dimensional interaction, and that's something that belongs to the theatre. Our field of work is telling stories and if we want to be exciting theatre story-tellers we have to be interested in film, tele-vision, and novels, because those forms of story-telling are changing how we tell stories. You have to have the humility to say, "This subject deserves this, or this," not try to imprison it or stifle it because you have a style, a way of doing things.'

30th September   Heard Peter Nichols on the radio telling a story about being in a taxi. 'Oh yeah,' said the taxi driver, 'I had another playwright in my cab. Whatsisname? . . . Don't tell me – the one who pulls all the birds.' Peter realised eventually it was Harold Pinter.

1st October   Eileen's reading (brilliantly) Virginia Woolf's Diaries on the radio. An irresistible intelligence: V.W. is funny, humane, snobbish, cruel, forgiving, and always acutely observant. She must have written them to practise for her fiction, or else she was effortlessly fluent. Also heard this on the radio, an interview with the woman who had invented *The Flowerpot Men*: 'Did you make lots of money?' 'None.' 'None. Why was that?' Very very long pause. 'I really don't know.'

3rd October   A meeting at the Garrick chaired by Melvyn Bragg about Labour Party policy for the arts: Richard Rogers, Stephen Daldry, Greg Dyke, Dennis Marks and Brian Wenham. It's a council of despair: no politician has an arts policy, no one is interested, no one wants to mention the arts until after the election – not a single word. Once again Stephen and I come out of a meeting about Labour and the arts and stand mournfully on the pavement and, as after the last meeting, Stephen says: 'Perhaps we should come out for the Tories.'

4th October We went to a Victoria Wood Concert at the Albert Hall: just her and a grand piano, a small figure asserting her control over an audience of about 3,000 by sheer talent.

6th October Sunday. Grey autumn day, leaves on the turn, bonfire smoke hanging in the air, a melancholy stillness, which reminds me of autumn at school, running joylessly on the 'slopes', the slap of plimsolls on damp road, the echoing distant cries from the games fields, and the meandering pointlessness of it all.

11th October Week spent fund-raising and trying to keep the theatre together. It's very centrifugal at the moment, flying apart because of fear of the future. But then it's always on the edge of flying apart: the effort is always to pull it together. But box office is good. I went to see *JGB*, somewhat in trepidation, but it was fine, stronger than ever. At the end – after Paul's hand of iron had gripped his heart and he'd died and lay stretched out on the bench, Eileen and Vanessa finally held hands and stood isolated against the falling snow, and the lights started to dim, and the last chords sounded, I heard (loudly): 'They've got a lot of clearing up to do.' I spoke to Ian Holm, who'd enjoyed *Borkman*, said he'd never seen anything like Paul. I told him that Stephen Rea had said that it was like looking into the eyes of a child suffering from Down's syndrome.

15th October Writers' Guild dinner. It had the air of a Rotary Club do, though perhaps with less flair. Our hostess, Rosemary Ann Sisson, offered us wine but said cheerily: 'I've ordered the cheapest.' I made a speech – a joke at the expense of directors (very popular) – and flattered writers shamelessly. The evening went on for a lifetime. Most recipients of awards didn't turn up, and Nigel Planer, who was the MC, said with eloquent bitterness that it was no longer fashionable to stay away.

16th October Paris. I saw *Les Fausses Confidences* [*Marivaux*] at the Comédie Française. I love going into that theatre, although I seldom like what I see there. I don't believe that in London the theatre has ever had the social cachet that it has in Paris – an indelible part of the ritual of haut bourgeois life, like going to the opera in London. The show was wholly inert, as was the audience, but they didn't seem to mind.

17th October I've been sent a further education prospectus: 'Shakespeare's texts are studied primarily from the point of view of the actors and directors whose job it is to make these plays signify to a modern audience. Attention is paid to Shakespeare's iconic status within world culture, particularly to such matters as the financial and educational power his name commands.'

18th October Been to a BBC meeting in Belfast. I'm sure that meetings in the chapter houses of medieval cathedrals strongly resembled these meetings: ideology, faith, schism, cynicism, optimism, moral imperatives, power, pragmatism, status and euphemism – as in an audience research response to Radio 4 in N. Ireland: 'A younger audience not yet in the mood to value the BBC's speech-based output.' Belfast looked wonderful: bright sun, hills above the lough, the city swelling with new buildings. An entirely artificial economy, bursting with subsidy and corruption.

20th October From the *Spectator*, almost at random: 'one of his most remembered *Spectator* speeches was a complaint about how too much was being done for the disabled . . . all those expensive ramps', and 'The Irish Republic has never been a proper country since it parted company with its mentor, England, and lost its natural ruling class . . .' The studied heartlessness of the English upper class and those mimicking it – i.e. Evelyn Waugh: 'She had written complaining that in Austria she was raped by a Cossack and got syphilis.' Complaining? I loathe that tone of voice, not least because it lurks somewhere deep within me as a genetic legacy. It's an inherited carapace, a defence against the indifference of your parents.

21st October *Guys and Dolls* has started rehearsals. It's probably as ill-advised as returning to an old love affair. I'm not sure it's right to be doing it again, without the excitement and danger of directing it for the first time, but everyone is full of good-will and generosity, the cast are immensely talented, and the piece *is* wonderful.

22nd October Stephen Daldry might have overplayed his hand in Hollywood. He had a project with Paramount and a meeting with big cheese, Sherry Lansing. 'Now, if anyone you meet confuses you, I

mean their function, just ask me what they do.' Stephen: 'OK, I'll start with you. What do you do?'

23rd October   I did a lunchtime 'conversation' in St Mary-le-Bow. It has two pulpits, and I 'conversed' with the Vicar, the Rev. Stock, across the nave, in front of a surprisingly largish and enthusiastic audience. Rev. Stock was rather like Streaky Bacon in *Racing Demon*, very bright, very nice. We had lunch in his house above the church: canary-yellow walls, good furniture, china, obviously family stuff. He's just given up 'a house in the country'. He told me about a meeting between the Archbishop and a group of police chief constables. They said: 'What we need is a moral lead.' To which Carey said, without a trace of irony: 'What are you looking at me for?' I asked the Rev. what he thought of Carey: 'He's not pretty enough.'

24th October   Dinner with Richard and Ruthie [*Rogers*] and the Blairs. Tony Blair was excessively effusive (again) about my visit to his school to talk to the sixth-form about theatre. He said it had made a deep impression on him – my enthusiasm and evangelical conviction. I felt excited and disappointed by him: excited that this man who is personable and plausible and energetic and intelligent and decent would be PM, and disappointed that he wasn't more extraordinary. I felt, in fact, that he was too much like one of us, when, quite unfairly, what I wanted was someone much brighter, wiser, more of a visionary. He's a good eater and drinker, in spite of Cherie's best efforts.

26th October   I did a platform with Peter Hall, chaired by Sue MacGregor. I'd forgotten how well-honed Peter's public manner is. He made running the NT sound like a noble battle, a welter of constant controversy and 'struggle'. Afterwards I was accosted by several loonies. 'There's always one,' said Bob. 'Well, actually, there's always five.'

27th October   The first preview of *Death of a Salesman*, directed by David Thacker, in the Lyttelton. It went well and was greeted with rapture, although the play is beginning to feel like a period piece, no longer a parable for our times, more about the destructive nature of

dreams than the corrosive effect of capitalism. The plot seemed over-neat – Biff becoming a drop-out when he discovers his father with another woman – and the funeral scene seemed sentimental, but Alun Armstrong and Marje Yates were luminously honest and thoughtful and unsensationally affecting.

3rd November   I've just heard that Peter Hall is going to do a production of *Lear* with Alan Howard. He's never done the play, and wanted to do it with Ian [*Holm*]. More and more I think of it as a play about a father being locked out of the house by his children. The fragility of our civilised lives, the terror of the destruction of that veneer. David Thomson: 'In life, we agonise over a scratch on our car or a leak in the roof. Those nagging bourgeois longings for wholeness and tidiness inspire a demon of resentment that is itching to break out in riots of mayhem, the lovely innocent plenty of ruin.'

5th November   David Toguri [*choreographer*] and I were at the Guildhall Academy of Music and Drama today to become Honorary somethings, and were talking to George Martin [*Beatles producer*]. David said to him: 'Why don't you do more pop records?' 'Pop,' said George, shaking his head ruefully, 'is for the young.'

13th November   Discussion at BBC Board about salaries. Much talk of 'comparators', but surely there *are* no comparators: public service is public service, it can't be compared to the City or to commercial TV. The only 'comparators' are the civil service, heads of cultural organisations like the British Museum (or even National Theatre), or government. How much does the Prime Minister get paid? Answer: less than a BBC top executive. It *may* be acceptable to receive huge salaries and bonuses and pension and redundancy payments and have cars and drivers paid for, but not in my universe. Most of the senior BBC managers have been enclosed within the BBC for the whole of their working lives and have no idea of what it feels like to be a freelance, or what 'public service' means in any area outside television. Nor, necessarily, do they have a market value outside the BBC. And their pensions – 50 per cent of their salary! For life!

14th November I've had a letter informing me, 'in strictest confidence, that Her Majesty may be graciously pleased to offer you a knighthood and the PM would like to know if it would be agreeable to you'. I can't help feeling that it would be agreeable to me but I have very mixed feelings about it. Sue had always said she would leave me if I accepted a knighthood and I swore I never would. Now I'm not robust enough, or am too vain, to refuse. Who does? Or who does without making it known that they have been offered it? So have I become soft or become corrupt? I'll become a fully paid-up member of the Establishment – but as Director of the *Royal* National Theatre haven't I been that for years? They've claimed me in the way they always do. It's important that writers, if they want to keep a critical distance, don't concede: they lose their independent voice, but I don't have the certainty of my own voice.

15th November The Chikamatsu play [*Fair Ladies at a Game of Poem Cards*] has started previewing. Almost the last thing that Peggy Ramsay said to me was 'Chikamatsu, dear, he's terribly good.' Clive Merrison was struck on the skull by a samurai sword and the show had to stop. He had a deepish gash, and was more shocked than in agony. Equally so the actor who'd done it. I went on stage to tell the audience what had happened; they were very good-humoured, and the show went on after a break. It's elegantly staged but doesn't quite get beyond the quaint: it's Japanoiserie.

19th November I introduced a lecture by Alan Yentob at BAFTA. Alan gave a good account of his life at the BBC and said that all the change there was for the better. Ken Trodd [*TV producer*] got up at the end and asked why – if it was all for the better – had so few people been convinced by it either in or out of the BBC. Ken started his question with the words: 'I don't want to spoil your evening . . . ' which should be the title of his autobiography.

21st November First run-through of *Guys and Dolls*. Exhilarating and fine. More than fine, and the only thing I missed was the sense of excitement and surprise that it could deliver such an impact, such a cumulative emotional gift. Never such innocence again.

26th November   I saw *Art*, which is a bewildering phenomenon. I'd heard it described in apocalyptic tones as crass, pernicious and philistine, but it seemed to me like a slight, bland but good-natured after-dinner sketch. I saw Albert Finney afterwards. 'Are you going to do it in New York?' 'No, it's not a theatre town. Anyway I did all that in the '60s.'

27th November   A Board meeting at the beginning of the week. Much talk about how to react to Lasdun's threat of litigation. All the Board are robust, although Stuart Lipton [*property developer*] hopes for some face-saving compromise. In the evening I had to give a speech at the ABSA Awards at the British Museum, following Virginia Bottomley, who told us that everything in the garden was lovely, and how grateful we should be for the Lottery. I'd been asked to say something inspirational about the arts, which was like standing on the pavement in the rain waiting for a sighting of Sharon Stone and shouting: 'Go on Sharon, do something sexy!' I said I felt we'd failed to convince the government that we were a sound investment, with a good return in VAT, in tax, in foreign currency, prestige, employment, tourism, and adding to the sum of human happiness, etc. etc. And how the consequences of the Lottery might be disastrous – new buildings, no art. I ended with what art did give us: two stanzas from Blake's 'Songs of Innocence'. I stepped down off the podium and went into the audience, but they went on and on applauding. It wasn't for me; it was to embarrass Bottomley, who stood rigid and furious, trapped in the middle of a political demonstration.

28th November   The Professor of Drama at Goldsmith's College, who used to teach at Nottingham University, said that when I was running Nottingham Playhouse he'd once been at a lunch at which the administrator of the Playhouse and his wife were present. She'd asked him if he could use his influence to get me removed since I was ruining the Playhouse with all these radical plays.

29th November   Lynn Redgrave has been doing her one-woman show about her father. Eileen said to Vanessa that she thought Lynn exaggerated the horrors of their father, based on the fact that Lynn's birth wasn't even registered in his diary. 'Maybe he had another

diary,' said Eileen. 'He did,' said Vanessa, 'Corin found it. And it recorded her birth and his feelings of joy about it.' 'Why didn't you tell Lynn that the other diary had been found?' said Eileen. 'It would have ruined her show,' said Vanessa.

30th November   I couldn't get to the *Evening Standard* Awards until 2 p.m., grateful to have missed all that nerve-jangling meeting and greeting people you haven't seen for a year possibly because you haven't wanted to. Martin McDonagh was legless. Sean Connery tried to sort him out, but Martin told him to fuck off, and was then heard to say that he was a fucking terrible actor who'd only made one decent film. Sam Mendes presented the Best Newcomer's Award to Martin. He introduced him as 'very talented, very assured, and very young' and a chorus of people muttered 'and very drunk'. Paul Scofield got an award for *JGB* from Maggie [*Smith*], who made a (gratuitous) joke about how nothing worked at the NT. In the evening I did a platform with Jenny. I'll miss her very much; she's been my professional north, south, east and west. I took her out to dinner at the Savoy, where I watched a young waiter absent-mindedly scratching his arse as he waited to serve a customer.

12th December   *The Cripple of Inishmaan* [*Martin McDonagh*] has started previewing. It needs time, which it has, and as the actors relax so will the audiences who, like the actors, haven't quite got the measure of its comedy. They will. Nick [*Hytner*]'s had problems with one of the actors who's been enthusiastically embracing the stereotype of the drunken Irish actor. He arrived late for rehearsals the other day with a livid scar on his nose, clearly the result of an encounter with a pavement. 'I got bitten by a chihuahua,' he said. He told friends that Nick was a 'divil' for making him learn his lines. 'You make bad choices if you learn your lines,' he said. The canteen's full of Irish these days – from several different shows. We're becoming known as The Abbey National. Two Irish jokes: Irishman goes into a Renault showroom. Salesman shows him a few of the bigger cars. He's not very interested. 'Ah,' says the salesman, 'what about the Renault 5?' 'They're innocent!' And: Irish boy in an optician. Optician says close your left eye. He closes his right eye. Close your right eye. He closes his left eye. Frustrated optician gets a cornflake packet and cuts eyeholes so that he can put his hand over the eyehole.

Boy bursts into tears. What's the matter? says the optician. I wanted a pair with frames, just like my brother's.

20th December   *Guys and Dolls* had a fairly painless tech – barring a heart-stopping moment when Stanley Townsend got struck on the head during 'Luck Be a Lady'. I'd forgotten just how big a show it was, and how complicated. Then a public dress rehearsal and the whole staff embraced it as the perfect morale booster. Then the first preview. The press had started to murmur that it was bad form to be reviving the show. Billington said it was 'scandalous' that we were reviving it, but then his paper published an editorial saying 'Why such negative thinking?' By the opening night there were only two ways it could go – a huge success (better than before) or a disaster (not as good). The first night swung, the audience stood at the end, and we were home and I should be saying to myself 'It doesn't get better than this,' but maybe it gets different. Or if it doesn't get better then it gets . . . um . . . worse.

21st December   I had a row with Bob [*Crowley*]'s agent over his availability for *Amy's View*. I said I don't want the short end of Bob's time, with a design done on the back of an envelope. Bob gave me an envelope on the first night of *G and D*, on the back of it: 'PRO-POSED DESIGN FOR AMY'S VIEW' – a drawing of a Chekhovian forest of BHS lamps. I showed it to David, who said that if I'd been Jonathan Miller I'd have accepted it.

24th December   Julian Mitchell has written an attack on the NT in the *Independent on Sunday*. He says there's no experiment, no new plays, too much reliance on stars. A few months ago I was being attacked for doing too *many* new plays. I turned down his last play. I liked it but not enough to want to do it. Should I have pretended to like it more than I did?

27th December   *JGB* has ended. When I saw it on the last night I was mildly disappointed. But then all last nights are always disappointing: it's one of theatre's invariable axioms. Last nights are like Christmas: they never quite live up to expectations.

28th December   Glos. Everyone's ill, except me – a particularly pernicious gastric flu. It's very cold outside and the house feels like a

field hospital in the Crimea. I've been watching a lot of TV: vast amount of effluent of hype and genuflection about showbiz, massive conspiracy to keep the liner of showbiz afloat – stars, stars, directors, technicians – films about the making of films, videos on the making of pop videos, the whole of showbiz joining hands and dancing round in a frantic frenzy of self-congratulation. It's a huge relief to watch *Ben Hur*, beautifully directed by William Wyler, fantastic chariot race, the film only subverted by the appearance of Jesus.

29th December   Alan Bennett on visiting a prison: 'Indeed one gets the impression that the only thing holding the prison service together and making it for the moment work is this shared hatred of Michael Howard.' A review of *Guys and Dolls*: ' "I dreamed last night I got on the boat to heaven," sings Nicely Nicely. Me too.' Another says: 'It gives you as high an endomorphine rush as you can have legally.' You can't imagine that being said of a play. I love the thing that Yip Harburg, who wrote 'Somewhere Over the Rainbow', said about musicals: 'Words make you think thoughts, music makes you feel a feeling, a song makes you feel a thought.'

30th December   On the *Today* programme an item about Alan Ayckbourn's theatre: a town councillor said it was a choice between funding the theatre and keeping the town's loos open. 'Our reserves are being drained away,' he said. Then a radio discussion about science in which art is talked of in the tone of atheists patronising Christians. Lewis Wolpert says science is progress, art is not. Science, he says, has nothing to learn from art. He slaps down Jude Kelly for talking 'art babble'.

31st December   Snow again, now sunlight – a thin peach light over the valley. It's official: I'm now a 'Sir'. Gorg rings me to say that she's pleased for me if that's what I wanted. She says she would want an honour in order to decline it – but decline it publicly. Alan Ayckbourn's got a knighthood. We're part of Major's lavender list – Paul McCartney, Lloyd Webber, Cilla Black, Joan Collins, Terry Wogan. I'm jolted out of churlishness and false humility by the genuine pleasure (and amusement) of many friends, some of whom ask: 'Will it change your life?' I feel like a man wandering about pulling a string with tin cans attached to it, as if I was just married.

1997

1st January Reading Alec Guinness's Diaries: 'I remembered my New Year resolution – "Cause me to know thy loving kindness in the morning."' I'm sad that I haven't worked with his generation – Gielgud, Ashcroft, Olivier, Richardson.

3rd January We're huddled round the fire because the central heating oil has run out, and there's a knock at the door. Sue answers it to a large mufflered and overcoated man: 'Is Sir Richard in?' Her Siberian peasant costume and look of utter confusion gave the impression of insanity, which wasn't helped when 'Sir' Richard appeared from the woodshed in a balaclava and First War flying helmet and three days' growth of beard. It's odd to change one's name: this is what it feels like to be a bride. The gentleman caller was after contributions to the local old people's home, which is, he pointed out, where I might like to end up.

4th January A postcard from Tony Harrison:

Only two days after our conversation where I swore I'd never be Poet Laureate & you swore that you'd never accept a knight-hood, I found this in a junk-shop in Newcastle and have been keeping it these past ten years for the day you changed your mind. I did make a poetic prediction in the *Guardian* of 11 Jan 1995. I actually wrote (or begun) a poem about our talk but never quite got it right for publication. I've been hunting the draft through my notebooks half the day and can't find it now so this is just to wish you a Happy New Year (and I promise I won't tell a soul!) (or finish the poem). With love as ever, Tony.

The postcard is embroidered with a crest of George V, circled by 'Honi Soit Qui Mal Y Pense', above two gold-threaded initials: R.E. Most English poets are rewarded with indifference at best and at worst with becoming Poet Laureate. Tony's often violated both ends of that spectrum: his poetry's provoked indignation, and outrage, and joy, and sorrow, pity perhaps, and with his front-page *Guardian* poems he's become the uncrowned Poet Laureate.

I ring Tony and he's genially mocking about the knighthood. He refuses everything he's offered, including seven doctorates (he's surprisingly specific). He says getting older should be about cutting away: adding baggage makes it harder to go back to the 'rag-and-bone shop of the heart'. It's true but that's the case with writers. How does it affect me, who borrows my voice – it affects the way I'll work because I'll no longer be a free agent. But all success, all fame, corrupts in that sense. Tony says I should plant (and emulate) a medlar tree: they're a hard fruit, Persian originally, which never soften. You 'blet' them in sawdust to ripen them, then eat them with yoghurt. Lawrence wrote a poem about them. I look it up, and barring the absence of rhyme and iambics, it's very Tony:

> So, in the strange resorts of medlars and sorb-apples
> The distilled essence of hell,
> The exquisite odour of leave-taking.

7th January I did a platform with Robert Lepage who was as beguilingly charming as ever. Robert is diffident about *Elsinore*, he says it's a doodle. It is: a brilliant sketch, with some marvellously vivid illuminations – like the closet scene played from the p.o.v. of Polonius.

8th January *Inishmaan* opened well. It's really found its pitch during previews and the actors and the audience enter into a wonderfully complicit enjoyment of Martin's black but not inhumane wit. Most of all I love the scene where the young girl gives a history lesson by breaking eggs on her kid brother's face: England v. Ireland. He ends up with three eggs yolks running down his face.

10th January Trevor [*Nunn*] is being very generous. I miss Jenny, greasing the cogs, oiling the wheels, and doing so much invisibly and

(almost) thanklessly. Having Trevor here has made me very aware of how many regular meetings I have, but it seems impossible to reduce them. Monday: technical meeting, Tuesday: planning, Wednesday: executive in the morning, scripts in the evening, Thursday: redevelopment, Friday: heads of department. Then there are budget meetings, development meetings, model meetings, production meetings, poster meetings, brochure meetings and sometimes even meetings about meetings. Not to mention the regular meetings we now have with the contractors about the redevelopment. I start rehearsing at twelve now, work straight through to six, which seems easier. I'm stuck with a number of unresolved problems: stage-management offices and their management, costume department and its management, the FOH, the education department. I went to an East End school recently, saw the education department at their very best – wonderful version of *The Tempest* – the whole project brilliantly conceived and executed, using scores of kids. Real education – for me as well.

11th January   Lunch with Miriam Stoppard and Chris Hogg. I said to M. (her flat's in Mayfair) that it was good to live in the centre of a city. Yes, she said, I went to look at a place in Holland Park and thought: I couldn't live in the suburbs. We talk about the lectures I'm going to be doing in Oxford. She said Tom (of course) did a brilliant one: a demonstration of a text in performance by showing how a scene in *Travesties* had been done in London and in Paris. In London it was thought to be dull, in Paris a huge success: the scene was performed by a beautiful actress who started the speech naked getting out of bed, dressing as she spoke.

12th January   Round-the-world yachtsman Tony Bullimore has been rescued after four days on his capsized hull, and when he got to dry land he was offered counselling. 'I'd rather have a beer,' he said.

13th January   Much discussion (*pace* Damien Hirst) about what art is. For me there has to be an element of craft, of visible skill. 'Creativity' by itself is nothing; it's no more to be applauded than being good-looking or having a sunny day. There must be distillation, form, expertise, meaning, and a desire to communicate.

14th January   Flu epidemic. Numerous understudies on in *G and D*. Yesterday it looked as though we'd have to put on an understudy for the understudy of Henry Goodman [*playing Nathan Detroit*]. Glen Baxter told me that he'd taken his son Harry – noted theatre sceptic aged seventeen – to *Guys and Dolls*. He'd overheard him recommending it on the phone: 'Yeah, it's dark, man.'

15th January   Tom's play has a title now: *The Invention of Love*. It's odd that he and David should be writing plays about homosexuality. Is it curiosity about an alien and exotic activity and the inaccessibility and criminality of homosexual sex in the late nineteenth century, or is it that they are both wanting to write about romantic love – and it somehow distils the issues to write about romantic love that's proscribed and that they haven't experienced?

16th January   Lunch with Michael Billington. We talk of his Pinter book, my plans, the state of newspapers, theatre, and the way theatre criticism is dominated by the vocabulary of the cocktail party: 'stunning', 'dazzling', 'glittering', 'fizzing', 'super', 'brilliant'. He said the one taboo word for theatre critics was 'interesting'. Throughout lunch I am transfixed by the toothpaste round his mouth.

Dinner with Robert Lepage. He asked me to work in his space in Quebec. He talked of his fear of assassination, when someone pointed a laser torch at the stage. He said he'd seen Peter's production of *Oh Les Beaux Jours* in Quebec: 'It was like hearing Beckett straight, in his non-French French.' I saw Simon Callow on the way into the restaurant. He'd been to see *Shopping and Fucking*. I said I'd been curious about the stage direction which read something like this: 'HE KNEELS DOWN, NAKED, PRESENTING HIS BUM. ANOTHER CHARACTER, ALSO NAKED, KNEELS AND RIMS HIS ARSEHOLE.' 'Oh that,' says Simon, 'that was perfectly fine, rather innocent.'

17th January   This week saw Alan [*Bennett*]'s double-bill of monologues. Maggie [*Smith*] was brilliant, on her own, in a class of her own. Penelope Wilton really good in *The Cherry Orchard*, also on her own, acting in a forest of preening. Also saw *Who's Afraid of Virginia Woolf* [*Edward Albee*]. I enjoyed Howard's production but found the

play melodramatic – I just didn't buy the stuff about the fictional child. I found the play overwhelmingly strong when I first saw it in the '60s with the extraordinary Uta Hagen and Arthur Hill.

18th January   *The Homecoming* has started previewing. Roger's done a really good production, excellent acting – particularly David Bradley and Lindsay Duncan. It's remarkable: mysterious, elusive and disturbing, particularly now in the light of Frederick West. I remember seeing it in 1963/4(?) when it was on tour before opening in London. I thought even then it was terrifying. When I saw it in Cambridge I sat across the aisle from a large, bearded man who scrawled furiously in large disordered writing on a pad illuminated by a small torch: Peter Hall.

19th January   Sunday. I start *Lear* tomorrow. I watched the Errol Flynn *Robin Hood* on TV after planting two acers and a climbing rose.

MAID MARION: You speak treason!
ROBIN: Fluently!

And Robin to Friar Tuck: 'Not so close, my ponderous one.' Also watch a documentary about Antonioni, who emerged as rather callow and pretentious, less than meets the eye. From a new film of his: 'What if I fell in love with you?' 'You'd be lighting a candle in a room full of light.'

I'm reading Gore Vidal's autobiography. It suffers from too much curl of the lip and painful contortions of snobbery, like a Daumier caricature. He's like those English snobs who say that the Queen is very middle class. But I did love this: 'Kissinger has a brother who came to America when he did. Recently the brother was asked why he had no German accent but Henry did. "Because," said the brother, "Henry never listens." '

20th January   The first day of *Lear*. I didn't talk much about the play, just a few ground rules, as much for me as for the cast:

1. You may be daunted by a play that appears to be about everything. At this moment it may appear to be a mountain

that is inaccessible and unscalable. But trust your own knowledge of the world: this is a play about two fathers – one with three daughters, the other with two sons. Everyone is an expert on the subject of families.

2. Believe that the writer is a playwright who understands what he's doing. However great Shakespeare's genius is, it doesn't help to treat him as a sort of holy fool or a Messianic seer. He was a playwright, and an actor, and a theatre manager. He was utterly pragmatic; his plays wouldn't and couldn't have worked if they had been shrouded in obscurity and abstract conceits. And remember that in spite of the play being in verse, each line is characterised. No two characters speak the same.

3. Treat the verse as an ally, not as an enemy. Look at the scansion, the line endings, the line breaks, the changes of rhythm: they are all aids to understanding the meaning and how to convey it.

4. Don't make judgements on the characters. Let us – and the audience – discover what the moral scheme of the play is. Don't describe anyone as good or evil; let us decide on the basis of their actions.

5. Rely on the evidence of the text, not on speculation, or psychological theory, or conceptualising, or spurious historical research.

6. Try to be simple; trust that Shakespeare is trying to do the same, however profound, eloquent, and complex is his intention. Be specific: all good art is derived from specific observations, all bad art from generalisations.

7. Our job is to discover and animate the meanings of the play: its vocabulary, its syntax, and its philosophy. We have to ask what each scene is revealing about the characters and their actions: what story is each scene telling us? We have to exhume, examine and explain: line by line, scene by scene. We have to understand the mystery of the play – in the light of that understanding.

And then we read the play and Ian did what he said he was going to do: he just 'does it', with an extraordinary daring and ferocity. He made the play seem short. He was only dull, surprisingly, when he played the mad scenes a bit 'mad'.

I've cast three of Ian's peers – Tim West, David Burke and Michael Bryant – which of course means three actors who'd consider themselves plausible candidates for the part of Lear. It's a tribute to their generosity that they agreed to play the parts, and it's also of course a tribute to their respect for Ian. Having Tim as Gloucester makes sense of the play being about two fathers and having Lear, Gloucester, Kent and the Fool the same vintage really highlights the theme of the young supplanting the old: 'The younger rises when the old doth fall,' says Edmund. It's a strong cast in all areas – three fantastic sisters [*Amanda Redman, Barbara Flynn, Anne-Marie Duff*].

23rd January BBC BOG meeting before rehearsals. I said it seemed logical that the BBC was going increasingly to shed its resources and end up as a commissioning house with a purely editorial function. John Birt hotly denied this and Christopher said never while he was Chairman. I got a cab back to the NT driven by an Alfred Doolittle: 'I know you, guv'nor,' etc. He kept up a continuous commentary about the NT; 'I 'ad that Peter Hall in the back of my cab, 'e's been at it a long time, and that Trevor Nunn, I s'pose 'e's been travelling a bit, wants the nine to five now, not that it is of course, guv'nor. That David Thacker, is 'e any good?'

25th January A week of *Lear* rehearsals. A few days of sitting around and talking. Partly as a means of trying to gain purchase on the mountainside, partly as a way of putting off the moment when the actors stand up and you start to draw on the blank sheet of paper, and partly as a way of finding out about each other. We talked about religion, about money, about monarchy, about hierarchy, about living conditions, about crime and punishment, about the climate, about the eclipse of the sun, about the geography, about the food, about the clothes. All assertions had to be supported by the evidence of the text; everyone had an equal voice in the discussions and even Michael Bryant, who always prefers doing to talking; joined in. Ian's like a fit dog, longing to gnaw at the bone. And when he does I begin to see how wonderful this play can be.

26th January Glos. Early morning. I watched the sun creep over the hill, a loud orange through the thin icy mist, then apricot, Gothic shadows across the iced grass, warm colour against the thin green.

Ian rang me to ask if I thought Lear had got Parkinson's disease. I say I don't think so. To me the story is about a father, a man, who is selfish, self-absorbed, impatient, irascible – a domestic autocrat. And a king. To make him in any way 'ill' seems to me to weaken the power of the play.

27th January   From the *Sunday Times*: two middle-aged men overheard in New York: 'Did you see *Trainspotting*?' 'No, did you?' 'No. Do you know what *Trainspotting* is?' 'No. Do you?' 'Yes, actually. I saw a whole programme about it recently, it's this craze among English kids for lying down on tracks and having trains run over them.' 'Really? How *British*.'

31st January   I had to break rehearsals to go to an awards lunch. *The South Bank Show* now have awards – why? They gave me an Award for Outstanding Achievement. Disraeli said that everyone liked flattery but with royalty you have to lay it on with a trowel; the same is true of directors. I was getting more and more anxious as speeches went on and on and I needed to go back to rehearsal. Finally my turn came and up popped Tony Blair to present it – to an explosively generous reception. He told the audience the story of me coming to his school and of seeing my production of *The Crucible*. Then he spoke feelingly of supporting the arts. I sat next to Salman and Jack Cunningham, who said if Labour got in he'd put a stop to the Dome.

1st February   Ian was playing the Dover scene beautifully, heart-breakingly, then he stopped in the middle of the scene: 'Give me an ounce of civet, good apothecary/ To sweeten my imagination. There's money for thee,' says Lear. 'O, let me kiss that hand,' says Gloucester. 'Let me wipe it first; it smells of –' And Ian stopped. Minutes seemed to pass, and I didn't dare breathe. This wasn't acting; this was *being*. This was possession – by madness. Then Ian turned to me, and he started to laugh: 'What's the word? Oh, mortality, of course.' Then, like a violinist picking up his bow, he returned to the same point in the scene, at the same pitch of intensity. That's the true actor: the true professional – experiencing the state of possession, enduring passion and yet, like a firewalker, remaining untouched by the experience.

2nd February   End of second week of *Lear*. Feeling optimistic, even though I still haven't got to the end of working through the play. Each page, each character, each speech, each line, requires so much attention. The *detail* is what is so remarkable.

4th February   Two theatre stories: Paul Scofield gets in a train. Man: 'You're Paul Scofield, aren't you?' Paul (reluctantly): 'Yes.' Man: 'I'm a bit of an actor myself.' Paul: 'Oh really?' Man: 'Yes.' PAUSE. Man: 'Why do we do it, Paul?' And a taxi driver picking up Alec Guinness. 'You're that – don't tell me – David Nixon, aren't you?' 'Well, no, as a matter of fact I'm Alec Guinness, not David Nixon.' 'I bet you wish you were.'

5th February   Harold and Antonia came to see *The Homecoming*. Harold was very cheery. The day before they'd had a wedding for one of Antonia's daughters and another had got engaged. Antonia said that Harold said at the end of the day: 'I think I've been very benign today.' 'Benign like a tumour,' said Antonia. She said she'd never seen Harold laugh so much.

6th February   We finally got to the end of working through *Lear*. It's taken nearly three weeks to work through the play from beginning to end, chipping away at the raw stone. I decided to have a run-through, so we could all feel the power of the play in the light of what we'd learned about it. We sat round in a circle: some actors read their parts, others performed them. Some stood up for their scenes in the middle of the circle, some remained seated. It was thrilling: fast, clear, intensely moving, played without a break: two hours forty-five minutes. We must achieve that in performance.

7th February   Peter Gill's play [*Cardiff East*] started previewing. It's very spare, very bleak, very touching and beautifully done. It couldn't have been written (or directed) by anyone else.

8th February   My first lecture as Cameron Mackintosh Professor at St Catherine's last night. I was slightly thrown by the absence of a lectern and the presence of historian Alan Bullock, who founded the college, sitting in the front row. At the end of the lecture he said: 'You've used the words "human", "humane", and "humanist" a lot.

If you were a student of mine I'd ask you to define your terms.' I tried, somewhat unsatisfactorily. Afterwards he deplored the lack of a lectern: 'It would never have happened in my day.' At dinner I sat next to the Vice Chancellor and Cameron Mackintosh. The VC talked a lot about funding problems, which he said were the same as for the arts. 'Can the government really give a damn for higher education?' he said. We both said we needed only 10 per cent more for stability.

11th February   Second of our regular meetings with the contractors and subcontractors. I told the assembled group (of fifteen-odd people) that we wanted to keep the theatre open during all the work, we didn't want to lose a single performance. We have to work to non-negotiable deadlines: if we advertise that we're opening a show at seven-thirty on such and such a night nine months ahead we're irrevocably committed to it. So could they work to the same criteria or would it be, forgive me, the see-you-next-Tuesday-John syndrome of the building trade? No, no, no, they guffawed, of *course* they could hit the deadlines. We'll see. Grisly cock-up later (not the contractors' fault) over the hoardings of playwrights that we'd put up outside the foyer while the building work is going on. I hadn't properly supervised it, so the pictures were either bad, misconceived, unrecognisable, or insulting to their subjects. Harold, Tom, David and Michael Frayn submitted to a badly organised photo-call and I writhed in embarrassment at Harold's castigation of the enterprise.

12th February   Very good piece on Enoch Powell in *LRB*. Tells story of him giving a talk in Oxford to a racially mixed audience who'd come to heckle and boo. He had them eating out of his hand, close to getting a standing ovation, then – with venom – he mentioned immigration and the audience reacted as if they'd been slapped in the face. Why had he done it? 'I could see that I'd won them over, so I thought, if you want to accept me, it's got to be the whole package, not just my views on devolution. So I showed them the cloven hoof. I don't want any easy victories.'

15th February   Now halfway through *Lear* rehearsals and I'm feeling optimistic. I asked Michael Ignatieff to write a piece for the programme. He came into rehearsals for a day and has written a

really good piece. He sent it to Lyn [*Haill, NT programme*] with a note that ended: 'This is going to be a great *Lear*.' Well, as Solti would say: it's too early to jubilate.

16th February There's a lot of restlessness at the theatre. Trevor's still sifting his plans and people are used to a different rhythm. It's as difficult for him as for them. It was the same when I took over. We both went to the start of rehearsals for *Caucasian Chalk Circle*, then to a meeting of the Public Art Development Trust, where we both felt the extraordinary remoteness and exclusivity of the language of contemporary art – or at least contemporary art criticism. Who are they speaking to except themselves? One of our 'experts' derided Anthony Gormley's work for its 'outdated humanism'. By that measure theatre's always going to seem 'outdated': it can't ever stop relying on the scale of the human figure and the sound of the human voice.

17th February I've seen Molly [*Dineen*]'s rushes for the party political broadcast. She's done really well, and Blair looks relaxed and authoritative. Molly says he's constantly nannied by Mandelson. 'Tie, Tony,' he says to him as he straightens his tie like a fussing mother. She thinks Mandelson and Campbell are destroying Blair, picking him to pieces. They behave as if they're indispensable to him. Maybe they are.

18th February Denys has complained to Chris Hogg at my reply to a letter from a man in a lobby group called the Twentieth-Century. Society, who'd written to me in an intensely patronising manner, explaining the aesthetics of the NT's carpet design, as if I had an IQ in single figures. There's a letter in an architectural magazine: '. . . What is instructive is how Lasdun exemplifies so many of the most awful manners of modernism (particularly urban ones) alongside some of the most refined (in composition and interior space). And if his good is not as good as Beethoven, his bad is every bit as bad. When I was a student Lasdun came to talk to us at UEA. He gave us the expected and seductive talk, with wonderful sunny slides of Italian holiday places and art history; then he was faced with a barrage of questions about sound insulation, rain penetration, sinks and shower taps. Lasdun seemed a bit bemused, his face a bit like

Ceauşescu when he first heard the jeering in the crowd that day: partly dismissive, and partly outraged that it should have been addressed to *him*.'

19th February *Ivanov* at the Almeida. Jonathan [*Kent*]'s production and David's version has made it come from the world of Gogol rather than Chekhov, banishing that elegiac water-colour of most English Chekhov. V. good acting from Harriet Walter, Billy Paterson and Oliver Ford-Davies. David did a good lecture about theatre in the Cottesloe and then we had a desultory conversation about casting for *Amy's View* and rehearsals for *Skylight*, after which he sent me one of his exocet faxes, in the tone of a stern father to a truculent child, about me being over-committed. I faxed him in fury in Berlin, where he's enduring penal servitude as a jury member for the Film Festival. We've made peace, but it's always very disturbing to row with friends. He's admitted he's getting more and more impatient about his plays – he wants them on as he writes them and the wait for this one has been unendurably long for him. Jonathan says David and I are like an old married couple, bickering affectionately; well, we've been friends for nearly thirty years – longer than most marriages.

20th February BBC Board. I worry away at the issue of training, ending up feeling like the resident clown. I achieve nothing except embarrassing myself.

21st February Harold wrote to me to complain about a newspaper display ad which he hadn't approved. He said I didn't care about living writers. I wrote back that I'd done everything for twenty-five years to prove that I *did*, and it was insulting to deny it. But he wrote to apologise and I felt intensely warm about him.

22nd February Jocelyn [*Herbert*]'s eightieth birthday party: a beautiful song by Harry Birtwistle – a setting of a Seamus Heaney poem, a wonderful speech from David Storey and a poem from Tony which made everyone cry as well as marvel at his rhyming ingenuity. I said to David S. that it was interesting that there were two Yorkshiremen celebrating Jocelyn. 'Aye,' he grinned, 'but Tony's from Leeds.' I sat on a sofa between Alan Bennett and Maggie Smith, with Alan Bates perching on the arm. Maggie said that at her

eightieth there wouldn't be enough people to fill a kitchen, and I thought: I'll read that in Alan's Diaries. Maggie said that at Alan's eightieth they'd have to hire the Albert Hall. I said there'd be choral recitals of his best lines. Alan said that was Larkin's nightmare – thousands of schoolkids in chorus chanting: 'They fuck you up, your Mum and Dad.' I danced with Jocelyn and marvelled at (a) how beautiful she is, and (b) how young she is. Denys Lasdun avoided me, but I confronted Sue Lasdun by accident and she gave me a look calculated to turn me to stone. I felt overwhelmingly sad that it had come to this. I wanted to say that I'd just read a brilliant short story written by her son, but I suppose that would have seemed an insult in the circumstances.

23rd February   Sunday. Ian Holm rang me at ten when I was half asleep. He wanted to change some moves. He's obsessed, can't erase the play, but he's always thinking constructively: he's never perverse or nit-picking. I'm beginning to see my way through the fourth and fifth acts. Shakespeare manages to keep all the characters' storylines going: Lear, Edgar, Edmund, Goneril, Regan, Cordelia, Kent and Gloucester. The aim must be to ensure that they are all equally interesting, and the audience don't keep craving the reappearance of Lear. I'm beginning to see what Shakespeare's plan is: he has a scene of unparalleled cruelty – the eye-gouging – the apotheosis of human hate, and follows it with a succession of scenes about love – sexual love (Regan, Goneril and Edmund), love of children for their father (Edgar and Cordelia), love of friend (Gloucester and Lear), love of surrogate daughter (Kent for Cordelia), love of father for daughter (Lear and Cordelia). The play's a symphony of love: flouted, refused, suppressed, unrequited, rewarded. And Lear at the beginning sees himself as the fount of patriarchal love.

26th February   Dinner with Ian Holm. He said formally and shyly: 'This is rather patronising, but can I say you're directing this very well.' I was very flattered. Ian's very open with his feelings and yet so reserved with them – and open about his reserve. He always forgets pain and the past.

1st March   I gave my second lecture at Oxford last night. I was very tired driving up the M40 and had to stop for twenty minutes to

sleep. I arrived just in time, walked on stage, and kept losing my place in my lecture. Afterwards I was buttonholed by a student who wanted to know what audition piece to do, and a woman who was writing a thesis on 'Peter Shaffer and the Divine'.

3rd March   Peter Gill is complaining that I haven't scheduled a proper run for his play, and it's suffering because of my patronage of what he calls 'Father Ted' – *Inishmaan* – and of *Closer* [*Patrick Marber*]. I haven't, as it happens, given it a long enough run, although Peter was initially more cautious and said that twenty-five performances was excessive. But I regret it (a) because the play is good (b) because it further corrodes my relationship with Peter who is fulminating against meretriciousness, musicals, marketing and my bad faith. And *Lady in the Dark* has started previewing, which justifies something of all Peter's complaints. When it works (about two-thirds of the time) it's really wonderful, but when it doesn't it's pure bathos. So it ends up as less than the sum of its parts. Marvellous score [*by Kurt Weill*], Francesca's [*Zambello, director*] done a great job, and Maria Friedman is superb.

4th March   I was rung latish by Glenn Close about 'a project with Meryl': they have a plan to do a film derived from Schiller's *Mary Stuart*. I give an unguardedly enthusiastic reaction. I really have no idea what I'll do when I leave the NT. I've said only that I'll do David's Oscar Wilde play. He's worried about the excess of Wilde, but I don't think it'll matter if we can get a good enough actor. Beyond that I haven't made plans, so a film with Glenn Close and Meryl Streep seems pretty irresistible.

5th March   The laying on of the sword at Buckingham Palace. We have a kneeling rehearsal in an ante-chamber before the ceremony. We all self-consciously test out the kneeling procedure on a little kneeling-rostrum with a small rail that looks like a prop exiled from a production of *The Yeoman of the Guard*. I don't know any of my fellow knights and dames, but I talk to Barbara Mills, who I think runs the DPP, and the man who runs the Marines. He's wearing a very tight dark-blue uniform with a red stripe down the trouser leg. I told him how much I liked his costume, and he looked at me as if I was about to ask him to take it off. Massive sense of bathos in the

ceremony: it's all pure D'Oyly Carte – wildly unglamorous, devised by a Victorian clerk, in desperate need of a designer, director and writer. The military string band played stridently out of tune, selections from *Lilac Time* and *My Fair Lady*. My conversation with HMQ was brief and to the point:

HMQ: So you're at the National Theatre.
ME: Yes, indeed.
HMQ: How interesting.

Then the handshake which turned into a mild shove to deter me from persisting in the lively interchange. In the evening I saw the Queen on the News opening a school computer centre wearing a purple hat that looked like a flying saucer: 'I have great pleasure in opening the royal website.'

6th March Interview with the European cultural correspondent of the *NY Times*. He had a thesis about the liveliness of British art: that we'd been radicalised by Thatcher. I said we had in the sense that the obsession with cost-effectiveness and management and self-reliance – 'There's no such thing as society' – had made the humanitarian and moral have a conspicuous importance. Hence the importance of art, which had been given a little continuity by government, but no security.

9th March I'm making notes for a lecture I said I'd give at Mayfest: 'Should Scotland Have a National Theatre?' Never been more true that I write in order to discover what I think. John Fowles: 'At heart write always for yourself, but make sure that you write from your real self, not one besotted with vainglorious dreams of a future self.'

10th March We spent the day on music for *Lear*. I felt very nervous for the first time. I suppose because of the 'affectation' of adding music, set against the sparse poetry of the rehearsal room. I don't want to manipulate the audience in any way.

12th March Dinner with Salman in order for Trevor to meet him; he wants to commission a play of *Haroun*. Much talk of football, a genial pissing competition – Trevor's love of Ipswich Town against

Salman's love of Spurs, and me mute in the face of a litany of statistics and players' names, lovingly invoked.

18th March   The tech for *Lear* starts today. Anxiety about putting it in the theatre and anxiety about Ian's voice. I'm sitting in the office waiting for the off. The election's been declared. Major said he'd asked the Queen for a dissolution: 'And I'm glad to say she consented.' He also said: 'I think it's going to be a lot of fun.' Never was a less true word spoken. The *Sun*'s come out for Labour. As has Thatcher (in Dalek voice): 'Mr Blair . . . won't . . . let . . . us . . . down.' A six-week campaign. Can the performance be sustained? Elections are all about the floating voters, the rest are forgotten; unless you're a swing voter in a marginal constituency, forget it. I heard on the radio, of the Tory Party: 'You can't polish a turd.' I also heard Redmond O'Hanlon talk about the need of Europeans to be loved by those they've colonised. He was in the jungle in Brazil with an Indian guide, who had captured and cooked a monkey. The guide pointed to the bottom of the pot and told him that it was the custom to eat the eyes out of the skull. O'Hanlon started to oblige, plucked out an eye, put it in his mouth, started to chew. The Indian looked disgusted: 'How can you do that? You Europeans will do anything to be liked.' As will politicians during an election.

19th March   *Lear* tech going OK. Still anxiety about Ian's voice and I could have been better tempered. Before the tech I had a call from Jeffrey Archer. He'd been to *G and D* with civil servant Robin Butler, said they'd behaved like children. He wants to transfer the show. 'You could make lots of money!' he said to me. I asked him who would capitalise it. 'I would! You see, I've got a cash problem: I've got too much of it!' He said he would be busy for the next six weeks (masterminding the election), but 'You can get me – anywhere I am – within five minutes!'

24th March   *Lear* has started previewing. My greatest anxiety was still Ian's voice: would it hold out? The specialist said it was psychosomatic, and that's what it proved to be. Ian started a little fast in the first scene, slightly ahead of the audience, but was utterly compelling in the second half. I talked to him just before the performance. 'I think I know how to do the "Howl" speech,' he

said. 'Ah,' I said. 'See what you think,' he said. And he did know how to do the 'Howl' speech. He carried Cordelia's body on – always an anxiety for every Lear – and instead of putting her down before he spoke, he stood with the body in his arms and howled at Kent, Albany and Edgar. The four 'howls' emerged as an order, a command, the indictment of a father – don't be indifferent to my suffering. It was a very charged night, and the audience called the actors back after the lights went up.

I went to Mezzanine to have dinner with Sue and Judy Daish and Nick Wright and Delia Fine [*American TV executive*]. They were all in tears and, like victims of a family tragedy, could talk about nothing but the play and the performance. Karel Reisz [*director*] and his family were having dinner at the next table. 'We had a joyous evening,' said Karel, and it took me a long time to realise they hadn't been to *Lear* but to *Guys and Dolls*.

25th March   Last night a much better performance. Just one scene where Ian raced ahead and the rest of the cast were sure-footed. The audience stood at the end.

28th March   My birthday: fifty-four going on thirty. I wish. Well, I don't actually. I remember this from Truffaut: 'This contempt that Hitch has for actors and, in spite of himself, for his characters, is his only present handicap and oddly enough, it's also what happened to Renoir, Rossellini and Hawks. Each of them does what he can to conceal it, but it's obvious with all of them, as soon as they reach their fifty-fifth year.'

John and Norma Major came to *G and D* for his birthday treat with the family. He and Neil Kinnock and I share the same birthday – and John Major is the same age as me. He was exasperated by the allegations of sleaze: 'There's a conspiracy, Richard, it can't be coincidence that they're all coming out now.' He said he was 'pragmatic'. 'Life's not over at fifty-four, is it, Richard?' 'You've climbed Everest,' said Norma. 'And I could find another mountain,' said John. I felt sympathy for this palpably nice man who's going into several weeks of misery for an election that he can't possibly win.

31st March   *Lear* has opened. Ian was possessed, a performance of sustained brilliance. After the show I went to see him in his dressing

room. He was lying contentedly in his bath. 'This is the best moment of my life,' he said and I said I'd never been prouder of anything. After the *Lear* party we went to a *Guys and Dolls* Havana-themed party in a bar along the Embankment. They greeted me with cries of 'Leader, leader' and sang 'Happy Birthday' and I drank too many margaritas and sang and sambaed with Imelda.

3rd April   Glos. Overheard in the pub – Tory woman with voice that carries across three counties: 'What *about* the election? I'm just going to write "bum bum bum" on my ballot paper, and I don't care who knows it.' She had been targeted by the Referendum Party: 'I've become a member. How did they know? It's amazing . . . I hope you're not going to say you're voting Labour.'

4th April   Robert Fox told me that his mother, who is recovering from a stroke, answered the door to an old woman who said: 'I don't know exactly where I am.' 'Neither do I,' said Angela, 'so fuck off.'

5th April   *Lear* is said to be the 'hottest ticket in town', 'audience glutted and gutted', 'tears and cheers', 'Lear of the century' in *The Times*. Somebody has given me a copy of the 'happy-ending Lear': at the end Lear lives, becomes King again, with Cordelia as Queen (shome mishtake surely), Edgar comes on with Gloucester sadly unable to restore his sight ('O my poor dark Gloster'), Kent is rewarded, Edgar is married to Cordelia, and Lear, Kent and Gloucester retire to some 'cool cell'. Edgar ends the play by saying that he prefers 'love' to 'empire' and that 'truth and virtue shall at last succeed'.

8th April

You must have been gladdened by that review in *The Times*. I have always thought that Ian Holm and Michael Bryant are two of the finest actors we have, and you have obviously provided a splendid occasion for them both. As to your double triumph, I always remember the first time I saw the Olivier auditorium: This will only suit 'The Miracle' and 'White Horse Inn' (both so much before your time) and your famous 'Guys and Dolls' is the result. Please don't dream of answering this. I do hope there will be a matinee of LEAR that I am simply

longing to see. All congratulations and admiration. Most sincerely, John Gielgud.

He was right about the Olivier. Last time Ian saw him, Gielgud said: 'I'm always worried about filming now for fear that I'll die in the middle of shooting and have to be replaced by Michael Denison.'

9th April Rehearsing *Skylight* for a tour with Bill Nighy and Stella Gonet: they're good, very good. Bill asked me if I'd agonised about accepting a knighthood, and said that Alec Guinness and his wife agonised about it when he was offered one because they anticipated that the grocer's bills would increase.

11th April Peter Brook came to *Lear* ('after some trepidation'), and he loved it, said it was the best Shakespeare he'd seen for ages, and it brought together the Elizabethan and the contemporary in an entirely modern fashion. Peter's production of *Lear* more or less dragged me into the theatre as a profession.

12th April After some nervousness about whether we would get a preview, we opened *Caucasian Chalk Circle* in the Olivier. The new auditorium – transformed into a theatre-in-the-round – is a triumph: it looks beautiful, it all works, and you can hear. The audience were excited, and so were the actors, who gave a fine performance. The show is too long and not clear enough yet, but Simon [*McBurney*]'s done a wonderful job – full of inventive ideas, great heart and true theatrical passion. Simon says I remind him of his father (so does Declan) and he wants to do well for me. He says I'm particularly like his father when I'm angry with him – which I often am because his wayward demands are often hard to deal with, and he often takes the technical staff (who have been brilliant with the in-the-round project) for granted. At the end of the show the audience went wild with delight and the cast sang a beautiful Georgian love song. Then they ran offstage like a football team after a 4–0 win.

13th April I got a letter from Norma Major thanking me for *G and D* – 'the perfect antidote to a trying few days . . . John joins me in sending our very best wishes for your future', which makes me feel guilty about mocking him in the *FT*. I said in the *FT* that he looked as

if he pined for the return of *Spitting Image*, so keen was he to mimic his model: one puppeteer appeared to operate his arms, while his hands flapped helplessly at their extremity and his voice appeared, in an ill-disguised piece of ventriloquism, to emerge from his ears. I don't have the brass neck to be a real journalist, even if I wanted to be: you can't afford to have *any* public affiliations or affections. 'Every writer has a chip of ice in the heart,' said Graham Greene.

14th April I've read *The Invention of Love*. The subjects, or at least the elements of the story, appear to be unpromising: academia, classical scholarship, unresolved (and unconsummated) love, but the play's very touching, incredibly dense, full of extraordinary observations and spattered with good (and one or two not so) jokes. At the moment I can't see the wood for the wood or the trees for the trees. I can't see the structure although I *know* that in Tom's mind all the connective tissues are there.

16th April Went to the Romanian Embassy to have dinner with Ion and his friends and cousin. The Embassy residence is a legacy of Ceaușescu's *folie de grandeur* – No. 1 Belgrave Square, a huge wedding cake of a house, stuffed with the ghosts of social aspirations. Now threadbare carpets, no staff, large echoing rooms. Ion is now Minister of Culture, has real power and is really changing things. His cousin has been in this country for about fifteen years. She told me that when she came here she was appalled that people had no books in their houses apart from ones on cookery and babycare. She found books prohibitively expensive; she was told that if she wanted to read anything she should go to a library. She used to go to the opera and theatre in Bucharest; it took seven years before she could afford to go in Britain.

18th April Got up at six to go on the *Today* programme to talk about the arts and the election. Waited outside the studio with the Bishop of Bath and Wells, who was doing 'Thought for the Day'. We both moaned about the infantilism of the election. Then we had evidence of it in the studio: a statement from me (Labour), a statement from Peter Gummer (Tory), back to me ('briefly') and out – one and a half minutes max – that's the *Today* programme on the arts. Jim Naughtie was nice and cheery, John Humphrys

superior. The day's big story: a Tory advertisement of Tony Blair sitting on Helmut Kohl's knee. Pathetic. The only party manifesto that has *anything* to say on the arts of any value is the Lib Dems'. The Tories treat the arts as a promo for GB plc. and trumpet the virtues of the Lottery; Labour talks of their social usefulness – rather as a nineteenth-century curate's wife might advocate distributing informative pamphlets to the deserving poor.

20th April Talked to David about Alan Rickman, who might be persuadable for *The Judas Kiss*. But I say that I don't think that you should ever try to persuade actors against their will. They only have the power to say yes or no, and they must be free to exercise it – however galling. David has a theory that you should never take an actor on after he's given a great performance. He cites Tony Hopkins: 'The only thing wrong with his Lear was his Lambert Le Roux.'

22nd April Dinner with Tom to talk about *The Invention of Love*. I don't think I'm much help to him because I still can't see how the play connects together. And some of it seems to me superfluous and yet I know that there's nothing gratuitous, everything is there for a reason. Tom wants to reverse the time scheme, and I can't say with authority whether that's right or not. But I think not. Of one thing I'm sure: the scene in which his old self confronts his young self is magical – wholly theatrical and very moving.

23rd April Lisa Jardine, who is a university English teacher, says in the *Independent* that she doesn't bother to go to the theatre to see Shakespeare – 'even Deborah Warner couldn't make *Lear* work' – so when she was invited by a friend to go to *Lear* at the Cottesloe she couldn't be bothered. But her friend e-mailed her: 'No sequins. They all took off their clothes, shouted, and died.'

24th April Labour are looking slightly dicey in the polls, and starting to get frazzled. Molly's party political broadcast has been shown. I think she did brilliantly within absurd constraints. At the press conference for the film Mandelson stood next to Molly and announced that he had had the idea of getting a leading documentary maker to make a film of Tony's 'frustrations'. Then he told a *Times* journalist what the film was about, and how he should feel about it.

The journalist obediently wrote it down. John Webster – from the ad agency – who worked with Molly on the film, says: 'Molly and I have emerged from the Tony Blair project as probable lifelong Referendum Party supporters. Suffice to say Rasputin would have been a doddle as a client compared to Mandelson.'

25th April   Anthony Blackstock has been offered a job at the British Museum and wants to take it. Trevor feels that he's been kicked by a horse. What to do? It's inevitable that people will move on, but it's very unfair considering that he took on a going concern and has lost Jenny, Nick Starr *and* Anthony.

26th April   At 10.15 a.m: 'Richard, Solti here. What a wonderful piece you wrote in the paper! Education, education, education! That's what I've been saying all my life. When are you going to be Prime Minister?' The papers today say that Labour is going to win. There's a story that several ex-cabinet ministers are asking if they can keep their red boxes – a sure sign that they're facing defeat. And the same papers that were crowing about a fall in the polls for Labour are now positioning themselves to be nice about their victory.

27th April   I spoke to Judi, who told me she'd just written to David complaining that there's a stage direction in *Amy's View* where she comes on 'seventy with white hair', then she realised it was another character. Judi once told me that when Finty [*her daughter*] had been doing a nativity play aged six, Judi had asked her: 'What are you playing?' 'A shepherd,' said Finty. 'What's the play about?' said Judi. 'Well, it's about this shepherd who goes on a long journey to see a baby.'

28th April   Oxford. Do some lighting for *Skylight* in the afternoon, then to St Catherine's to do a lecture, this time on acting. Afterwards the tech. Bill Nighy told me a story about Mary Wimbush (who plays Julia in *The Archers*), turning up at a friend's house, dressed for a party. 'But, Mary,' said the host, 'the party was last night, and you were at it.'

30th April   Oxford. In the morning a workshop with students. I ask them to talk about themselves before we start working. They

introduce themselves: 'I'm Jane, I'm eighteen, and I'm a history student.' 'I'm Richard, I'm fifty-four, I'm a theatre director.' In the afternoon, we finish the tech; in the evening a D/R. Next day, the first performance went well. We went back to London with David and Nicole in a car eating smoked salmon sandwiches and swigging champagne. Isn't this how it's always supposed to be?

1st May   Election day. Sunny, clear, buoyant weather and we walk to the polling station feeling like it was 1945. The polling station confirmed this feeling – a battered old black tin box, rickety wooden booth, bits of ill-printed paper with the candidates' names and stubby pencils attached to ratty string. Later we started rehearsals for *Amy's View*. Judi and Sam [*Samantha Bond*] are extraordinarily like mother and daughter, both supremely skilful.

To the BBC election party. A mixture of BBC grandees, showbiz and old politicians. Douglas Hurd was lounging, alone, watching the TV, tapping a silver propelling pencil on a small notepad, with a sly smile as he watched the collapse of the Tory party. *Après moi . . .* Ruthie Rogers told me that Blair's apparatchiks had been ringing the River Café to ask for meals to be sent over from Hammersmith to Islington. She didn't mind that nobody offered to pay, but a thank you would have been nice. She says that Alastair Campbell refers to the uselessness of the 'chattering classes' (i.e. us) and says there are only two serious papers: the *Mail* and the *Sun*. I went back to bed and dropped asleep, but Sue kept waking me to tell me of successive Tory collapses – Michael Forsythe, Portillo, and my last memory was of David Mellor losing his seat with ill grace while James Goldsmith, looking like a wolf on speed, clapped and chanted: 'Out! Out! Out!'

2nd May   Day one of the New Dawn. The mood reminds me of Romania after the Revolution: joy, astonishment, relief, bemusement – and perhaps some guilt that we'd all supinely put up with it for so long. Of course it's an absurd analogy, but we have been tyrannised by an orthodoxy of Tory expectations and assumptions for eighteen years, and an oppressively powerful media, who haven't (well, it's not their job) communicated the possibility of change, just accumulated an inventory of disdain. So no one has heard – except by anecdote – of the voices of the silent majority, who were all saying we've had ENOUGH, life isn't *all* about improving your income and

reducing your tax, and there *is* such a thing as society. They'd been disenfranchised by the media. I watched the news. All the politicians – in triumph or defeat – had gained eloquence and humanity, while during the election they had only bombast and opportunism. And in a day we've forgotten (or forgiven) all that. Got back home very late. There was a note from Harold, who had just been to see *Lear*: 'Your production was quite simply fucking marvellous.'

3rd May Tony Blair has announced his cabinet. No surprises except that Chris Smith has been made Secretary of State for the DNH. That's good news. Peter Hall called me to say how much he'd enjoyed *Lear*, which was characteristically generous of him, particularly as he's doing his own production of *Lear* in August. I've never known him to be mean-spirited. I talked to Neil. He said he hadn't allowed himself to grieve after his election failure last time, but he's done his mourning for himself in the last few days.

6th May Judi works through doubt, scepticism and instinct. She's never content until she's found something solid. It's like watching someone panning for gold in a stream. She and Sam have a remarkable facility and contact with their feelings. Judi told me about introducing John Gielgud in the BBC canteen at Acton to some awestruck young actors. Long silence, broken by John G.: 'Has anyone had any obscene phone calls recently?'

13th May I went to Guildford on Monday night to see *Skylight*. The audience didn't flinch at the 'fucks' and were warm and appreciative, and why should I patronise them? I got back from Guildford to find a message from Jenny McIntosh. I sensed real trouble and left a message. She called in the morning at seven-forty-five to say that she'd resigned from the ROH. I wasn't surprised. She was under intolerable strain – an organisation stuck in a nineteenth-century time warp, fuelled by *schadenfreude*, a series of mutually exclusive baronies, and presided over by a Board and development council of complacent meddlers. A total ideological mismatch with Jenny, and she couldn't adjust her values. But also, and more painfully for her, she had wanted to test her character and found it wasn't as robust as she'd hoped – but the test was so unfair. I found it unbearably touching when she said – in effect – 'I've broken my heart.' I can't forgive the people at the

ROH. There's a weasely press release saying she'll leave because of ill-health. I suppose Jenny agreed to that. There's been a ridiculous stitch-up and, bewilderingly, Mary Allen has been appointed her successor. In the end Jenny couldn't accept the audience as much as she couldn't accept the Board.

14th May   Rehearsals are surprisingly difficult. Judi doesn't hide her anxieties about learning her lines. It's not a pose – she's not using her pessimism to ward off ill spirits. She's a worker, a professional and of course a genius. When she turns it on it's breathtaking. Sam is invariably consistent, skilful, practical, hard-working, applied and very open. Ronnie [*Pickup*] is inspiringly inventive. Joyce [*Redman*] is – well, Joyce: beautiful, instinctive, thoughtful, but slightly scatty. And Eoin [*McCarthy*] is constantly undermined by his lack of confidence, which I try not to exacerbate. The play has to be played very light and fast and accurately; when the playing doesn't match the writing, it's painful.

15th May   John Gielgud came to the *Lear* matinée, and I went to see him afterwards, taking Judi with me. He was generous: 'Marvellously clear, terribly well spoken.' He knew of Judi's film, of Billy Connolly's stand-up act, of David's play. When Ian arrived Gielgud rose to his feet – ninety-three, dapper, light-grey suit, black satin tie – and hugged him.

16th May   Went to Oxford after rehearsals to do another lecture. It went OK and I saw Tom Paulin and Oliver Taplin afterwards. Tom described the Oxford Apollo Theatre as having all the atmosphere of a video store. I also saw David Birkin [*teenage actor in* White Chameleon] who's a student now and very tall and still formidably bright. He told me about the culture of gifts in Papua: 'If you give something it *must* be reciprocated. We should live like that – and put rubber tips on our arrow heads like they did after the missionaries came in.' At dinner I talked to the Bursar of St Catherine's, who'd been at the Ministry of Defence during the Falklands War. He said that *Tumbledown* had got it right: i.e. the war wasn't worth it. He said that the organisation was chaos: some SAS men were to be parachuted in around Port Stanley to give directions to the troops surrounding the town. There were no planes available to fly from Ascension Island, so they fitted a turbo prop with four extra tanks of

fuel which took up so much space in the fuselage that the soldiers couldn't sit down on the thirteen-hour flight. Then the tanks started to leak, so the soldiers had to brush down the gangway with a bristle broom to get rid of the fuel.

17th May   Judi's having a panic about learning her lines: she thinks her memory is going. I think it's exhaustion after going to the Cannes Film Festival and not sleeping. We talked for about an hour about her fear, then we worked. She was calmer, more focused, clearer, and very moving.

18th May   In the *Guardian* Mark Lawson said he'd been to *Lear*: brilliant, etc but had been distracted by the smallness of Ian's cock. It was, he said, all anyone was talking about in the interval. Ian is undisturbed: he says he's never had any complaints.

22nd May   BBC meeting – the annual Joint Boards Conference – was more encouraging than usual, more talk about programmes, and an occasional utterance of the words 'passion', 'particularity', 'brio' 'content' and 'quality', which sit oddly with the remorseless bullet points and the childish graphics of audience reach and market share. A recent T-shirt: 'TV IS FURNITURE, FILM IS LIFE, THEATRE IS ART.'

24th May   Bank Holiday weekend. The cast have three days' rest. I went to Glasgow to do my 'Should Scotland Have a National Theatre?' lecture. I pointed out (at length) my Englishness, that when we English speak of Britain we mean England, and that with our reticence – or is it arrogance – we fail to acknowledge that there are numerous people with whom we share no common assumptions about our nation or our culture. I tried to define who it is I meant by 'we', when it was unquestionably 'I' that I was speaking for, even if, at times, the assumptions of my 'we' would sometimes coincide with those of their 'we'. And how much I admired, even envied, Scottish culture – notwithstanding the tartan crap, and how being a 'National' theatre had its disadvantages and might raise expectations which couldn't be satisfied. All to no avail. Andy Byatt [*actor*] stood at the end in a white rage to say he disagreed with every word I said, was thoroughly disgusted and anyway we didn't need an Englishman to tell us what to do. I wanted to say that having a national theatre wouldn't make him

a better actor or a happier person. And he'll have to put up with remarks like this, from Edward Bond: 'Our theatre is dead. The men who run the NT and the RSC – I call them the floating dead. On the surface they float and appear to have a semblance of life because the current carries them along . . . The NT is an institution of total sleaze.'

28th May   Rehearsals have turned the corner. Judi is now optimistic and is enjoying playing the part. We still haven't got the first ten minutes right; I know what's required, but it's terribly difficult, like playing Mozart or juggling porcelain plates – or both if you believe Wagner, who said that Mozart's music was like the clatter of plates on a dinner table.

29th May   I'm doing preparation for *The Invention*, reading Housman's poetry and prose: 'The aim of science is the discovery of truth while the aim of literature is the production of pleasure, and the aims are not merely distinct but also incompatible, so that large departments of literature are also departments of lying.'

31st May   Rehearsals are going better. The play is good; the worry about it is, will the audience respond? The writing is very dense, but will the audience find this denseness hard to decode? *Closer* has gone really well in spite of a strained first performance. Patrick's a very assured writer, highly conscientious about the work, never complacent, constantly revising the play, tuning it.

1st June   David's very jumpy about the play. He's terrified of following a hit with a flop. He's had two years' peace after *Skylight*. There's a piece in the *Sunday Times* by Brian Appleyard, which could have been written by Dominic in *Amy's View*. He castigates the theatre for being an inferior medium, making extravagant claims for itself and being self-important. He's proud of his prejudices.

3rd June   Anxious start to the week with a run-through on Tuesday – promising and where I'd thought we'd be. David said we were very far behind. I found his response demoralising.

5th June   Good day's rehearsal yesterday, and had a good run today (David's fiftieth birthday). Nick Wright said it seemed effortless. I laughed: all this effort to conceal all this effort.

6th June   Company meeting. The first of many farewells for me. I went on stage in the Olivier-in-the-round to introduce Trevor. He started with a very good taxi story: 'You're that Trevor Nunn, aren't you? You directed *Sunset Strip*. And all that Lloyd Webber stuff. Now you're going to the National Theatre. Tell me, Trevor, what went wrong?'

7th June   *Closer* is a huge success. Universally good reviews. Patrick told me of two (sixty-plus) women coming out of the auditorium in the interval, the last line of the act ringing in their ears: 'THANK YOU FOR YOUR HONESTY. NOW FUCK OFF AND DIE, YOU FUCKED-UP SLAG.' Woman to her friend: 'I must have missed out on a lot in my youth.'

8th June   Depressing piece in the *Independent on Sunday*: 'Is David Hare really any good?' I hate those 'who's best' pieces, treating all art as if we were all at the same Islington dinner party, loud voices braying out prejudices: 'I really don't think the '86 is up to much, do you?' or 'Do you think early Marvin Gaye is as good as late Wordsworth?' The article describes the NT as 'an irredeemably bourgeois institution' – this from a paper with a readership of about 100,000 members of the metropolitan middle class, perfectly content to devote at least half of its pages to haute couture and cuisine, consumerism and interior decoration. But the apotheosis of the pot calling the kettle black is a recent leader in the *Guardian*: 'The BBC should be careful not to patronise its viewers.' Does no one there ever read their tabloid section, their 'Pass Notes'? A lovely party for David's birthday. Several of us make speeches and then, Joe [*Hare*]: 'Thing about my dad, right, is that he's always right, right? And he always gets angry with other drivers. But he makes me laugh a lot, and he's a great dad.'

9th June   Judi came to see me in my office before rehearsals. She got inside the door and burst into tears. 'Finty's had a baby,' she said. No warning, out of the blue. They'd been on holiday together in March: 'I thought she'd put on a little weight.' Judi insisted that she was going to go on rehearsing. We did a run-through in the afternoon, and almost every line – not just guessing at her daughter's pregnancy – seemed loaded with a double meaning. She endured

with a stoicism that you could only marvel at and be moved by, a heroic determination. What extraordinary mettle.

10th June On the show report from *Lady in the Dark*: 'A couple returned to the box office twenty minutes after the show had opened asking for a refund. They had assumed *Lady in the Dark* was a show about cyber sex.'

13th June First preview of *Amy's View* after a tense tech. After the preview a man came up to me: 'I enjoyed that. A mixture of the commonplace and the significant. Is it a great play?' Well, who knows? But it's a good one, and that's hard enough.

14th June I've spoken to Jenny who's decided to come back to the NT, though she's still smarting from what she sees as her failure. Peter Gummer is still telling anyone who listens that she couldn't have carried on. He's keen to justify his precipitate action in appointing Mary Allen. It's a mess and now there's to be an inquiry. Panic and fear rule. Peter Gummer said to Jenny: 'You're well out of it.'

15th June An article by Peter Hall about *Waiting for Godot*. He argues that Beckett made the revolution in *Godot* – 'freed the theatre from detailed naturalism. Metaphor once again filled the stage. And the way had been made for Harold Pinter, Joe Orton, Edward Bond . . .' He argues that John Osborne's 'revolution' was parochial: 'My generation heard more revolution than was ever there, largely because we needed to.'

17th June Very good meeting with Tom. The play is becoming clearer to me, although I'm still prevaricating about some scenes that I can't absorb – one of them a scene with three men in a boat, including Jerome K. Jerome – who, it appears, was responsible for stirring up an attack on 'decadence', alerting the public and Queensberry to Wilde's obsession with Douglas and ultimately detonating the infamous action for slander. Apropos men in boats Tom talked about Ken and Kathleen Tynan writing down the names of all the people they'd made love to; Ken baulked at the item 'Man in boat' on Kathleen's list.

18th June Last night the Gala. I'd dreaded it for months but it turned out to be quite genial. I stood with my arm round Peter Hall being photographed and thought how far I'd travelled in the ten years since I stood next to him so uncertainly at Olivier's eightieth. I had to make a speech before the show, and was applauded for saying we'd raised £400,000 from the Gala. And I said I'd never have imagined that I'd ever be standing on a stage of the National Theatre getting a round of applause for raising a sum of money. If I was running a theatre in the States, I would expect nothing more (or less), but it seemed to me a symbolic, and sad, watershed. So much for public funding. The audience turned out not to be at all as glacial as I'd feared; in fact the play proved itself very robust. It's moving, and funny, and theatrical. Shouldn't that be enough?

19th June Last night's preview rather relaxed since the Gala night had been like a first night – without the curse of reviews. David's very jumpy. He exploded at some sponsors in the VIP room. Told them not to fucking criticise the show while they were getting free drinks and sandwiches. They pointed out that they'd paid and what's more they weren't criticising the show. They weren't; they were discussing whether Eoin's accent was real or assumed. David was contrite today. He said that according to his diary the pattern of the previews was exactly the same for *Skylight*. 'Except for shouting at the sponsors,' I said. He faxed me a Tynan quote about *The Deep Blue Sea*: 'It has already been acclaimed as "brilliant theatre", but there is a patronising ring to that phrase which I must set about demolishing. It implies that for a play to suit the theatre is not quite enough; that it is somehow improper to write deliberately for the medium you have selected – not print, not pure sound, but for the upturned host of credulous faces in a darkened hall.'

20th June The show was relaxed and assured, even though Judi made a large cut in the third act. After the show I went to Salman's fiftieth birthday party. Most people were pissed by the time I got there. Matthew Evans and I were looking across the room at Melvyn Bragg. Matthew said Melvyn had got a lot of hair and it wasn't grey. 'Must be a wig,' he said and he rolled across the room, tugged at Melvyn's hair and was disappointed that it wouldn't come away in his hand.

23rd June   *Amy's View* opened to mixed reviews. Confused and slightly moany and unusually – and wrongly – for a new play some praise the production at the expense of the play. It's *very* rare that a production is better than the play: water doesn't rise above its source. Many critics see it as a play about a critic, rather than a play about loving and mothers and daughters, and how we never know how things will turn out.

24th June   Visit from the two queens to the NT: Glenn Close and Meryl Streep. Meryl is quick and witty and quite tough of mind. Glenn is more instinctive and more dogged. They're both perfectly charming, and it felt absurd to be sitting in my office with these two remarkable actresses, in a position of strength because they want to work with me. It gives a director immense confidence not to be, for once, in the position of a suitor. Over the next two days they saw *Lear* and *Amy's View* and we had five or six meetings. 'Do the actors here think we're auditioning?' said Meryl. 'Perhaps.' 'And we *still* haven't got the parts?'

26th June   *Skylight* has started previewing at the Vaudeville. On Tuesday a really listless performance, and the next day I gave notes in John Dexterish fashion to the cast. Poor Bill and Stella sat, hanging their heads in shame, humiliation and anger, as I brutally anatomised the previous night's performance. Then I had to go back to the NT to check that things were OK for Chris Smith's visit to *Inishmaan*. I ran into three actresses from the cast. 'We've got the Minister in tonight,' I said. 'Oh no,' said Doreen. 'Oh no,' said Anita. 'We had the little feller round knocking on our door. We told him we didn't need his services.' They thought I'd meant the new theatre chaplain, who is called, splendidly, Dick Truss. Then back to the Vaudeville where they were at their absolute best, playing with undecorated clarity and generosity. Then back to dinner with Chris Smith, who quizzed me about the BBC.

27th June   Lunch with Mark Thompson [*Controller BBC2*] and Kim Evans [*head BBC music and arts*] to talk about the series on the history of British theatre in the twentieth century. I found myself agreeing to do it to be broadcast in 2000. What am I taking on? In the evening I go to a dinner at the Middle Temple where the

Directors' Guild presented me with a Lifetime Achievement Award – incredibly generous speeches from Richard Wilson and Natasha [*Richardson*]. Natasha quoted Shaw, on what she described as my 'essence': 'This is the true joy of life, being used for a purpose recognised by yourself as a mighty one: being a force of nature instead of a feverish, selfish little clod of ailments and grievances, complaining that the world will not devote itself to making you happy.' I felt simultaneously grossly flattered and wholly undeserving.

3rd July   A listless dress rehearsal of *Guys and Dolls*. I told the cast not to sit back and assume that the show can play itself. Then the preview was like old times, so I felt I could go home. When I passed the Park Lane Hilton I noticed that the hotel was next to a security shop, a bookie and a pawnbroker.

12th July   Spain. Finished a biography of Cyril Connolly – the staggering insularity and infantilism of the English upper middle class. No wonder this country has been so crippled by self-regard and narcissism: 'The experiences undergone by boys at the great public schools, their glories and disappointments are so intense as to dominate their lives and to arrest their development. From this it results that the greater part of the ruling class remain adolescent, school-minded, self-conscious, cowardly, sentimental, and in the last analysis, homosexual.' This turns out to have been Connolly's canon all his life: a reflection on his youth, his failure, his rage at not having been born rich and aristocratic and thin, and talented as a novelist. The most revealing fact in the book is that he used to go to the Jack Barclay showroom in Berkeley Square and sit in the Rolls-Royces pretending he was a buyer.

17th July   We're staying in the finca of the mistress of a man who owned theatres in Barcelona in the Belle Epoque. Much tennis, and singing, and much discussion with John Mortimer about who the Board of the Royal Court should appoint as Stephen [*Daldry*]'s successor. We bought a plant (a Jerusalem daisy?) for John from a gypsy in the market that had to be soaked in water, and could then answer your questions about the future. I told him it was as good a method as any. The best of good days was when we were celebrating

our implausibly long (twenty-four years) marriage, garlanded and barbecuing by the pool. I went into the house, heard Lu on the phone, and then she came into the hall, breathless and tearful, and ran to me like a child: 'I've got a first!!!!!!!!!!' We hugged and cried and then went to the pool and I shouted the news and it will never be better than this. Which is why Lu's response – like mine – was to be mildly depressed soon after.

19th July   Back from holiday, mountains of correspondence and the less literal mountain of Tom's play to scale. I admire it hugely but can't (yet) love it: it's too *bright* for me – I'm dazzled by it at the moment. I walked across the bridge to the Strand to see *Skylight*, paying a toll to at least five beggars on the way. I keep hearing people crowing about how 'Britain as a civilised country can't be without an international opera house' – or National Theatre, for that matter – but I can't see how we can call ourselves civilised while we have homeless people on the streets. Is homelessness the price we pay for 'civilisation'?

23rd July   I had lunch with Liam [*Neeson*] to talk about *The Judas Kiss*. We talked a lot about the play, but as much about gardening. He said his mum had smuggled a suitcase into the US full of seed potatoes. When she arrived at his house it was like a scene from a heist. We swapped tales of diverticulitis. Liam won hands down, he'd had yards of his colon removed, and he lifted his T-shirt to show me his scar – to the immense delight of our fellow lunchers.

24th July   BBC BOG: 'Whither Radio 4?' Scheduling changes have been attacked in apocalyptic terms by the same broadsheet news-papers who change their format and dumb down indiscriminately. Got back to the theatre to hear that Brian Glover had died. The *Guardian* rang to ask if I'd write an 'appreciation' of him, and I sat at my desk and stared at a blank sheet of paper through a fog of tears. Then I went to the Studio to talk to some American students. Back at the office I wrote of Brian's personality, larger than life, or life smaller than Brian; of how he'd never lost his pleasure in being paid to do something that he regarded as an unexpected and undeserved privilege; of how he'd always underrated himself as an actor; of how he was large, sometimes loud, often boisterous, but everything he did

was touched with grace, and how anyone who'd seen him in *The Mysteries* would have been convinced that God was a big Yorkshireman. But then you'd have to ask why a God so utterly benign could be so limitlessly cruel as to give Brian a brain tumour.

26th July   My new laptop demands my attention like a persistent child. It creates a need which didn't exist before to format everything I write, to change fonts, to underline, to go bold, to italicise, to send faxes and e-mails. It's only a tool, but a tool that makes you obsessed with process at the expense of content; whatever else it doesn't make you write better.

27th July   Bob Crowley tells me of an impresario that Paul Simon sacked: 'I can't bear that man, he's too anecdotal.'

28th July   Board meeting. We discuss how we can carry on to attempt to square the circle without our grant increasing: we do fewer shows, we play out of repertoire, we raise our seat prices – all options which make us *less* worthy of increased grant. It's a vicious circle. Chris Hogg tells me after the meeting that we're like two rugby players who could anticipate each other's moves. Rugby players?

30th July   Brian's funeral. Outside the gates of the cemetery were a number of faintly familiar grey-haired men; it was many seconds before I realised many of them were friends I hadn't seen for years, paled by age. The chapel in Brompton Cemetery had been opened for the first time for fifteen years. A hot, clear day. In the round chapel maybe a hundred people, Tara and Gus looking white, washed out. Phil Jackson spoke brilliantly, marvelling at Brian's innocence, and joy in getting paid to be an actor. Told a story of he and Brian talking about someone's terrible teeth: 'I've seen better looking arseholes,' said Brian. Laughter. Pause. 'And he had.' Colin Welland spoke of him as the funniest man he'd ever known and his closest friend. Then Maddy Pryor sang. And Dave Hill read Brian's 'God' speeches from *The Mysteries*. And John Tams sang and then we walked behind the coffin for about 500 yards to the graveside. A few policemen strolled about, patrolling the cemetery for drug dealing and cottaging. A very young policeman stood to attention and saluted as the coffin passed him. And we stood round the grave wishing that the one man to

whom all this would have given so much pleasure could be with us and remembering Brian's laugh, a sound like a boiling kettle, bubbling, whistling, wheezing, lid tapping, tears of joy running down his giant jolly cherub face. Rog said he was going off to the Chelsea Arts Club for a drink. Brian used to say: 'They do a good wake – crying by tea-time, then it's biting noses.' I left to go to a lunch at the *Express* with the improbable editor – nice mild man, ex-monk – to talk about how the *Express* could acquire a cultural policy. As Brian would have said: a good lunch and (huge wheezing chuckle) it was all FREE!

31st July   Meeting at the newly christened Dept. of Culture with Mark Fisher [*Minister for the Arts*]. He talks of the ROH and the need to start again from scratch – abolishing ENO and getting Peter Jonas and Jenny McIntosh to run Covent Garden; of museum charges for 'Yanks and Japs'; of the Arts Council and the difficulty of creating a strategy for theatre, of the need for hard decisions, of the need to be unpopular (Chris Smith, he says, needs to be liked); and of the BBC as a cultural provider.

1st August   I did a talk for American theatregoers at a university hall of residence in Bloomsbury. On the way there I passed the Hotel Russell, which advertised its coffee shop: VIRGINIA WOOLF'S – PIZZAS, BURGERS, SNACKS. At the end of the talk I was asked what I would miss and how I would feel when I left the NT, and – in spite of myself – I was painfully moved. It's like the end of a summer holiday, all goodbyes. Later in the day I rehearsed with the *G and D* understudies. When we reached Sky's line: 'Obadiah, that's my real name,' Kieran (from Belfast – Clarke's understudy) said: 'When I was twelve I was given a new name. We'd had some trouble with the IRA and when I went off to school my mammy said: "You've got a new name, Kieran. It's Ken McElroy." So I wrote it on my palm, scared shitless I'd forget.'

2nd August   *Othello* has started previewing in the Cottesloe. It's the first time I've seen the play in a production where the performance of the Othello [*David Harewood*] is as strong as the Iago [*Simon Russell-Beale*]. Sam [*Mendes*] is very confident about the show. He's not fearless, but he's very smart, talented and lucky and – most impor-

tantly – has the wisdom (beyond his years) to take advantage of his luck. His production's very strong and clear, but needs cutting away. For me there are too many 'directorial touches' – radios, furniture, wind-up gramophone for the Willow Song – and the odd military solecism, that's conspicuous because it's in '30s costume. I talked to Sam. I remember Peter's advice to me: that as a producer you can only give advice to a director that a director can act on – i.e. you can't say you miscast it, or the design is wrong, etc. But the rider to this is that you can give advice, but will the director take it?

3rd August   Saw (and enjoyed) *Breaking the Waves*. Beautiful line when she is told that it would be better for her husband to die rather than to live paralysed, perfectly enunciated by Emily Watson in a Highland accent: 'You do not know Jan or you could not say such a thing.'

4th August   There's an article in the *Independent* about political correctness preventing white actors from playing Othello. It quotes me (accurately) as saying that Olivier's Othello was 'almost risible' and that I was alone in thinking that. I wasn't and I *did* admire his acting at the time – in particular in *Dance of Death*.

6th August   After a week of hectic activity *Guys and Dolls* isn't going to transfer, so I have to readjust my mental compass away from the West End and an income after the NT. Cameron has decided to keep *Martin Guerre* on: 'Sometimes a show can take ten years to get right,' he said. 'Look at *Sweeney Todd*.' Anyway, as he told me some time ago: '*Guys and Dolls* would never go in the West End, dear.'

7th August   Judi was told by Jeffrey Archer that Lloyd's should have been mentioned once only in *Amy's View* and then forgotten – a painful subject for him, no doubt. Also a woman told her that the boardroom of Lloyd's *isn't* oak-panelled. She's really enjoying the play now. 'Remind me,' she says to Trish [*Montemuro, stage manager*], 'that I was incredibly miserable during rehearsals.'

9th August   Glos. From today's paper: Henry James said the two most beautiful words in the English language were 'summer' and

'afternoon'. Yesterday the same paper credited Edith Wharton with saying the same thing. Actually I prefer summer morning – a hot day ahead of you, followed by a clear starry night. I look for the small satellite star on the turn of the handle on the Plough: it was the eyesight test for the Roman army. I heard the story of a man stopping to shake mud off his shoes, leaning on an electricity pylon. His son, walking some distance behind him, thought he was being electro-cuted because of his vigorous shaking and hit his father's arm with a large stick to make him break free, resulting in two broken bones.

11th August I started rehearsals for *The Invention* today, an-xious as ever. Tom said as I came into the rehearsal room: 'This must be just another day for you, you do it all the time. I only have one of these every five years.' A rather confident read-through – the aristocracy of British character actors – John Wood, Michael Bryant, Ben Whitrow, John Carlisle, Robin Soans, and some excellent younger actors led by Paul Rhys. We're instructed by a Latin professor, a friend of Tom's, in pronunciation and scan-sion. 'Of course,' he says, 'don't copy me exactly, I'm from Aberdeen.'

12th August The Head of Granada TV sales rings Viv Wallace [*head public affairs*] to ask if she knew anything about a proposal to make a TV film of *King Lear*. Yes, she said, it's Richard Eyre's production and it's one of the most successful NT productions ever. 'Well,' said the Granada TV exec, 'no one would ever want to watch it on TV.' 'Why don't you come and see it?' says Viv. 'Oh, I couldn't do that, I'm much too busy.'

14th August In the last three weeks I've been asked to do a film of a Trollope novel, a production of *A Month in the Country*, and musicals based on the lives of Hans Christian Andersen, Napoleon and Al Capone. Generous letter from Stephen Unwin about *Lear*: 'We directors need to overcome our customary and rather loathsome professional jealousy and support each other.'

15th August I'm hugely enjoying working with John Wood [*playing elder Housman*]: his skill and intelligence is prodigious, and there's something very touching about him underneath the

defensive-aggressive carapace that he often wears. And I'm enjoying the play more than I had feared. To my shame, I'd underestimated Tom's extraordinary ability to write for the *theatre*. I'm starting to understand the play and realise that the play's structure is symphonic: much of what I'd thought was decorative is thematic and indispensable. And I'd thought quite wrongly that much of the wit of the play lay on the page rather than in performance. 'Confession is an act of violence against the unoffending.' Is that yours or Housman? I asked Tom. Mine, said Tom. It'll be widely quoted, I said. Or misquoted, said Tom. It's been swelteringly hot everywhere but in our air-conditioned box of a rehearsal room. As the actors move around the room in their makeshift 'boat' on furniture casters I keep thinking that what we're doing is *playing*, like children, to make a 'play' and, paradoxically, it's the only part of my day at the NT that seems to make real sense. Everything else is receding. But the Studio is a problem: David Mirvisch [*owner the Old Vic*] called me to say he'd lost £1.5. m. on the Old Vic and it was time to call it a day. 'I can't run a theatre in London from Toronto,' he says, 'so we're going to sell.' So now we'll have to find a way of saving the Studio [*part of the Old Vic*]: £7.5. m. would buy the Old Vic.

16th August On the *Today* programme I heard an Australian diplomat saying that they were going to ship the head of an Aboriginal chief back home, and to get to the head – buried in Liverpool – they had to go through a pauper's grave. 'A *porpoise* grave? I never knew they buried porpoises,' said John Humphrys, and for once his ineffable bumptiousness was punctured.

19th August The density (and complexity) of the play is a problem that melts away when the actors play with absolute clarity – and John Wood sets the benchmark here. The more serious problem in rehearsals seems to be whether we can get the boat to appear to float effortlessly and accurately about the stage.

20th August Stephen Fay came to interview me about leaving the NT and having three 'hits', as he calls them, on at the same time. I always feel that as chronicler of the old regime (and semi-hagiographic biographer of Peter) that he disapproves of me. He followed me about the theatre before the shows began, watching me talking to

the actors, and I felt self-conscious and altogether unconvincing. After he left, I dotted between shows, like a bull going into a field of cows, uncertain which to mount first. One of the security guys said to me in the bar afterwards: 'How will you be able to live without this, Richard?' and I said, honestly, that I didn't know the answer. On my way to my office I saw a man in the corridor outside the lift turned away from me, his back arched over, his head bent into his shoulder, muttering to himself. I thought he was an actor rehearsing his Richard III audition. Then I realised he was talking on his mobile phone with his hands full.

21st August   Finally Alan Bennett's impossibly bad taste T-shirt slogan has been realised: an ungenerous remark about Judi. There's an envious, mendacious and bitchy piece in the *Telegraph*, which describes her 'tendency – no doubt unconscious – to upstage other actors by never remaining still'. This is like saying that Anton Mossiman uses Oxo cubes and can't boil an egg.

22nd August   Rehearsals get better for me as I understand the play better and admire it more. I smart still at the way in which I underestimated Tom's precise carefulness and his poetic skills. Everything connects – which is what Trevor had said to me was his discovery when he was rehearsing *Arcadia*. Tom's had flu and has been away for two days. He's a very genial and enthusiastic presence, although occasionally when he intervenes he says he 'overworks the power steering'.

30th August   First preview of *Chips with Everything* [*Arnold Wesker*]. Howard [*Davies*] has directed this beautifully – his best work since I became Director of the NT. His search for a style – a romantic expressionism – has occasionally made things seem over-cooked; this has real rigour, is marvellously staged, and has matched Arnold's still surprisingly bold and romantic play – surprising in that it *wasn't* written in a social-realist mode. The meaning of the play is elusive, apart from an assertion of the indelibility of the class system. It's about rite of passage more than anything. There's a problem with a noisy gravel floor, which can be cured in the time-honoured fashion: applying cash to the problem.

31st August   Sunday. I was lying in bed this morning – Sue had gone to make tea – and I switched on the radio. The tone immediately alerted me. Not sanctimonious, but shocked, panicked even. They were talking about Princess Di and I couldn't work out if she'd had a terrible accident – a landmine explosion – and was still alive, or if she'd committed suicide and was dead. It was twenty minutes before I discovered the truth, which was shocking in its commonplace plausibility; much later I discovered that the car had been racing to escape paparazzi. Then later still that the paparazzi had taken pictures *after* the accident and were trying to sell them. I watched a GMTV profile – rather beautifully edited, accompanied by the Adagio from Mahler's Fifth. She's had a short sad life, and now she'll be reconstituted as Evita. All the radio and TV is trying to respond to genuine grief. As children say: it's so unfair. What made her such an attractive public figure – and such an unstable one from the Royal Family's p.o.v. – was that she showed her feelings and refused to abide by their code of stoicism. The Ten o'clock News on ITV had Grieg's piano concerto, the BBC had Keith Jarrett's Köln Concert.

2nd September   It's like the death of Eva Peron. Massive public adoration. What does it say about us that we've canonised her? She touched the nation's heart, but what kind of heart is it? However devious she was, she was incapable in the end of dissembling: what she was was what you saw. She grew up in front of our eyes and made the rituals of the official royals look like bullying pomp. Having evicted her from the family, they of course reclaimed her by putting a royal standard over her coffin. Some people seem to believe that her death is a far far better thing than she's ever done. What's certainly true is that it's a far far better rest than she's ever known. No word from the Royal Family – no public expression of sympathy, no official statement. Blind protocol: it'll finish them.

3rd September   Trevor's just told me he has to cancel *Private Lives*, which Deborah was – or wasn't – going to do with Fiona [*Shaw*], but they couldn't get an actor who'd do it (or an actor they wanted). So Trevor wants to move *Invention* to the Lyttelton in December instead of March. I could see this coming – and no *schadenfreude*.

4th September   I talked to Alan Bennett, who's been very ill. The woman who lives opposite asked him how he was. 'All right,' he said, 'considering.' 'Considering what?' she said. 'Considering I've just had an operation.' 'Well, you should have another one. You look fine.' Crowds are gathering round Westminster Abbey. London is closing down. Who *are* the Dianistas? Is it grief or is it a need to be part of a historical moment, to show *something*, some feeling of importance of events – no matter what that feeling is. Talk to the actors about the Di effect. John Wood said that the funeral procession should go down Sloane Street and Beauchamp Place – an honour guard of shop assistants from designer clothes shops. Robin Soans says he saw three large construction workers in hard hats place a huge bunch of lilies at Kensington Palace. The card read: 'To darling, darling, darling Di. We'll miss you.'

5th September   We did our first run of *Invention* yesterday. It's long, full of marvellous squibs and protracted flights of brilliance, then shocks of intense feeling. At the end I felt unable to say anything to the cast and I let the cast dribble away unloved and insecure. I've been pinched by guilt ever since.

I've just heard on the radio that Georg Solti has died. It's hard to believe, even if he was eighty-four. We had hoped to do *Pelléas* in 1999 – 'If alive!'. I was hoping to see him conduct the Verdi *Requiem* this week. I've just heard Pavarotti on him: 'What you need as a conductor is millions of detail.'

6th September   I did a speech last night for the English Speaking Union of which Heather Brigstocke is Chairman. She was forthright and acerbic about the three boards that she chairs: 'I had to sack my chief executive. Totally inadequate.' She told me about sorting out St Paul's Girls' School. She had to expel a nymphomaniac, who went on to Cheltenham. 'The headmistress rang me to say that she was worried about the girl's mathematics. I said: "It's not her mathematics you need to worry about, it's the caretaker."'

7th September   I found the Diana funeral very moving. All the right decisions about music (even Elton John's ghastly kitsch and even more ghastly new lyrics), and the ceremony and the readings seemed right. Her brother spoke, seared by righteous anger and

unmodulated grief, and made the case that she was a victim of two establishments – rejected by royalty and hounded by the media. Why did the press want to bring her down? he asked (did they?): 'My own, and only, explanation is that genuine goodness is threatening to those at the opposite end of the moral spectrum.' Oddly little comment on this in today's newspapers. Bob Crowley's just got back from a week in New York. 'What country am I in?' he said. 'It's like India – religious, spontaneous, impulsive, mysterious. Who told anyone to throw flowers at the car? There was no model for it, no one taught them to do it.' What attracts me to theatre was displayed in the tension between the rival forms of mourning during the week: stoicism against passion. The theatre obliges you to embrace both philosophies – you have to be stoical; even when your heart is breaking the show must, and does, go on, that's the law of gravity. But it's only worth going on if when it goes on it's driven by passion.

8th September   I tried to get to Peter Eyre's flat last night on the Embankment but couldn't get down Kensington High Street. Huge crowds around Kensington Palace *and* round Harrods, which has become an object of veneration. This is an outpouring of religious feeling, but the old religion has been replaced by the new – it's no less an endorsement of the monarchy, just a different sort. It's revolt, or evolution – not revolution. John Mortimer was asked to do a piece on Diana for the *Mail*. He went to Kensington Palace and approached a mourner. 'Go away,' said the mourner, 'I don't want to talk to the paparazzi.' Will Boyd thinks that the hysteria is due to the myth of the fallen goddess – i.e. the goddess becoming mortal, dying in the under(pass)world, but I think it's religious passion: monarchy has *always* been the English religion, and the faith has been in crisis recently. New belief is reaffirmed in the New Religion, a better (and dead) Queen. I drove past Kensington and Buckingham Palaces in the morning, early. Crowds of mourners streaming towards the shrines – an Irish tricolour with the legend: 'WHEN IRISH EYES ARE CRYING'; a huge banner: 'DIANA OF LOVE'; a shield with the inscription 'DIANA, FAIRY GODMOTHER OF THE NEEDY COLOMBIANS IN MOURNING'.

9th September   At last a witty piece (by Craig Brown) about the hysteria in the *Guardian*: '. . . She taught us how to laugh, to cry, to

write, to eat, to rewrite "Candle in the Wind" . . . Heathrow Airport is to be renamed, and Big Ben, and the M25, and the *Guardian* – the *Guardiana.*'

10th September   The last night of *Lear*, and, as always with last nights, far from the best performance: too self-indulgent and plangent. The Blairs came with Dickie Attenborough. Tony Blair was very taken with Edgar's epitaph, which had been his dictum for the week:

> The weight of this sad time we must obey,
> Speak what we feel, not what we ought to say.

It was odd how insecure he seemed about whether he'd done the right thing, speaking as he did on the day of Diana's death. Cherie reassured us that he was speaking spontaneously, when I thought it was transparently clear that he couldn't have done otherwise. But no journalist seems to believe that.

12th September   Titanic performance of the Verdi *Requiem*. Colin Davis stood in for Solti and conducted in the character of Solti, whose presence spoke through every note of the music.

16th September   Bad day: argument over the filming of *Lear*, then drive to the garage, pay £30 for a new headlight bulb, have a jumpy rehearsal, give unpopular notes to *Amy's View* cast, go into a reading of *The Judas Kiss* and fail to meet Sue for the press night of *Othello*. *The Judas Kiss* is essentially a three-hander about romantic love, class, folly and honour. The play argues (convincingly) that it was Wilde's love of Bosie that prevented him from fleeing from his inevitable arrest. Also, it seems to me, he was tired of action. Like Hamlet, he wanted to distance himself from his own disaster, to be the spectator of his own tragedy. In our reading of the play – me as Bosie, Ian McDiarmid as Wilde, Jonathan Kent as Robbie Ross – it seems very entertaining, although I still can't hear David's voice in it. And I still can't quite focus on doing it: it's as if life after the NT is spectral.

17th September   Wittgenstein said there should be a verb 'to believe falsely'. I believed falsely that Trevor was talking about

Hamlet this morning. It turned out he was talking about 'Hamlyn' – the philanthropist. But perhaps there *could* be a production of *Hamlyn, Prince of Denmark*.

18th September   There's a huge graffito on the Lyttelton fly tower: 'WHAT THE FUCK'S GOING ON'? A fair question. Endless scratching around for the meaning of the reaction to Diana's death. Can it be that the English (is it just us?) are immensely sentimental, kitschy, callow and desperate? Very good reviews for *Othello*. *Enemy of the People* has started previewing: it's a busy, bustling, production [*by Trevor Nunn*]. Ian [*McKellen*] is flamboyant and restless, searching for a new way of using himself and visibly frustrated at not finding it.

19th September   Very good run-through: all parts of the play fitted together, John Wood is spectacular – a virtuoso, but more important a very touching one. I can't imagine anyone else being able to do what he does. And I'm now very fond of the play. Wendy Cope:

> I think I am in love with A.E. Housman
> Which puts me in a worse-than-usual fix.
> No woman ever stood a chance with Housman
> *And* he's been dead since 1936.

23rd September   Breakfast with Lindsay Doran, who runs United Artists, and produced *Sense and Sensibility*. She told me that she'd loved *Guys and Dolls* and could I do something like that on film? I said no one's done it since *Singing in the Rain*, and if they did, it wouldn't be me, I wouldn't know where to start. She told me about her dad (old Hollywood) who'd taken Mike Nichols to a studio when he was first in Hollywood, showing him how flats were made – with two-headed nails so that the nails could be pulled out and used again: everything is temporary.

26th September   Anxious tech for *Invention*. I'd meant to behave calmly and patiently but when I came to it I was too tired and too jumpy: too nervous about whether I could pull it off. The first hour of any technical is the worst for any director with any production: moving through mud wearing lead boots. Within the first hour you know if your staging is really going to work or whether you'll just be

engaged in day after day of remedial work because of your decisions made months ago, your original sins. I snapped at Tom when he was making a (perfectly sensible) suggestion, but we made it up the next day. One of the joys of this show has been Tom, droll and self-mocking, generous and sanguine. We didn't get a dress rehearsal but the first preview was very warmly received. It's exasperating that we don't seem able to make the first twenty minutes work the way we can imagine – or with the light-footedness of the rehearsal room. In the second preview there was an awed, bewildered silence. Is it because the theatre is too small, or the play too baffling early on? The audience aren't hostile, just curious.

27th September   I've packed up my office. Now bare walls, empty bookcases. I threw away ten years of programmes and ten years of my rehearsal scripts, chucked into bin bags in minutes. Tonight my leaving party, and fear of living up to the occasion.

28th September   The party: simply the best – and most over-whelming – party I've ever been to. I was sung at by Joanna and Clive and Sharon and Imelda and Janie and Di and Clarke and the whole cast of *G and D*. My heart was overloaded and when Judi sang to me it burst, and tears ran down my face unstoppably. Speeches from Oliver F.-D., Trevor N. and Ian McK. And from David, who was funny and warm, and said that he'd known good theatres that were happy and happy theatres that were bad, but this had been a happy and good theatre. And a blank canvas presented by Bob for my portrait to be painted by Tom Phillips. And I made a farewell speech in a blizzard of emotion, quoted William Shawn when he left *The New Yorker*: 'Whatever our roles, we did something quite wonderful together. Love was the controlling emotion; we did our work with honesty and love.'

Now I'm in a daze within a coma. Hangover in all senses. All my boxes arrive at home with labels on them: 'RICHARD EYRE – OUTGOING'. Lu said why didn't they put 'RICHARD EYRE – RESERVED'. The removals man delivered his epitaph on the NT: 'What a bloody place. Shouldn't be allowed.'

30th September   Working on *Invention*, trying to clear up anoma-lies and awkwardnesses in the production, which is at last letting the

play speak clearly. And saying goodbye to the workshop, thanking Trish for the party, wandering like a stranger into rooms and corridors that I've spent more time in than at home over the last ten years. Tennessee Williams was once asked what was his recipe for happiness. 'Oh,' he drawled, 'insensitivity, I guess.' If I'm asked what my recipe has been for running the National Theatre I'd have to say: 'Optimism, I guess.'

I did a platform with David in the Olivier. On my way I passed a poster for it outside the Gents by the Green Room. Some ill-meaning critic had written 'BORING' over my face, so at least it enabled me not to feel wholly misty-eyed about the staff of the NT. For years I've always felt trepidation about going into the Gents by the Green Room, where graffiti is so common it's practically a wall newspaper, for fear that I'd read a fruity insult. The nearest I've got was a comment written over an interview which had been stuck up on the press noticeboard. It mentioned that I had a cottage in Gloucestershire: 'JAMMY BASTARD'. The audience for the platform was very touching, David very generous, and the applause as much for him as me – we've been through most of a working life together.

1st October   My last night at the theatre and the first night of *Invention*. Like all first nights I was anxious, afraid really, full of expectation, relief, and in the end numbness, and like all first nights it left me feeling melancholy and incomplete. It was a parting – with the cast and the production and the stage management – but it was also a parting with a way of life. After the show we went to the party, picked some things up from my office, looked briefly round the empty shelves, turned off the lights, took in the view for the last time – Somerset House austere and stately across the treacly black river – locked the door and dragged the bin bags to the lift. There was no one at the stage door, except for a security man who I'd never seen before, but in the doorway, waiting for a cab, was Ian McKellen, who waved me off with a salute. So after years of plays, productions, meetings, complaints, negotiations, despair, joy and endless talk, I left at the stroke of midnight.

INDEX

A NOTE ON THE AUTHOR

Sir Richard Eyre was the Director of the National Theatre for ten years. He has directed numerous plays and films – most recently *Iris* – and is the author of *Utopia and Other Places*, and co-author of *Changing Stages* and of *Iris: A Screenplay*.

A NOTE ON THE TYPE

The text of this book is set in Linotype Sabon, named after the type founder, Jacques Sabon. It was designed by Jan Tschichold and jointly developed by Linotype, Monotype and Stempel, in response to a need for a typeface to be available in identical form for mechanical hot metal composition and hand composition using foundry type.

Tschichold based his design for Sabon roman on a fount engraved by Garamond, and Sabon italic on a fount by Granjon. It was first used in 1966 and has proved an enduring modern classic.